A Student Guide to the SEN Practice

In this essential textbook for students, Trevor Cotterill delves into the four broad areas of need identified in the SEND Code of Practice (2015), providing a spotlight on current research into a range of identified difficulties as well as outlining the appropriate pedagogical approaches required to support these needs in children and young people.

Closely mirroring the SEND Code of Practice (2015), each distinct area of need associated with cognition and learning, communication and interaction, physical and sensory issues and social, emotional and mental health difficulties features essential overviews of research and current thinking within each area. Supported with case studies, learning objectives and reflection points, this text includes discussions on autistic spectrum disorders, profound and multiple learning difficulties, ADHD, mental health, physical and sensory difficulties and adverse childhood experiences as they relate to the SEND Code of Practice (2015). Fully endorsed by evidence-based research involving children, young people, adults and their families, this text encourages students to understand that SEND is a complex area and provides opportunities to reflect on previous experience, harnessing them with knowledge for future practice.

Concise yet rigorous in its explanations and coupled with signposted activities and suggestions for further reading throughout, *A Student Guide to the SEND Code of Practice* will be invaluable to undergraduate students undertaking a programme of study incorporating special educational needs and disability as a single or joint honours.

Trevor Cotterill is Senior Lecturer in Education and SEND, and Programme Leader for the BA (Hons) Special Educational Needs and Disabilities degree at the University of Derby, UK.

A Student Guide to the SEND Code of Practice

Exploring Key Areas of Need

Trevor Cotterill

Routledge
Taylor & Francis Group

LONDON AND NEW YORK

Designed cover image: © Getty Images

First published 2024
by Routledge
4 Park Square, Milton Park, Abingdon, Oxon OX14 4RN

and by Routledge
605 Third Avenue, New York, NY 10158

Routledge is an imprint of the Taylor & Francis Group, an informa business

British Library Cataloguing-in-Publication Data
A catalogue record for this book is available from the British Library

Library of Congress Cataloging-in-Publication Data
Names: Cotterill, Trevor, author.
Title: A student guide to the SEND code of practice : exploring key areas of
need / Trevor Cotterill.
Other titles: Student guide to the special educational needs and disability code
of practice
Description: Abingdon, Oxon ; New York, NY : Routledge, 2024. |
Includes bibliographical references and index. |
Identifiers: LCCN 2023014927 (print) | LCCN 2023014928 (ebook) |
ISBN 9781032420752 (hardback) | ISBN 9781032420738 (paperback) |
ISBN 9781003361084 (ebook)
Subjects: LCSH: Children with mental disabilities--Education. |
Special education. | Sensory disorders in children. | Learning disabled
children--Education. | Education and state.
Classification: LCC LC4601 .C76 2024 (print) | LCC LC4601 (ebook) |
DDC 371.92--dc23/eng/20230517
LC record available at https://lccn.loc.gov/2023014927
LC ebook record available at https://lccn.loc.gov/2023014928

ISBN: 978-1-032-42075-2 (hbk)
ISBN: 978-1-032-42073-8 (pbk)
ISBN: 978-1-003-36108-4 (ebk)

DOI: 10.4324/9781003361084

Typeset in Galliard
by Taylor & Francis Books

Contents

Introduction

The SEND Code of Practice 0–25 (2015) is statutory guidance for organisations that work with and support children and young people with special educational needs and disabilities. It is a set of guidelines that the DfE say local authorities and schools should follow. It is not a legal document, but it does contain legal requirements and statutory guidelines as set out in the Children and Families Act (2014), the Equality Act (2010) and the Special Educational Needs and Disability Regulations (2014).

It is relevant to head teachers and principals, governing bodies, school and college staff, special educational needs (SEN) coordinators, early education providers, local authorities and health and social services staff. It identifies four broad areas of need as some children may have difficulties in one or more areas or it may not be clear which area their difficulty falls under. These are:

Communication and interaction

Children and young people with Speech, Language and Communication Needs (SLCN) have difficulty in communicating with others. This may be because they have difficulty saying what they want to, understanding what is being said to them or they do not understand or use social rules of communication. Autistic children and young people are likely to have difficulties with social interaction. They may also experience difficulties with language, communication and imagination, which can impact on how they relate to others.

Cognition and learning

Support for learning difficulties may be required when children and young people learn at a slower pace than their peers, even with appropriate differentiation. Learning difficulties cover a wide range of needs, including Moderate Learning Difficulties (MLD), Severe Learning Difficulties (SLD), through to Profound and Multiple Learning Difficulties (PMLD). Specific Learning Difficulties (SpLD) affect one or more specific aspects of learning and include a range of conditions such as dyslexia, dyscalculia and dyspraxia.

DOI: 10.4324/9781003361084-1

Social, emotional and mental health difficulties

Children and young people may experience a wide range of social and emotional difficulties which manifest themselves in many ways. They may become withdrawn or isolated, as well as displaying challenging, disruptive or disturbing behaviour. Other children and young people may have disorders such as Attention Deficit Hyperactivity Disorder or attachment disorder.

Sensory and/or physical needs

Many children and young people with vision impairment (VI), hearing impairment (HI) or a multisensory impairment (MSI) will require specialist support and/or equipment to access their learning, or habilitation support. Children and young people with an MSI have a combination of vision and hearing difficulties.

There are 12 chapters, divided into four parts which explore each of the four broad areas highlighting theory, research, lived experiences and approaches to support individuals. Within each part there are three chapters which explore:

- The underpinning theory and research evidence
- The impact of these needs on individuals and families
- Pedagogical approaches to support these needs

The first chapters of each part identify underpinning theories and research evidence in the aetiology of specific issues from the area, such as autism, dyslexia, ADHD, or speech language and communication needs. The second chapters of each part examine the impact that these needs have on children, young people, adults and their families. Case studies are drawn from areas such as education, employment and independence in adulthood. The final chapters of each part will review pedological approaches to support the area of need. These include generalised strategies such as the use of behaviourist approach involving SMART or SCRUFFY targets, personalised learning, supporting sensory issues, executive functioning and specific interventions such as comic strip conversations, social skills, PECS® and Social Stories™. Along with case studies, there are links to videoclips showing how the approaches are used in practice and the underpinning theory and research evidence.

Thus, you can follow a particular need or issue, such as attachment, or autism from identifying the characteristics, diagnosis and the aetiology or cause, through to explore the impact that this issue has on the lived experience of individuals and families and research into approaches which can be used to support these needs. The aim of each of the chapters is to provide you with an evidence base on which to discuss often competing discourses such as the existence of some of the issues identified, the use of diagnostic criteria and its impact on individuals. A key feature of the book is that it includes examples from both children, young people and adults, for example with respect to parenting a child and accessing employment. Although the SEND Code of Practice is aimed at ages 0–25, it is important to note that the issues discussed are not limited to that age range. The book has several features which allow you to reflect on what you have read, take part in activities to extend your understanding and identify key terms associated with the areas discussed. It is hoped that it will appeal to students on undergraduate courses, SEND practitioners, Initial Teacher Training trainees, employers and individuals and their families.

Part I

Exploring Cognition and Learning Needs

1 The underpinning theory and research evidence

Introduction

Support for learning difficulties may be required when children and young people learn at a slower pace than their peers, even with appropriate differentiation. Learning difficulties cover a wide range of needs, including Moderate Learning Difficulties (MLD), Severe Learning Difficulties (SLD), where children are likely to need support in all areas of the curriculum and associated difficulties with mobility and communication, through to Profound and Multiple Learning Difficulties (PMLD), where children are likely to have severe and complex learning difficulties as well as a physical disability or sensory impairment. Specific Learning Difficulties (SpLD) affect one or more specific aspects of learning. This encompasses a range of conditions such as dyslexia, dyscalculia, and dyspraxia (DfE, DoH, 2015).

Learning objectives

This chapter will:

- Introduce you to a range of learning difficulties associated with Cognition and Learning Needs including Profound and Multiple Learning Difficulties (PMLD), Severe Learning Difficulties (SLD), Moderate Learning Difficulties (MLD) and Specific Learning Difficulties (SpLD) including dyslexia, dyscalculia and dyspraxia
- Invite you to examine underpinning theory and research evidence in relation to Cognition and Learning Needs
- Introduce you to the aetiology of a range of issues identified in the continuum of needs
- Invite you to review how the characteristics of these issues are manifested
- Help you to understand the complexities associated with such a diverse area of need

Key terms

Moderate Learning Difficulty (MLD), Severe Learning Difficulty (SLD), Profound and Multiple Learning Difficulty (PMLD), aetiology, dyslexia, dyscalculia, neurobiology, genetics, Developmental Coordination Disorder (DCD)

DOI: 10.4324/9781003361084-3

Pause for reflection

- What links cognition to learning and how do these factors relate to SEND?

Activity

The SEND Code of Practice 2015 (DfE, DoH, 2015) refers to learning difficulties which cover a range of needs. You are applying for a post working with children, young people or adults who have learning difficulties and you must give a presentation on the following:

- What does the term mean and what specific issues does it relate to?
- The difference between learning difficulties and disabilities
- Examples of how these difficulties arise

The range of needs

Profound and Multiple Learning Difficulties (PMLD)

Learners with PMLD have severe and complex learning needs, in addition they have other significant difficulties, such as physical disabilities or a sensory impairment and may require a high level of adult support, both for their learning needs and for personal care. They are likely to need sensory stimulation and a curriculum broken down into very small steps. Some PMLD learners communicate by gesture, eye pointing or symbols, others by very simple language. These pupils will require a very high level of specialist support and a highly personalised curriculum. They are likely to communicate using gesture, eye pointing, symbols or very simple language. They are highly likely to have an Education Health and Care Plan and their needs are usually best met in specialist provision. According to the Department for Education (DfE) (2022), 10,877 pupils aged between 5 and 16 years are identified with PMLD as their primary need.

Severe Learning Difficulties (SLD)

Learners with SLD have significant intellectual or cognitive impairments. This has a major effect on their ability to participate in the school curriculum without support. They may also have associated difficulties in mobility and coordination, communication and perception and acquisition of self-help skills. Learners with

SLD will need support in all areas of the curriculum. They may also require teaching of self-help, independence, and social skills. Some may use sign and symbols, but most will be able to hold simple conversations and gain some literacy skills (Department of Education and Skills, 2003). Learners experience difficulties in acquiring skills and making progress in basic literacy and numeracy and in other areas of the curriculum.

They are likely to have additional difficulties in speech and language development, this can be in expressive and/or receptive language and be apparent in spoken and written communication. They are also likely to have immature social skills, memory and/or processing difficulties, with limited concentration and attention. Most of these learners will require direct and intensive intervention to support progress and development in relation to learning, developing, and maintaining motor skills, self-help skills and independence. They may require specialist support in the use of sign or symbols as a means of communication and are likely to have an Education, Health and Care plan and need specialist provision. According to the DfE (2022), 33,938 pupils aged between 5 and 16 years are identified with SLD as their primary need.

Moderate Learning Difficulties (MLD)

Learners with MLD will have attainments well below expected levels in all or most areas of the curriculum, despite appropriate interventions. Their needs will not be met by normal differentiation and the flexibilities of the National Curriculum. They may have much greater difficulty than their peers in acquiring basic literacy and numeracy skills and in understanding concepts. They may also have associated speech and language delay, low self-esteem, low levels of concentration and underdeveloped social skills (Department of Education and Skills, 2003). Learners with MLD have difficulties in learning across the curriculum, requiring support in all or most areas of the curriculum. This category can be used when difficulties are seen and evidenced as being wide ranging and with a significant impact on attainment. Attainment for these learners is well below that expected of their peers in all or most areas of the curriculum despite appropriate differentiation and intervention. Many of these learners' needs will be met by providing appropriate high-quality teaching, differentiation, and intervention. Therefore, the needs of most learners with MLD can be met without the need for an Education, Health and Care plan. According to the DfE (2022), 163,031 pupils aged between 5 and 16 years are identified with MLD as their primary need.

Specific Learning Difficulties (SpLD)

SpLD is an umbrella term which indicates that pupils display differences across their learning. Pupils with SpLD may have a particular difficulty in learning to read, write, spell, or manipulate numbers so that in these areas is below their performance in other areas. Pupils may also have problems with short-term memory, organisational skills, and coordination. Pupils with SpLD cover the whole ability range and the severity of their impairment varies widely. For most of these learners their needs will be met within a school's delegated notional SEN Budget and by providing appropriate high-quality teaching, differentiation, and intervention where the support and intervention is targeted on the specific area of need. Therefore, the needs of most learners with SpLD can be met without the need for an Education, Health and Care Plan. According to the DfE (2022), 163,031 pupils aged between 5 and 16 years are identified with MLD as their primary need.

Profound and Multiple Learning Difficulties

Defining the term PMLD

Discourses surrounding Profound and Multiple Learning Disabilities (PMLD) are debated throughout the literature. Whilst 'Profound and Multiple Learning Disabilities' is the most used terminology in contemporary literature in the UK (Simmons and Watson, 2014), other terms used include severe intellectual and motor disabilities, as well as complex and multiple disabilities (Goldbart, Chadwick and Buell, 2014). There is often an overlap in characteristics between PMLD and Severe Learning Disabilities (SLD) and they are regularly grouped together based on the similarities in cognitive difficulties; however, the significant difference is the medical and health complications that are attached to the definition of PMLD (Colley, 2020). Simmons and Watson (2014) define PMLD as a label presented to children who experience severe impairment to cognition resulting in significant developmental delay.

The term 'Profound and Multiple Learning Difficulties' (or Disabilities) (PMLD) is a description rather than a clinical diagnosis. It represents a hetero-geneous group of people with learning disabilities who have a complex range of difficulties. PMLD and SLD terminology is contested in both academic literature and policies, some definitions identify PMLD and SLD as 'disabilities' (NHS, 2018, Simmons and Watson, 2014), whilst others define PMLD and SLD as 'difficulties' (Public Health England, 2020; Department for Education and Department of Health, 2015). Gittens and Rose (2007) note that one of the problems in identifying individuals with PMLD is the confusion and lack of a generally accepted definition for this population.

Ware (2004) suggests that PMLD learners have a profound cognitive impair-ment/learning difficulty, leading to significant delay in reaching developmental milestones. Such learners will be operating overall at a very early developmental level and will display at least one or more of significant sensory impairments, complex health care needs/dependence on technology or significant motor impairments. Hogg (2004) refers to profound intellectual disability and complex health care needs identifying individuals whose developmental abilities fall within those characterising the first 18–24 months of typical development, and for whom communication is typically non-verbal. In addition to their intellectual disability, they have physical and/or sensory impairments that significantly limit adaptive behaviour. There is also a high probability of epilepsy, dysphagia and/or respiratory problems. Health care presents significant challenges to professionals and family carers. Lacey (1998) refers to PMLD learners as having more than one disability and that one of these is profound intellectual impairment. Often the multiplicity of disabilities includes sensory or physical impairment, but others may be involved, such as autism or mental illness. Behaviour which may be very challenging and/or self-injurious may also be present.

Samuel and Pritchard (2001) state that children and adults with profound learning disability have extremely delayed intellectual and social functioning with little or no apparent understanding of verbal language and little or no symbolic interaction with objects. They possess little or no ability to care for themselves. There is nearly always an associated medical factor such as neurological problems, physical dysfunction, or pervasive developmental delay. In highly structured environments, with constant support and supervision and an individualised relationship with a carer, people with profound learning disabilities have the chance to engage in their world and to achieve their optimum potential (which might even mean progress out of this classification as development proceeds). However, without structure and appropriate one-to-one support, such progress is unlikely.

Pause for reflection

- Why do you think that there are several definitions related to PMLD?
- Which ones would relate to an academic and practitioner discourse?

The aetiology of PMLD

Just as there is a range of difficulties experienced by the heterogeneous group identified as

PMLD, there is a range of causes that can be subdivided into those conditions that arise at

conception and those that arise during pregnancy, labour and after birth. However, the cause

of learning disabilities cannot be determined in 40–80 per cent of cases.

Pre- and peri-natal

Genetic abnormalities may be subdivided into chromosomal, single gene disorders and multifactorial disorders. Chromosomal disorders include Down's syndrome, Edwards syndrome and Patau's syndrome. Gene disorders include phenylketonuria (PKU), Prader-Willi syndrome and Fragile X syndrome. Multifactorial disorders include neural tube defects such as spina bifida and occur when both genetic and environmental factors combine.

Peri-natal

Chemicals, such as radiation, cigarette smoke, alcohol and drugs, and diseases (such as rubella and measles) can interfere with the normal development of the embryo or foetus. Prenatal alcohol exposure can lead to the occurrence of foetal alcohol syndrome (FAS).

Peri- and post-natal

Complications during labour and after birth include oxygen deprivation, low birth weight and prematurity which are strongly correlated to the later development of learning disabilities.

Activity

- From the list above, research one of the areas under each of the headings e.g. Prader-Willi syndrome and identify the cause and the consequences of the pre-, peri- or post-natal influence.

Specific Learning Difficulty: Developmental Dyscalculia

Dyscalculic learners show marked and persistent difficulties in grasping basic number concepts. The learner may have significant difficulties in learning number facts and calculation processes. Developmental Dyscalculia is a Specific Learning Difficulty that is characterised by impairments in learning basic arithmetic facts, processing numerical magnitude and performing accurate and fluent calculations. These difficulties must be quantifiably below what is expected for an individual's chronological age and must not be caused by poor educational or daily activities or by intellectual impairment.

Note that this chapter focuses on what is strictly called 'Developmental Dyscalculia' (DD). There is another type of dyscalculia called 'acquired dyscalculia', which is acquired (usually in adults) because of brain injury or stroke. Emerson and Babtie (2014) state that dyscalculia is an umbrella term that encompasses a variety of conditions that may result in difficulties specific to mathematics, such as difficulty understanding simple number concepts, lack an intuitive grasp of numbers, and have problems learning number facts and procedures. Calculation, like reading, is a culturally derived, specifically taught, slowly learned skill. It calls for the ongoing interaction of environmental experiences with the development of visual, spatial and language proficiency, working and long-term memory, focused attention, motivation, and other intellectual and executive competences (Rapin, 2016). These difficulties are not caused by lack of educational opportunities, and the degree of difficulty is evidenced to be below expectations for the individual's age (Dyslexia Association, 2023). The National Numeracy Strategy (DfES, 2001) defines developmental dyscalculia as a Specific Learning Disorder, an impediment in mathematics, evidencing problems with number sense, memorisation of arithmetic facts, accurate and fluent calculation and accurate maths reasoning. Developmental learning disorder with impairment in mathematics is not due to a disorder of intellectual development, sensory impairment (vision or hearing), a neurological disorder, lack of availability of education, lack of proficiency in the language of academic instruction, or psychosocial adversity (WHO, 2019). Mathematical difficulties are best thought of as a continuum, not a distinct category, with dyscalculia at the extreme end of this continuum. It should be expected that developmental dyscalculia will be distinguishable from general mathematical difficulties due to the severity of difficulties with symbolic and non-symbolic magnitude, number sense and subitising (British Dyslexia Association, 2018).

It is thought that between 5 and 6 per cent of people are born with the condition known as dyscalculia, which fundamentally impacts the individual's ability to use and understand numbers intuitively (Henderson, 2012). It is estimated that around 3 to 6 per cent of the population are affected by dyscalculia, yet that number could be significantly higher due to a lack of research. The British Dyslexia Association (BDA) suggests that 'mathematical learning difficulties' are extremely prevalent in the UK and could affect as many as 25 per cent of the population (BDA, 2018). There is general agreement that around 5 to 8 per cent of pupils have dyscalculia and, on average, each class of 30 children will have approximately two or three pupils who are affected by it (Hannell, 2005).

Aetiology of dyscalculia

Developmental dyscalculia results from differences in the parietal lobe of the brain, due to deficits elsewhere in the brain that cause working memory difficulties, a genetic link, or because of complications in pregnancy (Dehaene, 1997; Butterworth, Varma and Laurillard, 2011; Hornigold, 2015). Dyscalculia, like dyslexia, is not a single disorder attributable to a single gene or damage affecting one specific brain locus or pathway (Rubinsten and Henik, 2009).

Heritability

Kosc (1974) defined dyscalculia as a disorder affecting an individual's abilities in mathematics, originating in either areas of the brain that impact mathematical functioning negatively, while simultaneously having no impact on other mental functions, or because of the role of genetics. If one twin has dyscalculia, then 58 per cent of monozygotic twins and 39 per cent of dizygotic twins are also dyscalculic (Alarcón et al., 1997). Shalev et al. (2001) suggest that such an inherent deficiency has a genetic basis and familial aggregation may also be attributed to genetic factors. Shalev et al. (2001) have shown that it is common that a learner with dyscalculia often has a relative who also has similar difficulties in mathematics. However, Light and DeFries (1995) found that 49 per cent of monozygotic twins (who share all their genes) and 32 per cent of dizygotic twins had dyscalculia, which points to moderate genetic influence.

Neuroanatomy

Research on genetic and developmental disorders associated with dyscalculia, such as Turner's syndrome, foetal alcohol syndrome and low birth weight (Isaacs et al., 2001), shows impairment in areas of the brain known to process mathematics (specific parts of the parietal lobes). Developmental dyscalculics also show difficulties on basic cognitive tasks known to activate these areas. Like reading, calculation is an acquired skill that engages complex brain circuitry and individualised strategies and involves two major abilities, vision and language. The first ability is an innate visual sensitivity to small (two to four) numbers, which later blends into the autonomic nervous system (ANS) to create the ability to detect magnitude differences in numerosity between item displays and estimate an approximate number of items, with precipitously declining precision as the number grows. This innate spatial ability is analogous to gauging stimulus magnitude and intensity in other sensory modalities. The second, an exact cardinal and ordinal abstract number system, enables calculation and takes years to develop. Learning the visual symbols and algorithms for number competence requires extensive exposure and specific teaching and depends on other cognitive abilities like language and executive skills.

Von Aster and Shalev (2007) suggest that it is a dysfunction of developing neural networks specifically for the numerical domain and that the intraparietal sulcus (IPS) is involved in undertaking mathematical tasks. Calculation activates domain-specific networks centred on the interconnected intraparietal sulcus (IPS) and adjacent gyri of the left and right hemispheres. The IPS receives pre-processed visual inputs from occipital cortices, either directly (so-called 'where circuit') or after further pre-processing in ventral occipitotemporal and language cortices (so-called 'what circuit'). In addition, the IPS and adjacent multimodal cortical areas are reciprocally connected with prefrontal cortices activated by focused attention and working memory, and hippocampal circuitry involved in learning and retrieval from long-term memory stores, as well as with limbic and multiple subcortical nodes (Rapin, 2016). Imaging studies indicate that number processing activates interconnected number networks centred in both right and left parietal lobes, the IPS, with the left angular gyrus more involved in language-dependent manipulation of exact numbers and the right angular gyrus involved in continuous magnitude estimation, including ANS, although this remains disputed (Cappelletti et al., 2014).

Castelli, Glaser and Butterworth (2006) found differences in the thickness, surface area and volume of the brain in areas used in memory and keeping track of a task have been found and differences in mathematical ability because of dyscalculia may be situated in the parietal lobe (Dehaene, 1997; Butterworth, 1999; Hornigold, 2015). Simmons and Singleton (2008), however, suggest that dyscalculia originating in the parietal lobe is not yet a proven hypothesis, stating that there is still an ongoing debate questioning whether dyscalculia is caused by specific differences in the parietal lobe or if the difficulties are due to cognitive weaknesses elsewhere in the brain.

Pause for reflection

- How would a teacher, parent or student distinguish between dyscalculia, maths anxiety or lack of interest in maths?

Semantic memory, procedural memory and visuospatial skills and associated functions draw on specific regions of the brain to facilitate solving mathematical problems. The phonological loop, situated in the temporal regions, is required for retrieval of facts and for understanding word problems. Divided and sustained attention and the ability to manipulate and hold facts while calculating require the frontal lobes and the anterior cingulated regions. Visual, spatial and kinaesthetic information, comparing of quantities, estimating size and computation, require the intact functioning of the bilateral parietal regions. There are three main cognitive models that could be related to dyscalculia, with the numerical core deficit model responsible for the neurodiversity, which would suggest that all dyscalculic individuals would have similar characteristics. The other two models allow for a variety of mathematical difficulties, where differing mental processes could be responsible, giving rise to subtypes of dyscalculia (Kaufmann et al., 2013).

Activity

1 Numerical core deficit model
2 Numerical domain-specific deficit model
3 Domain-general deficit model

- Research the main points in relation to these models. How are they similar or different?
- What research evidence is given in support of each of these models?

Specific Learning Difficulty: Dyslexia

Dyslexia is a learning difficulty that occurs across the range of intellectual abilities and affects the skills involved in accurate and fluent word reading and spelling. The characteristic features of dyslexia are difficulties in phonological awareness, verbal memory and verbal processing speed, and it is best thought of as a continuum, not a distinct category, and there are no clear cut-off points. Co-occurring difficulties may be seen in aspects of language, motor coordination, mental calculation, concentration and personal organisation, but these are not, by themselves, markers of dyslexia. Learners may show marked and persistent difficulties in acquiring the skills for accurate and fluent reading. The learner may have significant difficulties in learning to spell, and may have poor comprehension, handwriting and punctuation. Their performance in these areas is likely to be below their performance in other areas.

Dyslexia can be either acquired, where language skills have developed typically and injuries or illness affecting the brain have caused them to deteriorate, or be developmental, where language difficulties are present from birth (Pumfrey, 2001). The discourse around the use of language can be traced to the view that 'dyslexia' originally came from the Greek terms 'dys', which means 'impairment', and 'lexis', which means 'word' (Brunswick, 2009). There are multiple definitions related to this learning difficulty, so dyslexia can be simply defined as a neurobiological impairment within the brain, which causes an individual to struggle more than their peers in reading, spelling and writing (Mather and Wendling, 2012).

Dyslexia is a specific learning disability that is neurobiological in origin characterised by difficulties with accurate and/or fluent word recognition and by poor spelling and decoding abilities. These difficulties typically result from a deficit in the phonological component of language that is often unexpected in relation to other cognitive abilities and the provision of effective classroom instruction. Secondary consequences may include problems in reading comprehension and reduced reading experience that can impede growth of vocabulary and background knowledge. As you would expect, there has been a substantial investigation of dyslexia, which has resulted in a wide range of definitions. The British Dyslexia Association's definition adopted in Sir Jim Rose's Report (Rose, 2009) states that dyslexia is a learning difficulty that primarily affects the skills involved in accurate and fluent word reading and spelling. Characteristic features of dyslexia are difficulties in phonological awareness, verbal memory and verbal processing speed and it is best thought of as a continuum (BDA, 2018). The Rose Report (2009) did not assign a cause to dyslexia but describes it in terms of the behaviours associated with it.

In DSM-5, dyslexia is included in the category 'Specific Learning Disorder' (SLD) and is described as problems with accurate or fluent word recognition, poor decoding and poor spelling abilities, difficulties with reading comprehension or maths reasoning (APA, 2013). According to DSM-5, SLD is a type of neurodevelopmental disorder that impedes a person's ability to learn and use specific academic skills, such as reading, writing and arithmetic, which serve as the foundation for most other academic learning. It refers to three specific learning disorders: impairment in reading, impairment in the written expression and impairment in mathematics. Diagnosis involves a range of methods, including medical history, clinical interview, school report, teacher evaluation, rating scales and psychometric tests.

In ICD-11, dyslexia is referred to as a Developmental Learning Disorder (WHO, 2019). There are subsections, including Developmental Learning Disorder with impairment in reading, and dyslexia is included within this section. It is characterised by significant and persistent difficulties in learning academic skills related to reading, such as word reading accuracy, reading fluency and reading comprehension. Reading is markedly below what would be expected for their chronological age and level of intellectual functioning, and results in significant impairment in the individual's academic or occupational functioning. Within the SEND Code of Practice: 0 to 25 Years (DfE and DoH, 2015), dyslexia is identified in Section 6.31 as a Specific Learning Difficulty (SpLD), affecting one or more specific aspects of learning, encompassing a range of conditions such as dyslexia, dyscalculia and dyspraxia.

Types of dyslexia

There is a range of types and subtypes of dyslexia identified in the literature. For example, the Balance Theory (Fawcett and Nicolson, 1999) identifies three dyslexia subtypes, Perceptual or P-type Linguistic or L-type and Mixed or M-type.

Activity

There are several types of dyslexia, including **Phonological dyslexia, Surface dyslexia, Rapid naming deficit dyslexia, Double deficit dyslexia** and **Visual dyslexia**.

- What are the key indicators of these types?
- What are the similarities and differences in how they refer to aspects of dyslexia?
- How do they account for the dyslexic characteristics seen?
- How do these relate to Perceptual or P-type Linguistic or L-type and Mixed or M-type?

Aetiology of dyslexia

Hereditability

Although developmental dyslexia apparently is seen to run families, and twin studies have confirmed that there is a substantial genetic contribution to poor reading, it is not caused by a single genetic mutation. Rather, it appears to involve the interaction of several genes and environmental factors. Chromosome numbers 6 and 18 have been implicated in dyslexia. Examining genetic markers, researchers have focused their attention on 15 brain-expressed genes located on chromosome 6, finding strong associations between one gene, named KIAA0319, and low performance in tests for reading, spelling, orthography and phonology. Other genes that contribute to verbal communication, phonology and memory difficulties associated with dyslexia have been recently discovered (Becker et al., 2017). On chromosome, Mueller et al. (2014) have located nine loci, fixed positions on a chromosome, which may have an impact in relation to dyslexia. Research involving twin studies has shown that 84 per cent of monozygotic (MZ) twins had a history of a reading difficulty, while 29 per cent of dizygotic (DZ) twins had a history of reading difficulties (Mather and Wendling, 2012). Snowling, Gallagher and Frith (2003) family histories research found that 61 per cent of children with a history of reading difficulties had one themselves, whereas 13.8 per cent of children with no family history of a reading difficulty had one themselves and Swagerman et al. (2015) conclude that genetics were the primary cause of dyslexia.

Neuroanatomy

There is now a great deal of evidence to support the theories that dyslexia is caused by abnormalities within the brain (Reid, 2011), such as the cerebellum and magnocellular neurones developing atypically, affecting reading and causing words to look blurred. Research suggests that the brain develops differently in individuals with dyslexia, causing problems with phonology and processing systems (Galaburda et al., 2006). MRI scans and post-mortem analyses of typical and atypical brains have shown that individuals with dyslexia do have differently structured brains, which occurs during early development. Studies on individuals who have had brain injuries affecting speech and language abilities have found that the left and right hemispheres each have a specific function (Reid, 2011).

The right hemisphere controls visual processes and the left hemisphere controls language processes and reading involves both hemispheres working together effectively (Robertson and Bakker, 2002). In individuals with dyslexia, these are typically larger and more developed (Reid 2011; Young and Tyre, 1983). Because of this, individuals with dyslexia often have difficulty with functions of the left hemisphere, but excel in those of the right hemisphere, leading researchers to believe that these individuals are more reliant on their right hemisphere. However, there is much debate about whether this is due to incomplete development of the left hemisphere or over-development of the right hemisphere. Individuals with dyslexia have difficulty passing information between the two hemispheres. This could be due to an excess of neurones, leading signals to be sent down the 'wrong' pathways. However, Protopapas and Parrila (2018) disagree with the theory that dyslexia is caused by an atypical development of the brain and suggest that there is an over-reliance on reading in society.

Brunswick (2011) suggests that the dyslexic brain could be viewed as functioning differently from the neurotypical brain, as it is 'wired' differently. There are three differences in the brains of dyslexic individuals compared to the brains of non-dyslexic individuals. First, the dyslexic brain is almost perfectly symmetrical, as opposed to a non-dyslexic brain, which will have one side of the brain larger than the other. Second, Hammond and Hercules (2007) state that nevertheless, individuals with dyslexia tend to be right brain thinkers, which involves creativity. Third, there are smaller neurones in the thalamus, which affect the timing of how information is transmitted across all the networks in the brain.

Activity

There are several theories relating to the neuroanatomy of dyslexia. These include:

1 **Rapid Auditory Processing Theory** (Tallal and Piercy, 1973) relating to impaired performance on auditory tasks.
2 **Phonological Theory** (Bradley and Bryant, 1983) relating to the representation, storage and/or retrieval of speech sounds.
3 **Visual Theory** (Lovegrove et al., 1980) relating to the processing of letters and words
4 **Cerebellar Theory** (Nicolson and Fawcett, 1990) relating to posture and balance and reading and writing.
5 **The insula-disconnection syndrome** (Paulesu et al., 1996) relating to speech and the comprehension of the written and spoken word.
6 **Magnocellular theory** (Stein and Walsh, 1997) relating to visual, learning and processing.
7 Identify the parts of the brain which these theories relate to.
8 How do they account for the range of characteristics seen in the dyslexic individual?

Cognition also plays a part in the development of dyslexia, including issues with processing sounds, the actual speed of processing information and working memory (Reid, 2011). Deficits in verbal memory span may have an impact on the storing of information in working memory also and these seem to continue into adulthood (Smith-Spark and Fisk, 2007). Executive functions, such as those which involve planning, problem solving, accessing information from the long-term memory store, and goal-directed behaviour, have also been shown to have an influence. Other functions such as inhibiting verbal and motor responses, accessing information in long-term memory in a controlled and adapting responses to meet the needs of the task, have also been shown to be relevant (Fisk and Sharp, 2004; Pennington and Ozonoff, 1996), with executive functioning impairments in dyslexia which are present in childhood, continuing into adulthood.

Activity

Neurodiversity describes the idea that people experience and interact with the world around them in many ways; there is no one correct way of thinking, learning, and behaving, and differences are not viewed as deficits. Neurodivergence is a term which relates to ADHD autism, dyslexia and dyspraxia.

- Who is cited as being responsible for the origin of the term and in what context?
- Neurodiversity can be a noun, or an adjective. How are they used to explain the experiences of individuals?
- What is the neurodiversity movement and how does neurodiversity relate to such issues such as ADHD, autism and dyslexia?

Specific Learning Difficulty: Developmental Coordination Disorder (DCD) (dyspraxia)

Developmental Coordination Disorder (DCD), also known as dyspraxia in the UK, is a common disorder affecting movement and coordination in children, young people and adults with symptoms present since childhood. DCD is distinct from other motor disorders such as cerebral palsy and stroke and occurs across the range of intellectual abilities. Individuals may present issues such as reaching motor milestones late, difficulty running, jumping, hopping, catching, etc.; being slow and hesitant in most actions, trips and falls easily, difficulty getting dressed, using cutlery, tying laces, etc.; poor understanding of spatial language/concepts and difficulty keeping friends/managing social behaviour. Dyspraxia can be defined as an impairment or immaturity of the organisation of movement. Associated with this may be problems of 'language, perception and thought' (Dyspraxia Foundation, 2023). It used to be called 'clumsy child syndrome', motor control deficit or 'minimal brain damage'. Motor coordination weaknesses may be primarily those of fine or gross motor control, or both; they are reflected in a range of everyday experiences, including bumping into objects and people, poor balance, and difficulty with everyday tasks such as housework and cooking. Dyspraxia also typically includes weaknesses in short-term memory, visual processing and visual tracking. These weaknesses are reflected in such everyday experiences as forgetfulness, disorganisation, difficulty following instructions and/or directions, and going off at tangents. In some instances, 'reading' non-verbal face and body signs may also be a challenge. Some dyspraxics are hyper-sensitive to touch, sound or light, and many report sleep difficulties (Grant, 2009).

Pause for reflection

Many people still refer to 'clumsy child syndrome' as it relates to motor coordination issues. However, it manifests in several characteristics.

- What impact might this have on social, emotional and mental health of a learner?
- How might it impact upon academic success or employability?

Diagnosis

Diagnostic testing for DCD requires first being referred for an assessment. Usually, assessment will involve a test called the Motor ABC which includes tests of gross and fine motor skills. Additionally, medical history will be looked at alongside general observations. The Wechsler Adult Intelligence Scale 4th Edition test battery (WAIS-IV) may also be used by psychologists to assess individuals for DCD for academic or occupational purposes. DSM -5 (APA, 2013) and ICD-11 (WHO, 2019) have inclusive and exclusive criteria in the definition of DCD. For DMS-5, the inclusive criteria include impairment in the development of motor coordination, which can be manifested in delays in milestones such as standing and walking; poor performance in sports activities; and untidy handwriting. To further complicate diagnosis, there is evidence to suggest a high probability that another specific learning disability will be present, for example, Kadesjö and Gillberg (1999) found in a study of seven-year-olds in Sweden that almost 50 per cent of children with dyspraxia had ADHD. As specific learning difficulties may share many overlapping features, this means that additional care needs to be taken when reaching a diagnosis. There have been many studies into the causes of DCD and whether genetics may be involved. Mountford et al. (2021) examined data from over 4,000 parents and their children who had their motor coordination tested at seven years old.

Developmental Coordination Disorder (DCD) DSM-5

(A) Motor performance that is substantially below expected levels, given the person's chronologic age and previous opportunities for skill acquisition.

(B) The disturbance in Criterion A, without accommodations, significantly and persistently interferes with activities of daily living or academic achievement.

(C) Onset of symptoms is in the early developmental period.

(D) The motor skill deficits are not better explained by intellectual disability (intellectual development disorder) or visual impairment and are not attributable to a neurological condition affecting movement (e.g., cerebral palsy, muscular dystrophy, degenerative disorder).

ICD-11

Developmental motor coordination disorder is characterised by a significant delay in the acquisition of gross and fine motor skills and impairment in the execution of coordinated motor skills that manifest in clumsiness, slowness, or inaccuracy of motor performance. Coordinated motor skills are substantially below that expected given the individual's chronological age and level of intellectual functioning.

Aetiology of Developmental Coordination Disorder

Hereditability

Nielsen et al. (2005) conducted a study into the shared genetic heritability of DCD and ADHD which found a substantial shared aetiology due to both genetic and common environmental factors. More recently, a 2011 study looking into the nature of DCD and its aetiology found issues in pregnancy to be a significant contributary factor to DCD (Vaivre-Douret et al., 2011). Other research suggests that there is disruption between the brain and the body with the outcome being the possibility of a compromised motor control system used when learning skills (Hill and Wing, 1999). Wilson et al. (2013) concluded that there were clear difficulties with executive function and working memory in children with DCD, and this is consistent with Piek et al. (2007) who found a generalised executive dysfunction. Developments in medical science have made it possible to use Neuroimaging to understand DCD (Fuelscher et al., 2018)

Neuroanatomy

DCD is a very heterogeneous condition, with distinctions in the type and level of motor skill impairment of everyone (Caçola and Lage, 2019). Children with DCD show increased activation in certain areas of the brain such as the fronto-central while performing some tasks. Zwicker, et al. (2010) conducted a study to explore whether children with DCD have different brain activity to those without the disorder. The results showed that the group with DCD relied on their visuospatial processing to complete the task, and the group without DCD used more regions which are associated with motor control, learning and error processing. This is significant because although there were no behavioural differences between the groups, the results show that DCD does impact the brain and how it is used when completing tasks.

Brown-Lum and Zwicker (2015) support the hypothesis that DCD is the result of atypical brain development and that children with DCD are neurobiologically different than TD peers. A potential cause of DCD could be deficits in planning motor actions and motor imagery. Motor imagery (MI) refers to the imagination of a motor task without actual movement execution and is believed to represent one's ability to accurately utilise forward internal models of motor control. Internal models (Adams et al., 2014) provide stability to the motor system by predicting the outcome of movements before sensorimotor feedback is available. Without that ability, movements are clumsy and disorganised, which explains most of the problems seen in DCD.

Activity

Debate: Let's not ask, 'Does dyslexia exist?' Let's instead concentrate upon ensuring that all children with literacy difficulties are served.

It was once a widely accepted way of explaining why some children struggled to read and write. But in recent years, some experts have begun to question the existence of dyslexia itself (Kale, 2020). Elliott and Gibbs (2008) argue that there is essentially no difference between a person who struggles to read and write and a person with dyslexia – and no difference in how you should teach them. Dyslexia is such a broad term, that it is effectively meaningless, and the current system entrenches inequality, because children from poorer backgrounds tend to be less likely to be diagnosed with dyslexia and about 50 per cent of the UK prison population have literacy difficulties, yet almost none of these prisoners will have a dyslexia diagnosis. The authors are sceptical about the value and validity of the dyslexia construct and suggest that it is a largely socially defined construct. They raise concerns about the fairness of allocating resources to those with a label of 'dyslexia' in ways that might leave those with reading difficulties (and without the label) less supported.

Snowling (2008) is alarmed by the practices of independent educational psychologists who are paid directly by parents to diagnose children with dyslexia and agrees that dyslexics and non-dyslexics can basically be taught to read and write in the same way. However, she states that dyslexia is a heritable disorder which affects the part of the brain that processes speech and sound. Dyslexia exists, she says, and it's a label that most people find useful. She argues that we need to identify the dyslexic type earlier so that we can research the genes and brains and children earlier, concluding that dyslexia is a major obstacle to success.

Watch the video 'Dyslexia: What we have learned from Family Studies' hosted by Maggie Snowling available at: www.youtube.com/watch?v= WPVqvUrbCik

Watch the video 'The Dyslexia Debate' available at: www.google.com/ search?client=safari&rls=en&q=Joe+Eliott+dyslexia+you+tube&ie=UTF-8& oe=UTF-8#fpstate=ive&vld=cid:ae26e084,vid:_Bhi5AuMBvQ

- What are the key points that they make?
- What evidence do they produce to support their arguments?
- What does this say about how dyslexia is viewed and the role of screening, resource allocation and social justice in education?

References

Adams, I. L., Lust, J. M., Wilson, P. H. and Steenbergen, B. (2014). Compromised motor control in children with DCD: a deficit in the internal model? A systematic review. *Neuroscience and Biobehavioral Reviews*, 47, pp. 225–244.

Alarcón, M., DeFries, J. C., Light, J. G. and Pennington, B. F. (1997). A twin study of mathematics disability. *Journal of Learning Disabilities*, 30 (6), pp. 617–623.

American Psychiatric Association (2013). *Diagnostic and Statistical Manual of Mental Disorders*. 5th ed. Washington, DC: American Psychiatric Publishing.

Becker, N., Vasconcelos, M., Oliveira, V., Santos, F. C. D., Bizarro, L., Almeida, R. M. M., Salles, J. F. and Carvalho, M. R. S. (2017). Genetic and environmental risk factors for developmental dyslexia in children: systematic review of the last decade. *Developmental Neuropsychology*, 42 (7–8), pp. 423–445.

Bradley, L. and Bryant, P. (1983). Categorizing sounds and learning to read: a causal connection. *Nature*, 301, pp. 419–421.

British Dyslexia Association (2018). *Dyslexia Friendly Schools Good Practice Guide.* 2nd ed. Bracknell: BDA.

Brown-Lum, M., Zwicker, J.G. (2015). Brain imaging increases our understanding of developmental coordination disorder: a review of literature and future directions. *Curr Dev Disord*, 2, pp. 131–140.

Brunswick, N. (2011). *Living with Dyslexia: Contemporary Issues.* 1st ed. New York: Rosen Publishing Group.

Brunswick, N. (2009). *Dyslexia: A Beginner's Guide.* Oxford: Oneworld.

Butterworth, B. (1999). *The Mathematical Brain.* London: Macmillan.

Butterworth, B., Varma, S. and Laurillard, D. (2011). Dyscalculia: from brain to education. *Science*, 332 (6033), pp. 1049–1053.

Butterworth, B and Reigosa-Crespo, V. (2007). Information processing deficits in dyscalculia. In: Berch, D. B. and Mazzocco, M. M. (eds.), *Why is Math So Hard for Some Children? The Nature and Origins of Mathematical Learning Difficulties and Disabilities.* Baltimore: Brookes, pp. 65–81.

Caçola, P., and Lage, G. M. (2019). Developmental Coordination Disorder (DCD): an overview of the condition and research evidence. *Motriz: Revista de Educação Física*, 25 (2), e101923.

Cappelletti, M. and Price, C. J. (2014). Residual number processing in dyscalculia. *NeuroImage: Clinical*, 4, pp. 18–28.

Castelli, F., Glaser, D. E. and Butterworth, B. (2006). Discrete and analogue quantity processing in the parietal lobe: a functional MRI study. *PNAS Proceedings of the National Academy of Sciences of the United States of America*, 103 (12), pp. 4693–4698.

Colley, A. (2020). To what extent have learners with severe, profound and multiple learning difficulties been excluded from the policy and practice of inclusive education? *International Journal of Inclusive Education*, 24 (6), pp. 721–738.

Dehaene, S. (1997). *The Number Sense: How the Mind Creates Mathematics.* New York: Oxford University Press.

Department for Education and Department of Health (2015). *Special Educational Needs and Disability Code of Practice: 0 to 25 years.* [online] Available at: www.gov.uk/government/publications/send-code-of-practice-0-to-25 [Accessed 25. 10. 2022].

Department for Education (2022). *Statistics: Special Educational Needs* (SEN). [online] Available at: www.gov.uk/government/collections/statistics-special-educational-needs-sen [Accessed 10. 12. 2022].

Department of Education and Skills (2003). *Data Collection by Type of Special Educational Need.* [online] Available at: https://dera.ioe.ac.uk/7736/1/DFES-1889-2005.pdf [Accessed 09. 12. 2022].

Department for Education and Skills (2001). *The National Numeracy Strategy. Guidance to Support Learners with Dyslexia and Dyscalculia.* London: DfES.

Department for Education and Skills (2001). *The National Numeracy Strategy.* [online] Available at: http://scotens.org/sen/resources/dyslexia_leaflet_maths.pdf [Accessed 03. 01. 2023].

Dyspraxia Foundation (2023). *Information Sheets.* [online] Available at: https://dyspraxia foundation.org.uk/advice/information-sheets [Accessed 02. 01. 2023].

Dyslexia Association (2023). *What Are the Signs of Dyscalculia?* [online] Available at: www. dyslexia.uk.net/specific-learning-difficulties/dyscalculia/the-signs-of-dyscalculia [Accessed 02. 01. 2023].

Elliott, J. and Gibbs, S. (2008). Does dyslexia exist? *Journal of Philosophy of Education*, 42 (3–4), pp. 475–491.

Emerson, J. and Babtie, P. (2014). *Dyscalculia Assessment.* 1st ed. London: Bloomsbury Publishing.

Fawcett, A. J. and Nicolson, R. I. (1999). Performance of dyslexic children on cerebellar and cognitive tests. *Journal of Motor Behavior*, 31 (1), pp. 68–78.

Fisk, J. E. and Sharp, C. A. (2004). Age-related impairment in executive functioning: updating, inhibition, shifting, and access. *Journal of Clinical and Experimental Neuropsychology*, 26 (7), pp. 874–890.

Fuelscher, I., Caeyenberghs, K., Enticott, P. G., Williams, J., Lum, J. and Hyde, C. (2018). Differential activation of brain areas in children with developmental coordination disorder during tasks of manual dexterity: an ALE meta-analysis. *Neuroscience & Biobehavioral Reviews*, 86, pp. 77–84.

Galaburda, A. M., LoTurco, J., Ramus, F., Fitch, R. H. and Rosen, G. D. (2006). From genes to behavior in developmental dyslexia. *Nature Neuroscience*, 9 (10), pp. 1213–1217.

Geary, D. C. (2004). Mathematics and learning disabilities. *Journal of Learning Disabilities*, 37 (1), pp. 4–15.

Gersten, R. and Chard, D. (1999). Number sense: rethinking arithmetic instruction for students with mathematical disabilities. *The Journal of Special Education*, 33 (1), pp. 18–28.

Kadesjo, K. and Gillberg, C. (1999). Developmental coordination disorder in Swedish 7-year-old children. *Journal of the American Academy of Child & Adolescent Psychiatry*, 38 (7) pp. 820–828.

Gittens, D. and Rose, N. (2007). An audit of adults with profound and multiple learning disabilities within a West Midlands community health trust: implications for service development. *British Journal of Learning Disabilities*, 36 (1), pp. 38–47.

Goldbart, J., Chadwick, D. and Buell, S. (2014). Speech and language therapists' approaches to communication intervention with children and adults with profound and multiple learning disability: SLT interventions with children and adults with PMLD. *International Journal of Language and Communication Disorders*, 49 (6), pp. 687–701.

Grant, D. (2009). *That's the Way I Think: Dyslexia, Dyspraxia, ADHD and Dyscalculia Explained.* Abingdon: Routledge.

Hammond, J. and Hercules, F. (2007). *Understanding Dyslexia: An Introduction for Dyslexic Students in Higher Education.* Scottish Higher Education Funding Council.

Hannell, G. (2005). *Dyscalculia Action Plans for Successful Learning in Mathematics.* London: David Fulton Publishers.

Henderson, A. (2012). *Dyslexia, Dyscalculia and Mathematics: A Practical Guide.* London: Routledge.

Hill, E. L. and Wing, A. M. (1999). Coordination of grip force and load force in developmental coordination disorder: a case study. *Neurocase*, 5 (6), pp. 537–544.

Hogg, J. (2004). Call for Papers for Special Issue of Journal of Policy and Practice in Intellectual Disabilities. www.iassid.org.

Hornigold, J. (2015). *Dyscalculia Pocketbook.* 1st ed. Alresford: Management Pocketbooks.

Isaacs, E. B., Edmonds, C. J., Lucas, A. and Gadian, D. G. (2001). Calculation difficulties in children of very low birthweight: a neural correlate. *Brain: A Journal of Neurology*, 124 (9), pp. 1701–1707.

Kadesjö, B. and Gillberg, C. (1999). Developmental coordination disorder in Swedish 7-year-old children. *Journal of the American Academy of Child and Adolescent Psychiatry*, 38 (7), pp. 820–828.

Kale, S. (2020). The battle over dyslexia. [online] Available at: www.theguardian.com/news/2020/sep/17/battle-over-dyslexia-warwickshire-staffordshire [Accessed 04. 12. 2022].

Kaufmann, L., Mazzocco, M. M., Dowker, A., von Aster, M., Göbel, S. M., Grabner, R. H., Henik, A., Jordan, N. C., Karmiloff-Smith, A. D., Kucian, K., Rubinsten, O., Szucs, D., Shalev, R. and Nuerk, H. C. (2013). Dyscalculia from a developmental and differential perspective. *Frontiers in Psychology*, 4, 516.

Kaufman, E., Lord, M., Reese, T. and Volkmann, J. (1949). The discrimination of visual number. *The American Journal of Psychology*, 62, pp. 498–525.

Kosc, L. (1974). Developmental dyscalculia. *Journal of Learning Disabilities*, 7 (3), pp.165–177.

Lacey, P. (1998). Meeting complex needs through collaborative multidisciplinary teamwork. In: P. Lacey and C. Ouvry (eds.), *People with Profound and Multiple Learning Disabilities: A Collaborative Approach to Meeting Complex Needs*. London: Fulton.

Landerl, K., Bevan, A. and Butterworth, B. (2004). Developmental dyscalculia and basic numerical capacities: a study of 8–9-year-old students. *Cognition*, 93 (2), pp. 99–125.

Light, J. G. and DeFries, J. C. (1995). Comorbidity of reading and mathematics disabilities: Genetic and environmental etiologies. *Journal of Learning Disabilities*, 28 (2), pp. 96–106.

Lovegrove, W. J., Martin, F., Blackwood, M. and Badcock, D. (1980). Specific reading difficulty: differences in contrast sensitivity as a function of spatial frequency. *Science*, 210, pp. 439–444.

Mather, N. and Wendling, B. J. (2012). *Essentials of Dyslexia Assessment and Intervention*. Hoboken: John Wiley and Sons Inc.

Mountford, H. S., Hill, A., Barnett, A. L. and Newbury, D. F. (2021). Genome-wide association study of motor coordination. *Frontiers in Human Neuroscience*, 15.

Mueller, B., Ahnert, P., Burkhardt, J., Brauer, J., Czepezauer, I., Quente, E., Boltze, J., Wilcke, A. and Kirsten, H. (2014). Genetic risk variants for dyslexia on chromosome 18 in a German cohort. *Genes, Brain and Behavior*, 13 (3), pp. 350–356.

Nicolson, R. I. and Fawcett, A. J. (1990). Automaticity: a new framework for dyslexia research? *Cognition*, 35 (2), pp. 159–182.

Nielsen, R., Williamson, S., Kim, Y., Hubisz, M. J., Clark, A. G. and Bustamante, C. (2005). Genomic scans for selective sweeps using SNP data. *Genome Res*, 15 (11), pp. 1566–1575.

Paulesu, E., Frith, C., Snowling, M., Gallagher, A., Morton, J. and Frackowiak, R. S. (1996). Is developmental dyslexia a disconnection syndrome? Evidence from PET scanning. *Brain*, 119 (1), pp. 143–157.

Pennington, B. F. and Ozonoff, S. (1996). Executive functions and developmental psychopathology. *Journal of Child Psychology and Psychiatry, and Allied Disciplines*, 37 (1), pp. 51–87.

Pick, J. P., Rigoli, D., Pearsall-Jones, J. G., Martin, N. C., Hay, D. A., Bennett, K. S. and Levy, F. (2007). Depressive symptomatology in child and adolescent twins with attention-deficit hyperactivity disorder and/or developmental coordination disorder. *Twin*

Research and Human Genetics: The Official Journal of the International Society for Twin Studies, 10 (4), pp. 587–596.

Protopapas, A. and Parrila R. (2018). Is dyslexia a brain disorder? *Brain Sci*, 8 (4), 61.

Public Health England (2020). Chapter 1: children's social care. [online] Available at: www.gov.uk/government/publications/people-with-learning-disabilities-in-england/chapter-1-education-and-childrens-social-care-updates [Accessed 10. 11. 2022].

Pumfrey, P. (2001). Specific Developmental Dyslexia (SDD): 'Basics to back' in 2000 and beyond? In: M. Hunter-Carsch (ed.), *Dyslexia: A Psychosocial Perspective* (pp. 137–159). London: Whurr.

Rapin, I. (2016). Dyscalculia and the calculating brain. *Pediatric Neurology*, 61, pp. 11–20.

Robertson, J. and Bakker, D. J. (2002). The balance model of reading and dyslexia. In: G. Reid, and J. Wearmouth (eds.), *Dyslexia and Literacy: Theory and Practice*. London: Wiley, pp. 99–114.

Reid, G. (2011). *Dyslexia*. 3rd ed. London: Continuum.

Rose, J. (2009). *Identifying and Teaching Children and Young People with Dyslexia and Literacy Difficulties*. Nottingham: DCSF.

Rubinsten, O. and Henik, A. (2009). Developmental dyscalculia: heterogeneity might not mean different mechanisms. *Trends in Cognitive Sciences*, 13 (2), pp. 92–99.

Samuel, J. and Pritchard, M. (2001). The ignored minority: meeting the needs of people with profound learning disability. *Tizard Learning Disability Review*, 6, pp. 34–44.

Shalev, R. S., Manor, O., Kerem, B., Ayali, M., Badichi, N., Friedlander, Y. and Gross-Tsur, V. (2001). Developmental dyscalculia is a familial learning disability. *Journal of Learning Disabilities*, 34 (1), pp. 59–65.

Simmons, F. R. and Singleton, C. (2008). Do weak phonological representations impact on arithmetic development? A review of research into arithmetic and dyslexia. *Dyslexia*, 14 (2), pp. 77–94.

Simmons, B. and Watson, D. (2014). *The PMLD Ambiguity Articulating the Life-Worlds of Children with Profound and Multiple Learning Disabilities*. London: Routledge.

Smith-Spark, J. H., and Fisk, J. E. (2007). Working memory functioning in developmental dyslexia. *Memory*, 15 (1), pp. 34–56.

Snowling, M. J. (2008). *State of Science Review: SR-D2: Dyslexia*. London: The Government Office for Science.

Snowling, M. J., Gallagher, A. and Frith, U. (2003). Family risk of dyslexia is continuous: individual differences in the precursors of reading skill. *Child Development*, 74 (2), pp. 358–373.

Stein, J. and Walsh, V. (1997). To see but not to read: the magnocellular theory of dyslexia. *Trends in Neurosciences*, 20 (4), pp. 147–152.

Swagerman, S., van Bergen, E., Dolan, C., Geus, E., Koenis, M., Pol, H. and Boomsma, D. (2015). Genetic transmission of reading ability. *Brain and Language*, 172, pp. 3–8.

Tallal, P. and Piercy, M. (1973). Defects of non-verbal auditory perception in children with developmental aphasia. *Nature*, 241, pp. 468–469.

Vaivre-Douret, L., Lalanne, C., Ingster-Moati, I., Boddaert, N., Cabrol, D., Dufier, J. L., Golse, B. and Falissard, B. (2011). Subtypes of developmental coordination disorder: research on their nature and etiology. *Developmental Neuropsychology*, 36 (5), pp. 614–643.

von Aster, M. (2000). Developmental cognitive neuropsychology of number processing and calculation: varieties of developmental dyscalculia. *European Child & Adolescent Psychiatry*, 9 (2), pp. 1141–1157.

von Aster, M. G. and Shalev, R. S. (2007). Number development and developmental dyscalculia. *Developmental Medicine and Child Neurology*, 49 (11), pp. 868–873.

Ware, J. (2004). Ascertaining the views of people with profound and multiple learning disabilities. *British Journal of Learning Disabilities*, 32, pp. 175–179.

Wilson, P. H., Ruddock, S., Smits-Engelsman, B., Polatajko, H. and Blank, R. (2013). Understanding performance deficits in developmental coordination disorder: a meta-analysis of recent research. *Developmental Medicine and Child Neurology*, 55 (3), pp. 217–228.

World Health Organization (2019). *International Statistical Classification of Diseases and Related Health Problems.* 11th ed.

Young, P. and Tyre, C. (1983). *Dyslexia or Illiteracy? Realizing the Right to Read.* Milton Keynes: Open University Press.

Zwicker, J. G., Missiuna, C., Harris, S. R. and Boyd, L. A. (2010). Brain activation of children with developmental coordination disorder is different than peers. *Pediatrics*, 126 (3), e678–e686.

2 The impact of Cognition and Learning Needs on individuals and families

Introduction

This chapter examines the impact that cognition and learning difficulties may have on an individual, their families and allies, utilising a series of case studies from a range of contexts and ages. Identifying the characteristics and issues involved in the examples given in Chapter 1, it examines the impact on children, adults and families of impact from the continuum Profound and Multiple Learning Difficulties, Developmental Coordination Disorder (DCD), dyslexia and dyscalculia. Specific cognitive issues such as working memory, executive function and theories of learning will be examined in Chapter 3.

Learning objectives

This chapter will:

- Invite you to apply your understanding gained from the previous chapter to the lived experience
- Introduce you to a wide range of consequences of Cognition and Learning Needs to individuals, families and allies
- Help you to understand how these needs impact the lives of children, young people and adults
- Invite you to review research evidence which supports our understanding of the impact on the lives of individuals, families and allies
- Invite you to review how dyslexia, Developmental Coordination Disorder (dyspraxia), and dyscalculia influence educational attainment and access to employment

Key terms

Profound and Multiple Learning Difficulties, COVID-19, Developmental Coordination Disorder (DCD), dyslexia, dyscalculia, children, adults, families, parents, education, employment

DOI: 10.4324/9781003361084-4

Pause for reflection

- What do you think may be the impact of cognitive and learning difficulties in relation to issues such as dyslexia or DCD (dyspraxia)?

Profound and Multiple Learning Difficulties (PMLD)

Impact of COVID-19 on PMLD families

The COVID-19 epidemic has had a profound effect on the lives of PMLD individuals and their families. Flynn et al. (2021) surveyed, first, 621 people with learning disabilities (Cohort 1) and second, 378 family carers or support staff of people with learning disabilities (Cohort 2). People with learning disabilities were more concerned about their family or friends catching COVID-19 than they were about themselves catching it. People with learning disabilities who were aged 45 and over were 1.6 times more likely to be (a little or a lot) concerned about leaving the house, compared to those aged 44 and under. Most participants in Cohort 1 reported experiencing low levels of well-being, with over 65 per cent of participants answering that they had felt angry or frustrated, sad, or down, and worried or anxious. Members of Cohort 1 living with their family were 1.5 times less likely to report feeling lonely and 1.7 times less likely to feel sad or down (at least some of the time) than people living elsewhere. Whilst over one-third of people with learning disabilities reported that they had not seen their partner (when they did not live with them) over the last four weeks, the majority had had some virtual contact.

There is no doubt that the specific coronavirus restrictions have clearly affected the lives of people with learning disabilities and their families across the UK. Social distancing restrictions are a barrier to the usual communication method of many people with profound and multiple learning disabilities as they prohibit physical touch. Shielding has significantly increased social isolation for both people with learning disabilities and their families, many of whom have been shielding since the outbreak of the pandemic. People with learning disabilities and their families feel society has forgotten about them. The increased anxiety around all the changes, including changes in support and access to medical care, has left people with learning disabilities and family carers experiencing a loss of control in their lives.

In another survey, the Scottish Commission for Learning Disability (SCLD, 2022) found that people with learning disabilities were worried about the coronavirus. Those who were interviewed were more concerned about their family or friends catching coronavirus than they were about catching it themselves. They also reported high levels of emotional distress and loneliness. The findings were similar for people with more severe learning disabilities. Carers reported that most people with more severe learning disabilities had felt worried, sad, and angry at the second wave of data collection, with little sign of improvement by August 2021. There was also an impact on carers who reported feeling tired, depressed, stressed, and had disturbed sleep. Lack of contact was a source of stress for family members and their loved ones who did not live with them. Restricted visiting for families and friends also had a negative impact on the person they supported.

Caton et al. (2022) reveal that around half of the people with PMLD had Internet access at home. Around half of the participants in their research interacted with others on video calls like Facetime or Zoom and most used the Internet for being with family and friends online and streaming TV and films. In the event of another lockdown, 27.5 per cent of the people supporting someone with PMLD said they would like support with technology to make seeing friends and family easier. For some the people, digital participation during the pandemic was not beneficial enough to want to continue when restrictions eased. For others, the new online experiences had the potential to be developed in their post pandemic lives. Flynn et al. (2021) reported that social isolation was the most reported worry for adults with learning disabilities, with other frequently reported worries including changes to or loss of routine, loss of support and services; and decreased health/well-being/fitness. A large proportion of participants indicated that nothing positive had happened because of COVID-19, but others reported some positive outcomes including digital inclusion, more time spent with important people improved health and well-being/fitness, and a slower pace of life.

Family carers of people with PMLD experienced a reduction in healthcare services due to the COVID-19 pandemic. Many subsequently turned to Non-Governmental Organisations (NGOs) who worked to support families. However, little research has sought to capture the experiences of family carers or identify effective interventions which might support them. Linden et al. (2022) sought the views of non-Governmental sector workers across the UK and Ireland who supported families of people with PMLD during the COVID-19 pandemic. NGOs provide ongoing care and support for families of individuals with disabilities and include supported living, residential services, day care, vocational training, supported employment, respite care and leisure. They reported that families were staying at home to protect their relative from the risk of coronavirus and have been doing so since March, and this group seem to have been forgotten about.

Hatton et al. (2021) suggest that complex communication challenges meant that it could be harder to identify health issues in people with PMLD and carers are mindful that many health issues are always attributed to the PMLD. Whilst some health issues can be identified through a remote consultation, people with PMLD are less likely to be able to access support in this way; their methods of communicating pain, distress and discomfort are likely to be idiosyncratic and health needs may need to be identified through a physical examination. The virus had resulted in restrictions on physical contact and many carers reported being unable to go and visit their relative if they are living in residential services. They did not describe 'social' distancing, but rather 'physically' distancing from other people.

Pause for reflection

The impact of COVID-19 is only one issue which may impact on a family with a child with complex needs.

- Can you think of any other significant factors such as finances, access to health services etc?

Activity

Read the following case studies.

Freddie is aged 22 and lives with his parents. He is a very sociable character and revels in the laughter and hubbub of spending time with his friends. He uses sounds in place of traditional speech due to deficit in motor skills of the mouth, regardless he is known for his skills in comedy. Freddie uses other cues in communication instead of speech: intonation- the rise and fall in pitch, face expressions, repetition of others and anticipation of laughter. Freddie shows high-functioning understanding of communication and social interaction, and he finds humour in such encounters.

Lin is aged seven and lives with her parents. She is a non-verbal communicator and does not recognise words but uses smiles in response to familiar voices. She will respond to stimuli; for example, Lin seems to like the soft textures in a sensory story but not the feel of cold water, although she will splash her hands in warm water. She will cry if she is supported by someone she doesn't know but will calm when one of the familiar staff takes over. She smiles if she sees or hears his taxi escort nearby. She is unable to support own body weight and cannot move her legs independently. She relies on others for personal care and has epilepsy.

Freddie wants to go to his local college, but his parents need to know that it can support his needs. Read the section on Further Education (Chapter 7), from the SEND Code of Practice (2015) (DfE, DoH, 2015).

- What would the college need to implement to support his needs?

Lin has complex needs.

- How would a multi-agency support network support her and her family?
- Which agencies would be involved?

Dyslexia

Dyslexia is a complex, multifaceted concept (van der Leij et al., 2013) that hinders literacy development in both children and adults and remains persistent across the lifespan. Without consensus regarding the specific definition, empirical and practical definitions will continue to have different foci and employ different assessment procedures (Tonnessen, 1997). The effects of dyslexia go beyond biological or genetic mechanisms to include psychosocial and cultural processes, which are influenced by society's reactions to the term (Elliott and Grigorenko, 2014). Modern classifications of dyslexia define the reading disorder along these lines of processing behaviours and the prevalence rates of dyslexia typically vary from 4 to 10 per cent depending on the definition employed and males are at least twice as likely to have the disorder as females. Dyslexia occurs across ethnicity, IQ and socio-economic status.

Dyslexia and education

Pitt and Soni (2017) argue that a positive dyslexic identity is conducive to academic success and found that their research participants accommodated their label of dyslexia and described it as a difference not a disability or neurological condition. In their view, this contributed to them becoming successful, determined university students. Armstrong and Humphrey (2009) corroborated this and cited the benefits of integrating dyslexia into identity including the motivation to study, use of educational support and success in academic work. However, when experienced daily at school, the painful feelings of inferiority, inadequacy, frustration and shame can weaken the motivation to learn of a dyslexic child, which can lead to issues with motivation. Gibson and Kendall (2010) interviewed five first-year university students, four with dyslexia, to explore factors that impact on academic achievement and self-esteem. Similarly, Glazzard (2010) interviewed nine secondary school pupils with dyslexia to investigate factors that affected their self-esteem. Both studies identified teachers and peers as key influencers. Participants had experienced mixed attitudes from teachers with some reporting negative teacher attitudes and some experiencing supportive teaching. About peers, participants in each study had experienced verbal abuse from peers in relation to their literacy difficulties. Both studies concluded that negative attitudes from teachers and peers led to detrimental effects on the self-esteem of children with dyslexia, with Gibson and Kendall (2010) arguing that teachers need to respond to the personal, social and emotional needs of young people with dyslexia, in addition to academic needs.

Pause for reflection

It is important to recognise that children, young people and adults may have a main area of need as identified within this book, but there may be other needs. For example, autism and dyslexia, or ADHD and dyspraxia.

- How would we examine the impact of multiple needs which may be identified?
- Who determines whether it is the main area of need?

Dyslexia and families

Dyslexia represents significant challenges not just for the student but can also be traumatic for their parents. Given that learning to read is a fundamental core skill of schooling and becoming literate opens doors to education, employment and adult well-being (Snowling and Hulme, 2012), parents of students with dyslexia show higher levels of anxiety than parents of non-dyslexic students (Snowling and Melby-Lervåg, 2016). Parents experience stress in coping with their child's apparent poor academic progress (Karande and Kuril, 2011), particularly if they lack understanding of the dyslexic implications. Mothers show higher levels of stress and depression and report significant impacts on family (Snowling, Muter and Carroll, 2007) and increased difficulties in everyday life.

The most common maternal worries involve both emotional and practical difficulties (Earey, 2013), as their child's chronic poor performance at school relates to the child losing self-esteem, getting frustrated and developing withdrawn or aggressive behaviour. In addition, maternal anxiety is increased when attempting to seek appropriate help for their child, especially when bureaucratic processes appear to move slowly in providing effective interventions to help students overcome dyslexic difficulties. Mothers, by necessity, become advocates for their child (Poon-McBrayer and McBrayer, 2014) and are frequently required to face schoolteachers who appear uncooperative and unconcerned about their child's dyslexia (Karande et al., 2009) requiring parents to return repeatedly to the schools to remind them of their child's needs (Earey, 2013). Mothers become emotionally and physically drained as they become heavily involved in their child's remedial education (Bonifacci et al., 2014) and worry for the child's future (Karande et al., 2009). Many mothers choose to quit their jobs to focus their energy and time attending to their child (Poon-McBrayer and McBrayer, 2014). Overall, the literature reports ongoing difficulties for parents as they struggle to support their child before, during and after the assessment of dyslexia.

Using Interpretative Phenomenological Analysis (IPA), Amiera Alias and Dahlan (2015) found that mothers reported that issues with time constraints were considered as one of the big challenges in raising children with dyslexia, along with negative feelings, such as sadness, denial, worry. Ongoing chronic stress can lead to negative parenting practices and adversely affect the parent–child relationships and outcomes (Karande and Kuril, 2011). Poor attachment to parents by dyslexic students may be due to a higher load of schoolwork straining the relationships within the family (Undheim and Sund, 2008). This is then compounded by higher parental distress related to the perception of having a relationship with a 'difficult child' (Bonifacci et al., 2014). Parental awareness of dyslexia as a lifelong disorder would empower parents to guide their child through to adulthood (Karande, Mehta and Kulkarni, 2007) and provide ongoing support to reconcile the complex array of emotions that are inherent in living with dyslexia (Nalavany and Carawan, 2012).

Delany (2017) showed the overarching core of this phenomenon was: 'A long difficult journey toward personal empowerment'. Five themes emerged from the data, which reflected aspects of how parents experienced this journey these being grieving the loss of normal, fierce but reluctant warriors, navigating system failures, the changing sense of self and hope for the future. Conceptualised through the theory of personal empowerment, these finding have highlighted that parents of children with dyslexia are able to evolve and develop strategies to cope with the many challenges they face along the difficult journey. Knight (2021) also revealed how the dyslexia label impacted whether the children believed that they would go to university. Not only did those labelled as dyslexic hold lower expectations about their likelihood of going to university, the parents and teachers of the labelled individuals also held significantly lower expectations for this group. Thus, the negative impact on future academic aspirations was not only found in the dyslexic child, but also their parent and teacher.

Dyslexia and children

A recurring theme in this research is the effect of labelling on young people: do they benefit from being labelled as dyslexic, or does it negatively impact on them? Riddick (2010) argued that whether a child has a 'label' attached to their difficulties makes little difference to their embodied classroom role. She believes that in attributing a child's difficulties to dyslexia, the child is empowered to better understand characteristics they possess. Other work by Gibby-Leversuch, Hartwell and Wright (2021) echoes this view that a label can be emancipatory. However, Solvang (2007) argues that although a diagnosis may help young people understand their difficulties, it can potentially be a source of oppression for them; they are pathologised, their condition 'treated' and 'remediation' of their difficulties sought.

Whether young people's relationships with others are negatively impacted by dyslexia is contested. Ingesson (2007) found that most young people reported that their dyslexia did not negatively impact on their relationships with their peers. However, they did report that many young people had been bullied due to their difficulties with literacy, which had in turn negatively affected their self-esteem. However, Gibby-Leversuch, Hartwell and Wright (2021) report that young people's relationships were influenced both positively and negatively by their dyslexia. Particularly influential within relationships was how young people conceptualise their own dyslexia. Their review found within several studies the importance of relationships in the sense-making process relating to dyslexia and the mutual importance of relationships in how young people make sense of their dyslexia. Teachers' understandings, empathy and pedagogy were crucial in supporting positive experiences for young people with dyslexia, as was early identification and openness with their peers. Young people often sought support from those who had experiential knowledge of dyslexia and the difficulties they faced.

Activity

Ross (2021) interviewed nine young people aged 11–14 to consider their own dyslexia and found that young people tended to draw on medicalised models of dyslexia. When describing it, it was a separate entity whilst concurrently part of them. Young people's conceptualisations of dyslexia were informed through both their own experiences of learning and through interaction with others. Young people's sense making of their own dyslexia drew upon others' understandings of it. Their views were largely located within medical conceptualisation of dyslexia as a condition that causes difficulties or differences in how their brains worked. They generally found it helpful to know that they had dyslexia and were able to locate their difficulties in it. It was freeing for the young people in this study to understand why they found things difficult, rather than them feeling they were intrinsically bad at learning or lacking ability. Several participants in this study chose to align themselves with others who have learning difficulties of varying types such as dyslexia, dyscalculia or autism. Their friendships were informed and influenced by their experiential knowledge of dyslexia and other learning difficulties. Thus, while young people have some agency and capacity to negotiate their own interactions at the 'interactional order,' they depend on others to support them in this process.

- What were the key findings from this study and what o they tell us about the complexities surrounding the impact of dyslexia?

  A researcher in dyslexia wants to hold a focus group looking at the lived experience of dyslexic students who attend a local university.

- Who could they invite to be a part of the group and why?
- What questions might be posed and why?
- Who should have access to the findings of the research?

Adult dyslexia

Research suggests that problems in reading fluency and spelling are the most prominent markers of dyslexia in adulthood (Nergård-Nilssen and Hulme, 2014). However, some studies indicate that dyslexic adults still differ significantly from those without dyslexia in terms of several cognitive skills, such as phonological short-term memory, phonological awareness and whole-word processing (Tamboer, Vorst and Oort, 2016). In a meta-analysis, Reis et al. (2020) suggest that the cognitive influences on dyslexia are multifactorial and involve reading and phonological processing deficits as well as weaknesses in other oral language skills such as vocabulary. Critically, these deficits in cognitive processes that underlie poor reading skills persist into adulthood. However, symptoms are more accentuated for reading and writing skills than for reading and writing associated processes, such as phonological awareness, rapid automatised naming, phonological memory, verbal working memory and vocabulary.

Dyslexia and the conundrum of failure

Tanner (2009) interviewed several dyslexic adults in Australia over a period of three years during a TAFE (Technical and Further Education) course specifically designed for adults with dyslexia. She investigated the conundrum of failure and, despite the efforts of so-called 'supportive others', the oppressive attitudes and beliefs which are institutionalised within schools and society devalue those whose literacy skills are deemed to be inadequate. Failure directly impacts on the self-perception and self-efficacy of dyslexic adults and their resultant attitudes regarding how society has failed and marginalised them. Failure, she argued, can be broken into at least five sub-types.

1   System Failure occurs when inappropriate educational opportunities have been provided to cater for specific learning needs. This causes academic or school failure due to ignorance, failure or inaccurate acknowledgement or identification of needs which results in low expectation, insensitive teaching and a weak curriculum

2   Constructed Failure results from the tunnelled view in which dyslexia is interpreted and 'treated', particularly in the educational context. A student must first fail in school before they are identified. This failure is determined by a 'diagnosis' which provides evidence to support funding to 'fix or treat' the problem

3   Public Failure is evident in all aspects of society. School contexts provide many opportunities for failure because demands are constantly placed on students to demonstrate their literacy skills within a public forum. Examples include reading out loud or reading text within a time frame and responding to it. For a dyslexic adult with dyslexia, public failure in life can be constant, from filling in forms, replying to emails, reading signs or reading instructions

4   Family Failure can be attributed to the attitudes of caregivers and siblings, as well as the individual's belief that they are failing their parents who believe that strong literacy skills are the key to academic success

5   Personal Failure is a culmination of failures beginning when a student with dyslexia enters an educational institution and realises they are not succeeding. This can eventually become a lifelong fear of learning and of new or unknown situations

Activity

Every year, the British Dyslexia Association (BDA) support Dyslexia Awareness Week and post answers to questions raised. The 2022 questions can be accessed via the link: www.youtube.com/playlist?list=PLT0AVTBsT BE5xJe7szduL1AyWw6KDZ7Q4 and the 2021 questions can be accessed via the link: www.youtube.com/playlist?list=PLT0AVTBsTBE5pvIA3TQ08 bA0aS721p8pN

The 2020 week was focused upon the theme Dyslexia Creates, and can be accessed via the link: www.youtube.com/playlist?list=PLT0AVTBsT BE4fT6Mmz56Wl9iXjUDpaqfo

- What do the questions posed tell you about living with dyslexia?
- You have been tasked to present a talk on the Dyslexia Creates theme from 2020. What messages would you want to send?

Dyslexia and employment

Deacon, Macdonald and Donaghue (2022) explored biographical narratives of dyslexic adults and found that all had experienced stigmatisation and exclusion, as well as discriminatory experiences in education and employment. Whilst in adulthood assistive technologies were often used to meet the legislative requirements of 'reasonable' adjustment in the workplace, participants very rarely reported that their employers actively attempted to foster an inclusive working environment. They concluded that the findings illustrate that the embodied experiences of dyslexia are defined within a disabling educational system and a discriminatory workplace, both of which have a psycho-emotional impact on a person's life course and personal identity.

Wissell et al. (2022) suggest that the nature of dyslexia may pose unique challenges for employers and managers. Their participants identified several literacy-based difficulties at a task level faced by dyslexic employees, including errors with spelling and grammar, length of time to complete work tasks, poor organisation and time management, and difficulties with reading comprehension and speed. In addition to the challenges that are common to all people, such as increased cognitive demand and an ability to respond in fast-paced work environments, employees with dyslexia must also contend with their literacy-based difficulties and this has the potential to put employees with dyslexia at a considerable disadvantage within the workplace. They suggested that the impact of dyslexia may not become apparent until work performance drops.

Activities in the workplace involving reading, writing or spelling, along with issues such as social relationships and personal factors such as self-disclosure and coping strategies, were identified as being important to a dyslexic employee (de

Beer et al., 2014). Managers may only suspect a problem when they see employees unable to keep up with speed of completing tasks or not coping with significant changes (e.g., new work procedures, managers, team, or equipment). This suggests that workplaces are currently reactive, rather than proactive, in their awareness and support of disabilities such as dyslexia, but when managers were empathetic and understanding, staff felt safe to disclose their dyslexia, and this resulted in positive outcomes for both the employee and the employer. They reported that it was the responsibility of the employee to self-identify or disclose to their managers that they had dyslexia. The participants identified several barriers that might prevent employees from disclosing dyslexia. At the organisation level, these barriers included a lack of awareness of dyslexia, minimal or no training opportunities to manage and support dyslexic workers, and an absence of workplace disability policies and/or procedures. In this study, participants acknowledged that those with dyslexia could be discriminated against across the employment lifecycle, starting at recruitment (e.g., during psychometric assessments and interview processes) and leading into onboarding and retention.

Locke et al. (2017) found that the impact of dyslexia on doctors can include writing and calculating prescriptions, writing patient notes, prioritising and making referrals. Adaptive strategies or 'workarounds' highlighted the use of adaptive technologies such as voice-activated software, spell checkers and practical strategies such as colour coding paperwork. Morris and Turnbull (2007) suggest that dyslexia provided a challenge to the everyday work of registered nurses, which was often met successfully using a range of individualised strategies. Career progression was achievable but, compared with peers, was perceived to take longer. Disclosure of dyslexia to work colleagues was selective and dependent on the perceived benefits. Informal support mechanisms were commonly utilised with formal management support less well defined.

Interestingly, Shaywitz et al. (2020) found that two groups of Yale graduates, dyslexic readers (DR) and typical readers (TR), were recruited, each at least five years after graduation. Participants' responses to questions about both their Yale experience and their work and life experiences since graduation suggest that if intellectually able and motivated students with dyslexia are given academic opportunity at a rigorous institution they can succeed academically, professionally, and personally. These findings offer an unexpected yet reassuring picture of the college and career success of individuals with dyslexia. The graduates with dyslexia appeared to compensate for their disability by accessing their strengths.

Activity

Read the following case studies.

Sue is aged 11 and always knew she had an issue with spelling and recognising letters, but it wasn't until entering secondary school that both teachers and she recognised that this might be having an impact on her work. She often has difficulty holding and retrieving information from her working memory. Her written work is messy with many crossings out and spellings attempted several times, with persistent reversal confusion, e.g., b/d, p/g, p/q, n/u, m/w and transposed letters. She is sometimes unable to recognise familiar words and hates reading aloud in class.

Jane is 40 years old and has been employed in the same organisation for four years. She has just been given a promotion into a more high-pressured department. She has already recognised that she had been having problems following this change in job role and line manager resulting from an office reorganisation. The new job role involves more written work than her previous job roles. Jane has a teenage daughter and son who had both recently been diagnosed with dyslexia at school. This led her to acknowledge that she had always needed to employ coping mechanisms to manage her work as she always felt that she was slower than most other people at reading and writing.

Her new line manager is exasperated by Jane's repeated clerical and arithmetic errors despite using a calculator or spreadsheet programme for calculations. He believes Jane is disorganised and that she cannot be trusted to carry out the requirements of her job and is now a liability in the department. Every piece of work she produces is checked for accuracy. Jane agrees she made unexplained errors but feels her manager's attitude results in her becoming very stressed and making even more errors.

Developmental Coordination Disorder (DCD) or Dyspraxia

Pause for reflection

- Apart from issues with motor coordination, what cognitive, social and emotional impact might DCD have on individuals and their families?

DCD and families

Stephenson and Chesson (2008) looked at long-term implications of having a child with DCD and parents who responded reported a high persistence of problems in their children. Difficulties spanned motor and academic performance, emotional/behavioural responses, and social interaction. Twenty-eight children (80 per cent) of respondents were reported as having difficulties in three or more areas. Bullying was a commonly identified problem. At interview mothers spoke at length about their experiences and reported feeling stressed and distressed. Mothers reported a lack of support and expressed feelings of isolation. They said that their time investment in their child with DCD had pronounced effects on themselves and other family members. Specifically, they highlighted time spent fighting the system, primarily for educational support.

A meta-ethnographic synthesis produced three themes: (a) 'It's harder than it should be': Navigating daily activities (b) Fitting in, and (c) 'So what? I drop things.' Participants experienced a wide array of challenges learning and performing new skills and activities, participating in school, and experienced social exclusion from activities such as play and leisure. The synthesis revealed that children with DCD experience bullying and various types of victimisation (O'Dea, Coote and Robinson, 2021), with Vaillancourt et al. (2010) finding issues including, verbal (name-calling, teasing), social (social exclusion, marginalisation) and physical (physical assault) in the school setting. The findings also highlighted that school sports and physical education were perceived as particularly challenging experiences, which led to incidents of ridicule, self-exclusion, marginalisation, and reluctance to participate due to poor teacher understanding and awareness.

The experience of struggling to learn and perform everyday activities and routines was frequently reported across the included studies. Typical childhood activities such as learning to ride a bicycle required additional support and extended periods of practice to master skills and build stamina. Children with DCD were able to report their perception that they did not feel competent in performing many daily activities. The specific choices that the children made indicated not only the impact of DCD on daily activities but also the fact that these young children were aware of its impact. For example, 18 children wanted to be able to tie their shoelaces 'by themselves' 'because everyone else can' (Dunford et al. 2005). Zwicker et al. (2018) interviewed 13 children (8–12 years) about their experiences and identified four themes. Two themes – milestones as millstones and the perils of printing – illuminated participants' challenges in completing everyday activities at home and at school. The third theme – more than a motor problem – revealed the social and emotional impact of these struggles and from being excluded from play. The fourth theme – coping strategies – described their efforts to be resilient.

Losse et al. (1991) examined whether problems of motor coordination in early childhood recede with age; they found that from a follow-up study of 17 children, identified by their teachers as having poor motor coordination at age six. At age 16, they found that most children still had difficulties with motor coordination, had poor self-concept and are experiencing problems of various kinds in school. Hessell, Hocking and Davies (2010) found that the gymnasts with DCD were successful participants in gymnastics in their study. Their participation, and their understanding of their participation, was influenced by internal and external factors. Wide-ranging activities are structured and graded to facilitate everyone's progress and assist in developing underlying movement patterns or abilities. The range of equipment, the coaching style, and the measures of success are all intended to support an individual's skill acquisition. The individuality of gymnastics makes it a good choice for children with DCD. However, they were intimidated by the number of people present, and had difficulty concentrating on the activity and staying out of the way of other gymnasts. Thus, they had to overcome more than simple coordination deficits.

Despite their movement difficulties, youngsters with Developmental Coordination Disorder (DCD) generally have sufficient capability for physical activity. However, they tend to be less physically active and less physically fit than their well-coordinated age peers. Barnett, Dawes and Wilmut (2013) semi-structured interviews were conducted with eight teenagers with DCD (aged 13–15) and their parents. Half of the children and all but one of the parents reported that the children did little physical activity. Although most children disliked competitive team games, they reported many physical activities that they did enjoy, and they reported wanting to be more physically active. Perceived internal constraints to participation included poor motor skill, lack of motivation and reports of fatiguing easily.

Using an IPA methodology, Payne et al. (2013) interviewed teenagers aged 13 years who felt that difficulties associated with DCD affected relationships with peers, parents and siblings and their social participation at home, at school and in other community settings. Participants identified themselves and their friendship group as either 'sporty' or 'not sporty'; some participants invested a lot of time and effort in team sports such as football, rugby and netball. Yet, despite their enjoyment of these sports, they were sometimes reluctant to participate in informal team games where their poor coordination might be exposed. Participants who identified themselves as 'not sporty' shared other interests with their friends, including music. The findings of this study support the suggestion that participation in non-physical activities may provide social experiences that are comparable to those offered by participation in team sports, and that participation in either type of activity could protect individuals with DCD from feelings of loneliness. Participants described various ways in which peers helped them manage practical and emotional challenges associated with DCD. Several participants were friends with peers who had additional needs of their own. They recognised that their relationship with their parents was different to people who did not have DCD. They felt they needed much more help, support and advocacy than even their younger siblings and generally felt that their fathers were less tolerant of their difficulties.

The literature highlights that children with motor coordination problems tend to have fewer friends and not be invited to play games with others. Children often still become the object of teasing, avoiding participation in environments that have physical activities and play in groups involved, making even more scarce opportunities to practice their skills and experiences with each other. De Medeirosa et al. (2019) found that difficulties when performing daily activities are not always related to the child's motor coordination problems. DCD is still poorly recognised and considered by parents and teachers when trying to explain children's performance. This is reinforced in the words of mothers: children are rated as lazy, disinterested, and stunted for not being able to perform the day-to-day activities that a child of the same age performs with mastery.

DCD and adults

Adults with dyspraxia often have improved their motor coordination skills over the years, and their chief difficulties in education and employment are more likely to be related to the cognitive aspects of dyspraxia, such as difficulty with sequencing and structuring information, organisational skills, timekeeping, and sometimes social skills (Moody, 2014). Self-reported levels of life satisfaction, general health and symptoms of anxiety and depression were investigated in a group of adults with a diagnosis of DCD and those with suspected DCD using several published self-report questionnaire measures. A comparison between those in and out of employment was undertaken. As a group, the unemployed adults with DCD reported significantly lower levels of life satisfaction. Whilst there was no significant difference between those who were employed and unemployed on General Health Questionnaire scores, both groups reported numbers of health-related issues reflective of general health problems in DCD irrespective of employment status. While both groups reported high levels of depressive symptoms and rated their satisfaction with life quite poorly, the unemployed group reported significantly more depressive symptoms and less satisfaction. Additionally, the results identified high levels of self-reported anxiety in both groups, with the majority sitting outside of the normal range using the Hospital Anxiety and Depression Scale (Kirby et al., 2010).

Activity

- Watch this video noting how dyspraxia impacts Tim and his family as well as others in the film. It can be accessed via: www.youtube.com/watch?v=zidXDVfdGms
- Watch the video 'What Is It Like Having Dyspraxia? Zarah's Story' and note any similarities with the impact that dyspraxia has on Tim. It can be accessed via: www.youtube.com/watch?v=pQhf23DJRU0

DCD and education

Cantell, Smyth and Ahonen (2003) examined perceptual motor, educational and social outcomes in a group of 17–18-year-old Finnish adolescents, with significant motor problems (or developmental coordination disorder, DCD), minor motor problems and 20 controls. The results showed that at age 17, all perceptual motor tasks differentiated the three groups. The DCD group performed less well than the control group on all tasks, with the intermediate group situated between these two. Discriminant function analyses showed that more classification errors occurred between the control and intermediate groups suggesting that the distinction between these groups becomes more difficult with age. In the educational domain, the adolescents with DCD had the lowest Wechsler Adult Intelligence Scale (WAIS) scores and shortest school careers of the three groups. In the social domain, the DCD group had the lowest perceptions of athletic and scholastic competence while the intermediate and control groups did not differ. In addition, the interview results indicated that the three groups were in different stages of identity development. The research suggested two developmental paths for those with early perceptual motor problems: 'persistence' and 'catching up'. The term quality of life refers to a multidimensional concept incorporating various psychological and physical components including physical ability, functional performance, emotional well-being, social relationships, and occupational experience. Overall, the group of adults with DCD reported significantly lower levels of quality-of-life satisfaction across all domains on the scale.

Furthermore, it is apparent that in late childhood and adolescence, the emotional impact of this disorder may be more severe than the primary motor difficulties that are experienced (Hill, Brown and Sorgardt, 2011). Thus, as individuals with DCD age, the presentation of difficulties may begin to include more psychosocial issues that are more than likely to affect one's quality of life. Also, the DCD only group lives at home with parents more and has a significantly greater reported motor and executive functioning difficulty than the other two groups (Kirby et al., 2008). Current functioning of 19 young adults with DCD was examined using the Adult Dyspraxia/DCD Checklist (Kirby et al., 2010) and parents' views of their child's current functioning was also obtained. Results suggest that whilst some motor skills such as handwriting continue to impact in emerging adulthood, not all skills are as problematic, such as self-care skills. Additionally, executive functioning and social skills seem to be a key area of concern for both young adults and their parents. Results provide guidance for areas of intervention that need to be considered, especially focusing on executive functioning skills. Also, they highlight the need for gathering information from more than one source to gain a complete picture of functioning.

Activity

Read the following case studies.

Peter is 14 years of age and was diagnosed with DCD (dyspraxia) at the age of 10. He struggles with his fine motor skills such as holding a pen to write and doing up his shoelaces. He finds it difficult to coordinate activities such as using a knife and fork and choosing a song to play on his iPhone. He is anxious when he must work in groups to demonstrate an activity, say in PE or Music. His writing is very untidy, and he tends to be slower to complete tasks than other learners, such as copying from the Smartboard. Peter really loves sport, but he has difficulty in organising himself and getting out equipment. When teachers are explaining tasks which involve sequencing of activities, he finds it hard to concentrate, especially when it comes to time constraints. He finds activities that involve eye-hand and eye-foot coordination particularly frustrating, and he often exhibits tantrums if he cannot succeed.

Abi is aged 34 and works in an estate agent's office. She oversees booking in viewings and showing clients around potential homes. She has lived with dyspraxia for several years but still finds some activities at work difficult. In the office she has poor posture and fatigue and difficulty in standing for a long time because of weak muscle tone. She has difficulty with typing and handwriting and has issues with working memory and poor sequencing causes problems with maths, reading and spelling and writing reports at work. At times she can be distracted and has difficulty in following instructions. Abi sometimes tries to do too many things at once and is slow finish a task. When showing clients around she tends to fall, trip and bump into things and people. Abi also has difficulty with concentration and may be easily distracted if they are asking questions.

- What do you think are the key issues that both Peter and Abi face in the everyday lives?
- Take one of the case studies and suggest some strategies to support them at school or at work
- What strengths do you think your case studies may have and how could these be utilised?

Dyscalculia

Pause for reflection

- How would you as a teacher or student distinguish between maths anxiety and DD?

A large-scale cohort study in England Ritchie and Bates (2013) revealed that poor mathematical ability is associated with major psychosocial and economic risks. They found that 70–90 per cent of the affected persons ended their schooling prematurely at age 16; at age 30, very few of them were employed full-time. Their probability of being unemployed and of developing depressive symptoms was twice as high as that of persons without dyscalculia. Achievement in mathematics and reading was also significantly associated with intelligence scores, academic motivation, and duration of education. Siugzdaite et al. (2020) found that the brain differences did not map onto any labels the children had been given – in other words, there were no brain regions that predicted having autism or ADHD, for example. More surprisingly, they found that the different brain regions did not even predict specific cognitive difficulties – there was no specific brain deficit for language problems or memory difficulties, for example. Instead, the team found that the children's brains were organised around hubs, like an efficient traffic system or social network. Children who had well-connected brain hubs had either very specific cognitive difficulties, such as poor listening skills, or had no cognitive difficulties at all. By contrast, children with poorly connected hubs – like a train station with few or poor connections – had widespread and severe cognitive problems. They argue that rather than thinking there are specific brain regions that predict having a particular learning disorder or difficulty, it's much more important to consider how these brain areas are connected – specifically, whether they are connected via hubs. They go onto suggest that the severity of learning difficulties is strongly associated with the connectedness of these hubs in playing play a key role in sharing information between brain areas.

Dyscalculia and adults

Kaufmann et al. (2020) suggest that DD in adults involves both number-specific and number-un-specific (i. e., domain-general) cognitive deficits such as alerting and executive attention. The ability to deal with numbers is fundamental in our modern society. From managing money to remembering PIN numbers or codes, numerical skills are continuously needed during an adult's daily life. People with Developmental Dyscalculia (DD) often have poor mathematical skills that may have an impact also in their daily lives. Even if children and adults with DD present similar deficiencies, the implications of this disorder might be different at an older age. While during childhood poor arithmetical skills affect school attainment, mental health, and self-esteem, in adulthood, their impact on daily living might concern additional life spheres, such as money usage or job seeking. Bruine de Bruin and Slovic (2021) state that numeracy was associated with being among the poorest 20 per cent of one's country, and with difficulty living on one's income, even after accounting for income, education, and demographics. Vigna et al. (2022) assessed numerical skills in both formal and informal contexts and showed that adults with DD had poorer arithmetical skills in both formal and informal settings. Adults with DD presented difficulties in time and measure estimation as well as money usage in real-world numerical tasks. In contrast, everyday tasks regarding distance estimation were preserved. In addition, the assessment revealed that adults with DD were aware of their numerical difficulties, which were often related to emotional problems and negatively impacted their academic and occupational decisions.

Activity

Read the following case studies.

Deepak is aged 15, is studying for his GCSE in Maths but finds some aspects of the lessons difficult which causes him anxiety. He has confusion with number direction, has a challenge in understanding mathematical symbols and takes a long time to complete mathematical tasks. He particularly has an issue with the planning of activities and using working memory when he is trying to follow multiple instructions. To avoid 'being shown up' in front of his mates, he tries to keep his head down and does not catch the eye of the teachers.

Shaun is 21 years of age and works for an engineering firm. He has bought his own house and needs to shop for himself and likes to engage socially with friends after work. However, there are several issues which impact upon his life out of work. He finds that he has difficulty in using money and seeks support from his family with respect to budgeting. He buys packaged fruit and vegetables as he finds he lacks understanding of weight and measurement. When meeting friends, he is often late as he finds time keeping difficult. He is fearful of using the cash machine as he cannot remember his pin number and is afraid that he 'holds everyone up'.

Both Deepak and Shaun have voiced the impact of their DD has upon their friends.

- What advice could you offer to them to increase their understanding that DD has on individuals?

Deepak is worried about how he will perform in his GCSE mock exams as he also has difficulty in understanding data questions in Science.

- Who may be able to support him in school?

Shaun is highly regarded by his employer and work mates.

- How could he transfer the skills from his job to his everyday life?

References

Amiera Alias, N. A. and Dahlan, A. (2015). Enduring difficulties: the challenges of mothers in raising children with dyslexia. *Procedia – Social and Behavioral Sciences*, 202, pp. 107–114.

Armstrong, D. and Humphrey, N. (2009). Research section: reactions to a diagnosis of dyslexia among students entering further education: development of the 'resistance–accommodation' model. *British Journal of Special Education*, 36, pp. 95–102.

Barnett, A. L., Dawes, H. and Wilmut, K. (2013). Constraints and facilitators to participation in physical activity in teenagers with Developmental Co-ordination Disorder: an exploratory interview study. *Child Care Health Dev*, 39 (3), pp. 393–403.

Bonifacci, P., Montuschi, M., Lami, L. and Snowling, M. J. (2014). Parents of children with dyslexia: cognitive, emotional and behavioural profile. *Dyslexia*, 20 (2), pp. 175–190.

Bruine de Bruin, W. and Slovic, P. (2021). Low numeracy is associated with poor financial well-being around the world. *PLoS One*, 6 (11), e0260378.

Cantell, M. H., Smyth, M. M. and Ahonen, T. P. (2003). Two distinct pathways for developmental coordination disorder: persistence and resolution. *Hum Mov Sci*, 22 (4–5), pp. 413–431.

Caton, S., Bradshaw, J., Gillooly, A., Hatton, C., Flynn, S., Oloidi, E., Jahoda, A., Maguire, R., Marriott, A., Mulhall, P., Taggart, L., Todd, S., Abbott, D., Beyer, S., Gore, N., Heslop, P., Scior, K., and Hastings, R. P. (2022). Digital participation of people with profound and multiple learning disabilities during the Covid-19 pandemic in the UK. *British Journal of Learning Disabilities*, pp. 1–12.

de Beer, J., Engels, J., Heerkens, Y. and van der Klink, J. (2014). Factors influencing work participation of adults with developmental dyslexia: a systemic review. *BMC Public Health*, 14 (77), pp. 1–22.

de Medeirosa, C. C. M., Buffonea, F. R. R. C., Schochatb, E. and Araújoa, C. R. S. (2019). Transcending the problem: perceptions of mothers and children about the impact of developmental coordination disorder in everyday life. *Cad. Bras. Ter. Ocup.*, 27 (4), pp. 792–805.

Deacon, L., Macdonald, S. J. and Donaghue, J. (2022) 'What's wrong with you, are you stupid?' Listening to the biographical narratives of adults with dyslexia in an age of 'inclusive' and 'anti-discriminatory' practice. *Disability & Society*, 37 (3), pp. 406–426.

Delany, K. (2017). The experience of parenting a child with dyslexia: an Australian perspective, *Journal of Student Engagement: Education Matters*, 7 (1), pp. 97–123.

Department for Education and Department of Health (2015). *Special Educational Needs and Disability Code of Practice: 0 to 25 years.* [online] Available at: www.gov.uk/government/p ublications/send-code-of-practice-0-to-25 [Accessed 25. 10. 2022].

Dunford, C., Missiuna, C., Street, E. and Sibert, J. (2005). Children's perceptions of the impact of developmental coordination disorder on activities of daily living. *The British Journal of Occupational Therapy*, 68, pp. 207–214.

Earey, A. (2013). Parental experiences of support for pupils with dyslexia: ignoring the effect on parents. *Support for Learning*, 28 (1), pp. 35–40.

Elliott, J. G. and Grigorenko, E. L. (2014). *The Dyslexia Debate*. Cambridge: Cambridge University Press.

Flynn, S., Caton, S., Gilhooly, A., Bradshaw, J., Hastings, R., Hatton, C., Jahoda, A., Mulhall, P., Todd, S., Beyer, S. and Taggart, L. (2021). The experiences of adults with learning disabilities in the UK during the COVID- 19 pandemic: qualitative results from Wave 1 of the Coronavirus and people with learning disabilities study. *Tizard Learning Disability Review*, 26 (4), pp. 224–229.

Gibby-Leversuch, R., Hartwell, B. K. and Wright, S. (2021). Dyslexia or literacy difficulties: what difference does a label make? Exploring the perceptions and experiences of young people. *Educational Psychology Research and Practice*, 7 (1), pp. 1–15.

Gibson, S. and Kendall, L. (2010). Stories from school: dyslexia and learners' voices on factors impacting on achievement. *Support for Learning*, 25, pp. 187–193.

Glazzard, J. (2010). The impact of dyslexia on pupils' self-esteem. *Support for Learning*, 25 (2), pp. 63–69.

Hatton, C., Bailey, T., Bradshaw, J., Caton, S., Flynn, S., Gillooly, A., Jahoda, A., Maguire, R., Marriott, A., Mulhall, P., Oloidi, E., Taggart, L., Todd, S., Abbott, D., Beyer, S., Gore, N., Heslop, P., Scior, K and Hastings, R. P. (2021). The willingness of UK adults with intellectual disabilities to take COVID-19 vaccines. *J Intellect Disabil Res*, 65 (11), pp. 949–961.

Hessell, S., Hocking, C. and Davies, S. (2010). Participation of boys with developmental coordination disorder in gymnastics. *New Zealand Journal of Occupational Therapy*, 57 (1), pp. 14–21.

Hill, E. L., Brown, D. and Sorgardt, S. K. (2011). A preliminary investigation of quality of life satisfaction reports in emerging adults with and without developmental coordination disorder. *Journal of Adult Development*, 18 (3), pp. 130–134.

Ingesson, S. G. (2007). Growing up with dyslexia: interviews with teenagers and young adults. *School Psychology International*, 28 (5), pp. 574–591.

Karande, S. and Kuril, S. (2011). Impact of parenting practices on parent-child relationships in children with specific learning disability. *J Postgrad Med*, 57, pp. 20–30.

Karande, S., Kumbhare, N., Kulkarni, M. and Shah, N. (2009). Anxiety levels in mothers of children with specific learning disability. *Journal of Postgraduate Medicine*, 55, pp. 165–170.

Karande, S., Mehta, V. and Kulkarni, M. (2007). Impact of an education program on parental knowledge of specific learning disability. *Indian J Med Sci*, 61 (7), pp. 398–406.

Kaufmann, L., von Aster, M., Göbel, S. M., Marksteiner, J. and Klein, E. (2020). Developmental dyscalculia in adults: current issues and open questions for future research. *Lernen und Lernstörungen*, 9 (2), pp. 1–12.

Kirby, A., Edwards, L., Sugden, D. and Rosenblum, S. (2010). The development and standardization of the Adult Developmental Co-ordination Disorders/Dyspraxia Checklist (ADC). *Res Dev Disabil*, 31 (1), pp.131–139.

Kirby, A., Sugden, D., Beveridge, S. and Edwards, Lisa. (2008). Developmental Co-ordination Disorder (DCD) in adolescents and adults in further and higher education. *Journal of Research in Special Educational Needs*, 8, pp. 120–131.

Knight, C. (2021). The impact of the dyslexia label on academic outlook and aspirations: an analysis using propensity score matching. *Br J Educ Psychol*, 91 (4), pp. 1110–1126.

Linden, M. A., Forbes, T., Brown, M., Marsh, L., Truesdale, M., McCann, E., Todd, S. and Hughes, N. (2022). Impact of the COVID-19 pandemic on family carers of those with profound and multiple intellectual disabilities: perspectives from UK and Irish Non-Governmental Organisations. *BMC Public Health*, 22, 2095.

Locke, R., Alexander, G., Mann, R., Kibble, S. and Scallan, S. (2017). Doctors with dyslexia: strategies and support. *Clin Teach*, 14 (5), pp. 355–359.

Losse, A., Henderson, S. E., Elliman, D., Hall, D., Knight, E. and Jongmans, M. (1991). Clumsiness in children – do they grow out of it? A 10-year follow-up study. *Dev Med Child Neurol*, 33 (1), pp. 55–68.

Moody, S. (2014). Dyslexia, dyspraxia, and ADHD in adults: what you need to know. *The British Journal of General Practice*, 64, 252.

Morris, D. and Turnbull, P. (2007). A survey-based exploration of the impact of dyslexia on career progression of UK registered nurses. *J Nurs Manag*, 15 (1), pp. 97–106.

Nalavany, B. A. and Carawan, L. W. (2012). Perceived family support and self-esteem: the mediational role of emotional experience in adults with dyslexia. *Dyslexia*, 18 (1), pp. 58–74.

Nergård-Nilssen, T. and Hulme, C. (2014). Developmental dyslexia in adults: behavioural manifestations and cognitive correlates. *Dyslexia: An International Journal of Research and Practice*, 20 (3), pp. 191–207.

O'Dea, Á., Coote, S. and Robinson, K. (2021). Children and young people's experiences of living with developmental coordination disorder/dyspraxia: study protocol for a qualitative evidence synthesis. *HRB Open Res*, 2 (28).

Payne, R. A., Abel, G. A., Guthrie, B. and Mercer, S. W. (2013). The effect of physical multimorbidity, mental health conditions and socioeconomic deprivation on unplanned admissions to hospital: a retrospective cohort study. *CMAJ*, 185 (5), E221–228.

Pitt, S. and Soni, A. (2017). Students' experiences of academic success with dyslexia: a call for alternative intervention. *Support for Learning*, 32 (4), pp. 387–402.

Poon-McBrayer, K. and McBrayer, P. (2014). Plotting Confucian and disability rights paradigms on the advocacy–activism continuum: experiences of Chinese parents of children with dyslexia in Hong Kong. *Cambridge Journal of Education*, 44, pp. 93–111.

Reis, A., Araújo, S., Morais, I. S. and Faísca L. (2020). Reading and reading-related skills in adults with dyslexia from different orthographic systems: a review and meta-analysis. *Ann Dyslexia*, 70 (3), pp. 339–368.

Riddick, B. (2010). *Living With Dyslexia: The Social and Emotional Consequences of Specific Learning Difficulties/Disabilities*. 2nd ed. London: Routledge.

Ritchie, S. J. and Bates, T. C. (2013). Enduring links from childhood mathematics and reading achievement to adult socioeconomic status. *Psychological Science*, 24 (7), pp. 1301–1308.

Ross, H. (2021). 'I'm dyslexic but what does that even mean?': young people's experiences of dyslexia support interventions in mainstream classrooms. *Scandinavian Journal of Disability Research*, 23, pp. 284–294.

Scottish Commission for Learning Disability (SCLD). (2022). The Coronavirus and people with learning disabilities survey. Coronavirus and people with learning disabilities in Scotland Policy brief. [online] Available at: www.scld.org.uk/wp-content/uploads/2022/01/Coronavirus-and-people-with-learning-disabilities_Policy-brief_15.03.22.pdf [Accessed 02. 02. 2023].

Shaywitz, S., Holahan, J., Kenney, B. and Shaywitz, B. (2020). The Yale outcome study: outcomes for graduates with and without dyslexia. *Journal of Pediatric Neuropsychology*, 6, pp. 189–197.

Siugzdaite, R., Bathelt, J., Holmes, J. and Astle, D. E. (2020). Transdiagnostic brain mapping in developmental disorders. *Curr Biol*, 30 (7), pp. 1245–1257.

Snowling, M. J. and Hulme, C. (2012). Interventions for children's language and literacy difficulties. *International Journal of Language & Communication Disorders*, 47 (1), pp. 27–34.

Snowling, M. J. and Melby-Lervåg, M. (2016). Oral language deficits in familial dyslexia: a meta-analysis and review. *Psychological Bulletin*, 142 (5), pp. 498–545.

Snowling, M. J, Muter, V. and Carroll, J. (2007). Children at family risk of dyslexia: a follow-up in early adolescence. *J Child Psychol Psychiatry*, 48 (6), pp. 609–618.

Solvang, P. (2007). Developing an ambivalence perspective on medical labelling in education: case dyslexia. *International Studies in Sociology of Education*, 17, pp. 79–94.

Stephenson, E. A. and Chesson, R. A. (2008). 'Always the guiding hand': parents' accounts of the long-term implications of developmental co-ordination disorder for their children and families. *Child Care Health Dev*, 34 (3), pp. 335–343.

Tonnessen, F. (1995). On defining 'dyslexia'. *Scandinavian Journal of Educational Research*, 39, pp. 139–156.

Tamboer, P., Vorst, H. C. M. and Oort, F. J. (2016). Five describing factors of dyslexia. *Journal of Learning Disabilities*, 49 (5), pp. 466–483.

Tanner, K. (2009). Adult dyslexia and the 'conundrum of failure'. *Disability and Society*, 24 (6), pp. 785–797.

Undheim, A. M. and Sund, A. M. (2008). Psychosocial factors and reading difficulties: students with reading difficulties drawn from a representative population sample. *Scandinavian Journal of Psychology*, 49 (4), pp. 377–384.

van der Leij, A., van Bergen, E., van Zuijen, T., de Jong, P., Maurits, N. and Maassen, B. (2013). Precursors of developmental dyslexia: an overview of the longitudinal Dutch Dyslexia Programme study. *Dyslexia: An International Journal of Research and Practice*, 19 (4), pp. 191–213.

Vaillancourt, T., Trinh, V., McDougall, P., Duku, E., Cunningham, L., Cunningham, C., Hymel, S. and Short, K. (2010). Optimizing population screening of bullying in school-aged children. *Journal of School Violence*, 9 (3), pp. 233–250.

Vigna, G., Ghidoni, E., Burgio, F., Danesin, L., Angelini, D., Benavides-Varela, S. and Semenza, C. (2022). Dyscalculia in early adulthood: implications for numerical activities of daily living. *Brain Sciences*, 12, pp. 373.

Wissell, S., Karimi, L., Serry, T., Furlong, L. and Hudson, J. (2022). 'You don't look dyslexic': using the job demands-resource model of burnout to explore employment experiences of Australian adults with dyslexia. *Int J Environ Res Public Health*, 19 (17), 10719.

Zwicker, J. G., Suto, M., Harris, S. R., Vlasakova, N. and Missiuna C. (2018). Developmental coordination disorder is more than a motor problem: children describe the impact of daily struggles on their quality of life. *British Journal of Occupational Therapy*, 81 (2), pp. 65–73.

3 Pedagogical approaches to support these needs

Introduction

This chapter explores approaches to support issues associated with Cognition and Learning Needs, and will highlight examples for PMLD, SLD and dyslexic individuals. There are several websites, organisations and textbooks which identify a range of approaches in relation to cognition and learning. This chapter will instead focus on the theoretical underpinning, research studies and evidence-based research and practice, for some of the main approaches used in an educational context. It will signpost you to videoclips showing how the approach is being used in practice. It must be remembered that although an approach is identified in a specific chapter, it can be used in other areas of need. For example, although Intensive Interaction is included in this area of need in relation to PMLD, it is also utilised in relation to Communication and Interaction needs.

Learning objectives

This chapter will:

- Introduce you to a number of specific approaches which can be used to support Cognition and Learning Needs
- Invite you examine underpinning theory and research evidence in relation to approaches from the continuum related to this area of need (PMLD, SLD and SpLD)
- Introduce you to the paradigms and principles involved in cognition and learning
- Help you to understand how these approaches can support individuals in the classroom
- Invite you to review the approaches with respect to evidence-based research and practice

Key terms

Paradigms, SMART and SCRUFFY targets, Assessment of and for Learning, evidence-based research, Objects of Reference, Intensive Interaction, eye gaze, TEACCH®, dyslexia

DOI: 10.4324/9781003361084-5

Paradigms related to cognition and learning

The behaviourist paradigm considers positive actions to be rewarded and negative behaviours to be sanctioned to promote classroom performance and to encourage positive social behaviours. Wheldall and Carter (1996) argue that some believe those that follow a behaviourist approach to teaching are merely following the academic status quo without making their teaching meaningful. However, teacher support and attention can be a large factor in establishing a sense of control for the individual. The interactionist approach follows a widely social model in which learning is achieved through social interaction with peers or teachers and therefore is not directly teacher led but is a collaboration between student and teacher (Wheldall and Carter, 1996). Karkou (2009) suggests that all therapeutic intervention should function with the intention of maintaining a clear psychological intent as opposed to focusing on the product of the activity. Some may argue that the use of therapeutic intervention may be costly due to the need for therapists and equipment. However, a therapeutic approach to teaching does not necessarily require teachers to have therapy qualifications but looks at bringing the concepts of therapy and relating them to the curriculum (Waters, 2015).

SMART and SCRUFFY targets

A common approach in planning for learning is by setting SMART targets, which despite differing definitions, generally involves specific, measurable, achievable, realistic, or relevant and time-bound or time-related targets, which facilitates a thorough understanding of expectations for the student. They aim to set out outcomes which are measurable and ordered and by following these targets, students should develop in a structured format. For example, they may focus on skills such as eating, drinking, and noticing stimuli and target setting can be done by carrying out formative assessment to examine gaps in knowledge (Dixson and Worrell, 2016), then creating targets based upon these gaps to create a focus to learning (Imray and Hinchcliffe, 2013). SMART targets are less time consuming as they do not require the same level of justification as SCRUFFY targets, planning is very specific, and learning is always relevant to specific outcomes.

Learning for students with PMLD is not a linear process due to delays in development, therefore SMART targets are potentially too specific and rigid to educational outcomes set out by the curriculum. Imray and Hewett (2015) state that for a young person with SEND, targets, abilities, skills, and competencies are fluid. Lacey (2010) recognises that PMLD learners are 'poor consumers of SMART targets' and so created alternative SCRUFFY targets, as learning at a very early cognitively developmental level is irregular, random and comes from all experiences in a holistic manner.

However, these types of targets are less focused on individual needs, may hinder learning for individuals with SLD and PMLD and limit the opportunity for the student to play a role in their planning (Day and Tosey, 2011). Moreover, Imray and Hewett (2015) argue that the world of SLD and PMLD teaching is littered with discarded SMART targets which have never been achieved. These targets can often be downgraded so often that the target becomes meaningless or becomes a skill which the learner already had (Van Walwyk, 2011; McNicholas, 2001). Learning is not guaranteed to be linear nor developmental (Carpenter, 2010; Lacey, 2010) due to 'spikey' cognitive profiles (Rees, 2017), thus the subject-driven, skills-based, and target-centred models may not be the best fit (Imray and Hinchcliffe, 2013). SCRUFFY targets, which are student led, creative, relevant and unspecified fun for youngsters, may be more effective for individuals with SLD and PMLD, as they may be more adaptable to their learning needs. These targets set out general aims for an individual, but they are not time-bound, and allow the student to progress at their own pace. It is, therefore, student led and children undertaking SCRUFFY targets are typically more engaged in the process than when completing SMART targets and staff can be more imaginative with their work, students are more motivated, and more support is available to students.

Assessment of and for Learning

Assessment allows for pupil-centred planning to build upon the knowledge and interests that the child with PMLD already has and have high expectations for their future (Cartwright and Wind-Cowie, 2005). Two types of assessment often used are Assessment of Learning (AoL) (summative assessment) and Assessment for Learning (AfL) (formative assessment). AoL has been the typically accepted form of assessment, in which learners are tested at the end of a period of learning with the purpose of determining their outcomes. AoL ties to behaviourist approaches to planning, using skills such as chaining and task analysis (Boyd, McDonough and Bodfish, 2012). A learner's progress must be clear, achievable, and quantifiably measurable, so setting targets is often the next step taken but these can tend to be limiting to pupils' progress and don't promote learning if they are not able to be met.

Assessment for Learning is the process of seeking and interpreting evidence for use by learners and their teachers to decide where the learners are in their learning, where they need to go, and how best to get there. It is a more personalised approach whereby students are assessed throughout the learning process, to the purpose of involving the student in their own learning and providing feedback which governs future interventions (Anderson and Östlund, 2017). AfL is seen in the interactionist approach to learning where the learner decides on the pace and direction of teaching and is particularly useful when planning activities for a student with SEND as it allows for the lessons to be fully personalised and for them to decide their own goals based upon their interests. Both approaches are extensively used to support cognition and learning

---

Activity

Assessment of and for Learning in context
In this clip a specialist teacher explains how the Assessment for Learning Framework can be adapted to enable pupils in a special school to self-assess

and/or understand how well they have done. It can be accessed via the link: http://complexneeds.org.uk/modules/Module-2.1-Planning-to-meet-needs/All/m05p060b.html

- How does this approach support Assessment for Learning?

An example of Assessment of Learning and the breaking down of a complex task into smaller steps is task analysis. Task analysis breaks down the target behaviour into smaller steps that can be more easily taught. It involves 'forward chaining' and 'backward chaining'.

- Research what is meant by these two terms

Watch the video 'How To: Task Analysis' which can be accessed via the link: www.youtube.com/watch?v=mIAJ8SKLkGY
Identify a complex task from a context such as school, home, work, etc.

- Show how a child, young person, or adult could be supported using targets and task analysis

Objects of Reference (OoR)

Objects of Reference (OoR) were first used to develop communication in people with dual hearing and visual impairments and subsequently, they have been used with PMLD learners (Jones, Pring and Grove, 2002). OoR are objects to which meanings are assigned, such as activities, places, or people, which aids communication. They are resources that connote a special meaning, representing a person, object, location, or event (POLE). A multi-dimensional intervention initially designed for those with sensory impairment, they can be utilised for a range of needs in many settings (Park, 1995). For OoR to be used effectively, it should be used in an activity – such as using a spoon to represent mealtime, and not objects whose association with the activity is arbitrary (McLarty, 1995). This will increase awareness of associations with activities, people, and places using objects and can ultimately lead to their expressive use (Joffee and Rikhye, 1991). For instance, communicating and expressing choice-making by choosing the OoR of their choice. Another advantage of using OoR to develop communication is that it allows advancement from non-symbolic to symbolic levels of communication, like how pupils with PMLD progress from non-intentional to intentional communication.

For example, a class is undertaking a visit to a swimming pool. In the classroom a symbol timetable is displayed showing the events of the day but with the addition of using an OoR in conjunction further supports understanding (Park, 1995).

The students engage with the timetable by interacting with the resource and sticking it next to the symbol representing the activity to bridge visual and tactile understanding. The OoR could be individualised for each student as every person has different interpretations of symbols. For example, one object could be a swimming bag to prepare their responses on the journey to the pool. Another student's target may be to get dressed independently with no prompts, so their OoR could be a distinctive part of the changing room such as a lock to signify their need for privacy. Many people with PMLD are unable to anticipate what is occurring, therefore they have no basis relying on previously learned schemes to respond accordingly. OoR help to organise external information with symbolic understanding providing a sense of prediction to alleviate the risk of anxiety that comes with not being aware of what is happening around you.

Research evidence

Harding et al. (2011) monitored two children with PMLD and found that both children improved their communication skills when objects of reference were introduced, but also there is a need to consider children's cognitive abilities to carry out the most effective intervention. Stadskleiv et al. (2018) highlight that individuals with PMLD are significantly restricted in their exploration of objects which could imply that objects remain subject to interpretation by the caregiver and are not as accessible as eye-gaze technology. Nevertheless, guidance encourages that the use of objects should not be cognitively demanding and must be differentiable regarding tactile and visual representation. This allows for objects to act as anticipation cues and provide choice to the individual through increased awareness. However, Stadskleiv et al. (2018) suggest that objects must be meaningful to the individual, otherwise they are meaningless. In practice, passing a paintbrush around may highlight that we are going to begin 'Art', but a learner may not associate Art with the paintbrush and may reference Art to a pair of safety scissors. Goldbart, Chadwick and Buell (2014) showed objects of reference and Intensive Interaction to be two of the most popular interventions used with people with PMLD: 77.1 per cent of Speech Language Therapists (SLTs) used OoR with adult provision and 69 per cent of SLTs informing pedagogy in schools prescribed OoR in the classroom. However, although OoR are used extensively, there remains inadequate research evaluating the effectiveness of this communication aid.

Activity

Sebastian is aged seven and has been given an activity to pick out objects of reference from a visual story of visiting the park. Sebastian is asked to identify the flower.

- How could you use Objects of Reference to support this activity?

Watch the video 'How to use objects of reference' which can be accessed via the link:

www.youtube.com/watch?v=NlBMB6A3Axs

- What key points does the SLT raise about OoR?

Watch the video 'Introducing Objects of Reference' which can be accessed via the link:

www.youtube.com/watch?v=vetUsvdJX1A

- Identify the four stages involved in the implementation and give an example of how this approach could be used with a child, young person, or adult.

Intensive Interaction

Intensive Interaction is a technique of communication with people who do not use words. The approach uses pre-verbal communication techniques, for instance responsive eye contact, facial expressions, vocal mirroring and joint focus activities (Nind and Hewett, 2001). Intensive Interaction was initially developed in the 1980s by professionals working in long-stay education settings, who wanted to gain a better rapport with their pupils. This interactionist approach is designed to improve the communication, initially between the learner and the teacher, and following on from this, the learner, and the wider community (Hutchinson and Bodicoat, 2015), by basing the teaching around the learner's intentions and wishes. Intensive Interaction aims to teach the basic principles of communication that would normally be taught during the first two years of life, where a baby develops critical understanding and abilities by interacting with the adults around them. Studies into child and parent interactions have shown that by allowing a baby to guide the interaction, and by the parent imitating that action, babies learn to understand and communicate, therefore the theory suggests that this same method can be used to develop communication in learners with a range of needs, including autism. The intention is to create the fundamentals of communication such as:

- Enjoying being with another person
- Concentration and attention span
- Taking turns exchanging behaviour
- Sharing personal space
- Using and understanding eye contacts; and
- Using and understanding non-verbal communication

When using Intensive Interaction with PMLD learners it is important to seize opportunities, for example when the learner is feeling more social, plan time for the session, and ensure that there is time to reflect on the session. This level of interaction requires an in-depth knowledge of the young person, to ensure that the practitioner understands when the young person is enjoying the activity and when they require rest. This level of understanding is known as 'tuning-in'. Another difficulty of this approach is that this process can be physically and mentally exhausting for the practitioner, making it vital that rest time is enabled. Finally, it is important that the practitioner does not rush the process of Intensive Interaction to ensure that the sessions are experienced at the rate the learner intends (Hewett, 2012).

Kellett and Nind (2003) recommend that a practitioner makes an initial assessment and collects baseline data first, making a clear distinction when the approach is being used and when it is not. Therefore, the individual would be given the space and prompts to interact with the practitioner at their own pace, getting verbal feedback the whole time to engage them. It is up to the practitioner to decide on codes for one-to-one interactive sessions such as eye contact, smiles, and contingent vocalisations, but this is the extent to which the practitioner takes the lead. Sessions may look different every time, but an example of an Intensive Interaction session could be a practitioner working to recognise different emotions and sounds. When the practitioner mimics the child it then becomes a conversation that they are both participating in, and the practitioner will be able to gauge which sounds and faces they prefer. A session would include mutually enjoyable interactive games where the child is encouraged to explore conversation and mutual interactions, with her expressions and vocalisations being acknowledged and listened to.

Research evidence

When carried out successfully, research demonstrates that individuals with PMLD have the potential to master skills in self-involvement to initiate social contact (Nind, 1996). Nevertheless, this can only be achieved if practitioners carry out the same methodology of Intensive Interaction. Barber (2007) stated that often practitioners misunderstand Intensive Interaction as just imitation. Consequently, this can limit interaction and provides little variation to introduce new communicative skills. Describing Intensive Interaction as a process could ultimately discourage practitioners when working with individuals with PMLD who are not meeting the expected milestones. However, a review of literature examining practitioners' experiences across a range of settings with Intensive Interaction suggested that staff find Intensive Interaction rewarding and judge that those they work with benefit from it (Berridge and Hutchinson, 2021). Clegg et al. (2020) investigated how staff used Intensive Interaction and found that barriers of staffing, management and organisational structure must be reduced by services to enable care staff to use Intensive Interaction. They also found that care staff were able to identify changes and progress in communicative behaviours and comment that Intensive Interaction promotes social inclusion for adults with PMLD.

Activity

Watch these three videos related to Intensive Interaction:

'How to do Intensive Interaction – the principles of the approach.' The video can be accessed via the link: www.youtube.com/watch?v=Epp QXyI5FX0

'How does Intensive Interaction help people with ASD?' The video can be accessed via the link: www.youtube.com/watch?v=rjKxu6QKjAo

Look at this Intensive Interaction film for parents and carers. The video can be accessed via the link: www.youtube.com/watch?v=9FEOeG-9Zpo

- How could the steps seen in the videos be used to support James and Julie?

James is aged 10 and has a diagnosis of Foetal Alcohol Syndrome, resulting in a global developmental delay and behavioural issues. It is difficult for communication to occur between him and professionals, as verbal communication does not produce responses.

Julie is aged 14 and has cerebral palsy and does not use spoken language or sign to communicate. She does not take interest in other children playing around her and has a significant cognitive delay.

Eye gaze

Whilst many interventions such as those above work on the premise of working with practitioners and individual commitment, there are interventions which make use of technology to assist their users. A prominent and rising technology-based intervention is eye gaze. This is an eye-driven communication system which uses eye-tracking cameras to observe the movement of an individual's eye. This requires a user to look at specific tiles on a screen such as letters of the alphabet for sustained periods of time to allow the system to complete the command, for example, forming a sentence (Lariviere, 2015). This system is typically used by children and adults who have significant physical disabilities which prevent them from communicating verbally or through signed languages. The most prevalent disability types who benefit from this are cerebral palsy (CP), muscular dystrophy, motor neurone disease and PMLD (Cañigueral and Hamilton, 2019). The main premise of EG technology is to allow these individuals to communicate with their peers independently without needing to rely on assistance from practitioners or family. It also aids children who do not verbally communicate to understand the rules of language and communication such as turn taking, and sentence structures (Degutyte and Astell, 2021). Ball et al. (2010) state that the most prevalent language skills and tasks that are supported by eye-gaze technology are face-to-face interaction, group communication and making phone calls.

Karlsson et al. (2018) suggest that eye-gaze technology is effective at supporting communication and improving quality of life for people with physical disability – who cannot access spoken or signed languages – and, for some, is the only technology that is appropriate and effective at supporting access to independent communication. Eye-gaze technology supports communication for individuals who demonstrate severe limitations to control purposeful speech and voluntary movements to converse meaning. Without such intervention, the caregiver is typically responsible for interpreting and decoding pre-linguistic behaviours such as hand movements and facial expressions. These gestures are typically interpreted as attention-seeking behaviours to request, refuse or make a choice (Townend, et al., 2016). Eye-gaze technology contributes as a form of expressive language for individuals with PMLD by tracking eye movements to select choices on a computer screen or accompanying interactive white boards. Although eye gaze is accessible to a huge range of physical disabilities, there are many challenges that come with complex AAC such as eye gaze. The communication partner plays a vital role in supporting communication with AAC, and without a competent communication partner, assistive technology may be abandoned.

Research evidence

Karlsson et al. (2018) stated that there is evidence of increased quality of life, achieving communication goals and higher self-esteem in children after usage. Additionally, Karlsson et al. (2018) found that in children with dyskinetic CP, there was an improved goal achievement and communication-based skill mastery. This would suggest that for those individuals who cannot verbally communicate, using this technology can allow them to participate more freely with their peers and develop their communication skills. Hsieh et al. (2021), who studied the communication skills of children with severe speech impairments, found that the group who had access to EG technology and used it frequently were more likely to initiate communication and made greater contributions to conversations than those who did not use EG technology. However, Perfect et al. (2020) found that this success greatly depended on the degree of comprehensive professional and familial support that the individuals received. Borgestig et al. (2016) stated that it can take between 15 and 20 months for individuals to fully adapt to the way that EG technology works, therefore, it is a long process from obtaining the technology to becoming completely efficient in working it. Hahn, Brady and Versaci (2019) found that outcomes for children with learning disabilities were hugely variable and therefore eye gaze may not always be effective means of communication for children with SLCN.

Activity

Developments in technology mean that there are more AAC eye-pointing devices than ever before, from the more traditional Eye Transfer Frame to bespoke eye-tracking systems that enable those with very limited physical movement to communicate.

The video 'AAC strategies: Eye pointing' can be accessed via the link: www.complexneeds.org.uk/modules/Module-3.1-Communication—augmentative-and-assistive-strategies/B/m09p070bcd.html#

- What range of technologies are highlighted?
- How are these being used in the videoclips?

Treatment and Education of Autistic and related Communications Handicapped Children (TEACCH®)

Division TEACCH® started in 1966 as part of the Department of Psychiatry of the School of Medicine at the University of North Carolina in the USA. It began as a Child Research Project to provide services to children on the autism spectrum and their families. In 1972, the North Carolina General Assembly passed legislation which enabled Division TEACCH® to become the first comprehensive statewide community-based programme of services for autistic children and adults and other similar developmental conditions and disorders.

The key features of TEACCH® are:

- Focusing on a child's individual skills, interests and needs creating a child-centred plan to meet their specific needs
- The use of visual structures allow organisation to flow through an environment to meet five elements (physical structure, visual structure, working systems, task organisation and routines)
- Allowing flexible teaching to suit the needs of all learners
- Providing support to allow children to thrive in all environments

(National Autistic Society, 2023)

TEACCH® is an organisational teaching strategy used to support autistic individuals using workboxes, routines and visual timetables. Practitioners can create an independent and effective working environment for learners, encouraging children to complete work tasks, knowing that they will be rewarded for this (Mesibov, Shea and Schopler, 2005). The systematic approach of teaching autistic children was devised from a series of observations, showing that they share a pattern of neuropsychological deficits and strengths, that are now known as the 'Culture of Autism' (Mesibov, 1997). Studies show that using visuals, routines and workstations, autistic children can thrive in the consistent and structured environment, due to the removal of barriers to encourage and support positive development (Mesibov, Shea and Schopler, 2005). Although this strategy is built from the use of behaviourist reinforcers, it is also important for the practitioner to use a more child-centred approach, to ensure a child's individual skills, interests and needs are used to create a child-centred plan.

A typical classroom can generally be one space where children are expected to learn and play; however, for an autistic learner it can be overwhelming, therefore, the use of zonal organisation can break a room up into different areas, allowing children to begin to associate and understand the expectations of each zone, as some zones are dedicated to completing work, and some to play and choose. As a result of different zones, children can begin to build a routine and in turn lessen their anxieties, knowing what to expect and how to respond (D'Elia et al., 2014). This is achievable when professionals are consistent with spatial delegation; however, this approach will lose meaning if the professional has a limited understanding of the strategy, showing the importance of practitioner training when delivering support strategies (Orellana, Martínez-Sanchis and Silvestre, 2014). Along with the organisation of the room, it is also important to declutter spaces and limit the number of distractions in each zone.

Consistent visual schedules are used which include visual timetables for the whole class and individual student schedules. Visual supports can ease certain challenges people with autism face, such as emotional expression and recognition, by augmenting communication with visual cues which therefore help to complete with tasks and engage in social interactions. Visual timetables create an accessible system for children to use to understand when and where they need to be in different areas; this can reduce anxiety for many children as they are able to see what is next and manage their emotion based on this change, instead of dwelling on the unknown. It is likely that visual timetables will co-exist with the communicational intervention of Picture Exchange Communication System PECS, enhancing a learner's communication and understanding, therefore allowing children at early stages of development to understand their timetable of pictures accompanied by symbols.

There is clear empirical support for the benefits of structure and predictability in the environment for autistic individuals. Work systems establish expectations and activity measurements and detail the expected tasks each day. According to Mesibov, Howley and Naftel (2015) work systems are a way of structuring tasks or task elements that students are expected to do, how much work is expected and how to know they are making progress. Structured teaching strategies such as visual schedules and work systems may support autistic individuals to stay on-task and navigate transitions. Task boxes contain details of activities which are individualised for the student and filled with visual cues and reminders. There is evidence that both expressive and receptive language skills of children within a TEACCH® environment were progressively developed compared to previous inputs. However, there are debates around whether this strategy is too structured for those with mild autistic characteristics, and they may become reliant on the rigid routine which they may not have access to when entering adulthood (Braiden et al., 2012).

Research evidence

Butler (2016) found that communication skills became more frequent, and were spontaneous, as opposed to being teacher led. However, others suggest that the impact of TEACCH is marginal at best, particularly relating to cognition, communication, motor, and daily living activities, with Virués-Ortega, Julio and

Pastor-Barriuso (2013) finding that the response is dependent on the skill being targeted. Studies have shown a range of benefits of TEACCH® programmes, including reducing parental stress (Sanz-Cervera et al., 2018) developing perception, motor and cognitive skills (D'Elia et al., 2014) and social behaviours (Virués-Ortega, Juilo and Pastor-Barriuso, 2013) – studies show large support for child and parent behaviours. This includes improvement in independence and self-efficacy for the child and their work skills, parent ability to understand and structure their environment. Research shows children with ASD struggle to with interpersonal relationships, time passing, abstract concepts and gestures, but the programme makes reality as clear as possibly from preconceptual viewpoints by using continuous visual aids, giving them more independence in handling their own space, time and thoughts (Panerai, Ferrante and Zingale, 2002).

A longitudinal study of 28 Italian autistic children were exposed to a TEACCH® oriented practice to evaluate the best age to begin an intervention. The study showed that after a six-month review, developmental abilities significantly improved, and a 12-month follow-up period showed that children 60 months and under showed improvement of motor skills and cognition, showing that early intervention strengthens the effectiveness of the programme (Fornasari et al., 2012). A Chinese longitudinal study of pre-school autistic children mirrored these findings as they found TEACCH principles developed perception, fine motor skills, eye- hand coordination and gross motor skills, as well as cognitive functioning (Tsang et al., 2007).

Comparing TEACCH® with LEAP and standardised teaching showed that each of the methods provided significant benefits and improvements with communication and social interactions (Boyd et al., 2014). Callahan et al. (2010) analysed results comparing practitioners' and parents' preference of TEACCH® and Applied Behaviour Analysis Training (ABA) and found there were no preference. However, they found teachers with 'higher functioning' autistic learners rated TEACCH® interventions higher than ABA. Panerai, Ferrante and Zingale (2002) compared two groups of eight children matched by genders, chronological and mental age, and diagnosis. One experimental group had the programme applied while the other controlled group were integrated with a support teacher and found the TEACCH® group improved test scores after a year. Ozonoff and Cathcart (1998) state that TEACCH® notably increased social communications for autistic children and Siu, Lin and Chung (2019) found that children with mid-moderate learning disabilities showed improvements in functional skills. Virués-Ortega et al. (2013) performed a meta-analysis of intervention studies including TEACCH® and concluded that the method had a large improvement of social and maladaptive behaviours, but with perceptual, motor, cognitive and verbal skills they found it had small/lower effects.

Activity

This video is an introduction to a TEACCH® classroom. It can be accessed via the link:

www.youtube.com/watch?v=vkymZzmg4jw&t=3s

- Can you identify the five principles of TEACCH® in this classroom?

You have been asked to help a new teacher to plan a classroom following these principles.

- Where would you go for advice and how would you support them?

Dyslexia

There are several strategies which may support dyslexic learners. One approach is to ensure that the approaches could benefit all learners in an inclusive classroom, so-called Wave 1 – what can every teacher do in every classroom. For example:

Reading

- Arrange for any lengthy text reading to be supported by a 'buddy' or a support assistant, or tape recorded in advance
- Ensure that a dyslexic learner can read a text easily before expecting him/her to read aloud
- Use cream or pastel-coloured paper (ask learners what colour they prefer)
- Use blue, brown, red, green or purple board markers in preference to black
- Use colour to separate key information written on the board

Accessibility of text

- Use an uncluttered layout with accessible key words and ideas
- Use shorter sentences rather than longer ones
- Ensure that high-frequency words are used
- Use active verbs rather than passive ones
- Use colour to separate key information

Writing

- Use writing frames, cloze procedure exercises and jumbled text
- Ensure learners have a model close by to copy from
- Allow students with literacy difficulties to write directly onto worksheets
- Provide key words
- Encourage the use of spellcheckers and word mats

Grouping

- Pair the learner with a competent, supportive peer
- Ensure all students are facing you when you are giving instructions
- Vary seating arrangements
- Use 'study buddies', e.g. if a dyslexic pupil has good ideas for writing, put him/her with a child who is strong at transcription but weaker at composition

Activity

The 'Train the Trainer: Teaching for Neurodiversity project' was funded by the Department for Education and ran until 31 March 2017. It was led by the BDA in partnership with the Dyspraxia Foundation, Dyslexia Action, Helen Arkell, Manchester Metropolitan University and Patoss. The aim of the project was to provide training and quality-assured information about dyslexia and other SpLD for teachers and support staff, and for dyslexic individuals and their families.

It can be accessed via the link:

www.thedyslexia-spldtrust.org.uk/4/resources/2/schools-and-local-a uthorities/387/teaching-for-neurodiversity-resources-ndash-engaging-lea rners-with-send

The materials are broken down into the following sections:

1 Seeing the whole picture
2 Understanding neurodiversity
3 Dyslexia Action: Understanding neurodiversity Post 16/FE
4 Dyslexia Action: Train the Trainer Classroom support strategies (Primary)
5 Teaching for Neurodiversity, Classroom support strategies (Secondary)
6 Teaching for Neurodiversity Classroom support strategies (Post 16/FE)
7 Take an area which interests you or one in which you are working and suggest how the resources could support both your teaching and learners

The following examples are strategies which could be used to support dyslexic learners:

Multisensory teaching

The use of visual, auditory, and kinaesthetic information to improve the reading and generally the learning ability has a long history. The use of multisensory teaching can help dyslexic children become independent learners and boost their self-esteem and children are encouraged to believe in themselves and to become independent learners from an early age.

Metacognition

Dyslexic learners may have difficulty with the metacognitive aspects of learning. This implies that they need to be shown how to learn, for example, through identifying connections and relationships between different learning tasks. This essentially means the emphasis should not only be on the content or the product of learning but also on the process – that is, how learning takes place.

Repetition approach

Repetition, the implementation of multisensory techniques and the word identification strategies are the essential factors to acquire reading ability. The repetitive reading of a certain text with the guidance of a computer, an educator or even another auditor has proven effective at the early years of education. There are two ways of effective repetition, echo reading, where the learner repeats what he/she hears from the teacher or a fellow student and cooperative reading, where the learner reads paired with a non-dyslexic learner.

The Aural-Read-Respond-Oral-Write (ARROW) approach

This is a multisensory learning system and based upon the idea that when someone hears his/her own voice, reading comprehension is improved. During this programme, children with dyslexic learners record their voices on a computer while reading a small text and play them back. Then they write down exactly what they heard. The programme is advised for 30 minutes a day for a sum of ten hours.

Peer reading

Peer reading is an intervention model where the dyslexic learner who has reading difficulties is paired to a non-professional, who reads to the student, reads simultaneously with them, and then listens and guides. In this way, the learner will understand the meaning of the text and enjoy the reading procedure as they gain in confidence and fluency.

Metacognition

Strategies for developing metacognition in reading include:

1   Teacher-modelling, in which the teacher demonstrates the application of a reading strategy, such as self-questioning or summarising, explaining both the procedure for implementing the strategy, and the purpose and utility of the strategy.
2   Think-alouds, in which the learner verbalises their processing as they read a text.

3 Reciprocal teaching, in which the teacher and learner take turns at (a) asking questions during reading, (b) summarising the text at appropriate points, (c) clarifying what has been read, noting any inconsistencies and (d) predicting the next part of the text.
4 Semantic mapping, in which the learner uses a teacher-made graphic representation or mind map as a guide to the organisation of the material in the text and how the ideas of the content are related. Later, the learner learns to mind map the text's content while they read.

Useful videoclips:

Using multisensory methods: www.youtube.com/watch?v=qWBjBq73oR4
Repetition: www.youtube.com/watch?v=uST7Yj-3YrQ
ARROW: www.youtube.com/watch?v=2h0qqBrnVMM
Metacognition: www.youtube.com/watch?v=VaiiNCoLDcU
Approaches and strategies for teaching spelling: www.youtube.com/watch?v=Fcy_MTDWo6I

Structured literacy
A structured literacy approach is a highly explicit and systematic way to teach all components of literacy including oral and written language alongside focusing on phonological awareness, spelling, syntax and reading comprehension. www.youtube.com/watch?v=mCf5hSuav18&t=465s

---

References

Anderson, L. and Östlund, D. (2017). Assessments for learning in grades 1–9 in a special school for students with intellectual disability in Sweden. *Problems of Education in the 21st Century*, 75 (6), pp. 508–524.

Ball, L. J., Nordness, A. S., Fager, S. K., Kersch, K., Mohr, B., Pattee, G. L. and Beukelman, D. R. (2010). Eye-gaze access to AAC technology for people with amyotrophic lateral sclerosis. *Journal of Medical Speech-Language Pathology*, 18 (3), pp. 11–23.

Barber, M. (2007). Imitation, interaction and dialogue using Intensive Interaction: tea party rules. *Support for Learning*, 2 (3), pp. 124–130.

Berridge, S. and Hutchinson, N. (2021). Staff experience of the implementation of intensive interaction within their places of work with people with learning disabilities and/or autism. *J Appl Res Intellect Disabil*, 34 (1), pp. 1–15.

Borgestig, M., Sandqvist, J., Parsons, R., Falkmer, T. and Hemmingsson, H. (2016). Eye gaze performance for children with severe physical impairments using gaze-based assistive technology: a longitudinal study. *Assist Technol*, 28 (2), pp. 93–102.

Boyd, B. A., McDonough, S. G. and Bodfish, J. W. (2012). Evidence-based behavioral interventions for repetitive behaviors in autism. *Journal of Autism and Developmental Disorders*, 42, pp.1236–1248.

Boyd, B. A, Hume, K., McBee, M. T., Alessandri, M., Gutierrez, A., Johnson, L., Sperry, L. and Odom, S. L. (2014). Comparative efficacy of LEAP, TEACCH and non-model-specific special education programs for preschoolers with autism spectrum disorders. *J Autism Dev Disord*, 44 (2), 366–380.

Braiden, H. J., McDaniel, B., McCrudden, E., Janes, M. and Crozier, B. (2012). A practice-based evaluation of Barnardo's Forward Steps Early Intervention Programme for children diagnosed with autism. *Child Care in Practice*, 18 (3), pp. 227–242.

Butler, C. (2016). The effectiveness of the TEACCH approach in supporting the development of communication skills for learners with severe intellectual disabilities. *Support for Learning*, 31, pp. 185–201.

Callahan, K., Shukla-Mehta, S., Magee, S. and Wie, M. (2010). ABA versus TEACCH: the case for defining and validating comprehensive treatment models in autism. *J Autism Dev Disord*, 40 (1), pp.74–88.

Cañigueral, R. and Hamilton, A. F. d. C. (2019). The role of eye gaze during natural social interactions in typical and autistic people. *Frontiers in Psychology*, 10, Article 560.

Carpenter, B. (2010). *Children with Complex Learning Difficulties and Disabilities: Who are They and What are Their Needs?* (Complex Needs Series). London: SSAT.

Cartwright, C. and Wind-Cowie, S. (2005). *Profound and Multiple Learning Difficulties, (SEN)*. New York: Continuum.

Clegg, J., Black, R., Smith, A. and Brumfitt, S. (2020). Examining the impact of a city-wide intensive interaction staff training program for adults with profound and multiple learning disability: a mixed methods evaluation. *Disability and Rehabilitation*, 42 (2), pp. 201–210.

D'Elia, L., Valeri, G., Sonnino, F., Fontana, I., Mammone, A. and Vicari, S. (2014). A longitudinal study of the TEACCH program in different settings: the potential benefits of low intensity intervention in preschool children with autism spectrum disorder. *J Autism Dev Disord*, 44 (3), pp. 615–626.

Dixson, D. D. & Worrell, F. C. (2016) Formative and summative assessment in the classroom. *Theory Into Practice*, 55 (2), pp. 153–159.

Day, T. A. and Tosey, P. (2011). Beyond SMART? A new framework for goal setting. *The Curriculum Journal*, 22, pp. 515–534.

Degutyte, Z. and Astell, A. (2021). The role of eye gaze in regulating turn taking in conversations: a systematized review of methods and findings. *Front Psychol*, 7 (12), 616471.

Fornasari, L., Garzitto, M., Fabbro, F., Londero, D., Zago, D., Desinano, C., Rigo, S., Massimo, M. and Brambilla, P. (2012). Twelve months of TEACCH-oriented habilitation on an Italian population of children with autism. *International Journal of Developmental Disabilities*, 58, pp. 145–158.

Goldbart, J., Chadwick, D. and Buell, S. (2014). Speech and language therapists' approaches to communication intervention with children and adults with profound and multiple learning disability. *International Journal of Language & Communication Disorders*, 49, pp. 687–701.

Hahn, L. J., Brady, N. C. and Versaci, T. (2019). Communicative use of triadic eye gaze in children with down syndrome, autism spectrum disorder, and other intellectual and developmental disabilities. *Am J Speech Lang Pathol*, 28 (4), pp. 1509–1522.

Harding, C., Lindsay, G., O'Brien, A., Dipper, L. and Wright, J. (2011). Implementing AAC with children with profound and multiple learning disabilities: a study in rationale underpinning intervention. *Journal of Research in Special Educational Needs*, 11, pp. 120–129.

Hewett, D. (2012). *Intensive Interaction: Theoretical Perspectives*. London: SAGE.

Hutchinson, N. and Bodicoat, A. (2015). The effectiveness of Intensive Interaction, a systematic literature review. *Journal of Applied Research in Intellectual Disabilities*, 28 (6), pp. 437–454.

Hsieh, Y.-H., Borgestig, M., Gopalarao, D., McGowan, J., Granlund, M., Hwang, A.-W. and Hemmingsson, H. (2021). Communicative interaction with and without eye-gaze technology between children and youths with complex needs and their communication partners. *International Journal of Environmental Research and Public Health*, 18 (10), p. 5134.

Imray, P. and Hinchcliffe, V. (2013). *Curricula for Teaching Children and Young People with Severe or Profound and Multiple Learning Difficulties*. London: Routledge.

Imray, P. and Hewett, D. (2015). Challenging behaviour and the curriculum. In: P. Lacey, R. Ashdown, P. Jones, H. Lawson and M. Pipe (eds.), *The Routledge Companion to Severe, Profound and Multiple Learning Difficulties*. London: Routledge.

Joffee, E. and Rikhye, C. H. (1991). Orientation and mobility for students with severe visual and multiple impairments: a new perspective. *Journal of Visual Impairment & Blindness*, 85, pp. 211–216.

Jones, F., Pring, T. and Grove, N. C. (2002). Developing communication in adults with profound and multiple learning difficulties using objects of reference. *International Journal of Language & Communication Disorders*, 37 (2), pp. 173–184.

Karkou, V. (2009). *Arts Therapies in Schools: Research and Practice*. London: Jessica Kingsley.

Karlsson, P., Allsop, A., Dee-Price, B. J. and Wallen, M. (2018). Eye-gaze control technology for children, adolescents and adults with cerebral palsy with significant physical disability: findings from a systematic review. *Dev Neurorehabil*, 21 (8), pp. 497–505.

Kellett, M. and Nind, M. (2003). *Implementing Intensive Interaction in Schools: Guidance for Practitioners, Managers and Coordinators*. London: David Fulton.

Lacey, P. (2010). Smart and scruffy targets. *The SLD Experience*, 57 (1), pp. 16–21.

Lariviere, J. A. (2015). Eye tracking: eye-gaze technology. In: I. Söderback (ed.), *International Handbook of Occupational Therapy Interventions*. 2nd ed. Cham, Switzerland: Springer International Publishing, pp. 339–362.

McLarty, M. (1995). *The Education of Dual Sensory Impaired Children*. London: Routledge.

McNicholas, J. (2001). Assessment: the assessment of pupils with profound and multiple learning difficulties. *British Journal of Special Education*, 27, pp. 150–153.

Mesibov, G. B. (1997). Formal and informal measures on the effectiveness of the TEACCH programme. *Autism*, 1 (1), pp. 25–35.

Mesibov, G. B., Shea, V. and Schopler, E. (2005). *The TEACCH Approach to Autism Spectrum Disorders*. New York: Springer.

Mesibov, G., Howley, M. and Naftel, S. (2015). *Accessing the Curriculum for Learners with Autism Spectrum Disorders: Using the TEACCH Programme to Help Inclusion*. London: Routledge.

National Autistic Society (NAS) (2023). TEACCH. [Online] Available at: www.autism.org.uk/what-we-do/professional-development/the-teacch-approach [Accessed 02. 02. 2023].

Nind, M. (1996) Efficacy of Intensive Interaction: developing sociability and communication in people with severe and complex learning difficulties using an approach based on caregiver-infant interaction. *European Journal of Special Needs Education*, 11 (1), pp. 48–66.

Nind, M. and Hewett, D. (2001). *A Practical Guide to Intensive Interaction*. Birmingham: British Institute of Learning Disabilities.

Orellana, L. M., Martínez-Sanchis, S. and Silvestre, F. J. (2014). Training adults and children with an autism spectrum disorder to be compliant with a clinical dental assessment using a TEACCH-based approach. *J Autism Dev Disord*, 44 (4), pp. 776–785.

Ozonoff, S. and Cathcart, K. (1998). Effectiveness of a home program intervention for young children with autism. *Journal of Autism and Developmental Disorders*, 28, pp. 25–32.

Park, K. (1995). Using objects of reference: a review of the literature. *European Journal of Special Needs Education*, 10 (1), pp. 40–46.

Panerai, S., Ferrante, L. and Zingale, M. (2002). Benefits of the Treatment and Education of Autistic and Communication Handicapped Children (TEACCH) programme as compared with a non-specific approach. *Journal of Intellectual Disability Research*, 46 (4), pp. 318–327.

Perfect, E., Hoskin, E., Noyek, S. and Davies, T. C. (2020). A systematic review investigating outcome measures and uptake barriers when children and youth with complex disabilities use eye gaze assistive technology. *Dev Neurorehabil*, 23 (3), pp. 145–159.

Rees, K. (2017). Models of disability and the categorisation of children with severe and profound learning difficulties: informing educational approaches based on an understanding of individual needs. *Educational and Child Psychology*, 34, pp. 30–39.

Sanz-Cervera, P., Fernández-Andrés, M. I., Pastor-Cerezuela, G., and Tárraga-Mínguez, R. (2018). The effectiveness of TEACCH intervention in autism spectrum disorder: a review study. *Papeles del Psicólogo*, 39 (1), 40–50.

Siu, A. M. H., Lin, Z. and Chung, J. (2019). An evaluation of the TEACCH approach for teaching functional skills to adults with autism spectrum disorders and intellectual disabilities. *Res Dev Disabil*, 90, pp. 14–21.

Stadskleiv, K., Jahnsen, R., Andersen, G. L. and von Tetzchner, S. (2018). Neuropsychological profiles of children with cerebral palsy. *Dev Neurorehabil*, 21 (2), pp. 108–120.

Tsang, S. K., Shek, D. T., Lam, L. L., Tang, F. L. and Cheung, P. M. (2007). Brief report: application of the TEACCH program on Chinese pre-school children with autism – does culture make a difference? *J Autism Dev Disord*, 37 (2), pp. 390–396.

Townend, G. S., Marschik, P. B., Smeets, E., van de Berg, R., van den Berg, M and Curfs, L. M. (2016). Eye gaze technology as a form of augmentative and alternative communication for individuals with rett syndrome: experiences of families in the Netherlands. *J Dev Phys Disabil*, 28, pp. 101–112.

Van Walwyk, L. (2011). Measuring progress in children with profound and multiple learning difficulties. *SLD Experience*, 60, pp. 9–16.

Virues-Ortega, J., Julio, F. M. and Pastor-Barriuso, R. (2013). The TEACCH program for children and adults with autism: a meta-analysis of intervention studies. *Clin Psychol Rev*, 33 (8), pp. 940–953.

Waters, L. (2015). Why positive education? *Teaching and Learning Network*, 22 (3), pp. 16–19.

Wheldall, K. and Carter, M. (1996). Reconstructing behaviour analysis in education: a revised behavioural interactionist perspective for special education. *Educational Psychology*, 16, pp. 121–140.

Part II

Exploring Sensory and/or Physical Needs

4 The underpinning theory and research evidence

Introduction

The SEND Code of Practice 2015 (DfE and DoH 2015) describes the broad area of need of 'Sensory and/or Physical Needs' as including those pupils with hearing impairment (HI), visual impairment (VI), multisensory impairment (MSI) or physical disability (PD). Many children and young people with vision impairment (VI), hearing impairment (HI) or a multisensory impairment (MSI) will require specialist support and/or equipment to access their learning, or habilitation support. Children and young people with an MSI have a combination of vision and hearing difficulties. Some children and young people with a physical disability (PD) require additional ongoing support and equipment to access all the opportunities available to their peers. The Equality Act (2010) defines a disability as a physical or mental impairment which has a long-term and substantial adverse effect on their ability to carry out normal day-to-day activities. Long-term is defined as 'a year or more', substantial is defined as 'more than minor or trivial'. This definition includes sensory impairments such as those affecting sight or hearing, and long-term health conditions such as asthma, diabetes, epilepsy, and cancer.

Learning objectives

This chapter will:

- Introduce you to a range of Sensory and/or Physical Needs including hearing impairment (HI), visual impairment (VI), multisensory impairment (MSI) and physical disability (PD)
- Invite you examine underpinning theory and research evidence in relation to Sensory and/or Physical Needs
- Introduce you to the aetiology of a range of Sensory and/or Physical Needs
- Invite you to review how the characteristics of these issues are manifested
- Help you to understand the complexities associated with such a broad area of need

DOI: 10.4324/9781003361084-7

Key terms

Sensory Needs, Physical Needs, hearing impairment, visual impairment, multi-sensory impairment, physical disability, barriers, aetiology, congenital glaucoma, retinitis pigmentosa, sensory processing difficulties, Sensory Modulation Disorder, Sensory Processing Disorder, cerebral palsy, Duchenne muscular dystrophy

---

Pause for reflection

- What do you think are the main barriers for disabled children, young people and adults that prevent access to education, employment and everyday life?
- What are the origins of such barriers?

Barriers

Barriers are factors in a person's environment that, through their absence or presence, limit functioning and create disability. These include aspects such as a physical environment that is not accessible, a lack of relevant assistive technology negative attitudes of people towards disability, and services, systems and policies that are either non-existent or that hinder the involvement of all people with a health condition in all areas of life. Centers for Disease Control and Prevention (CDC, 2020) refer to the following barriers:

1 Attitudinal barriers can contribute to other barriers and include stereotyping, stigma, prejudice, and discrimination
2 Communication barriers are experienced by people who have disabilities that affect hearing, speaking, reading, writing, and or understanding, and who use different ways to communicate
3 Physical barriers are structural obstacles in natural or manmade environments that prevent or block mobility (moving around in the environment) or access and include steps and curbs
4 Policy barriers are frequently related to a lack of awareness or enforcement of existing laws and regulations. Examples of policy barriers include denying individuals with disabilities the opportunity to participate in or benefit from services, or other benefits, denying individuals with disabilities access to programmes, services, benefits, or opportunities to participate because of physical barriers
5 Programmatic barriers limit the effective delivery of healthcare programmes and include attitudes, knowledge, and understanding of people with disabilities
6 Social barriers are related to the conditions in which people are born, grow, live, learn and work and include access to employment

7   Transportation barriers are due to a lack of adequate transportation that interferes with a person's ability to be independent and to function in society and include lack of access to accessible or convenient transportation

---

Activity

Take each of the seven barriers identified in relation to physical and sensory needs and complete the table.

Barrier	Example(s) of specific barriers	Impact on education or employment	Impact on social and family life
Attitudes			
Communication			
Physical			
Policy			
Programme			
Social			
Transport			

Hearing impairment (HI)

Hearing impairment (HI) can have a significant impact on a child's educational development, in some cases resulting in learning delay and reduced curricular access. Hearing impairment spans a range from mild/moderate to severe/profound. It can be temporary or permanent. A significant proportion of students have some degree of hearing difficulty at some time. Temporary hearing loss in the early years is usually caused by the condition known as 'glue ear'. Such hearing losses fluctuate and may be mild to moderate in degree. They can compound other learning difficulties. Occasionally a significant hearing loss may be caused by a long-term conductive loss in both ears. Significant permanent hearing losses are usually bilateral (both ears) and sensori-neural (due to problems with the auditory nerve or the cochlea) in origin. They may be severe or profound and may give rise to severe and complex communication difficulties. A permanent loss in one ear and a temporary loss in the other may also cause significant hearing impairment. Listening to language through hearing aids and cochlear implants and the visual concentration required for following lip reading and sign language is very tiring.

Children and young people with HI range from those with a mild hearing loss to those with a profound hearing loss. The impairment can be temporary or permanent and may affect one ear or both ears. It is often identified at a very early age through neo-natal screening and can occur across the whole ability range. Learning and difficulties in learning relate to the difficulties experienced in the auditory environment, both in the classroom and the wider school environment. These learners may experience difficulties in hearing, understanding, responding to instructions and any interactions.

- These learners may experience high levels of anxiety and have low self-esteem
- These learners are likely to need hearing aids, adaptations to the environment and teaching strategies to support the access to and understanding of language and concepts
- They may also need support in developing social skills and building relationships with peers
- They may also need support in developing emotional resilience and ensuring their well- being

Within the first few weeks of a child's life, a healthcare professional will undertake a hearing screening test called an automated otoacoustic emission test identifying a response when clicking sounds are played into their ear. If the results from the test show possible signs of deafness or hearing loss, a referral is made to a hearing specialist to complete further tests (NHS, 2021). At this stage, two types of deafness could be identified: sensori-neural or conductive hearing loss. Conductive hearing loss is caused by issues with sound passing from the outer/middle ear to the cochlea due to a build-up of fluid or wax in the middle ear often known as glue ear. Conductive hearing loss can be permanent but is more regularly a fluctuating hearing loss. However, sensori-neural hearing loss is permanent due to a fault in the inner ear usually because of damaged hair cells in the cochlea itself, meaning sound can't be converted to electrical impulses for the brain to understand.

Apart from hearing loss associated with ageing, congenital factors such as inherited genes or infection/illness in the pre-natal and post-natal stages of development can also lead to deafness. Some of these include rubella in pregnancy, severe jaundice, meningitis or even trauma in childbirth. Kubba et al. (2004) researched the effect of low birth rate because of socio-economic deprivation and its contribution to deafness. In their study they found that prematurity and low birth rate were more likely in economically poorer families. As a result, premature babies additionally have a higher risk of suffering from illnesses which could lead to deafness or hearing loss.

If a hearing impairment or deafness is identified at birth, hearing specialists along with specialist support workers including teachers of the deaf will be identified to create a multidisciplinary team supporting the family and the child. Options such as whether the family want to introduce technological aids, the use of sign language or bilingualism, and potential education and schooling options can all be discussed with the team. One of the options often discussed is the use of technological aids such as hearing aids or cochlear implants. Hearing aids are devices worn on the outside of the ear to amplify sound whereas cochlear implants are inserted into the ear and directly send sounds to the hearing nerve (Williams, 2019). However, the negative societal attitude towards the use of them can lead to a lowered confidence and self-esteem, resulting in individuals not wanting to use them. Parents may make the decision to use sign language as a method of communication with their child, but the older the child is when learning sign language, the poorer accuracy and vocabulary they will have, providing evidence that even language development through signing is developed early in life (Brice, 2008).

Activity

The Royal Association for Deaf people have produced a report entitled 'Deaf Advance: Deaf people, employment and career progression'. It can be accessed via the link: www.royaldeaf.org.uk/wp-content/uploads/2021/04/DeafAdvance-Report.pdf

- Read the report, or watch the BSL videos embedded within the report and summarise the key points it makes about deaf people and employment

They suggest that Deaf people consider themselves a linguistic minority and not disabled; to the Deaf community, deafness is not a problem that needs to be fixed. Also, that many words and expressions have been used over the years to describe Deafness but most have no place in modern society, for example, 'deaf and dumb' and 'hearing impaired'.

- Research the use and meaning of the terms: deaf, Deaf, BSL, deafened and Deafblind

---

Visual impairment (VI)

Pause for reflection

- Most blind people are not born blind, they become blind. This means that, having learned to rely on their sight in order to recognise and relate to the world, they must now radically revise their basic assumptions about that world. It is not surprising that blindness is usually an overwhelming personal and family catastrophe affecting the patient's mobility, work, personal relationships and much else. What impact might this have on an individual and their family?

Visual impairment(s) are when an individual experiences sight loss; some children may be blind and unable to see anything, whereas others may have reduced vision. For example, they may not see from a specific distance, they may have difficulties distinguishing colour or have issues with their peripheral or central vision. Visual impairments are more common in the older population, affecting one in two of those over the age of 90 years (Slade and Edwards, 2016). According to Sivaprasad et al. (2012), people who are African or Asian have double the risk of having severe visual impairments compared to white people. The term 'visual impairment' (VI) is used to describe any kind of vision loss, ranging from the degree of blindness to partial vision loss because of the dysfunction, anomaly or injury to the optic and visual pathways (Barton, 2011). Besides the loss of central or peripheral vision, the other functional effects of VI include poor image sharpness, low contrast sensitivity or adaptability to light, colour loss, and impaired eye movement (Alagaratnam et al., 2002). VI can also be classified as congenital – where vision loss is present at birth due to genetic reasons or infections transmitted from the mother to the foetus during pregnancy or acquired – where vision loss is later in life because of degenerative conditions, illnesses or accidents. They can be caused by cataracts, uncorrected refractive errors, glaucoma and from eye diseases in the trachoma and cornea and can also arise due to diabetes, for example diabetic retinopathy can be caused by having either type 1 or 2 diabetes and results in complications in the retina. Age-related macular degeneration is where the macula in the retina which is responsible for clear and central vision experiences changes to the blood flow and structure due to ageing (Ma and Liutkevičienꟷ, 2021). The number of people with this condition is increasing and is more prevalent in people over the age of 65 (Bennion, Shaw and Gibson, 2012). Children with neurodevelopmental disorders like autism and cerebral palsy are more likely to have visual impairments because their disorder affects their brain and cerebral visual impairments are caused when part of the brain is damaged (Williams et al., 2021). ICD11 (WHO, 2019) classifies visual impairments into different categories, including distance vision ranging from mild, where the visual acuity is 6/12 to 6/18, to blindness where the visual acuity is 3/60 to 1/60, and near vision, where visual acuity is worse than M0.8 or N6.

Types of visual impairment

In 2015, it was estimated that there were 253 million people worldwide with a visual impairment (including 36 million classified as blind and 217 million with a moderate to severe visual impairment); this is set to significantly increase over time due to an ageing and growing population as well as factors such as increases in diabetes (Ackland, Resnikoff and Bourne, 2017). In 2021, more than two million people are estimated to be living with sight loss in the UK. This level of sight loss is severe enough to have a significant impact on their daily lives (Royal National Institute of Blind People, 2022). ICD-11 (WHO, 2019) references distance vision impairment, which can range from mild (visual acuity worse than 6/12) to blindness (visual acuity worse than 3/60) and near vision impairment – classified as having near visual acuity worse than N6 or M.08 with existing correction. Globally, the leading causes of vision impairment are uncorrected refractive errors, cataracts, age-related macular degeneration, glaucoma, diabetic retinopathy, corneal opacity and trachoma. However, there are some differences across countries due to level of income. Visual impairment in low/middle-income countries is more likely to be caused by cataract; however, in higher-income countries visual impairment is more likely to be caused by glaucoma, age-related macular degeneration or diabetic retinopathy (WHO, 2022).

Activity

The Royal National Institute of Blind People (RNIB) are running a campaign entitled 'See the person, not the sight loss'. Watch the video featuring Ava, a typical teenager, an avid gamer, with dreams of working in technology, who has a visual impairment. It can be accessed vis the link: www.rnib.org.uk/our-campaigns/see-the-person

• What messages does the video attempt to get across?

The RNIB website can be accessed via the link: www.rnib.org.uk
Using the dropdown menu under the link 'Living with sight loss', suggest the impact of sight loss on the following:

• Education and learning
• Employment and equality
• Independent living
• Community connection and well-being

Congenital glaucoma

Congenital glaucoma is a condition caused by the draining system in the eye not developing correctly and can be primary or secondary congenital glaucoma (Alanazi et al., 2013). Primary congenital glaucoma is a rare condition which can cause blindness in children. Its cause is largely genetic and has been linked to several different genes including autosomal recessive and dominant genes (Ling et al., 2020). Aziz, Denis and Matonti (2012) found that 14 per cent of children in their study had a close relative with the condition. Congenital glaucoma is an increase in the intraocular pressure caused by poor drainage of fluid in the eye which leads to damage of the optic nerve. Children with the condition typically have enlarged eyes, clouding of the cornea and atrophied irises as well as a restricted field of vision (Badawi et al., 2019). Parents may also notice their child has a sensitivity to light, head or eye pain or has consistently red eyes. It is diagnosed by an ophthalmologist, but if it is left untreated for too long it can lead to irreversible loss of sight. Medication and surgery which lower intraocular pressure such as angle surgery, which aims to allow for proper drainage of the fluid in the eye, can be used to manage the condition.

Retinitis pigmentosa (RP)

Retinitis pigmentosa (RP) is a type of visual impairment that causes progressive vision loss. This type of disorder effects the retina, which is the layer of light-sensitive tissue at the back of the eye. Retinitis pigmentosa is an inherited disorder as an abnormal gene is inherited from either parent. Genes related to retinitis pigmentosa act as an important role in the structure and function of specialised light receptor cells in the retina. Gradual loss of rods and cones in the retina are caused by mutations in any of the genes responsible for retinitis pigmentosa; rods usually break down before cones, which explains why loss of night vision is one of the first signs of this impairment (Hamel, 2006). The most prominent indicator of RP in childhood is usually a developed loss in night vision, this takes individuals longer to adjust to darkness as many individuals tend to trip over objects in dim light (Berson, 1993). Most individuals may gradually lose their peripheral vision where they have a reduced ability to see through their side vision, this is known as tunnel vision where you are unable to see to the side without turning your head. Some people with retinitis pigmentosa may have trouble seeing different colours. As the impairment progresses individuals will eventually lose their central vision and be completely blind (Altinbay and Taskin, 2021). Research has identified that most adults with visual impairments experience co-morbid conditions; current studies highlighted that 70 per cent of adults with visual impairments reported experiencing at least one co-morbid condition that include a variety of additional disabilities or health conditions (Haegele et al., 2021).

RP is generally identified when children grow and develop, as characteristics and symptoms of retinitis pigmentosa tend to become more prominent. During the assessment pathway it is crucial for electrophysiological alternations to be included as electroretinography is one of many methods used to diagnose and follow up individuals with RP. Electroretinography studies are conducted by an ophthalmologist, it is used to measure the individual's response to flashes of light through electrodes. RP individuals show a decrease in the amplitude of five electroretinography (ERG) which includes the rod, maximum, oscillatory, cone and flicker (Chang et al., 2014). As dysfunctions in the cone system occurs in the early stages of RP, the examination of flicker ERG can detect and characterise cone system dysfunctions in the RP as high frequencies of the flicker provides an enhanced assessment of cone photoreceptor integrity in RP (Hassan-Karimi et al., 2012). Visual electrophysiologists most frequently concentrate on scotopic and mesopic results to identify RP earlier on as reduction of the scotopic rod response is predominantly one of the first signs that the electroretinography highlights. Most individuals with RP normally display prolonged b-waves implicit times; however, during early stages of this impairment the ERG will fail to identify this as it will show normal amplitude and implicit time values, thus other signs of RP will be used in making a diagnosis. (Hamel, 2006).

Activity

Retinitis pigmentosa (RP) is the most common group of inherited retinal dystrophies (IRD) which is a genetic eye condition which affects the light-sensitive cells in the retina at the back of your eyes, which over time stops them from working. The RNIB have produced a document called 'Understanding Inherited retinal dystrophies'. It can be accessed via the link: https://media.rnib.org. uk/documents/Understanding_Inherited_retinal_dystrophies_PT_2022_i0scuYn.pdf

- Research autosomal dominant, autosomal recessive and X-linked inheritance of an IRD
- Read the case studies of Rupa and Bill and suggest what impact RP has had on their everyday lives

---

Sensory processing difficulties

Our bodies and the environment send our brain information through our senses. We process and organise this information so that we feel comfortable and secure. Some individuals may experience the sensory inputs as overwhelming and upsetting, leading to 'sensory overload'. Individuals may be over-sensitive to sensory input, under-sensitive, or both. When a child has difficulty coping with these demands, they may have sensory processing difficulties. A child may be under-sensitive or over-sensitive in the five areas:

- Proprioception (ability to perceive the body's position in space and movement)
- Vestibular (sense of balance and spatial orientation)
- Auditory (reaction to certain sounds)
- Oral sensory (taste, texture, and temperature of food)
- Tactile (reaction to touch – e.g., light touch or deep pressure)

Sensory modulation difficulties

Problems with sensory modulation occur when our brain either over responds or under responds to sensory information. It has been found that people can be over-responsive or under-responsive in all the different senses, or they can be over-responsive in one sense and under-responsive in another. The term 'sensory modulation' refers to a complex process of perceiving sensory information and generating responses that are appropriately graded to, or congruent with, the situation. It describes the ability to regulate and organise reactions to sensory input, filter out unnecessary stimuli, and attend to relevant stimuli while maintaining an optimal level of arousal. This capacity is a critical component of human function that affects the efficiency of one's interactions with the physical and human environment, ability to adapt to daily life challenges, and quality of life (Schoen et al., 2009). Individuals may display a wide range of unusual behaviours ranging from over- to under-responsiveness to sensory stimuli and/or actively seeking sensation. Typical and benign sensory stimuli may be experienced as unpleasant, painful, or irritating, with defensive behaviours or withdrawal from specific daily living tasks accompanied by increased stress levels. As a result, this can negatively affect developmental and functional abilities, resulting in interference with efficient participation.

Sensory Processing Disorder (SPD)

Altered neurological sensory integration results in Sensory Processing Disorder (SPD), also known as Sensory Regulation Dysfunction, Sensory Integration Dysfunction or Sensory Dysfunction Disorder. Sensory Processing Disorder (SPD) refers to the difficulty that some individuals' nervous systems have in integrating and making use of sensory information and thus creating atypical responses. This neurological disorder can exist either when there are no other underlying health conditions, or in combination with alternative neurological or psychological diseases. Mitchell at al. (2015) have categorised SPD into a combination of processing challenges: Sensory Modulation Disorder (SMD), Sensory Discrimination Disorder (SDD), and Sensory-Based Motor Disorder (SBMD). Sensory Modulation Disorder (SMD) is the most common type of processing disorder among children and is primarily acknowledged by parents and teachers. Ahn et al. (2004) found a prevalence of 5 per cent of SPD in younger children and Ben-Sasson et al. (2009) found that 16 per cent of 7- to 11-year-olds had symptoms of SPD. While the exact causes of SPD have not yet been identified, it is typically a result of the disorganisation around the nervous system affecting processing in a few different ways that affects the development of an individual. SPD can affect one sense, or it can even affect multiple senses, such as hearing, touch or taste and like many illnesses, the symptoms exist on a spectrum. The most common signs and symptoms for SPD are being overly sensitive or under reactive to touch, movement, sights or sound, becoming easily distracted and difficulty making transitions.

There remains debate about whether SPD is an independent diagnosable disorder, or the result of observable symptoms linked to well-established disorders. For example, sensory sensitivities are part of the diagnostic criteria for autism. Symptoms include abnormal reactions, such as heightened or reduced emotional, behavioural, or psychological responses to sensory stimuli at normal intensities. However, SPD is not included in DSM-5 (APA, 2013) or ICD11 (WHO, 2019).

Dysfunction in sensory processing is more commonly known as a feature of autism spectrum disorder or other developmental disorders. Children with difficulty tolerating or processing sensory information may go on to receive a diagnosis of autism spectrum disorder.

However, there are children who present with significant sensory processing deficits but who do not meet criteria for other disorders. Investigators found that the brains of children with SPD were measurably different from those of neuro-typical control subjects, specifically noting white matter abnormalities in the posterior regions involved in sensory processing. Chang et al. (2014) compared the brains of boys with SPD with those with autism spectrum disorder. They found shared white matter disruption in the sensory pathways but divergent connectivity in the socio-emotional pathways, indicating that SPD may exist distinctly from autism spectrum disorder. Comparing sensory processing characteristics of children with SPD to the characteristics of those with autism spectrum disorder. Schoen et al. (2009) found lower physiologic arousal and sensory reactivity in the autism spectrum disorder group and higher reactivity after each sensory stimulus in the SPD group. This group showed specific reduction in the white matter microstructure primarily affecting posterior cerebral tracts. Additionally, the reduced posterior white matter microstructural integrity in children with SPD correlates directly with the atypical sensory behaviour. From a clinical perspective, these findings suggest that children with SPD have a specific imaging biomarker for their clinical disorder and the pattern of their shared structural difference (i.e., posterior decrease in white matter microstructural integrity) suggests that this disorder may be distinct from other overlapping clinical diagnoses, specifically ADHD and autism (Owen et al., 2013).

Pause for reflection

Discourses within this, and other areas of need, include terms such as disability, difficulty, impairment and disorder.

- How are these terms used in relation to SEND and how do they differ?

Sensory Modulation Disorder (SMD)

One subtype of Sensory Processing Disorder is called Sensory Modulation Disorder (SMD). It is characterised by difficulty responding to sensory input in a flexible and adaptive manner to participate successfully in daily life. Children with SMD can display a range of sensory symptoms. One nosology of SMD includes three subtypes, Sensory Over-responsivity, Sensory Under-responsivity and Sensory Seeking/Craving (Miller et al., 2007). Individuals with Sensory Over-responsivity often display negative responses to touch, sound or bright lights. Behaviourally they avoid certain sensory experiences or have extreme emotional reactions to typically non-aversive sensory stimuli (Bar-Shalita, Vatine and Parush, 2009). On the other hand, individuals with Sensory Under-responsivity ignore or do not notice typical sensory stimuli. They appear passive, uninterested in the environment and often lazy or lethargic, which is hypothesised to be caused by the inability of the sensory information to reach their threshold for awareness. Lastly, individuals with Sensory Seeking/Craving excessively crave sensory experiences and are described behaviourally as 'always on the go', often appearing reckless and dangerous in their attempts to fulfil their sensory needs. There is also a wide range of normal responses to sensory input. Therefore, individuals are only considered to have a disorder when their responses to sensory input are so extreme that it interferes with daily functioning at home (i.e., self-care, eating, sleeping), in school and in interactions with peers or adults (Schoen et al., 2009). Bar-Shalita, Vatine and Parush (2009) examined participation dimensions of children with SMD and compared with their typically developing peers; the level, degree of enjoyment, and frequency of participation in functional activities of children with SMD is significantly lower.

Scheerer et al. (2021) were able to identify five categories of sensory processing phenotypes in autism which were linked to common behavioural traits including socialisation difficulties, communication issues, repetition or compulsions, and clinical traits found in attention deficit hyperactivity disorder and obsessive-compulsive disorder. They suggest that an autistic child might perform poorly in the classroom, not because they have cognitive difficulties, but because they process sensory information differently than their peers. Thus, the sensory environment in their classroom may interfere with their ability to concentrate and perform cognitively. These categories were:

1   Sensory adaptive
2   Generalised sensory differences
3   Taste and smell sensitivity
4   Under-responsive and sensation seeking
5   Movement difficulties with low energy

Pause for reflection

There are a range of issues and disorders associated with sensory issues.

- What does this tell you about the importance of these needs in relation to individuals?
- Have you seen evidence of the five categories of sensory processing phenotypes in autism?

Difficulties with praxis: dyspraxia or Developmental Coordination Disorder

Praxis is the medical term for how our brain plans for and carries out movements we have not done before. For children this could be learning to jump; for adults, it may be learning to drive or use chopsticks. When sensory information is not properly processed it can make new movements very difficult, because the child does not have the ability to make sense of the different incoming sensory information. So, they struggle to work out where their body is and how much force, speed and direction is needed to do a new movement. Developmental Coordination Disorder (DCD), also known as dyspraxia in the UK, is a common disorder affecting movement and coordination in children, young people and adults with symptoms present since childhood.

Multisensory impairment (MSI)

Individuals with MSI have a combination of visual and hearing difficulties, may have complex needs and are sometimes referred to as 'deafblind', but they may have some residual vision and/or hearing. They may have additional difficulties in perception, communication and understanding their environment. They may need an alternative method of communication, are likely to experience high levels of anxiety and have low self-esteem, are likely to require a very high level of specialist support to make progress and develop and they may also need support in developing emotional resilience and ensuring their well-being.

Physical disability (PD)

The NHS (2022) describes a physical disability as a limitation on a person's physical functioning, mobility, dexterity or stamina. Physical disability may be present from birth or acquired later in life, it may remain the same throughout life or get worse over time. Some disabilities are hidden.

For a person to be offered protection under the Equality Act (2010), their disability must be substantial, long-term and affect day-to-day activities. Some physical disabilities are short-term and respond to treatment, others are permanent. Some children and young people with physical disabilities will have been disabled since birth while others may have become disabled, perhaps after an accident. Learners with physical disabilities are likely to experience high levels of anxiety and have low self-esteem and may need adjustments and adaptations in enable them to access the various classrooms and wider school environment. They may also need support in practical subjects to enable them to access the lessons, sometimes needing more time or space and in developing emotional resilience and ensuring their well-being. Examples of physical disabilities include dystrophies, brittle bones, cerebral palsy, spina bifida, hydrocephalus and acquired brain injury from illness or injury, e.g., brain tumour or road traffic accident.

Activity

This chapter focuses upon two physical disabilities, that of cerebral palsy (CP) and Duchenne muscular dystrophy (DMD). However, there are many more which may impact the lives of individuals. Research the aetiology and impact of the following:

- Spina bifida
- Multiple sclerosis
- Parkinson's disease
- Fibromyalgia

Cerebral palsy (CP)

Hereditability in cerebral palsy

Güvener et al. (2021) identified that monozygotic twins were found to have a higher concordance rate compared to dizygotic twins and the risk of a child having cerebral palsy was 2.5 times higher if it was present in the family, suggesting that genetic factors are a strong risk factor. The aetiology of CP is not fully understood yet; however, many studies state that it is caused by genetic variations within certain genes. Zhu et al. (2018) identified three pathways (axon guidance, transmission across chemical synapses, protein-protein interactions at synapses) with 23 genes that were identified to be highly correlated with CP. Initially it was found that there are six genes that are likely to contribute to the risk of cerebral palsy, these were the SCN1A, ATM, DOCK6, PPT1, SMARCB1 and ZSWIM which are all associated with walking and movement difficulties (May et al., 2021).

Peri- and post-natal risks

The aetiology of CP often remains unclear due to the complexities of symptoms used in the diagnosis (Jacobsson and Hagberg, 2004) but it is frequently created by the joint effects of several factors genetic factors, foetal infection, and problems occurred during or after childbirth (Alberman and Peckham, 2006). Development of the brain during pregnancy may include damage to the white matter, or an infection caught by the mother. Also damage may be a result of the brain temporarily not getting enough oxygen (asphyxiation) during a difficult birth or an infection of the brain, such as meningitis. Risk factors can include being born prematurely (before the 37th week of pregnancy), having a low birthweight, or being part of a multiple birth, such as a twin or triplet (CDC, 2022).

CP can be defined as a persistent but forever changing disorder of physical movement, often appearing in early years due to interference in the brain, relating to injury in the white matter (Rosenbaum et al., 2007). Neuroimaging research has improved understanding of abnormalities in brain development with 83 per cent of children with CP having white matter damage (Korzeniewski et al., 2008) possibly because of reduced blood or oxygen supply. The white matter holds importance as it is the portion of the brain that coordinates communication between different regions of the brain. Eighty-five to 90 per cent of children diagnosed with CP results from abnormal brain development or damage occurred during or shortly after birth (CDC, 2022).

Birth asphyxia is a factor that is strongly linked to cerebral palsy and it is when oxygen and blood is lost during birth which can lead to hypoxia (MacLennan, Thompson and Gecz, 2015). A meta-analysis to examine whether birth asphyxia was associated in preterm children with cerebral palsy suggested that there was a link between birth asphyxia and CP (Yang et al., 2021). However, other studies suggest that there is not a link between cerebral palsy and birth asphyxia, for example Ellenberg and Nelson, (2013) reviewed 23 studies and concluded that the current data does not support that most cases of cerebral palsy are due to birth asphyxia, because of the inability to accurately identify asphyxia at birth.

Diagnosis

The symptoms of CP are not usually obvious just after a baby is born but become noticeable during the first two or three years of a child's life. Symptoms can include delays in reaching development milestones, seeming too stiff or too floppy, weak arms or legs, fidgety, jerky or clumsy movements, random, uncontrolled movements and walking on tiptoes. CP can be identified as unusual fidgety movements, abnormalities in skin tone, slow motor development like not sitting up or crawling at the expected age and difficulties when being fed. If a child shows these signs or if they are at risk of cerebral palsy then they must be assessed (NICE, 2017). A child can be assessed by using various brain scans, such as a CT scan, a cranial ultrasound or an MRI scan. Morgan et al. (2019) argued that it is beneficial to perform multiple different tests on children with CP to help improve the accuracy of the diagnosis. To assist the early diagnosis of CP, neuroimaging techniques can be utilised to measure underlying brain abnormalities and the impact this has upon an individual (Palmer, 2004). Neuroimaging techniques can increase the validity of the diagnosis and early and accurate identification allows prompt access to early intervention during critical periods of early brain development (Morgan et al., 2018). The diagnostic process combines clinical history, examination by professionals, neuroimaging, and genetic testing to improve the accuracy. Within the diagnostic process, developmental monitoring, screening, and medical evaluations may be utilised by professionals to examine a child's development in relation to peers of a similar age (CDC, 2018), to determine if physical progress is delayed.

There are a range of characteristics associated with cerebral palsy, but in terms of movement, the main characteristics are tremors, muscle spasms, frail arms and legs, jerky movements and they may walk on their tiptoes. CP is presented as different types, these are spastic, dyskinetic and ataxic (NHS, 2021). ICD-11 (WHO, 2019) states that dyskinetic cerebral palsy is when the muscles become stiff and floppy which creates muscle spasms, whereas spastic cerebral palsy is when the muscles stretch and tighten, which creates resistance and makes it difficult to move. Ataxic cerebral palsy is the least common type and is caused by damage to pathways in the brain which results in coordination problems and shaky movements (Berelowitz and Franzsen, 2021). Cerebral palsy also has co-morbidities with other conditions like epilepsy and hearing impairments, therefore not everyone with cerebral palsy will display the same characteristics (NICE, 2019).

According to the ICD-11 (WHO, 2019), CP is categorised by increased muscle tone, associated with hyperactivity in specific muscles and characteristics include issues with movement, coordination, and development; however, the severity and portrayal of characteristics can vary significantly between individuals. Alongside delayed development of physical movement, disturbances of brain activity may also affect sensation, perception, communication and behaviour (Richards and Malouin, 2013). Co-morbidities to CP include epilepsy, occurring in 32.5 per cent of individuals (Gabis et al., 2015), anxiety and depression.

Activity

Three strangers with CP open up about their experiences. The video can be accessed via the link: www.youtube.com/watch?v=cFQmS2JWKNY

- What has been the impact of CP on their lives?
- Are there any mutual experiences?

Lee Ridley, aka Lost Voice Guy, is a disabled comedian with cerebral palsy. He studied journalism at university, wrote a book called *I'm Only in It for the Parking: Life and Laughter from the Priority Seats* and won *Britain's Got Talent* in 2018.

- How did CP impact his early life and how has he used his disability to become a successful writer and comedian?

Duchenne muscular dystrophy (DMD)

Duchenne muscular dystrophy (DMD) is the most common type of MD in boys. Symptoms can be present from birth, but usually appear between 12 months and three years of age. For example, a child may have difficulty walking or climbing stairs, they fall more frequently than other children, learn to speak later than usual, be unable to climb the stairs without support and have behavioural or learning difficulties (NHS, 2021). There is progressive wasting of skeletal muscles, with the limb-girdle muscles first showing weakness by the age of five years, followed by an inability to walk by the ages of 8 to 12 years (Brooke et al., 1989). A child may also find it difficult to stand up from sitting on the floor and may use what's known as Gowers' manoeuvre to do this where they start by facing the floor, placing their feet wide apart, lifting their bottom first and using their hands to 'walk up' their legs by first placing their hands on their knees and then on their thighs. At the cellular level, pathological changes include the absence of dystrophin at the membrane of the muscle fibres, increased adipose and connective tissue between muscle fibres, increased variability in muscle fibre size, infiltration of inflammatory cells, and centrally located nuclei, which are indicative of degenerating and regenerating muscle fibres. Dividing myoblasts are required for muscle growth and maintenance, and the limited capacity of DMD myoblasts to grow is directly related to the progressive muscle degeneration characteristic of the disease (Pavlath et al., 1989).

Hereditability of DMD

DMD has an X-linked recessive inheritance pattern and is passed on by the mother, who is referred to as a carrier. MD is inherited in an X-linked pattern because the gene that can carry a DMD-causing mutation is on the X chromosome. Every boy inherits an X chromosome from his mother and a Y chromosome from his father. Girls get two X chromosomes, one from each parent. Each son born to a woman with a dystrophin mutation on one of her two X chromosomes has a 50 per cent chance of inheriting the flawed gene and having DMD. Each of her daughters has a 50 per cent chance of inheriting the mutation and being a carrier. A man with DMD cannot pass the flawed gene to his sons but he will certainly pass it to his daughters. They will then be carriers, and each of their sons will have a 50 per cent chance of developing the disease and so on. Although DMD often runs in a family, it is possible for a family with no history of DMD to suddenly have a son with the disease. This may be due to a genetic mutation leading to DMD which may have existed in the females of a family for some generations without anyone knowing, or that no male children were born with the disease. The second possibility is that a child with DMD has a new genetic mutation that arose in one of his mother's egg cells (ova). The genetic changes prevent the body from producing dystrophin, a protein that increases the strength of muscle fibres and help protect them from damage. People who have DMD (mostly boys and adult men) therefore lack muscle strength, which often leads to movement difficulties, speech delay, and eventually heart or lung failure.

DMD severity may be partly determined by the types (or variants) of dystrophin that are absent from the body. The dystrophin gene is the largest gene yet identified in humans and is in the short arm of the X chromosome, in the Xp21.2 locus (a locus is the position of a gene on a chromosome).

All boys with DMD lack a variant of dystrophin called Dp427, which is found mainly in our muscles. However, some boys with DMD also lack variants called Dp140 and/or Dp71, which are found mainly in the brain. The absence of Dp140 and Dp71 has previously been associated with learning disabilities in boys with DMD but boys with DMD who are missing Dp140 and Dp71 have been found to struggle in a range of complex movement tasks compared to boys with DMD who could produce these dystrophin variants (Tran et al., 2013).

Most mutations of the dystrophin gene are deletions of one or more parts of it. DMD occurs because the mutated DMD gene fails to produce virtually any functional dystrophin. Individuals with BMD genetic mutations make dystrophin that is partially functional, which protects their muscles from degenerating as badly or as quickly as in DMD. The dystrophin protein transfers the force of muscle contraction from the inside of the muscle cell outward to the cell membrane.

Because it connects the centre of the muscle cell to the edge of the cell, the dystrophin protein is extremely long. One end is specialised for linking to the muscle cell interior and the other end is specialised for linking to a variety of proteins at the cell membrane. The long middle section, called the rod domain, is taken up by a series of repeating units called spectrin repeats. The repeated spectrin units in the middle of the protein play an important role in linking the two ends, but studies have shown that the exact number of these units is not critical for the function of the protein. Many cases of DMD are caused by mutations in the part of the gene that encodes this middle section. Production of the entire protein stops when the mutation is encountered (Gao and McNally, 2015).

The absence of dystrophin sets in motion a cascade of harmful effects. Fibrous tissue begins to form in the muscle, and the body's immune system increases inflammation. In addition to its force-transfer role, dystrophin provides the scaffold for holding numerous molecules in place near the cell membrane. Loss of dystrophin displaces these molecules, with consequent disruptions in their functions. Lack of dystrophin causes muscle damage and progressive weakness, beginning in early childhood. Furthermore, in a parallel experiment, mice without Dp427, Dp140, and Dp71 showed reduced grip strength in comparison to mice lacking Dp427 only. Accordingly, these findings suggest that the severity of DMD is not just due to the absence of dystrophin in muscles. Instead, lack of dystrophin in the brain also worsens the ability to move for people with DMD (Chesshyre et al. 2022).

Pause for reflection

- Having read that physical and sensory needs cover a range of issues, reflect upon the importance that this area has on education, families, employment and everyday lives of individuals
- What role do organisations such as the Royal National Institute of Blind People and Royal Association of Deaf play in supporting sensory needs?
- Are there any organisations which could support physical needs?

Activity

Debate: Meares-Irlen's Syndrome (MIS), or Visual Stress
Meares (1980) described the visual distortions reported by some children and young adults when reading from white paper. Irlen (1983) described the use of coloured overlays aiding reading abilities of some adults and refers to 'scotopic sensitivity', a previously unknown visual-perceptual problem that interfered with a person's ability to process full spectrum light. The condition has subsequently been referred to as 'Meares-Irlen Syndrome',

'Irlen Syndrome', Scotopic Sensitivity and most recently, Visual Stress. Symptoms of Irlen Syndrome include sensitivity to bright and fluorescent lighting and glare, slow or inefficient reading, poor reading comprehension, poor attention and concentration, eye strain, fatigue, headaches and migraines and poor depth perception. The reading difficulties include symptoms of eye strain, headache, and visual-perceptual distortions such as blurring, doubling, patterns, and movement of print on the page.

MIS is a magnocellular system disorder that induces visual stress and distortion, causing reading difficulties by hypertransmission of a specific light wave. Coloured overlays and tinted lenses are purported to improve reading ability and visual perception and eliminate symptoms associated with reading, such as light sensitivity, eyestrain, headaches, blurring of print, loss of place, and watery eyes (Robinson and Miles, 1987). Affected individuals have a low threshold to perceptual distortions when viewing striped patterns of lines with high contrast and spatial frequencies not unlike black text on white paper. Studies have identified hyperexcitability of the visual cortex as a major factor (Wilkins, Huang and Cao, 2004) or a magnocellular pathway deficiency, leading to disrupted synchronisation of signals conveyed to the visual cortex (Stein, 2003). Williams et al. (2003), confirmed activation in the left middle and superior temporal gyri during sentence reading after wearing colour-tinted lenses which could explain the effectiveness of colour-tinted lenses in patients with Meares-Irlen Syndrome.

However, some researchers have noted the absence of objective scientific evidence that Scotopic Sensitivity Syndrome exists. The Institute of Optometry claimed that the symptoms are not detectable by standard vision examinations. Consequently, Irlen Syndrome is not recognised in ICD-11 (WHO, 2019) or DSM-5. (APA, 2013). The American Academy of Pediatrics (2009) stated that scientific evidence does not support the efficacy of eye exercises, behavioural vision therapy, or special tinted filters or lenses for improving the long-term educational performance in these complex paediatric neurocognitive conditions. Diagnostic and treatment approaches that lack scientific evidence of efficacy are not endorsed, and should not be recommended. The concepts underlying Irlen Syndrome are vaguely defined, and several groups insist that the visual stress associated with this syndrome might be responsible for dyslexia as well as other disorders. These ambiguous criteria may be responsible for the criticism over the validity of this condition.

- Research the evidence for and against the existence of MIS
- Which side of the debate is the most convincing?
- Where could a parent go for advice if they wanted to look into tinted lenses and coloured overlays for their child?

References

Ackland, P., Resnikoff, S. and Bourne, R. (2017). World blindness and visual impairment: despite many successes, the problem is growing. *Community Eye Health*, 30 (100), pp. 71–73.

Ahn, R. R., Miller, L. J., Milberger, S. and McIntosh, D. N. (2004). Prevalence of parents' perceptions of sensory processing disorders among kindergarten children. *Am J Occup Ther*, 58 (3), pp. 287–293.

Alagaratnam, J., Sharma, T. K., Lim, C. S. and Fleck, B. W. (2002). A survey of visual impairment in children attending the Royal Blind School, Edinburgh using the WHO childhood visual impairment database. *Eye (Lond)*, 16 (5), pp. 557–561.

Alanazi, F. F., Song, J. C., Mousa, A., Morales, J., Al Shahwan, S., Alodhayb, S., Al Jadaan, I., Al-Turkmani, S. and Edward, D. P. (2013). Primary and secondary congenital glaucoma: baseline features from a registry at King Khaled Eye Specialist Hospital, Riyadh, Saudi Arabia. *Am J Ophthalmol*, 155 (5), pp. 882–829.

Alberman, E. and Peckham, C. (2006). Cerebral palsy and perinatal exposure to neurotropic viruses. *BMJ*, 332 (7533), pp. 63–64.

Altinbay, D. and Taskin, I. (2021). Evaluation of vision-related quality of life in retinitis pigmentosa patients with low vision. *Jpn J Ophthalmol*, 65 (6), pp. 777–785.

American Academy of Pediatrics (2009). Learning disabilities, dyslexia, and vision. *Pediatrics*, 124 (2), pp. 837–844.

American Psychiatric Association (2013). *Diagnostic and Statistical Manual of Mental Disorders*. 5th ed. Washington, DC: American Psychiatric Publishing.

Aziz, A., Denis, D. and Matonti, F. (2012). Epidemiology of primary congenital glaucoma: a study lasting 11 years. *Acta Ophthalmologica*, 90.

Badawi, A. H., Al-Muhaylib, A. A., Al Owaifeer, A. M., Al-Essa, R. S. and Al-Shahwan, S. A. (2019). Primary congenital glaucoma: an updated review. *Saudi J Ophthalmol*, 33 (4), pp. 382–388.

Bar-Shalita, T., Vatine, J. J. and Parush, S. (2009). Sensory modulation disorder: a risk factor for participation in daily life activities. *Developmental Medicine and Child Neurology*, 50, pp. 932–937.

Barton, J. J. (2011). Disorders of higher visual processing. *Handb Clin Neurol*, 102, pp. 223–261.

Bennion, A. E., Shaw, R. L. and Gibson, J. M. (2012). What do we know about the experience of age related macular degeneration? A systematic review and meta-synthesis of qualitative research. *Social Science and Medicine*, 75 (6), pp. 976–985.

Ben-Sasson, A., Hen, L., Fluss, R., Cermak, S. A., Engel-Yeger, B. and Gal, E. (2009). A meta-analysis of sensory modulation symptoms in individuals with autism spectrum disorders. *J Autism Dev Disord*, 39 (1), pp. 1–11.

Berelowitz, S. and Franzsen, D. (2021). Visual perceptual deficits in different types of cerebral palsy. *South African Journal of Occupational Therapy*, 51 (1), pp. 18–26.

Berson, E. L. (1993). Retinitis pigmentosa. The Friedenwald Lecture. *Invest Ophthalmol Vis Sci*, 34 (5), pp. 1659–1676.

Brice, P. (2008). 'Well, it is complicated...'. In: L. Edwards and S. Crocker (eds.), *Psychological Processes in Deaf Children With Complex Needs: An Evidence-Based Practical Guide*. London: Jessica Kingsley Publishers.

Brooke, M. H., Fenichel, G. M., Griggs, R. C., Mendell, J. R., Moxley, R., Florence, J., King, W. M., Pandya, S., Robison, J., Schierbecker, J., Signore, L., Miller, J. P., Gilder, B. F., Kaiser, K. K., Mandel, S. and Arfkenet, C. (1989). Duchenne muscular dystrophy:

patterns of clinical progression and effects of supportive therapy. *Neurology*, 39 (4), pp. 475–481.

Centers for Disease Control and Prevention (CDC) (2020). *Common Barriers to Participation Experienced by People with Disabilities.* [online] Available at: www.cdc.gov/ ncbddd/disabilityandhealth/disability-barriers.html [Accessed 09. 02. 2023].

Centers for Disease Control and Prevention (CDC) (2022). *Cerebral Palsy.* [online] Available at: www.cdc.gov/ncbddd/cp/features/cerebral-palsy-11-things.html [Accessed 09. 02. 2023].

Chang, Y. S., Owen, J. P., Desai, S. S., Hill, S. S., Arnett, A. B., Harris, J., Marco, E. J., and Mukherjee, P. (2014). Autism and sensory processing disorders: shared white matter disruption in sensory pathways but divergent connectivity in social-emotional pathways. *PLoS One*, 9 (7), e103038.

Chesshyre, M., Ridout, D., Hashimoto, Y., Ookubo, Y., Torelli, S., Maresh, K., Ricotti, V., Abbott, L., Gupta, V. A., Main, M. and Ferrari, G. (2022). Investigating the role of dystrophin isoform deficiency in motor function in Duchenne muscular dystrophy. *Journal of Cachexia, Sarcopenia and Muscle*, 13 (2), pp.1360–1372.

Department for Education and Department of Health (2015). *Special Educational Needs and Disability Code of Practice: 0 to 25 years.* [online] Available at: www.gov.uk/gov ernment/publications/send-code-of-practice-0-to-25 [Accessed 25. 10. 2022].

Ellenberg, J. H. and Nelson, K. B. (2013). The association of cerebral palsy with birth asphyxia: a definitional quagmire. *Dev Med Child Neurol*, 55 (3), pp. 210–216.

Gabis, L. V., Tsubary, N. M., Leon, O., Ashkenasi, A. and Shefer, S. (2015). Assessment of abilities and comorbidities in children with cerebral palsy. *J Child Neurol*, 30 (12), pp. 1640–1645.

Gao, Q. Q. and McNally, E. M. (2015). The dystrophin complex: structure, function, and implications for therapy. *Compr Physiol*, 5 (3), pp.1223–1139.

Güvener, O., Sezgin, M., Tezol, Ö., Barlas, İ. Ö., Özdemir, A. A. and Kanık, E. A. (2021). Are COL4A1 and COL4A2 gene polymorphisms associated with cerebral palsy? *Turk J Phys Med Rehabil*, 67 (2), pp. 242–249.

Haegele, J. A., Kirk, T. A., Holland, S. K. and Zhu, X. (2021). 'The rest of the time I would just stand there and look stupid': access in integrated physical education among adults with visual impairments. *Sport, Education and Society*, 26 (8), pp. 862–874.

Hamel, C. (2006). Retinitis pigmentosa. *Orphanet J Rare Dis*, 1 (40).

Hassan-Karimi, H., Jafarzadehpur, E., Blouri, B., Hashemi, H., Sadeghi, A. Z. and Mirzajani, A. (2012). Frequency domain electroretinography in retinitis pigmentosa versus normal eyes. *J Ophthalmic Vis Res*, 7 (1), pp. 34–38.

Irlen, H. (1983). *Successful treatment of learning disabilities.* 91st Annual Convention of the American Psychologists Association, August 1983, Anaheim, California. 1983.

Jacobsson, B. and Hagberg, G. (2004). Antenatal risk factors for cerebral palsy. *Best Pract Res Clin Obstet Gynaecol*, 18 (3), pp. 425–436.

Korzeniewski, S. J., Birbeck, G., DeLano, M. C., Potchen, M. J. and Paneth, N. (2008). A systematic review of neuroimaging for cerebral palsy. *J Child Neurol*, 23 (2), pp. 216–227.

Kubba, H., Swan, I. R. and Gatehouse, S. (2004). The Glasgow Children's Benefit Inventory: a new instrument for assessing health-related benefit after an intervention. *Ann Otol Rhinol Laryngol*, 113 (12), pp. 980–986.

Legislation.gov.uk (2010). *Equality Act 2010.* [online] Available at: www.legislation.gov. uk/ukpga/2010/15/contents [Accessed 02. 02. 2023].

Ling, C., Zhang, D., Zhang, J., Sun, H., Du, Q. and Li, X. (2020). Updates on the molecular genetics of primary congenital glaucoma (Review). *Exp Ther Med*, 20 (2), pp. 968–977.

Ma, H. H. and Liutkevičien, R. (2021). Age-related macular degeneration: what do we know so far? *Acta Med Litu*, 28 (1), pp. 36–47.

MacLennan, A. H., Thompson, S. C. and Gecz, J. (2015). Cerebral palsy: causes, pathways, and the role of genetic variants. *Am J Obstet Gynecol*, 213 (6), pp. 779–788.

May, H. J., Fasheun, J. A., Bain, J. M., Baugh, E. H., Bier, L. E., Revah-Politi, A., Roye, D. P., Jr, Goldstein, D. B. and Carmel, J. B. (2021). Genetic testing in individuals with cerebral palsy. *Dev Med Child Neurol*, 63, pp. 1448–1455.

Meares, O. (1980). Figure/background, brightness/contrast and reading disabilities. *Visible Language*, 14, pp. 13–29.

Miller, L. J., Anzalone, M. E., Lane, S. J., Cermak, S. A. and Osten, E. T. (2007). Concept evolution in sensory integration: a proposed nosology for diagnosis. *Am J Occup Ther*, 61 (2), pp. 135–140.

Mitchell, A. W., Moore, E. M., Roberts, E. J., Hachtel, K. W. and Brown, M. S. (2015). Sensory processing disorder in children ages birth-3 years born prematurely: a systematic review. *Am J Occup Ther*, 69 (1), 6901220030.

Morgan, C., Fahey, M., Roy, B. and Novak, I. (2018). Diagnosing cerebral palsy in full-term infants. *J Paediatr Child Health*, 54 (10), pp. 1159–1164.

Morgan, C., Romeo, D. M., Chorna, O., Novak, I., Galea, C., Del Secco, S. and Guzzetta, A. (2019). The pooled diagnostic accuracy of neuroimaging, general movements, and neurological examination for diagnosing cerebral palsy early in high-risk infants: a case control study. *J Clin Med*, 8 (11), p. 1879.

National Health Service (NHS) (2021). Hearing loss. [online] Available at: www.nhs.uk/conditions/hearing-loss [Accessed 02. 02. 2023].

National Health Service (NHS) (2021). Muscular dystrophy. [online] Available at: www.nhs.uk/conditions/muscular-dystrophy [Accessed 02. 02. 2023].

National Health Service (NHS) (2022). Disability. [online] Available at: https://digital.nhs.uk/data-and-information/data-collections-and-data-sets/data-sets/mental-health-services-data-set/submit-data/data-quality-of-protected-characteristics-and-other-vulnerable-groups/disability [Accessed 02. 02. 2023].

National Institute for Health and Care Excellence (NICE) (2017). Cerebral palsy in under 25s: assessment and management. [online] Available at: www.nice.org.uk/guidance/ng62 [Accessed 10. 02. 2023].

Owen, J. P., Marco, E. J., Desai, S., Fourie, E., J., Hill, S. S., Arnett, A. B. and Mukherjee, P. (2013). Abnormal white matter microstructure in children with sensory processing disorders. *NeuroImage: Clinical*, 2, pp. 844–853.

Palmer, F. B. (2004). Strategies for the early diagnosis of cerebral palsy. *J Pediatr, Suppl*, 145 (2), S8–S11.

Pavlath, G., Rich, K., Webster, S. and Blau, H. (1989). Localization of muscle gene products in nuclear domains. *Nature*, 337, pp. 570–573.

Richards, C. L. and Malouin, F. (2013). Cerebral palsy: definition, assessment and rehabilitation. *Handb Clin Neurol*, 111, pp. 183–195.

Robinson, G. L. and Miles, J. (1987). The use of coloured overlays to improve visual processing-a preliminary survey. *The Exceptional Child*, 34 (1), pp. 65–70.

Rosenbaum, P., Paneth, N., Leviton, A., Goldstein, M., Bax, M., Damiano, D., Dan, B. and Jacobsson B. (2007). A report: the definition and classification of cerebral palsy. *Dev Med Child Neurol*, 49 (6), pp. 8–14.

Royal National Institute of Blind People (2022). Key information and statistics on sight loss in the UK. [online] Available at: www.rnib.org.uk/professionals/health-social-ca re-education-professionals/knowledge-and-research-hub/key-information-and-statistics-on-sight-loss-in-the-uk [Accessed 02. 02. 2023].

Scheerer, N. E., Curcin, K., Stojanoski, B., Anagnostou, E., Nicolson, R., Kelley, E. and Georgiades, S. (2021). Exploring sensory phenotypes in autism spectrum disorder. *Molecular Autism*, 12 (67),

Schoen, S. A., Miller, L. J., Brett-Green, B. A. and Nielsen, D. M. (2009). Physiological and behavioral differences in sensory processing: a comparison of children with autism spectrum disorder and sensory modulation disorder. *Frontiers in Integrative Neuroscience*, 3, Article 29.

Sivaprasad, S., Gupta, B., Crosby-Nwaobi, R and Evans, J. (2012). Prevalence of diabetic retinopathy in various ethnic groups: a worldwide perspective. *Surv Ophthalmol*, 57 (4), pp. 347–370.

Slade, J. and Edwards, R. (2016). My Voice 2015: The views and experiences of blind and partially sighted people in the UK. [online] Available at: www.rnib.org.uk/professionals/ health-social-care-education-professionals/knowledge-and-research-hub/research-archive/ my-voice [Accessed 10. 02. 2023].

Stein, J. (2001). The magnocellular theory of developmental dyslexia. *Dyslexia*, 7 (1), pp.12–36.

Tran, T. H., Zhang, Z., Yagi, M., Lee, T., Awano, H., Nishida, A., Okinaga, T., Takeshima, Y. and Matsuo, M. (2013). Molecular characterization of an X(p21.2;q28) chromosomal inversion in a Duchenne muscular dystrophy patient with mental retardation reveals a novel long non-coding gene on Xq28. *J Hum Genet*, 58 (1), pp. 33–39.

Wilkins, A. J., Huang, J. and Cao, Y. (2004). Visual stress theory and its application to reading and reading tests. *Journal of Research in Reading*, 27, pp. 152–162.

Williams, L. (2019). Untreated severe-to profound hearing loss and the cochlear implant situation: how policy and practice are disabling New Zealand society. *The New Zealand Medical Journal*, 132 (1505), pp. 73–78.

Williams, M. J., Stuart, G. W., Castles, A. and McAnally, K. I. (2003). Contrast sensitivity in subgroups of developmental dyslexia. *Vision research*, 43 (4), pp. 467–477.

Williams, C., Pease, A., Warnes, P., Harrison, S., Pilon, F., Hyvarinen, L., West, S., Self, J., Ferris, J. and CVI Prevalence Study Group. (2021). Cerebral visual impairment-related vision problems in primary school children: a cross-sectional survey. *Dev Med Child Neurol*, 63 (6), pp. 683–689.

World Health Organization (2019). *International Statistical Classification of Diseases and Related Health Problems*. 11th ed.

World Health Organization (2022). Blindness and vision impairment. [online] Available at: www.who.int/news-room/fact-sheets/detail/blindness-and-visual-impairment [Accessed 02. 02. 2023].

Yang, S., Xia, J., Gao, J. and Wang, L. (2021). Increasing prevalence of cerebral palsy among children and adolescents in China 1988–2020: a systematic review and meta-analysis. *J Rehabil Med*, 53 (5), jrm00195.

Zhu, Q., Ni, Y., Wang, J., Yin, H., Zhang, Q., Zhang, L., Bian, W., Liang, B., Kong, L., Xuan, L. and Lu, N. (2018). Identification of pathways and genes associated with cerebral palsy. *Genes Genomics*, 40 (12), pp. 1339–1349.

5 The impact of Sensory and/or Physical Needs on individuals and families

Introduction

This chapter examines the impact Sensory and/or Physical Needs may have on an individual, their families and allies, utilising a series of case studies from a range of contexts and ages. Identifying the characteristics and issues involved in the examples given in Chapter 4, it examines the impact on children, adults and families of these needs and invites you to apply the knowledge gained with respect to a range of sensory and physical needs.

Learning objectives

This chapter will:

- Invite you to apply your understanding gained from the previous chapter to the lived experience
- Introduce you to a wide range of consequences of Sensory and/or Physical Needs for individuals, families and allies
- Help you to understand how these needs impact the lives of children, young people and adults
- Invite you to review research evidence which supports our understanding of the impact on the lives of individuals, families and allies
- Invite you to review how hearing, visual and multisensory impairments, cerebral palsy and muscular dystrophy influence educational attainment and access to employment

Key terms

Hearing impairment, visual impairment, multisensory impairment, cerebral palsy, muscular dystrophy, impact, children, adults, families, parents, education, employment

DOI: 10.4324/9781003361084-8

Pause for reflection

- Do you agree with the statement 'people with congenital disabilities are generally assumed to be better adapted than people with acquired disabilities'?
- Where would you look for evidence in defence or refutal of this view?

Activity

Attitudes and disability

Scope is the disability equality charity in England and Wales. They have produced a number of documents and campaigns which relate to issues faced by disabled people. One such campaign is the Disability Perception Gap, the report of which can be accessed via the link: www.scope.org.uk/campaigns/disability-perception-gap.

- Read the report and identify the main issues raised

They also produced research on families with disabled children underpins the Now is the Time campaign. The report can be accessed via the link: www.scope.org.uk/campaigns/now-is-the-time

- Read the report and identify the main issues raised
- How would you research the attitude of both peers and teachers towards disabled children and young people?

Hearing impairment (HI)

Conductive hearing loss involves the middle/outer ear, rarely causes severe to profound hearing loss and sensori-neural hearing loss involves the inner ear, most frequently the cochlea, with damage to Corti's organ or to the auditory nervous system and in most cases is a result of a recessive gene. These individuals may experience high levels of anxiety, have low self-esteem, are likely to need hearing aids and teaching strategies to support the access to and understanding of language and concepts. They may also need support in developing social skills and building relationships with peers along with support in developing emotional resilience.

Impact on individuals and their families

Zaidman-Zait et al. (2016) found that parents of children who are deaf or hard of hearing (D/HH) face unique long-term challenges that can place the parents at a greater risk for elevated levels of parenting stress. Adaptation of families to the various challenges presented by childhood hearing loss is influenced by their personal and social coping resources available for managing these stressors and challenges. The current study examined differences in parenting stress and personal (i. e., acceptance of the child who is deaf/hard of hearing (D/HH) and parents' sense of parenting self-efficacy) and social (i.e., formal and informal social support) coping resources between mothers and fathers of children who are D/HH in the Arab sector in Israel. Findings revealed no significant differences between mothers and fathers regarding parenting stress, child acceptance, or parental support systems. However, mothers reported significantly higher self-efficacy.

Zaidman-Zait and Curle (2018) indicated that parents of children with implants might experience various stressors that are specifically associated with raising an implanted child. These stressors may stem from contextual factors, factors related to the child, and factors associated with parenting a child with an implant. Quittner et al. (2010) showed that parents of deaf children do not report elevated levels of general parenting stress when compared to parents of hearing children. Szarkowski and Brice (2019) identified a range of positive aspects in parenting a deaf child. These included internal factors such as finding becoming an advocate for their child empowering, having a greater level of involvement and an understanding of the way that children learn and the complex learning that takes place. External positive factors included having a supportive partner or spouse and social aspects of meeting similar parents.

Deafness does not in itself cause emotional/behavioural or cognitive problems or psychiatric disorders. However, children with hearing impairment are at greater risk of developing emotional/behavioural problems and neurodevelopmental disorders. The incidence of both seems to be higher in deaf children from hearing families. Most prelingual deafness is caused by recessive genes; hence, most deaf individuals come from hearing families, the majority of whom do not use sign language. Numerous studies, in both hearing and deaf populations, show how the lack of access to language has an impact on the emotional development of children. Children with severe hearing impairment are at greater risk of developing psychiatric disorders and of poor psychosocial adjustment compared with their hearing peers. The reason for this is the barrier to efficient language acquisition (Gentili and Holwell, 2011). Hearing loss was found to be associated with substantially reduced mental health ratings among some young and middle-aged persons, but did not affect mental health much among older persons (Tambs, 2004). Spouse hearing loss increased the likelihood of subsequent poorer physical, psychological and social well-being in partners. The negative impact of husbands' hearing loss on wives' well-being appears stronger than the reverse (Wallhagen et al., 2004).

D/HH adolescents experience more peer problems and lower levels of friendships than their hearing peers. Stevenson et al. (2015) stated that children and adolescents with HI have scores on emotional and behavioural difficulties and the scores for parent, teacher, and self-rating of peer problems consistently indicated more peer problems in D/HH children than in their hearing peers. Stevenson et al. (2017) later found that D/HH children and adolescents were at increased risk of emotional and behavioural difficulties and that adolescents with no long-term health conditions other than their hearing loss identified themselves as experiencing a significantly higher level of problems with peers and friends. Xie, Potměšil and Peters (2014) describe how D/HH children interact with hearing peers in inclusive settings, illustrate the difficulties and challenges faced by them in interacting with peers, and identify effective interventions that promote their social interaction in inclusive education. The research indicated that children who are D/HH face great difficulties in communicating, initiating/entering, and maintaining interactions with hearing peers in inclusive settings.

Wolters et al. (2012) found that well-being in school was stable during the transition for mainstreamed hearing children, but not for deaf children. In mainstream schools, school well-being increased for deaf boys but decreased for deaf girls. In contrast, in special education schools, school well-being increased for deaf girls but decreased for deaf boys. Peer acceptance, popularity, and relationship with the teacher had different effects on well-being for deaf early adolescents in mainstream schools compared to the effects on those in special education schools. Wolters and Isarin (2015) investigated the effect of quality of friendship on the well-being of 12 Dutch D/HH 13- to 19-year-olds and found that, compared to their hearing peers, they scored lower on positive qualities of friendships, such as intimacy and companionship. The few studies that compare the quality of friendship of D/HH adolescents with that of their hearing peers suggest that they tend to report lower levels of positive features in their friendships.

D/HH adolescents in schools for the deaf show more difficulties in relationships with D/HH and hearing peers than D/HH children in mainstream schools or in specialist-support provisions. Musselman, Mootilal and MacKay (1996) examined the social adjustment of deaf adolescents enrolled in segregated, partially integrated and mainstream settings, comparing them with a control group of hearing students. Segregated students showed the lowest levels of adjustment overall. Partially integrated students reported better adjustment overall. Partially integrated students reported better adjustment than mainstreamed students with deaf peers; mainstreamed students reported better adjustment than partially integrated students with hearing peers, showing the same levels of adjustment with hearing peers as hearing students.

Terlektsi et al. (2020) suggest that when adolescents are in mainstream schools, they are often the only, or one of very few, D/HH people in the school. A sample of 30 13- to 19-year-old DHH adolescents with a moderate to profound hearing loss underwent semi-structured interviews. Participants reported that, overall, they had developed positive and rewarding relationships with their peers, notwithstanding their earlier experience of being bullied. Conflicts and infrequency of interaction in their friendships were mainly reported by girls. Adolescents with moderate hearing loss were identified as facing the same or even more barriers than adolescents with severe to profound hearing loss in making new friends.

The backgrounds of deaf individuals are vastly diverse. It is not uncommon for these individuals to find themselves in a situation where they must figure out how they identify themselves within their own family before they even have a chance to identify themselves in the world. Furthermore, their identity within their family may have a large influence on how involved they might choose to be within the deaf community. Some D/HH individuals are naturally born into the deaf community, but 95 per cent are born to hearing families (Brice and Strauss, 2016). Identity is a term that is heard often in the deaf community. Although there may be two opposite positions a person can take in their community (as a member or as a separate individual), DHH individuals tend to lie along a spectrum and McIlroy and Storbeck (2011) found that deaf identity is not a static concept but a complex ongoing quest for belonging, bound up with the acceptance of being deaf in a hearing-dominant society.

Pause for reflection

- Discourses surrounding the concept of inclusivity and choice are evident throughout the literature pertaining to SEND. What should a parent consider if they were looking to place the D/HH or VI/blind child in a school?

Activity

The National Institute for Health and Clinical Excellence (NICE) is fundamental to the NHS. It is the primary and authoritative source for defining specific physical and sensory conditions.

In addition, it sets out the formal identification and assessment pathways for these needs. As such, this is used by all health-based professionals in the UK.

The website can be accessed via the link: www.nice.org.uk

- Use the search tool on the NICE guidance to find information about the examples of sensory and physical needs identified in this chapter, as well as one other area of need identified in the book

---

Visual impairment (VI)

The level to which someone's visual impairment impacts their daily lives is dependent on several factors such as inaccessibility, for example buildings or written information, access to products such as glasses or white canes for assistance and access to interventions and preventions through treatment (World Health Organization, 2022). Kurtović and Ivančić (2019) suggest the level to which a person with a visual impairment is affected depends on factors such as personality, co-morbidity, the level of impairment and age of onset, societal attitudes and support from others/assistive technology. They found that depression was negatively related to the level of education, optimism, self-liking, self-competence, support from friends, family and coworkers, and positively related to co-morbidity and pessimism. Martiniello, Haririsanati and Wittich (2020) highlight that there is stigma around blindness which is evident from several inaccurate and problematic depictions of blindness in both literacy and visual culture. They explored the experiences of working-age and older adults with acquired visual impairment who pursue braille rehabilitation training. Findings showed that a variety of personal, social and institutional factors characterise the adult braille learning experience including the role of prior identity and experience, the impact of access to resources and the cost of materials and devices needed to maintain braille skills. Findings also emphasised invisible barriers, including the role of societal perceptions towards braille, the level of support provided by family and friends, and the influence of unconscious biases towards braille.

Slade and Edwards (2015) reported that over a third of blind and partially sighted people reported they sometimes, frequently or always experienced negative attitudes in relation to their visual impairment from the general public. Sight loss was associated with the biggest barriers for accessing employment, travel, leisure and technology even if individuals had other disabilities/impairments. Kurtović and Ivančić (2019) suggest that negative attitudes around someone with a visual impairment in the workplace and their ability to carry out tasks may lead to retiring unnecessarily or not seeking employment, which can be prevented by promoting acceptance and value to allow those individuals to feel accomplishment. Stevelink, Malcolm and Fear (2015) suggested that there may be many challenges for those who acquire a visual impairment such as adjusting to the consequences of vision loss and its impact on areas of life such as relationships, work, well-being and mobility. They found that younger ex-Service personnel applied a number of different strategies to overcome their loss of vision and its associated consequences. Coping strategies varied from learning new skills, goal setting, integrating the use of low vision aids in their daily routine, to social withdrawal and substance misuse. Vision loss affected all aspects of daily life and ex-Service personnel experienced an ongoing struggle to accept and adjust to becoming visually impaired which included the need to depend more on others, loss of confidence and freedom and having lower self-worth.

VI can significantly decrease the quality of life by affecting the child's mobility and daily activities, social participation and emotional state, and cognitive and educational achievements. Non-correctable visual impairment was associated with reduced functional status and well-being, with a magnitude comparable to major medical conditions (Chia et al., 2004). It can affect mobility and day-to-day activities due to issues with spatial orientation, coordination, balance and body awareness along with motor development. VI can also affect cognitive functioning as visual experience and information is extremely paramount for the building of concepts and it is generally acknowledged that it provides the main reference frame for organising incoming sensory data. Patients who had been deprived of pattern vision for at least the first five months of their life as a result of congenital binocular cataracts showed reduced audio-visual interactions in later life, although their visual performance in control tasks was unimpaired (Putzar et al., 2007).

Academic progress can be hampered because visual acuity affects the speed of learning/working. Children with VI may take more time to read and write because language – the vehicle for learning – is code-related (e.g., alphabets) and meaning-related (e.g., vocabulary). Without the ability to see word prints and relate them to alphabets or pictures, abstract learning can be difficult. Research showed that children with VI have delayed development in social cognition due to their disadvantages in establishing perspective taking and joint attention behaviours in early childhood. McAlpine and Moore (1995) cite the performance of 16 visually impaired children, aged 4–12, on tasks designed to assess their understanding of false belief, a central aspect of social understanding. The study found that the development of understanding of another's false belief is delayed in children with severe visual impairments and that the degree of vision loss seems to be a key variable in that development. The inability to readjust their gaze to follow an adult's changed focus of attention or the difficulty to look and explain what another person might see contributes to the delayed understanding of the mental states of others. Bigelow, (1988) found that when two totally blind children, ages four and five, were asked to show objects to sighted people and to each other, the children's performance indicated that they were aware that blind people see differently than sighted people; blind persons need to feel objects in order to gain a sense of them but sighted persons do not. In fact, many social cues take the form of body language and therefore require vision to be understood, which might be partially or not at all accessible for children with VI.

Children with VI may also have difficulty maintaining attention or eye contact and thus are unable to sustain interactions long enough for a social exchange to take place (DeLuzio and Girolametto, 2011). Furthermore, as children with VI may not have access to visual modelling to self-monitor and shape expected social behaviour patterns, others could easily misunderstand their behaviours. Therefore, with inappropriate pragmatic uses, decreased social-perceptual ability to interpret the thoughts, emotions and intentions of others, inadequate strategies to gain access to a group, and multiple failed communication initiations, children with VI may not follow conversations and find it difficult to express themselves. This may hinder their relationship with others and lead to rejection, bullying and non-acceptance by peers and even isolation. However, Khadka et al. (2012) suggested that children and young people with a VI have similar lifestyles to their fully sighted counterparts but are more restricted in some specific activities. Children and young people also reported that sometimes these restrictions were imposed by those supporting them rather than their own abilities.

Pause for reflection

- How do the differing models of disability relate to this area of need?
- How do they differ in how they view the impact of physical or sensory needs on individuals and their families?

Activity

Intersectionality

Intersectionality is a means for understanding how different aspects of a person's identity combine to create different experiences of both discrimination and privilege. The term was initiated by Kimberlé Williams Crenshaw in 1989, noting multiple factors of advantage and disadvantage that shape the lived experience. Examples of these include gender, sex, race, class, sexuality, religion, disability, and physical appearance. Research the following examples of disability and intersectionality:

- Disability and gender
- Disability and race
- Disability and gender
- Disability and sexuality

Multisensory impairment (MSI)

Individuals who have sight and hearing impairments are said to be deafblind. This combination of impairments actually causes additional difficulties – such as problems with balance and spatial awareness – which is why we talk of multisensory impairment (MSI). The combined sight and hearing impairment causes difficulties with communication, access to information and mobility. This includes people with a progressive sight and hearing loss. Aitken (2000) separates the three main causes of congenital or early-onset deafblindness into the categories of infection, genetic or chromosomal and birth trauma, discussing how many of these causes will often lead to additional or multiple physical or learning difficulties. In 2022 it was estimated that there are over 450,000 people in the UK who are deafblind. This is expected to increase to over 610,000 by 2035 (Sense, 2022). Someone who is deafblind, particularly congenitally deafblind, will not be able to acquire information about the world around them in the same way as hearing and sighted counterparts (Aitken 2000).

It has been long recognised by practitioners that children with sensory impairments can experience delays in gross and fine motor skills which could be attributed to the withdrawal of children with deafblindness from their environment due to the lack of incidental learning. Furthermore, if a child is deafblind, not only do they experience the fear of the unknown of their surroundings but also, they do not have positive motivating factors to move – such as a brightly coloured toy – that typical children experience (Aitken, 2000). The lack of motivation to explore environments can also be impacted by physical difficulties, frequently seen in children with congenital deafblindness. An example of a congenital cause of deafblindness which may also compound difficulties in moving around and exploring environments is CHARGE syndrome which may, alongside multisensory impairment, lead to physical impairments (Aitken, 2000). CHARGE syndrome has an incidence rate of around one in every 10,000 births (Hsu et al., 2014) and is recognised as one of the most common causes of genetic congenital deafblindness.

Having a deafblind member has consequences for the family as a whole. Björk et al. (2022) describe the lived experience of family life from the perspective of one parent when the other has deafblindness. When one parent has deafblindness, communication within the family and with people outside the family is affected. The non-deafblind partners tried to integrate deafblindness into everyday family life and constantly strove to compensate for the losses caused by deafblindness. They tried to enhance participation and engagement in everyday family life for the parent with deafblindness by facilitating communication and taking a greater part in some areas of their shared responsibilities at home. Huus et al. (2022) explored how children experience their everyday family life when having a parent with deafblindness. They found that the children experience that their family is like any other family, although having a somewhat different everyday life, which at times affects the children both positively and negatively. Thus it was living an ordinary life, like their friends, although they could identify some differences. One positive reflection on being a child of a parent having deafblindness was that the children felt that they had something special within their family, that they were unique and that the parent's disability created a closeness between the child and the parent. However, they also have taken on caring activities to a much higher degree than their friends. These activities and emotional work prevent the young person from engaging in social and educational activities.

Activity

Deafblind UK is a national charity in the United Kingdom supporting people with sight and hearing loss to live the lives they want. Their website can be accessed via the link: https://deafblind.org.uk

There are a number of stories hosted on the site, including Jean, Jim and Mark.

- Choose three stories and describe the impact that deafblindness has on their lives

- How are deafblind individuals supported by volunteers, friends and the organisation?
- Choose two resources relating to issues such as communication, or accessibility and identify how the impact of deafblindness could be lessened

Cerebral palsy (CP)

Impact of cerebral palsy on the individual

Research shows that children with CP are less likely than their peers to participate in formal and informal social, physical, arts and day-to-day activities, despite evidence that inclusion in these activities improves physical and mental health and encourages physical and cognitive development. In their research, Zwier et al. (2010) found that 93 per cent of the children with CP were insufficiently physically active according to the Dutch recommendation for physical activity and that younger age and lower educational level of the mother were significantly associated with lower levels of physical activity, while severity of CP was not associated with physical activity levels. Parkes, McCullough and Madden (2010) found that children with CP participate less well in school, in maintaining their personal care and in mobility when compared to their participation rates in relationships, fitness and communication and that individuals with CP were likely to be passively involved in activities. This added pressure, on top of the daily struggles of caring, often leads to poor mental and physical health and lower quality of life for parent and child (Davis et al., 2009).

Some individuals with CP also have visual impairments, specifically regarding colour vision; however, other difficulties incurred by cerebral visual impairment (CVI) include seeing moving targets, underdeveloped reaching and knocking over objects (Salavati et al., 2014). It is typically more pronounced in children with spastic CP, in terms of colour vision being reduced compared with controls and developmentally impaired, than children with other CP sub-types (Costa and Pereira, 2014). One of the most difficult to overcome challenges faced by people with CP is the stigma and attitudes of others. Research by Read, Morton and Ryan (2015) found that many cognitively able people with CP often feel patronised and are treated as cognitively impaired by family, peers and professionals, often due to personal care and physical needs, as people forget that these do not reflect cognitive functioning. Mudge et al. (2016) found that many adults with CP experience strangers, friends and family completing tasks or helping without being asked, believing that CP renders individuals helpless.

Pause for reflection

It has been said that disabled children may have less contact with other people than non-disabled children, because they have fewer out-of-school opportunities than their peers, less access to transport, amongst other issues.

- How true is this statement with respect to disabled adults and are there any specific issues which adults may face?

Cerebral palsy and education

Children with CP can have a range of issues including with communication, cognitive and learning issues, hearing or sight issues, and difficulties with sensory processing, and therefore it should not be considered as purely a physical disability. People with CP present a predisposition to show working memory (WM) and executive function (EF) deficits. Bottcher, Flachs and Uldall (2010) found that greater impairment was observed in executive function in general and in inhibition and shifting in particular performance of all timed tasks was slower which may indicate a general impairment in efficiency of information processing in relation to white-matter lesions. Impairments in attention and executive functions are present in children with CP and may help to explain why these children have increased social and learning problems, alongside a deficit in anticipatory planning.

Unlike automatic processes, EFs require effort and the use of self-regulation (SR) competences. EFs show two forms as follows: Core EFs (i.e., inhibition interference control, working memory, and cognitive flexibility) and High Order EFs (i.e., reasoning, problem solving, and planning). Due to motor limitations, children are likely to struggle to follow school routines and show limited participation in school activities, and may have issues with behavioural, emotional and cognitive engagement in activities. They may show mild to moderate deficits in visuospatial functions, attention, and/or executive functions which relate to academic performance and everyday social participation (Fluss and Lidzba, 2020). There may also be co-occurring conditions such as intellectual disability, early-onset epilepsy and speech and language problems. There is a high prevalence of associated learning and cognitive difficulties with CP which impact upon the functioning of daily life. Approximately 50 per cent of children with CP have Moderate Learning Difficulties (MLD) and 25 per cent have Severe Learning Difficulties (SLD) (Novak et al., 2012). Children with CP frequently demonstrate difficulties in communication as a result of language skills, which are often influenced by the motor impairment and linked to the cognitive and/or sensory processing deficits associated with CP (Pennington, Goldbart and Marshall, 2005). Approximately 20 per cent of children with CP are unable to produce intelligible speech (Straub and Obrzut, 2009). Pennington and McConachie (2001) recognise that children with CP and co-morbid speech disorders have been described as passive communicators, whose conversation partners control and dominate interaction. Being assigned the role of the 'passive communicator', individuals with co-occurring communication deficits are least likely to receive pain management and therefore are the most at risk of enduring high levels of undetected pain. This is evidenced by Riquelme, Pades Jiménez and Montoya (2018) who found that practitioners who are regularly involved in the lives of children with CP seem to detect less frequently chronic pain in non-communicative individuals.

Cerebral palsy and families

Vadivelan et al. (2020) reported that due to the difficulty in balancing family and work, caregivers had significant financial burdens. They also perceived a lack of knowledge and awareness about possible options for the treatment of their child. At the interpersonal level, the mothers lacked support from their husband and family in the process of caregiving and suffered the ill effects of alcoholism and domestic violence from their husbands. Sipal et al. (2010) found that for many individuals with CP, motor disorders are accompanied by other disturbances, including emotional and behavioural problems. Levels of behaviour problems are elevated but diminish during adolescence for children with CP. Behaviour problems of children with CP started significantly higher than in the general population but diminished over the three-year period. Older children showed fewer problems overall, and girls showed fewer externalising problems than boys. In a literature review, Guyard et al. (2011) identified seven parental impact dimensions were distinguished, these being time spent, occupational restrictions, social relationships, family relationships, psychological well-being, physical health and financial burden. Guyard et al. (2017) found that parents living with an adolescent with CP showed clinically significant high stress requiring professional assistance, with the main stressors being the level of motor impairment and behavioural disorders.

Activity

Raina et al. (2005) found that although impaired motor function is the hallmark of CP, many children with this development disorder also experience sensory, communicative, and intellectual impairments and may have complex limitations in self-care functions. Although caregiving is a normal part of being the parent of a young child, this role takes on an entirely different significance when a child experiences functional limitations and possible long-term dependence. One of the main challenges for parents is to manage their child's chronic health problems effectively and juggle this role with the requirements of everyday living. The psychological and physical health of caregivers, who in this study were primarily mothers, was strongly influenced by child behaviour and caregiving demands. Child behaviour problems were an important predictor of caregiver psychological well-being, both directly and indirectly, through their effect on self-perception and family function. Caregiving demands contributed directly to both the psychological and the physical health of the caregivers. The practical day-to-day needs of the child created challenges for parents. The influence of social support provided by extended family, friends, and neighbours on health outcomes was secondary to that of the immediate family working closely together.

- What does this study tell us about the impact on families in relation to the need for support, the health of caregivers and everyday challenges?
- If you were a researcher, what kind of questions would you ask with respect to the challenges of CP on families?
- How would you seek information about the benefits that a child with CP bring to a family?

Activity

Read the following case studies.

Danny is 29 years old and has cerebral palsy, which affects his mobility and ability to control his upper limb and head movement. He uses a wheelchair and requires support in all aspects of his life. Until three years ago, Danny's only method of expressing himself had been through facial expression, vocalising and a somewhat haphazard yes/no response using one blink for 'yes' and two for 'no'. Everyone involved in Danny's life had always felt that he should have been able to use a communication aid. However, the difficulties he experienced in controlling his limbs and his many involuntary movements had meant that no one had ever been able to establish a method of assessing his level of understanding and therefore, never attempted to introduce such a system.

Three years on, Danny now uses a sophisticated electronic speech output aid which allows him to express needs, wishes, opinions, emotions and social language.

Heidi is a very sociable 14-year-old who enjoys being with her friends both at school and at home. Everyone who knows her says that she is happy and great fun to be around. She has a very inquisitive nature and enjoys learning. Heidi is very clear that she wants to be like everyone else in her class – she wants to achieve, do well and to be as independent as possible. Like all other teenage girls, Heidi enjoys make-up, clothes, the latest pop group and chatting about boys. She has a diagnosis of cerebral palsy affecting all four limbs. This means that she finds walking and using her hands difficult as well as using her voice to communicate. Heidi also has moderate learning difficulties and is attaining about Level 2 of the National Curriculum for all subjects. To help Heidi access the curriculum and learning opportunities at school, she has a transdisciplinary team consisting of her family, teacher, classrooms assistance, her enabler, physiotherapist, OT and, of course, Heidi herself.

Heidi uses a powered chair at school to take herself to lessons. As she finds speech difficult, she uses a combination of 'high tech and low tech' communication aids such as her Tough Book and Communication File. Heidi's enabler works in partnership with the teachers to ensure that all her communication systems are programmed and have the relevant vocabulary for the lessons.

- How do these case studies evidence the impact of CP?
- Why is the issue of communication important and how do you see the use of technology supporting individuals?
- Research one low and medium technological aid which would support a young person and an adult with CP

Duchenne muscular dystrophy (DMD)

Social isolation is identified as a major concern for youth transitioning to adulthood by parents, patients and healthcare providers. Forming friendships with peers is a developmental milestone of adolescence and decreases in the quality of life can result from social isolation and missing friends. Travlos et al. (2019) found that non-ambulant youth reported relatively high mental well-being compared with the general population, despite more than half experiencing severe co-morbidities across cardiorespiratory, musculoskeletal, renal and gastrointestinal systems. Above average academic achievement and greater perceived family support influenced mental well-being the most, beyond effects of physical co-morbidities. Many patients with DMD also have depression and anxiety. Pangalila et al. (2015) found that fatigue, pain, anxiety, and depression, potentially treatable symptoms, occur frequently in adults with DMD and significantly influence health-related quality of life. They found that fatigue, pain, anxiety and depression occur frequently in adults with DMD and significantly influence health-related quality of life. Lindsay, Cagliostro and McAdam (2019) found that individuals with DMD and neuromuscular disorders engage in meaningful occupations in a variety of ways. Occupational enablers were supports and accommodations and self-care skills and coping strategies, while occupational barriers involved societal expectations of a normative adulthood, discrimination and inaccessible environments, lack of supports and resources, medical challenges, fatigue, lack of motivation, and social isolation and depression.

Impact on families

Schwartz et al. (2021) examined the impact of DMD on family-member caregivers in terms of quality of life, life stress, and indirect costs, as compared to a stratified comparison group of parents of similar-age children without DMD.

Compared to parents without a DMD child, DMD caregivers reported better physical health but worse mental health, positive affect/well-being, environmental mastery, difficulty paying bills, and more hours missed from work. Providing caregiving support for DMD teenagers was the most challenging. DMD caregivers curtailed their educational and professional ambitions and modified their homes to accommodate the disability associated with DMD. Their non-DMD children had to make sacrifices as well. Nonetheless, in resilience and life stress, DMD caregivers were comparable to the comparison group, and showed consistent levels of positive emotions across the age of their DMD child.

Uttley et al. (2018) identified that phases of decline during the disease, the importance of accessible services and family resources, and the impact on the family were key to the measurement of Quality of Life (QoL). Gagliardi (1991) studied three families for ten weeks with a follow-up at one year. Six themes recurred in the common experiences in the families: the erosion of hope for normalcy; society's confirmation of the impossibility of normalcy; the dynamics of the family; a smaller world; letting go or hanging on; and things must change. Buchanan et al. (1979) found chronic emotional stress experienced by families of DMD children was found to be a significant problem in the overall management of the illness. Boström, Ahlström and Sunvisson (2006) focused upon the next of kin's experiences, when an adult family member has muscular dystrophy, as partners or parent. The results showed the meaning of being close to a person with DMD included the span between obligation and love, being vigilant, protective, and supportive, along with striving for an ordinary life.

Despite the presence of DMD deeply impairing health-related quality of life, some areas of well-being are present both in children and caregivers. Longo-Araújo de Melo and Moreno-Valdés (2007) showed a good QoL perception among DMD children and a strong agreement between children and their caregivers especially regarding to the happiness requirements question. The most import life domains identified were physical function, family and leisure activity. Magliano et al. (2014) found that parents of patients with DMD reported feelings of loss, stigma and neglect of their hobbies. Despite the burden, parents stated the caregiving experience had a positive impact on their lives, while a minority of parents thought it had a negative influence on the psychological and social life of unaffected children. However, burden correlated with duration of illness and parent age, and burden was higher among parents with lower social contacts and support in emergencies.

Activity

Ableism

The disabled people rights movements in the United States and Britain introduced the concept of 'ableism' to question and highlight the normative expectation. The concept is aimed at challenging the prejudice and negative treatment people experience when their body-linked abilities are seen as sub-species-typical and therefore labelled as impaired or deficient (Wolbring,

2012). This approach and conceptual shift should be seen in similar ways that previous/current groups seen as 'non-normative' have challenged prejudice and pervasive normalcy in society e.g., racism, sexism and homophobia.

'Disabling Ableism: The Modern Pathway to Inclusion'. This video focuses on shifting perceptions of what is perceived possible by disabling ableism, a social prejudice against people with disabilities based on the belief that typical abilities are superior. It can be accessed via the link: www.you tube.com/watch?v=ah_NWrE291o

- What are your thoughts about the messages that the presenter wishes to get across?

References

Aitken, S. (2000). Understanding deafblindness. In: S. Aitken., M. Buultjens, C. Clark, J. T. Eyre and L. Pease (eds.), *Teaching Children who are Deafblind: Contact, Communication and Learning*. London: David Fulton.

Bigelow, A. (1988). Blind children's concepts of how people see. *Journal of Visual Impairment & Blindness*, 82 (2), pp. 65–68.

Björk, M., Wahlqvist, M., Huus, K. and Anderzén-Carlsson, A. (2022). The consequences of deafblindness rules the family: parents' lived experiences of family life when the other parent has deafblindness. *British Journal of Visual Impairment*, 40 (1), pp. 18–28.

Boström, K., Ahlström, G. and Sunvisson, H. (2006). Being the next of kin of an adult person with muscular dystrophy. *Clinical Nursing Research*, 15, pp. 86–106.

Bottcher, L., Flachs, E. M. and Uldall, P. (2010). Attentional and executive impairments in children with spastic cerebral palsy. *Developmental Medicine & Child Neurology*, 52 (2), pp. e42–e47.

Brice, P. J. and Strauss, G. (2016). Deaf adolescents in a hearing world: a review of factors affecting psychosocial adaptation. *Adolesc Health Med Ther*, 7, pp. 67–76.

Buchanan, D C, LaBarbera, C. J., Roelofs, R and Olson, W. (1979). Reactions of families to children with Duchenne muscular dystrophy. *Gen Hosp Psychiatry*, 1 (3), pp. 262–269.

Chia, E. M., Wang, J. J., Rochtchina, E., Smith, W., Cumming, R. R. and Mitchell, P. (2004). Impact of bilateral visual impairment on health-related quality of life: the Blue Mountains Eye Study. *Invest Ophthalmol Vis Sci*, 45 (1), pp. 71–76.

Costa, M. F. and Pereira, J. C. (2014). Correlations between color perception and motor function impairment in children with spastic cerebral palsy. *Behav Brain Funct*, 10 (22).

Davis, E., Shelly, A., Waters, E., Mackinnon, A., Reddihough, D., Boyd, R. and Graham, H. K. (2009). Quality of life of adolescents with cerebral palsy: perspectives of adolescents and parents. *Dev Med Child Neurol*, 51 (3), pp. 193–199.

DeLuzio, J. and Girolametto, L. (2011). Peer interactions of preschool children with and without hearing loss. *J Speech Lang Hear Res*, 54 (4), pp. 1197–1210.

Fluss, J. and Lidzba, K. (2020). Cognitive and academic profiles in children with cerebral palsy: a narrative review. *Ann Phys Rehabil Med*, 63 (5), pp. 447–456.

Gagliardi, B. A. (1991). The impact of Duchenne muscular dystrophy on families. *Orthop Nurs*, 10 (5), pp. 41–49.

Gentili, N. and Holwell, A. (2011). Mental health in children with severe hearing impairment. *Advances in Psychiatric Treatment*, 17 (1), pp. 54–62.

Guyard, A., Fauconnier, J., Mermet, M. A. and Cans, C. (2011). Impact sur les parents de la paralysie cérébrale chez l'enfant: revue de la littérature [Impact on parents of cerebral palsy in children: a literature review]. *Arch Pediatr*, 18 (2), pp. 204–214.

Guyard, A., Michelsen, S. I., Arnaud, C. and Fauconnier, J. (2017). Family adaptation to cerebral palsy in adolescents: a European multicenter study. *Res Dev Disabil*, 61, pp. 138–150.

Hsu, P., Ma, A., Wilson, M., Williams, G., Curotta, J., Munns, C. F and Mehr, S. (2014). CHARGE syndrome: a review. *J Paediatr Child Health*, 50 (7), pp. 504–511.

Huus, K., Sundqvist, A. S, Anderzén-Carlsson, A., Wahlqvist, M. and Björk, M. (2022). Living an ordinary life – yet not: the everyday life of children and adolescents living with a parent with deafblindness. *Int J Qual Stud Health Well-being*, 17 (1), 2064049.

Khadka, J., Ryan, B., Margrain, T. H., Woodhouse, J. M. and Davies, N. (2012). Listening to voices of children with a visual impairment: a focus group study. *British Journal of Visual Impairment*, 30 (3), pp. 182–196.

Kurtović, A. and Ivančić, H. (2019). Predictors of depression and life satisfaction in visually impaired people. *Disability and Rehabilitation*, 41 (9), pp. 1012–1023.

Lindsay, S., Cagliostro, E. and McAdam, L. (2019). Meaningful occupations of young adults with muscular dystrophy and other neuromuscular disorders. *Canadian Journal of Occupational Therapy*, 86 (4), pp. 277–288.

Longo-Araújo de Melo, E. and Moreno-Valdés, M. T. (2007). Evaluación de la calidad de vida de los niños con distrofia muscular progresiva de Duchenne. *Revista de Neurología*, 45 (2), pp. 81–87.

Magliano, L., D'Angelo, M. G., Vita, G., Pane, M., D'Amico, A., Balottin, U., Angelini, C., Battini, R., Politano, L., Patalano, M., Sagliocchi, A., Civati, F., Brighina, E., Vita, G. L., Messina, S., Sframeli, M., Lombardo, M. E., Scalise, R., Colia, G., Catteruccia, M., Berardinelli, A., Motta, M. C., Gaiani, A., Semplicini, C., Bello, L., Astrea, G., Zaccaro, A. and Scutifero, M. (2014). Psychological and practical difficulties among parents and healthy siblings of children with Duchenne vs. Becker muscular dystrophy: an Italian comparative study. *Acta Myol*, 33 (3), pp. 136–143.

Martiniello, N., Haririsanati, L. and Wittich, W. (2020). Enablers and barriers encountered by working-age and older adults with vision impairment who pursue braille training. *Disabil Rehabil*, 44 (11), pp. 2347–2362.

McAlpine, L. M. and Moore, C. L. (1995). The development of social understanding in children with visual impairments. *Journal of Visual Impairment & Blindness*, 89 (4), pp. 349–358.

McIlroy, G. and Storbeck, C. (2011). Development of deaf identity: an ethnographic study. *The Journal of Deaf Studies and Deaf Education*, 16 (4), pp. 494–511.

Mudge, S., Rosie, J., Stott, S., Taylor, D., Signal, N. and McPherson, K. (2016). Ageing with cerebral palsy; what are the health experiences of adults with cerebral palsy? A qualitative study. *BMJ Open*, 6 (10), e012551.

Musselman, C., Mootilal, A. and MacKay, S. (1996). The social adjustment of deaf adolescents in segregated, partially integrated, and mainstreamed settings. *The Journal of Deaf Studies and Deaf Education*, 1 (1), pp. 652–663.

Novak, I., Hines, M., Goldsmith, S. and Barclay, R. (2012). Clinical prognostic messages from a systematic review on cerebral palsy. *Pediatrics*, 130 (5), e1285–1312.

Pangalila, R. F., van den Bos, G. A., Bartels, B., Bergen, M., Stam, H. J. and Roebroeck, M. E. (2015). Prevalence of fatigue, pain, and affective disorders in adults with Duchenne muscular dystrophy and their associations with quality of life. *Arch Phys Med Rehabil*, 96, pp. 1242–1247.

Parkes, J., McCullough, N. and Madden, A. (2010). To what extent do children with cerebral palsy participate in everyday life situations? *Health & Social Care in the Community*, 18, 304–315.

Pennington, L. and McConachie, H. (2001). Predicting patterns of interaction between children with cerebral palsy and their mothers. *Dev Med Child Neurol*, 43 (2), pp. 83–90.

Pennington, L., Goldbart, J. and Marshall, J. (2005). Direct speech and language therapy for children with cerebral palsy: findings from a systematic review. *Dev Med Child Neurol*, 47 (1), pp. 57–63.

Putzar, L., Goerendt, I., Lange, K., Rösler, F. and Röder, B. (2007). Early visual deprivation impairs multisensory interactions in humans. *Nat Neurosci*, 10 (10), pp. 1243–1245.

Quittner, A. L., Barker, D. H., Cruz, I., Snell, C., Grimley, M. E., Botteri, M. and the CDaCI Investigative Team. (2010). Parenting stress among parents of deaf and hearing children: associations with language delays and behavior problems. *Parent Sci Pract*, 10 (2), pp. 136–155.

Raina, P., O'Donnell, M., Rosenbaum, P., Brehaut, J., Walter, S. D., Russell, D., Swinton, M., Zhu, B. and Wood, E. (2005). The health and well-being of caregivers of children with cerebral palsy. *Pediatrics*, 115 (6), e626–636.

Read, S. A., Morton, T. A. and Ryan, M. K. (2015). Negotiating identity: a qualitative analysis of stigma and support seeking for individuals with cerebral palsy. *Disabil Rehabil*, 37 (13), pp. 1162–1169.

Riquelme, I., Pades Jiménez, A. and Montoya, P. (2018). Parents and physiotherapists recognition of non-verbal communication of pain in individuals with cerebral palsy. *Health Commun*, 33 (12), pp. 1448–1453.

Salavati, M., Rameckers, E. A., Steenbergen, B. and van der Schans, C. (2014). Gross motor function, functional skills and caregiver assistance in children with spastic cerebral palsy (CP) with and without cerebral visual impairment (CVI). *European Journal of Physiotherapy*, 16 (3), pp.159–167.

Schwartz, C. E., Stark, R. B., Audhya, I. F. and Gooch, K. L. (2021). Characterizing the quality-of-life impact of Duchenne muscular dystrophy on caregivers: a case-control investigation. *J Patient Rep Outcomes*, 5 (1), 124.

Sense (2022). Deafblindness statistics in the UK. [online] Available at: www.sense.org.uk/about-us/statistics/deafblindness-statistics-in-the-uk [Accessed 12. 02. 2023].

Sipal, R. F., Schuengel, C., Voorman, J. M., Van Eck, M. and Becher, J. G. (2010). Course of behaviour problems of children with cerebral palsy: the role of parental stress. *Child: Care, Health and Development*, 36, pp. 74–84.

Slade, J. and Edwards, R. (2015). My voice. [online] Available from: www.rnib.org.uk/myvoice [Accessed 16. 02. 2023].

Stevelink, S. A., Malcolm, E. M. and Fear, N. T. (2015). Visual impairment, coping strategies and impact on daily life: a qualitative study among working-age UK ex-service personnel. *BMC Public Health*, 15, 1118.

Stevenson, J., Kreppner, J., Pimperton, H., Worsfold, S. and Kennedy, C. (2015). Emotional and behavioural difficulties in children and adolescents with hearing impairment: a systematic review and meta-analysis. *Eur Child Adolesc Psychiatry*, 24 (5), pp. 477–496.

Stevenson, J., Pimperton, H., Kreppner, J., Worsfold, S., Terletski, E. and Kennedy, C. (2017). Emotional and behaviour difficulties in teenagers with permanent childhood hearing loss. *Int J Paed Otolarnyngol*, 101, pp. 186–195.

Straub, K. and Obrzut, J. E. (2009). Effects of cerebral palsy on neuropsychological function. *Journal of Developmental and Physical Disabilities*, 21 (2), pp. 153–167.

Szarkowski, A. and Brice, P. (2019). Positive aspects of parenting a deaf child: categories of potential positive influences. *JADARA*, 37 (2).

Tambs, K. (2004). Moderate effects of hearing loss on mental health and subjective well-being: results from the Nord-Trøndelag Hearing Loss Study. *Psychosomatic Medicine*, 66, pp. 776–782.

Terlektsi, E., Kreppner, J., Mahon, M., Worsfold, S. and Kennedy, C. R. (2020). Peer relationship experiences of deaf and hard-of-hearing adolescents. *The Journal of Deaf Studies and Deaf Education*, 25 (2), pp. 153–166.

Travlos, V., Downs, J., Wilson, A., Hincee, D. and Patmana, S. (2019). Mental wellbeing in non-ambulant youth with neuromuscular disorders: what makes the difference? *Neuromuscular Disorders*, 29, pp. 48–58.

Uttley, L., Carlton, J., Woods, H. B. and Brazier, J. (2018). A review of quality of life themes in Duchenne muscular dystrophy for patients and carers. *Health Qual Life Outcomes*, 16 (1), 237.

Vadivelan, K., Sekar, P., Sruthi, S. S. and Gopichandran, V. (2020). Burden of caregivers of children with cerebral palsy: an intersectional analysis of gender, poverty, stigma, and public policy. *BMC Public Health*, 20, 645.

Wallhagen, M. I., Strawbridge, W. J., Shema, S. J. and Kaplan, G. A. (2004). Impact of self-assessed hearing loss on a spouse: a longitudinal analysis of couples. *J Gerontol B Psychol Sci Soc Sci*, 59 (3), S190–196.

Wolbring, G. (2012). Expanding ableism: taking down the ghettoization of impact of disability studies scholars. *Societies*, 2, 75–83.

Wolters, N., Knoors, H., Cillessen, A. H. and Verhoeven, L. (2012). Impact of peer and teacher relations on deaf early adolescents' well-being: comparisons before and after a major school transition. *The Journal of Deaf Studies and Deaf Education*, 17 (4), pp. 463–482.

Wolters, N. and Isarin, J. (2015). Reciprocity in school peer relationships of deaf and hard-of-hearing early adolescents: promoting empowerment. In: H. E. T. M. Knoors (ed.), *Educating Deaf Learners: Creating a Global Evidence Base*, pp. 311–336.

World Health Organization (2022). Blindness and vision impairment. [online] Available at: www.who.int/news-room/fact-sheets/detail/blindness-and-visual-impairment [Accessed 19. 02. 2023].

Xie, Y. H., Potměšil, M. and Peters, B. (2014). Children who are deaf or hard of hearing in inclusive educational settings: a literature review on interactions with peers. *The Journal of Deaf Studies and Deaf Education*, 19 (4), pp. 423–437.

Zaidman-Zait, A., Most, T., Tarrasch, R., Haddad-eid, E. and Brand, D. (2016). The impact of childhood hearing loss on the family: mothers' and fathers' stress and coping resources. *The Journal of Deaf Studies and Deaf Education*, 21 (1), pp. 23–33.

Zaidman-Zait, A. and Curle, D. (2018). Complexity: an interpretative phenomenological analysis of the experiences of mothers of deaf children with cochlear implants and autism. *Journal of Health Psychology*, 23 (9), pp. 1173–1184.

Zwier, J. N., van Schie, P. E., Becher, J. G., Smits, D. W., Gorter, J.W. and Dallmeijer, A. J. (2010). Physical activity in young children with cerebral palsy. *Disabil Rehabil*, 32 (18), pp. 1501–1508.

6 Pedagogical approaches to support these needs

Introduction

This chapter explores approaches to support issues associated with Sensory and/or Physical Needs. There are several websites, organisations and textbooks which identify a range of approaches in relation to communication and interaction. This chapter will instead focus on the theoretical underpinning, research studies and evidence-based research and practice, for some of the main approaches used in an educational context. It will signpost you to videoclips, case studies and policies showing how the approach is being used in practice. It must be remembered that although an approach is identified in a specific chapter, it can be used in other areas of need.

Learning objectives

This chapter will:

- Introduce you to a number of specific approaches which can be used to support Physical and/or Sensory Needs
- Invite you examine underpinning theory and research evidence in relation to approaches related to this area of need
- Introduce you to the paradigms and principles involved in Physical and Sensory Needs
- Help you to understand how these approaches can support individuals in the classroom
- Invite you to review the approaches with respect to evidence-based research and practice

Key terms

Sensory and Physical Needs, Little Room, multisensory curriculum, Multisensory Environments (MSEs), immersive and sensory rooms, tactile illustrated books, cerebral palsy, assistive technology

DOI: 10.4324/9781003361084-9

Little Rooms

The concept of a 'Little Room' was first developed by Dr Lilli Nielsen with the purpose of giving children with multiple and complex disabilities an opportunity to gain experience in exploring their environments, understanding space and a concept of objects (Newton, 2012). It is an environment that allows the child to play and explore without distraction or interference. Someone who is deafblind will not be able to acquire information about the world around them in the same way as hearing and sighted counterparts (Aitken, 2000). Broadbent et al. (2018) indicate the importance of information from multiple senses to construct meaningful understanding of the world around us. Unsurprisingly, the inhibiting of information from sight and hearing – the senses which provide information about things at a distance to the individual (Haring and Romer, 1995) – can lead to withdrawal by the child as the outside world becomes unknown, scary and dangerous.

It has long been recognised by practitioners that children with sensory impairments can experience delays in gross and fine motor skills (Parker, 2017) which could be attributed to the withdrawal of children with deafblindness from their environment due to the lack of incidental learning. An important way to reduce the anxiety that multisensory impaired children face around their surrounding is to maintain structure and predictability (Wheeler and Griffin, 1997). The lack of motivation to explore environments can also be impacted by physical difficulties, frequently seen in children with congenital deafblindness. An example of a congenital cause of deafblindness which may also compound difficulties in moving around and exploring environments is CHARGE syndrome which may, as well as multisensory impairment, lead to physical impairments.

Parker (2017) considers the close link between movement and communication including the specific behavioural components of communication which require movement such as initiating reaching to locate, grasp and release objects as well as locating and moving towards communication partners, by encouraging independent movement to explore an environment, we can teach deafblind children about the communication and feedback they can receive from exploring their environment and combat the withdrawal seen in deafblind children. The items in the Little Room, made of materials such as wood, metal and fabric, are suspended from the walls with elastic cords. They are within easy reach, and the child can comfortably examine and play with them. When the child releases an item, it returns to its original location. Therefore, the child can locate the item again and repeat the activity. This repetition builds memory for the child.

Teachers and caregivers tend to place children on soft surfaces such as blankets or rugs. However, a soft surface doesn't provide much information to a blind child. For instance, when the child drops a toy, there is no sound to indicate where it landed, so a resonance board could be used. This is a thin, flexible sheet of wood that gives tactile and auditory feedback whenever the child moves. When the child kicks the board, there is a sound and a vibration and this feedback encourages the child to repeat the movement, and eventually to experiment with other movements as well. The child moves independently, without an adult manipulating his or her body. Resonance boards provide vibro-tactile feedback amplifying any auditory feedback using vibration that can be felt through the whole body. Resonance work can be an initial method of encouraging communication, giving the child an awareness of themselves and their actions. The child is also able to explore independently but also the items have rich sensory experiences which are applicable to everyday life (Urosevic and Cross, 2003) and the use of tactile experience and texture encourages movement, as it removes the focus from the movement and into the purpose of the movement, which can be constructed to provide the child with information about their environment.

Activity

Here is a short video which shows Zoe in the Little Room. It can be accessed via the link: www.youtube.com/watch?v=X7_S4dfN_-U

The Welsh Government (2019) have published a document entitled 'Support for children and young people with multi-sensory impairment in educational settings'. It can be accessed via the link: www.gov.wales/sites/default/files/publications/2019-12/191209-support-for-children-and-young-people-with-multi-sensory-impairment-in-educational-settings.pdf

It identifies twelve educational strategy areas, each with an introduction, a brief discussion of the relevant intervention literature, and a summary of relevant strategies and approaches.

- Take two strategy areas and suggest how the research may support curriculum design in these areas

---

Multisensory curriculum

A multisensory curriculum seeks to improve learning experiences by providing an environment of relaxation and enjoyment through the administering of valuable stimulation for those with impairments and learning difficulties (Houghton et al., 1998). It is underpinned by the Sensory Integration Dysfunction theory present in pupils with SEN that explains their inability to appropriately receive and process environmental stimuli to provide a coherent response to the brain. Such a disorder leads to disorganised, maladaptive interactions with the environment from which faulty internal sensory feedback is produced that affects the development, learning and behaviour of an individual. Therefore, the aim of a multisensory curriculum is to stimulate the senses in a controlled way to enable the brain to organise these sensations and elicit adaptive responses (Case-Smith et al., 2015). In addition, it uses all learning pathways in the brain simultaneously to enhance memory and learning which compensates for the loss or reduction in one or more sensory areas exhibited in some SEND individuals and encourage the development of other communication channels. Davis (2001) states that a sensory curriculum is where activities are delivered in a 'fun' environment where the enjoyment of the activity is the motivating factor and not the outside pressure of achievement.

Sensory stories

A sensory story is storytelling that is supported by the use of relevant objects chosen for their sensory qualities and appeal that has been identified as enjoyable for the pupil to enhance engagement (Preece and Zhao, 2015). Sharing a sensory story enables the storytelling to convey meaning through sensory experience as well as spoken language and receive comment through the responses and reactions of the learner and in doing so, enter a conversation; the success of this activity is assessed when their responses increase over time (Watson, 2002). The approach begins with having a familiar adult deliver the story, who knows the learner and is aware of their sensory abilities and preferences and thus is able to interpret their communicative behaviour more accurately.

Next, the story should be delivered in the same way and order and the teller should refrain from adding extra language. This burst-pause activity is similar to the intent-respond communication model of Intensive Interaction which will develop anticipation and build understanding of the story at the learner's pace, enabling interaction with the stimuli and focus on the experience (Grace, 2014). When they interact with the stimuli, such as touching, manipulating in terms of exploring, moving, vocalising or changing facial expression in response to some aspect of the story, it is an opportunity for the facilitator to feedback by adjusting the level of response to the pupil, such as increasing pitch of vocalisations, exaggerating facial expressions and imitating movements, so as to enrich emergent communication skills. The facilitator should not deliver the story without considering that the learner plays an active part and controls as much of the action consequent on the narrative as possible. This implies that the facilitator should focus on what the learner is doing at the moment.

Multisensory Storytelling (MSST)

MSST is an intervention method which involves using sensory stimulation alongside a verbal story. The approach is used in general teaching practice for those with PMLD/SLD to enhance their engagement and understanding in aspects of the curriculum (Mercieca and Mercieca, 2009). However, it is also often used as a direct intervention for individuals with PMLD, SLD and other difficulties to overcome barriers around sensitive issues such as dental visits, living with epilepsy or managing sexual behaviour (Lambe and Hogg, 2013; Young et al., 2011), presenting these issues in social contexts to facilitate understanding. While it has been argued by some that MSST is used more effectively as a pedagogical tool rather than an intervention (Preece and Zhao, 2015), high success rates have been seen in other studies with regards to MSST as a method of intervention with specific goals being achieved. For example, a boy with PMLD and autism was able to overcome his anxieties about trips to the dentist and began to cooperate during these visits because of the MSST (Lambe and Hogg, 2013). The combination of sensory stimuli, listening to the rhyme and rhythm and the repetitive structure of a multisensory story supports memory and aids learning, playing a crucial role in the development of early communication skills, eye contact, and shared attention. It promotes language development through alternative communication systems, Makaton, sign language and to facilitate PECS exchanges.

Multisensory storytelling (MSST) is an approach to storytelling in which stories are not simply told but can be experienced with all our senses, they can support the development of literacy skills in PMLD (Fornefeld, 2013) and provide such individuals with opportunities for interaction and enjoyment (Park, 2013). The act of narration is supported by the use of relevant objects, chosen for their sensory qualities (e.g., feel, smell, sound, weight, temperature) and for their appeal and relevance to those experiencing the story. Many schools and teachers have adapted their own multisensory versions of existing stories, developed their own stories to suit a particular need, or both. Furthermore, commercially produced multisensory stories are also available both as complete activities such as 'Bag Books' (2011) and 'Story Sacks' (Grace, 2014). Multisensory storytelling for individuals with PMLD embodies the inclusion of learners into storytelling, allowing learners to take part by experiencing sensory stimuli alongside verbal text (Fornefeld, 2013).

Ten Brug et al. (2016) compared the attention levels of learners using regular storytelling and multisensory storytelling and found that learners with PMLD paid more attention to the book when reinforced with personalised and sensory stimuli. Grove (2011) suggests that by capturing our senses and feelings, only then can a judgement be made. In practice this can be reinforced into storytelling, for example learning hot and cold would require us to touch stimuli, such as ice and a hot mug to reinforce meaning of words which can be a crucial part of understanding and development. It is also particularly useful to incorporate everyday life experiences of the individual into the story telling to attract attention and encourage exploration (Ten Brug et al., 2016).

Research evidence

Studies have been undertaken by researchers associated with the Profound and Multiple Impairment Service (PAMIS) (2023), to evaluate the impact of MSST in helping individuals with PMLD deal with and understand sensitive issues, including living with epilepsy, undergoing dental treatment, and managing sexual behaviour. Further research in the United Kingdom using the Storysharing® approach has identified that MSST can be used to support the development of both fictional stories and personal narratives (Grove, 2014). Preece and Zhao (2015) found that MSST was viewed positively, and that it was considered to contribute to the curriculum access, assessment, learning and socialisation of students across a wide range of SEN. Kamei-Hannan, Chang and Fryling (2022) examined the effectiveness of the approach on listening comprehension and language use in three bilingual children with visual impairment. The results suggest that the MSST approach is a promising intervention for children with visual impairment in increasing their language skills.

Tactile illustrated books

In tactile illustrated books, the reader must explore the tactile picture to interpret its meaning and to associate it with the text content. As is the case with sighted children (Carney and Levin, 2002), tactile illustrations could be beneficial for language and literacy development of visually impaired (VI) children (Heller and Gentaz, 2014). Examining the effect of tactile illustrations on comprehension of storybooks by three children with VI, Bara, Gentaz and Valente (2018) found that few tactile illustrated books exist, and they are often inadequate, since they are mainly based on a visual approach (converting a visual picture into bidimensional tactile representation). They advise teachers of students with visual impairments and other practitioners to add 3-D elements with which children with visual impairments can interact (for example, miniaturised objects or pop-up illustrations). In our point of view, these 3-D illustrations that are based on real environmental objects, available both to children who are sighted and to those who are visually impaired, could create communication bridges between these two communities during shared book-reading activities in class.

Activity

The video 'Introduction to multi-sensory storytelling' shows a MSST in practice. It can be accessed via the link: www.youtube.com/watch?v=0Y-jRGAyYw4

Teachers can adapt existing stories following a sequence of six steps. The article can be accessed via the link:

https://senmagazine.co.uk/content/activities/multi-sensory/18029/multisensory-storytelling

- Choose a story that you are familiar with and perhaps have used in the past and describe how it could be adapted to become a MSST experience

---

Multisensory Environments (MSEs), immersive and sensory rooms

A sensory space is a designated area within a school which can support a student's sensory preferences and needs. It is a space which aims to provide students with the individualised sensory input they need to self-regulate, so they can be better prepared for learning and interacting with others. A sensory space addresses the primary senses of sight, hearing, smell, touch, vestibular and proprioceptive. Other terms used to describe a sensory space include sensory room, calm space, chill-out room, Multisensory Environments (MSEs) and sensory garden. They allow children to explore places and environments safely, removing barriers which otherwise in the 'real world' may trigger a behavioural challenge, anxiety or resistance. A sensory space in the school environment promotes a positive school culture and climate in supporting students' health and well-being. Sensory spaces can benefit all students, especially those who have been exposed to trauma, chronic stress, and those with specified sensory needs. They can provide a safe environment where the student can be supported to calm and regulate, therefore optimising learning and participation in the school environment. The sensory space should be flexible, changeable and adaptable to meet the needs of students. There are many benefits to creating a sensory space; they can reduce sensory overload for students who may find the school day overwhelming and enable them to achieve a calmer state for learning and provide increased sensory input for students who require more stimulation to enable them to regulate their sensory and emotional needs. Sensory spaces can incorporate mindfulness activities to support interceptive awareness to facilitate self-regulation and support social and emotional learning, promote self-care, self-nurturance, empowerment, skill development, resilience and recovery (Champagne, 2006) and can also be used as part of a school's trauma-informed approach to supporting students who have experienced loss of a consistent caregiver, neglect, different forms of abuse and maltreatment, and chronic stress (Whiting, 2018).

MSEs have become a standard feature in special educational needs schools in the UK with government building guidelines now stipulating the inclusion of at least one sensory room within any such provision. Increasingly found in school classrooms, it provides alternative real-world experiences which promote students' level of understanding and encourages innovative thinking in education. The idea of a sensory curriculum was first developed by Longhorn (1988) who identified that learners with PMLD needed sensory stimulation to make sense of their environment and experiences (Mount and Cavet, 1995). Hulsegge and Verheul (1987) developed the Snoezelen® philosophy, which was essentially a sensory environment in which recreation for individuals with PMLD was the primary focus, with learning being a secondary motive. These environments adopted an interactive approach where the individual with PMLD was in control and the non-disabled person was a facilitator (Pagliano, 2001). Since then, the concept of multisensory environments has been criticised, with Hulsegge and Verheul (1987) describing their own work as lacking a firm theoretical underpinning and Mount and Cavet (1995) describing multisensory environments as dumping grounds where people with PMLD are contained and ignored and suggest that the value of these environments are over-estimated and raise concerns over a lack of focus on their educational benefits.

Research evidence

Multisensory Environments (also called sensory or Snoezelen® rooms) are rooms that contain equipment which can create light, sound and touch experiences.

MSEs are often used with autistic children, particularly in schools, but there is no evidence for how best to use them. Unwin, Powell and Jones (2022) found that when autistic children could control the sensory equipment, they paid more attention and performed fewer repetitive and sensory behaviours. They also used less stereotyped speech, produced fewer vocalisations and showed lower levels of activity. Other behaviours were not affected. They suggest that a MSE can impact behaviour and that providing control of sensory changes to autistic children may help create better conditions for learning. Fava and Strauss (2010) compared the effects of the Snoezelen® and the Stimulus Preference environment on the behaviour of adults with profound mental retardation. Results showed that the Snoezelen® intervention decreased disruptive behaviours only in individuals with autism, while Stimulus Preference increased pro-social behaviours only in participants with profound mental retardation with co-occurring poor motor and linguistic abilities. Hill et al. (2012) found that there was greater engagement in the MSE when their ID participants were provided with high levels of caregiver attention.

Unwin, Powell and Jones (2021) interviewed and surveyed practitioners who believed that the MSE had an effect on autism symptomatology, including increasing social and communication behaviours and decreasing RMBs. Other outcomes were also reported, including improvements to focus and attention and enjoyment, and a reduction in challenging behaviours. Practitioners additionally believed in the anxiety reducing effect of the MSE for autistic children. Stephenson and Carter (2011) interviewed five teachers from two special schools who agreed to be videorecorded while using the room with their classes and who were interviewed about their perspectives on MSEs and about the activities observed in their classes. Most teachers seemed to believe that use of the MSE or the equipment in it would have automatic and remarkably wide-ranging benefits for their students. Teachers at School 2 seemed to adopt part of the original Snoezelen® philosophy in their conception of the MSE as a safe, semi-structured environment where students could experience or use the pieces of equipment that they enjoyed, without a strong focus on direct teaching or prompting.

A meta-analysis conducted by Lotan and Gold (2009) reported improvements in adaptive functioning, maladaptive behaviour and daily interactions following sensory room use. Included studies encompassed people of a wide range of ages (5–65 years) with most participants having moderate to severe intellectual disability, some with co-occurring autism. Similarly, a study by Shapiro et al. (2009) found that a physical sensory room (termed 'sensory adapted environment') reduced anxiety in children with and without developmental disability (n = 32, mean age eight) by utilising lighting, tactile, auditory and somato-sensory stimulation during dental treatments. Breslin et al. (2020) reported a range of positive outcomes for people with intellectual and developmental disabilities accessing MSEs in clinical settings showed improvements in behaviour, alertness and anxiety following use of a sensory room using a range of measures including that of distress, discomfort, and maladaptive behaviours (e.g., aggression, stereotypy, self-injury), as well as positive behaviours (e.g., communication, engagement, cooperation). Mills et al. (2023) investigated the impact of a VR sensory room intervention on anxiety, depression, personal well-being, sensory processing, and adaptive behaviour for adults with disability. Quantitative findings indicated improvements in anxiety and depression from pre- to post-, with changes in sensory processing, but no significant changes in adaptive behaviour or personal well-being. Qualitative findings indicated that participants perceived there was a positive impact on anxiety as well as enhanced social participation.

Activity

Watch these three videos which show children accessing examples of such rooms. They can be accessed via the links:

www.youtube.com/watch?v=8OVBgE-aNbY&t=70s
www.youtube.com/watch?v=iTjgR3L_Dxg
www.youtube.com/watch?v=R-WDBECYuy0&t=14s

- Compare the experiences of the learners in the rooms
- Are there any similarities and differences in their experiences and interactions?

Sensory diets

A sensory diet is several activities, specifically included in a child's daily planning to help his/her attention, arousal, and adaptive responses. The activities are selected according to the child's needs and based on the theory of sensory integration. The sensory diet uses a variety of proprioceptive, motor, tactile, auditory, auditory, vestibular, taste, and oral stimuli at different times of the day to help the brain regulate attention and the right level of arousal. These stimuli release neurochemicals that can last up to two hours depending on the type and intensity of the stimulus. To maintain the flow of these neurochemicals in the brain, it is essential to plan a sensory diet throughout the day.

Sensory diets are derived from the principles of sensory integration (SI) and sensory processing theories. SI theory hypothesises that some individuals with intellectual and developmental disabilities have trouble processing and integrating sensory information (e.g., auditory, vestibular, proprioceptive, tactile, visual), affecting their adaptive and maladaptive repertoires (Ayres, 1989).

Sensory processing theory was developed by Dunn (1997) and is based on occupational and educational counselling principles. Specifically, sensory processing theory proposes four sensory processing patterns (i.e., low registration, sensory avoiding, sensory seeking, and sensory sensitivity), which characterise the perceptual process. Sensory diet interventions assume that individuals (with or without autism) need certain types of passive and active sensorimotor experiences to stay alert, stay organised, and to successfully participate in many aspects of life. Sensory diets can provide controlled sensory input or utilise already existing sensory input for an individual to maintain a regulated behavioural state (Wilbarger and Wilbarger, 2002). Specifically, a sensory therapist will provide the individual with a schedule of sensory-based activities (e.g., brushing, joint compression, climbing, weighted vest) to be implemented across all environments (e.g., home, school) throughout the day, that aim to fulfil that individual's sensory needs (Baranek, 2002). A sensory diet is therefore a personalised activity plan that suggests the sensory input a child/young person needs to stay focused and organised throughout their day. A sensory diet includes activities that help the child to feel calm, alert and in an optimal state of arousal. It can help modulate behaviour, mood and level of arousal, thus enabling the child to engage and participate in the activities they want and need to do. An effective sensory diet can only be achieved by using a collaborative/team approach, involving all those responsible for the care of the child, at home and in care/educational settings.

Research evidence

Sensory diet interventions were developed for individuals displaying behaviours associated with a diagnosis of sensory processing disorders. Sensory diets administered in brief sessions in the school day appear to be effective in improving children's sensory processing, psychosocial, and classroom engagement behaviours and may have a continued beneficial effect (Pingale, Fletcher and Candler, 2019). Sensory diets may have changed participants' sensory processing, psychosocial skills, and classroom engagement behaviours. However, target behaviours for each participant responded to sensory diets differently. Control intervention of non-therapeutic fine-motor visual activities did not change these behaviours. Pingale et al. (2022) noted positive and individualised changes in sensory processing, psychosocial, and classroom engagement behaviours were noted for children when sensory diets were administered in brief sessions throughout a school day. Pingale, Fletcher and Candler (2019) found a decrease in problematic behaviours with introduction of the sensory diet that persisted after intervention withdrawal. She concluded that sensory diets administered in brief sessions in the school day appear to be effective in improving children's sensory processing, psychosocial, and classroom engagement behaviours and may have a continued beneficial effect. Sensory diet intervention has also been used with ADHD children and found to improve performance in various social situations and is recommended to use in combination with other therapeutic interventions in rehabilitation centres and schools, amongst other settings (Shabdini, Azizi and Peymani, 2022). However, sensory processing disorders are not recognised in DSM-5. The National Clearinghouse on Autism Evidence and Practice (Steinbrenner et al., 2020) recently published their review of autism treatments and levels of evidence. It indicated that there has been no empirical study published on the effectiveness of sensory diets since 2011, but that there have been publications suggesting it is not evidence-based, and so recommends caution when considering the diet.

Cerebral palsy (CP)

Chaitow et al. (2010) suggest that the arts could potentially begin to change negative attitudes towards disability, by showing that those with severe physical disabilities are creative and need to express the same thoughts and emotions as the able bodied through dance, music or art. Skills and music therapy can be used to encourage emotional and creative expression and that vibrations caused by different frequencies can have a profound effect on mood, relax muscles, reduce spasms and lower blood pressure. Traditional medical treatments struggle to achieve this, leaving those with severe spastic movements in high levels of pain and discomfort (Shamsoddini et al., 2014). Research by Nasuruddin (2010) found that encouraging individuals with CP to engage in playing instruments led to improved posture, concentration, cognition, gross motor skills, muscle development and control, and confidence through enjoyment and independent participation. This aligns with research by Hoare et al. (2007) into constraint-induced movement, whereby those with CP are encouraged to make use of limbs affected by their CP to participate in rewarding physical activities, e.g., playing a drum. This encouragement to move unused limbs is important to prevent stiffness and pain and to ensure higher levels of physical health and comfort (Davis et al., 2017). Percussive instruments lend themselves to rhythmical beats; research by Efraimidou et al. (2016) and Schweizer, Eylon and Katz-Leurer (2020) found that children with CP who have better rhythmic perception and understanding of beat make greater progress in development of gait, walking, motor and cognitive skills.

Some individuals with CP also have visual impairments specifically regarding colour vision; however, other difficulties incurred by cerebral visual impairment (CVI) include seeing moving targets, underdeveloped reaching and knocking over objects (Salavati et al., 2014). It is typically more pronounced in children with spastic CP, in terms of colour vision being reduced compared with controls and developmentally impaired, than children with other CP sub-types (Costa and Pereira, 2014). Another impairment that this resource considered was lack of finger dexterity and finger sensory perception by using large handles. Guedin, Fluss and Thevenot (2018) found that children with hemiplegia exhibited finger dexterity deficit in both hands while children with diplegia exhibited finger dexterity deficit only in their dominant hand. These are two different types of spastic CP, which state the number of limbs that are affected.

Assistive technology

Assistive technologies (AT) are specialised products designed for people with SEND. The objective of assistive technology is to make information, programmes and services, and facilities more accessible to the user of the equipment. The DfE published its Education Technology (EdTech) strategy (DfE, 2019) in April 2019 on realising the potential of technology in education, which was supported by £10 million in funding. As a result, the DfE launched a series of EdTech challenges to encourage change in the use of technology across the education system in

England. They produced a report on 'Insights on the use of assistive technology in educational settings by pupils and students with SEND' (DfE, 2020). Assistive technology (AT) is an umbrella term for products and related services used by persons with disability to enable and enhance their inclusion in all domains of participation. AT can be used by people of all ages and with all types of impairment (loco-motor, visual, hearing, speech or cognition) and all sorts of limitations in activities, and for short or long periods of time (de Witte et al., 2018). Physical disabilities, also known as orthopaedic impairments, are those that affect an individual's motor abilities. Examples include cerebral palsy, spinal cord injury, multiple sclerosis, spina bifida or amputation. Relevant types of AT for this group include alternative methods for accessing the computer keyboard and mouse such as switches and eye gaze, speech to text, wheelchairs, wearable AT and writing aids. Assistive devices currently available include:

- Mobility aids – include wheelchairs, walkers, scooters, crutches, canes, and prosthetic and orthotic devices
- Hearing aids – include devices to enable hearing or help an individual hear more clearly
- Software aids – persons with sensory impairment or mobility issues can use computer software-aided mobile devices, screen readers, voice recognition tools and screen enlargement apps
- Cognitive aids – examples include electrical or software-backed assistive devices that help persons with attention, comprehension and reading impairments
- Educational aids – adapted pencil grips, book holders, auto page-turners, and other assistive devices for learners with physical disabilities
- Sports aids – high-performance, lightweight mobility devices to enable people with physical disabilities to participate in sports and other physical activities
- Adaptive aids – assistive devices, such as adaptive utensils and switches, enable persons with limited motor skills to drink, eat, play, and perform other activities
- Innovations in assistive devices for physical disabilities
- Adaptive switches – an assistive device that enables a person with a physical disability to activate switch-based devices like cell phones on their own. Some of the latest digital adaptive switches allow people with mobility impairments of the upper body to access various types of smart devices, including home automation systems. These switches allow the user to pair them with multiple Bluetooth-enabled devices and switch between them easily by activating the switch

Activity

Caleb, who has cerebral palsy, lacks the motor skills to play with blocks, but he can stack digital blocks using an app on a tablet. While the goal remains to use real-world materials, the tablet offers Caleb valuable play experiences not possible before.

A group of children are working on a slideshow of photographs they have taken on a digital camera. Frank is autistic and doing most of the editing work on the computer while the other children are excitedly chiming in with suggestions... the student who has been doing the editing has autism, and this was an area where he excelled (Puerling and Fowler, 2015).

- Is the experience of Caleb and Frank equal to the experiences of the others?

A useful website to examine the range of technologies to support Sensory and Physical Needs can be accessed via the link:
www.accessibility.com/blog/assistive-technology-for-physical-disabilities

- Take an example from the list of assistive devices and suggest how it would allow inclusivity in the life of an individual

References

Aitken, S. (2000). Understanding deafblindness. In: S. Aitken., M. Buultjens, C. Clark, J. Eyre and L. Pease (eds.), *Teaching Children who are Deafblind: Contact, Communication and Learning*. London: David Fulton Publishers.

Ayres, A. J. (1989). *Sensory Integration and Praxis Tests Manual*. Los Angeles: Western Psychological Services.

Bag Books (2011). *Bag Books: Training Notes*. London: Bag Books.

Bara, F., Gentaz, E. and Valente, D. (2018). The effect of tactile illustrations on comprehension of storybooks by three children with visual impairments: an exploratory study. *Journal of Visual Impairment & Blindness*, 112 (6), pp. 759–765.

Baranek, G. T. (2002). Efficacy of sensory and motor interventions for children with autism. *Journal of Autism and Developmental Disorders*, 32, pp. 397–422.

Breslin, L., Guerra, N., Ganz, L. and Ervin, D. (2020). Clinical utility of multisensory environments for people with intellectual and developmental disabilities: a scoping review. *Am J Occup Ther*, 74 (1), p. 12.

Broadbent, H., Osbourne, T., Rea, M., Peng, A., Mareschal, D. and Kirkham, N. (2018). Incidental category learning and cognitive load in a multisensory environment across childhood. *Developmental Psychology*, 54 (6), pp. 1020–1028.

Carney, R. N., and Levin, J. R. (2002). Pictorial illustrations still improve students' learning from text. *Educational Psychology Review*, 14 (1), pp. 5–26.

Case-Smith, J., Weaver, L. L. and Fristad, M. A. (2015). A systematic review of sensory processing interventions for children with autism spectrum disorders. *Autism*, 19 (2), pp. 133–148.

Chaitow, L., Rogoff, T., Mozgala, G., Chmelik, S., Comeaux, Z., Hannon, J., Lederman, E. and Myers, T. (2010). Modifying the effects of cerebral palsy: the Gregg Mozgala story. *J Bodyw Mov Ther*, 4 (2), pp. 108–118.

Champagne, T. (2006). Creating sensory rooms: environmental enhancements for acute inpatient mental health settings. *Mental Health Special Interest Section Quarterly/American Occupational Therapy Association*, 29 (4), pp. 1–4.

Costa, M. F. and Pereira, J. C. (2014). Correlations between color perception and motor function impairment in children with spastic cerebral palsy. *Behav Brain Funct*, 10 (22).

Davis, J. (2001). *A Sensory Approach to the Curriculum for Pupils with Profound and Multiple Learning Difficulties*. London: David Fulton.

Davis, E., Reddihough, D., Murphy, N., Epstein, A., Reid, S. M., Whitehouse, A., Williams, K., Leonard, H. and Downs, J. (2017). Exploring quality of life of children with cerebral palsy and intellectual disability: what are the important domains of life? *Child Care Health Dev*, 43 (6), pp. 854–860.

de Witte, L., Steel, E., Gupta, S., Ramos, V. D. and Roentgen, U. (2018). Assistive technology provision: towards an international framework for assuring availability and accessibility of affordable high-quality assistive technology. *Disability and Rehabilitation: Assistive Technology*, 13 (5), pp. 467–472.

Dunn, W. (1997). The impact of sensory processing abilities on the daily lives of young children and their families: a conceptual model. *Infants & Young Children*, 9, pp. 23–35.

Department for Education (2019). EdTech Strategy marks 'new era' for schools. [Online] Available at: www.gov.uk/government/news/edtech-strategy-marks-new-era-for-schools [Accessed 01. 02. 2023].

Department for Education (2020). Assistive technology (AT) stakeholder reports. Insights on the use of assistive technology in educational settings by pupils and students with special educational needs and disabilities (SEND). [Online] Available at: www.gov.uk/government/publications/assistive-technology-at-stakeholder-reports [Accessed 01. 02. 2023].

Efraimidou, V., Tsimaras, V. K., Proios, M., Christoulas, K.I., Giagazoglou, P. F., Sidiropoulou, M. P. and Orologas, A. (2016). The effect of a music and movement program on gait, balance and psychological parameters of adults with cerebral palsy. *Journal of Physical Education and Sport*, 31 (2), pp. 1357–1364.

Fava, L. and Strauss, K. (2010). Multi-sensory rooms: comparing effects of the Snoezelen and the Stimulus Preference environment on the behavior of adults with profound mental retardation. *Research in Developmental Disabilities*, 31 (1), pp. 160–171.

Fornefeld, B. (2013). Storytelling with all our senses: mehr-Sinn Geschichten. In: N. Grove (ed.), *Using Storytelling to Support Children and Adults with Special Needs*. Abingdon: Routledge.

Grace, J. (2014). Sensory stories: literature for service users. *Learning Disability Practice*, 17 (1), pp. 36–38.

Grove, N. (2011). Odyssey now: not only words – literacy stories. In: B. Fornefeld (ed.), *Multi-Sensory Storytelling: An Idea Gets Through*, pp. 123–140. Münster: LIT Verlag.

Grove, N. (2014). Personal oral narratives in a special school curriculum: an analysis of key documents. *British Journal of Special Education*, 41 (1), p. 624.

Guedin, N., Fluss, J. and Thevenot, C. (2018). Dexterity and finger sense: a possible dissociation in children with cerebral palsy. *Percept Mot Skills*, 125 (4), pp. 718–731.

Haring, N. and Romer, L. (1995). *Welcoming Students who are Deafblind into Typical Classrooms: Facilitating School Participation, Learning and Friendships*. Baltimore: Paul H. Brookes Publishing Co.

Heller, M. A. and Gentaz, E. (2014). *Psychology of Touch and Blindness*. New York: Psychology Press.

Hill, L., Trusler, K., Furniss, F. and Lancioni, G. (2012). Effects of multisensory environments on stereotyped behaviours assessed as maintained by automatic reinforcement. *Journal of Applied Research in Intellectual Disabilities*, 25 (6), pp. 509–521.

Hoare, B., Imms, C., Carey, L. and Wasiak, J. (2007). Constraint-induced movement therapy in the treatment of the upper limb in children with hemiplegic cerebral palsy: a Cochrane systematic review. *Clin Rehabil*, 21 (8), pp. 675–685.

Houghton, S., Douglas, G., Brigg, J., Langsford, S., Powell, L., West, J., Chapman, A. and Kellner, R. (1998). An empirical evaluation of an inter-active multi-sensory environment for children with disability. *Journal of Intellectual and Developmental Disability*, 23 (4), pp. 267–278.

Hulsegge, J. and Verheul, A. (1987). *Snoezelen: Another World*. Chesterfield: Rompa.

Kamei-Hannan, C., Chang, Y.-C. and Fryling, M. (2022). Using a multisensory storytelling approach to improve language and comprehension: a pilot study. *British Journal of Visual Impairment*, 40 (2), pp. 175–186.

Lambe, L. and Hogg, J. (2013). Sensitive stories: tackling challenges for people with profound intellectual disabilities through multisensory storytelling. In: N. Grove (ed.), *Using Storytelling to Support Children and Adults with Special Needs: Transforming Lives through Telling Tales*. London: Routledge, pp. 86–94.

Longhorn, F. (1988). *Sensory Curriculum for Very Special People: A Practical Approach to Curriculum Planning*. London: Souvenir Press.

Lotan, M. and Gold, C. (2009). Meta-analysis of the effectiveness of individual intervention in the controlled multisensory environment (Snoezelen®) for individuals with intellectual disability. *Journal of Intellectual and Developmental Disability*, 34 (3), pp. 207–215.

Mercieca, D. and Mercieca, D. P. (2009). Literacy with parents for children with profound and multiple learning difficulties. *Educational and Child Psychology*, 26 (4), p. 55.

Mills, C. J., Tracey, D., Kiddle, R. and Gorkin, R. (2023). Evaluating a virtual reality sensory room for adults with disabilities. *Sci Rep*, 13 (1), p. 495.

Mount, H. and Cavet, J. (1995). Multi-sensory environments: an exploration of their potential for young people with profound and multiple learning difficulties. *British Journal of Special Education*, 22 (2), pp. 52–55.

Nasuruddin, M. G. (2010). The confluence between arts and medical science – music and movement therapy for children with cerebral palsy. *Malays J Med Sci*, 17 (3), pp. 1–4.

Newton, G. (2012). The active learning approach: using the resonance board and the little room with young blind and multiply disabled children. [Online] Available at: https://nfb.org/sites/default/files/images/nfb/publications/fr/fr31/4/fr310416.htm [Accessed 01. 02. 2023].

Pagliano, P. J. (2001). *Using a Multisensory Environment: A Practical Guide for Teachers*. London: David Fulton.

Profound and Multiple Impairment Service (PAMIS) (2023). [online] Available at: https://pamis.org.uk [Accessed 02. 03. 2023].

Park, K. (2013). Interactive storytelling. In: N. Grove (ed.), *Using Storytelling to Support Children and Adults with Special Needs*. Abingdon: Routledge.

Parker, A. (2017). Considering a practical orientation and mobility framework to design communication interventions for people with visual impairments, deafblindness and multiple disabilities. *Perspectives of the ASHA Special Interest Groups*, 2 (3), pp. 89–97.

Pingale, V., Fletcher, T. S. and Candler, C. (2019) The effects of sensory diets on children's classroom behaviors. *Journal of Occupational Therapy, Schools, & Early Intervention*, 12 (2), pp. 225–238.

Pingale, V., Fletcher, T. S., Candler, C., Pickens, P. and Dunlap, K. (2022) Effects of sensory diets: a single subject study. *Journal of Occupational Therapy, Schools, & Early Intervention*, 15 (2), pp. 165–180.

Preece, D. and Zhao, Y. (2015). Multi-sensory storytelling in special school settings. *British Journal of Special Education*, 42 (4), pp. 429–443.

Puerling, B. and Fowler, A. (2015). Technology tools for teachers and teaching: innovative practices and emerging technologies. In: C. Donohue (ed.), *Technology and Digital Media in the Early Years: Tools for Teaching and Learning*. New York: Routledge.

Salavati, M., Rameckers, E. A. A., Steenbergen, B. and van der Schans, C. (2014). Gross motor function, functional skills and caregiver assistance in children with spastic cerebral palsy (CP) with and without cerebral visual impairment (CVI). *European Journal of Physiotherapy*, 16 (3), pp. 159–167.

Schweizer, M., Eylon, S. and Katz-Leurer, M. (2020). The correlation between rhythm perception and gait characteristics at different rhythms among children with cerebral palsy and typically developing children. *Gait Posture*, 82, pp. 83–89.

Shabdini, S., Azizi, M. P. and Peymani, J. (2022). The effect of sensory diet on the impulsivity of children with attention deficit hyperactivity disorder. *Journal of Modern Rehabilitation*, 16 (4), pp. 364–371.

Shamsoddini, A., Amirsalari, S., Hollisaz, M. T., Rahimnia, A. and Khatibi-Aghda, A. (2014). Management of spasticity in children with cerebral palsy. *Iran J Pediatr*, 24 (4), pp. 345–351.

Shapiro, M., Sgan-Cohen, H. D., Parush, S. and Melmed, R. N. (2009). Influence of adapted environment on the anxiety of medically treated children with developmental disability. *The Journal of Pediatrics*, 154 (4), pp. 546–550.

Steinbrenner, J. R., Hume, K., Odom, S. L., Morin, K. L., Nowell, S. W., Tomaszewski, B., Szendrey, S., McIntyre, N. S., Yücesoy-Özkan, S. and Savage, M. N. (2020). Evidence-based practices for children, youth, and young adults with Autism. The University of North Carolina at Chapel Hill, Frank Porter Graham Child Development Institute, National Clearinghouse on Autism Evidence and Practice Review Team.

Stephenson, J. and Carter, M. (2011). The use of multisensory environments in schools for students with severe disabilities: perceptions from teachers. *J Dev Phys Disabil*, 23, pp. 339–357.

Ten Brug, A., Van der Putten, A. A., Penne, A., Maes, B. and Vlaskamp, C. (2016). Making a difference? A comparison between multi-sensory and regular storytelling for persons with profound intellectual and multiple disabilities. *J Intellect Disabil Res*, 60 (11), pp. 1043–1053.

Unwin, K. L., Powell, G. and Jones, C. R. (2021). A sequential mixed-methods approach to exploring the experiences of practitioners who have worked in multi-sensory environments with autistic children. *Research in Developmental Disabilities*, 118, p. 104061.

Unwin, K. L., Powell, G. and Jones, C. R. (2022). The use of Multi-Sensory Environments with autistic children: exploring the effect of having control of sensory changes. *Autism*, 26 (6), pp. 1379–1394.

Urosevic, J. and Cross, L. (2003) Creating educational toys and activities for children who are blind or visually impaired. [Online] Available at: http://caseyscircle.org/downloads/Crafts4SpecialKids.pdf [Accessed 01. 02. 2023].

Watson, M. (2002). *Developing Literacy Skills through Multisensory Storytelling in Children and Young Adults with Profound and Multiple Learning Disabilities*. Dundee: University of Dundee.

Wheeler, L. and Griffin, H. (1997). A movement based approach to language development in children who are deafblind. *American Annals of the Deaf*, 142 (5), pp. 387–390.

Whiting, C. C. (2018). Trauma and the role of the school-based occupational therapist. *Journal of Occupational Therapy, Schools, & Early Intervention*, 11 (3), pp. 291–301.

Wilbarger, J. and Wilbarger, P. (2002). Clinical application of the sensory diet. In: Bundy, A., Lane, S. J. and Murray, E. A. (eds.), *Sensory Integration: Theory and Practice*. 2nd ed. Philadelphia, PA: F.A. Davis, pp. 339–341.

Young, Y., Fenwick, M., Lambe, L. and Hogg, J. (2011) Multi-sensory storytelling as an aid to assisting people with profound intellectual disabilities to cope with sensitive issues: a multiple research methods analysis of engagement and outcomes. *European Journal of Special Needs Education*, 26 (2), pp. 127–142.

Part III

Exploring Social, Emotional and Mental Health Difficulties (SEMH)

7 The underpinning theory and research evidence

Introduction

The SEND Code of Practice: 0 to 25 Years (DfE and DoH, 2015) states that some children and young people may experience a wide range of social and emotional difficulties which manifest themselves in many ways. These may include becoming withdrawn or isolated, as well as displaying challenging, disruptive or disturbing behaviour. These behaviours may reflect underlying mental health difficulties such as anxiety or depression, self-harming, substance misuse, eating disorders or physical symptoms that are medically unexplained. Other children and young people may have disorders such as attention deficit disorder, attention deficit hyperactive disorder or attachment disorder.

Learning objectives

This chapter will:

- Introduce you to discourses surrounding mental health and associated terminology
- Invite you examine underpinning theory and research evidence in relation to SEMH, attachment disorders and ADHD
- Introduce you to the aetiology of SEMH, attachment disorders and ADHD
- Help you to understand the importance of Adverse Childhood Experiences and trauma
- Invite you to review the belief that ADHD is a social construct

Key terms

Social, Mental and Emotional Health Difficulties, Adverse Childhood Experiences, mental health, mental ill-health, mental illness, well-being, trauma, attachment, Reactive Attachment Disorder, Disinhibited Social Engagement Disorder, mentalizing, epistemic trust, neuroception, Attention Deficit Hyperactivity Disorder, hereditability, neurobiology, neurotransmitters, cognition

DOI: 10.4324/9781003361084-11

Pause for reflection

- What do you think are the key issues to consider when examining the relationship between SEMH and SEND?
- Why has the issue of mental health become a prominent discourse?

Mental health, mental ill-health and mental illness

Mental health, like physical health, is not a fixed concept and can be affected by different factors, including life events such as relationship breakdowns, bereavement and work stress, as well as mental health conditions such as depression or anxiety. Mental illness refers to a diagnosable condition that significantly interferes with an individual's cognitive, emotional or social abilities – and is perceived as a positive state of well-being (Pilgrim, 2017) and associated with psychological, emotional well-being (Mental Health First Aid, 2014). Keyes (2002) suggested the renaming of mental health to imply positivity, proposing the 'promotion of' mental health. The World Health Organization (1948) placed mental health as a fundamental component of health, advocating that there is no health without mental health, with Jahoda (1958) proposing six indicators of ideal mental health personal attitude, self-actualisation, integration, autonomy, perception of reality and mastery of the environment. Keyes (2005) suggests that there has been a move away from such definitive categorisation and proposed the notion of 'lavishing' or the experience arising from a variety of stressors. Joseph and Wood (2010) state the fact that the absence of flourishing health increased the likelihood of depression and highlighted the risk of prolonged periods of mental ill-health which could increase the likelihood of developing into mental illness.

DSM-5 (APA, 2013) states that mental illness is distinct from mental ill-health, in that it lasts for prolonged periods of time and that it is generally considered to emerge from biological, chemical imbalances, infections, brain injury or defects. Stigmatisation surrounding mental illness has the potential for long-lasting damaging effects on the discourse of mental health, beyond the point of recovery. According to the World Federation for Mental Health (2011), individuals recovering from a mental health problem continue to have wider societal challenges, particularly around employment, housing, and general acceptance within the community. With respect to psychoses, for example, negative assumptions that such individuals are incapable of experiencing positivity have been challenged and it has been shown that they do have the ability to experience positive well-being (Mankiewicz, Gresswell and Turner, 2013).

Approximately 20 per cent of school children experience social, emotional and behavioural difficulties such as anxiety, depression and ADHD and this may rise to 50 per cent for pupils from socially deprived backgrounds (Cefai and Camilleri, 2015). The chances of experiencing mental ill-health are increased by children having more than five of the predicators which include poor communication skills, poor relationship with peers and teachers, low expectations, behaviour problems and parenting issues. According to the Department for Education (DfE) (2022), 258,441 pupils aged between 5 and 16 years are identified with PMLD as their primary need. Behavioural difficulties do not necessarily mean that a child or young person has a possible mental health problem or SEN.

Models of mental health

Various factors can be conducive to the development of a mental illness, including psychological, environmental and biological origins (Healthwell, 2023). Psychological elements which may influence the individual's behaviour include acute trauma experienced during childhood such as abuse and neglect, a significant early loss like the death of a parent and lacking the capacity to interact and relate to other people. Environmental factors include a maladjusted family life, drastic life changes, and cultural and social expectations. Biological influences include brain injury, infections which can lead to brain damage, prenatal brain damage and genetics. For many people, abuse or neglect in childhood, social isolation and disadvantage, work stress and redundancy, long-term health issues and the death of a loved one will be the most influential on behaviour (MIND, 2023). There are several models which have been applied to mental health and ill-health, including the following:

The **medical model** attributes mental abnormalities to physiological, biochemical or genetic causes, and attempts to treat these abnormalities by way of medically grounded procedures.

In the **psychodynamic model**, the core assumption of this approach is that the roots of mental disorders are psychological. They lie in the unconscious mind and are the result of the failure of defence mechanisms to protect the self (or ego) from anxiety. Problems are determined by the history of a person's prior emotional experiences, such as negative childhood experiences.

The **behavioural model** emphasises the role of observable behaviour and learning, while the cognitive-behavioural model suggests that mental ill-health is a result of errors or bias in thinking and explains how thoughts and information processing can become distorted and lead to maladaptive emotions and behaviour.

The **humanistic model** sees mental health problems as a signal that an individual is failing to reach his or her potential. The model emphasises present conscious processes and places strong emphasis on each person's inherent capacity for responsible self-direction.

The **social model** suggests that the ways in which societies are organised can be considered as causal factors in mental illness. People should not be held responsible for their behaviour because they are victims of society and that social forces are the most important determinants of mental illness.

The psychosocial model explains the causation of mental illness being a result of the interaction of psychological and social factors. Psychosocial causal factors include early deprivation or trauma, inadequate parenting styles, marital discord and maladaptive peer relationships.

The **family therapy model holds** the view that individuals with mental illness are the victims of a pathological family process. Attention is paid to family interactions, especially to alignments and discord, and the engagement and disengagement of the different group members.

Pause for reflection

- Why is it important that practitioners working with this primary area of need understand these models of mental health and ill-health?
- How might the underpinning assumptions impact upon how we support individuals who experience issues with social, emotional and mental health difficulties?

Well-being

There is little doubt that the concept of mental health is complex and it is a common misconception that mental ill-health denotes the absence of mental health or vice versa (Keyes, 2002). Well-being, closely linked to mental health, is equally complex, with no concrete definition and a plethora of suggested models (Dodge et al., 2012).

Bradburn (1969) moved away from the diagnosis of psychiatric cases to the psychological reactions of ordinary people in their daily lives. Numerous efforts to define well-being have focused on how it can be measured, but it remains undecided how it should be defined (Dodge et al., 2012). However, many researchers are now in agreement that well-being is a 'multifaceted construct' incorporating social, emotional and functional elements (Forgeard et al., 2011). Seligman (2002) incorporates positive emotion, engagement, relationships, meaning and accomplishment (PERMA), which are described as blocks that can be built up to achieve a thriving life (Seligman, 2011). The NHS (2022) suggests that there are five steps to well-being:

1   Connect with people and develop relationships
2   Engage in physical activity and be active regularly
3   Learn new skills to create a sense of achievement and develop confidence
4   Be altruistic and carry out small and large acts of kindness
5   Practise mindfulness and become more aware of the 'moment' and your thoughts and feelings

There are two principal ways of measuring well-being – objectively, based on indicators about people's lives, and subjectively, using people's own assessments of their lives. For example, subjective well-being is about people's own assessments of how their lives are progressing. It consists of two key elements, life satisfaction and the experience of positive and negative emotions – or 'affect' – at a particular point in time. Keyes (2002) investigated the concepts associated with subjective well-being and surmised that subjective well-being equates to happiness and human potential that, when realised, results in positive functioning.

The concern of individuals in the first approach is with their happiness and general satisfaction with life, whereas in the second approach individuals are more concerned about becoming well-functioning citizens. By contrast, a person is said to be languishing if they lack positive functioning and merely exist from day to day (Liddle and Carter, 2010). Individuals who are neither languishing nor flourishing are said to be experiencing moderate mental health. Languishing is a state of being that occurs at the lower end of the mental health spectrum. Individuals with the most positive state of mental health are at the higher end of the spectrum and are deemed to be flourishing with most people, having a state of being that is located between languishing and flourishing.

Adverse Childhood Experiences (ACEs)

Adverse Childhood Experiences (ACEs) can be described as potentially traumatic events that can have negative lasting effects on health and well-being and may include several maltreatment and/or abusive practices, as well as living environments that may be harmful to the child's development (Boullier and Blair, 2018). There are three types of ACEs: neglect, abuse and household dysfunction. Ross, Coambs and Johnson (2022) found an increase in the frequency of negative ACEs was associated with a decrease in secure attachment and an increase in insecure attachments. Toxic stress can change brain development and affect how the body responds to stress and are linked to chronic health problems, mental illness and substance misuse. Exposure to ACEs can impact upon the ability to recognise and manage different emotions, the capacity to make and keep healthy friendships and other relationships as well as difficulties coping with emotions safely without causing harm to self or others. The response begins in the amygdala, which is part of the brain that can be impacted by consistent stress as well as the prefrontal cortex and hippocampus (Rayner, Jackson and Wilson, 2016). The prefrontal cortex is linked to an individual's behaviour as well as speech and language reasoning (Fuster, 2009). Many individuals who have experienced ACEs develop Speech, Language and Communication Needs (SLCN) (Westby, 2018).

ACEs can cause a large amount of stress and can lead to trauma which is the type of response that we have to a traumatic event, which you feel overwhelmed or lack control over. Research has shown that 12.8 per cent of children between the ages of 5 and 19 have a mental health condition (Sadler et al., 2018). Although these are not all due to ACEs, individuals who experience frequent trauma are more likely to have poor mental health. The National Autistic Society (NAS, 2018), which references a correlation between mental health and autism, found around 20 per cent of autistic individuals also have depression. This could be due to views of peers or stress, but it could also be due to the differences in their brain structure and brain function. Two main types of traumas are acute trauma, usually a single incident, such as a car accident, and complex trauma, which relates to a reoccurring incident such as abuse and usually has more of a long-term impact on an individual's mental health. The 'fight, flight and freeze' response may occur frequently when someone has experienced ACEs. This response is a natural reaction to danger meaning that when it occurs, adrenaline and cortisol are released, leading to an increase in heart rate and a fight or flight response.

Pause for reflection

- Why is it important that practitioners working with individuals with SEMH difficulties reflect on the importance of early experience on later development, including adulthood?
- How could families be supported if Adverse Childhood Experiences (ACEs) have been identified?

Adverse Childhood Experiences, trauma and attachment

The interplay between childhood adversity and attachment is complex and will include socio-economic, intergenerational and psychological factors. Importantly, some adverse health outcomes for parents (such as problem substance use or suicide) will simultaneously act as risk factors for their children (Smith, Dalgleish and Meiser-Stedman, 2019). Secure and healthy relationships between caregivers and children are likely to provide protection from negative effects of trauma experienced in childhood. A secure parental attachment has been shown to help children effectively regulate emotional arousal and Weinfield et al. (1999) identify positive effects including the ability to build safe and secure relationships, and the establishment of positive self-esteem. Children who have been subject to trauma have certain imperfections in terms of developmental domains, particularly in the sense of social and emotional development (Cook et al., 2005). These include an inability to make and sustain friendships, being distant from or exhibiting oppositional behaviour towards parents, caregivers, and authorities and difficulties in developing trust, intimacy and affection.

Key research

Fonagy (2010) emphasised that the most destructive factor in an attachment relationship is trauma. Structuring of the brain will be delayed in terms of the development process and when children experience frightening events with their parents, they are likely to develop representations of them in their mind and develop angry and frightening figures leading to constant pain and bad feelings. Such behaviours conducted by the caregivers confront the children with a dilemma of how to safely approach or avoid the person they are attached to. Disorganised attachment appears to be related to more extreme traumas or neglect which brings together the characteristics of the avoidant and ambiguous strategies. Negative and pathogenic caregiving may result in seriously disturbed attachments both in infants and young children who may show very abnormal relational behaviours, namely emotionally withdrawn/inhibited or socially indiscriminate/disinhibited behaviours. There are significant positive relationships between physical abuse, emotional abuse, physical neglect, emotional neglect and sexual abuse sub-dimensions of childhood trauma and insecure types of attachment.

Activity

As described above, Fonagy (2010) suggests that the most destructive factor in an attachment relationship is trauma.

- Look back at the models of mental health described earlier in the chapter and suggest how these could be used to explain the causes and effects of trauma on attachment

---

Attachment

Attachment is a bond or connection between two people, such as a mother and their child. It is extremely important as it allow individuals to feel safe and secure within their environment (Prior and Glaser, 2006). Attachment-based relationships are established in the early months and become gradually more complex and sophisticated while developing towards adult maturity. The attachment behavioural system presents children with a clear survival advantage by maintaining a balance between exploratory behaviour and proximity-seeking behaviour. By the second half of the first year, infants have become attached to familiar people who have responded to their needs (Berk, 2013). From his research, Bowlby (1973) concluded that the primary caregiver has a particular role in providing the infant and child with a sense of safety: a secure base from which to thrive and flourish. He went on to argue that the quality of attachment between the primary carer and infant created an 'internal working model' (IWM) a mental model from which the child (and later adult) engages with the world. The suggestion being that the quality of the earliest relationship(s) will inform the way in which the child (and later the adult) not only relates to others, but also explores and engages with life's opportunities.

Bowlby (1973) posits that children develop beliefs and behavioural patterns based on the relationship they have with their primary caregiver (Bretherton, 1992), that makes the child feel safe, secure, and protected (Benoit, 2004). The attachment to the caregiver can be seen through the proximity-seeking behaviours by the infant toward the mother or other primary caregiver (Shilkret and Shilkret, 2011) as the child uses the caregiver as a secure base from which he can explore his surroundings and have a source of comfort (Benoit, 2004; Bowlby, 1973). The quality of this attachment is based on the responsiveness and attunement of the caregiver to the infant's needs and depending on how the caregiver responds, the child will learn to anticipate similar responses in the future and organise their own behaviours accordingly.

Ainsworth developed a technique for analysing the quality of an attachment and concluded with a categorisation of three types of attachment: secure, insecure avoidant, and insecure resistant or ambivalent (Ainsworth et al., 1978). Ainsworth and Bell (1970) assessed the attachment between infants and their parents through the 'strange situation', which was when they put an infant and their mother into a small room, then adding a stranger and monitoring the reaction of the child when the mother left them. This work was advanced by Main and Solomon (1986), who added a fourth category – insecure disorganised attachment. However, Chess and Thomas (1991) believed that we are born with one of three temperaments, which were: the 'easy child', the 'difficult child' and the 'slow-to-warm-up child'. They believed that an 'easy child' would adapt to people and certain environments easier, meaning that they would naturally have a better relationship with their parents compared to a 'difficult child' who would have intense reactions and often a negative mood.

Activity

There have been several researchers who have studied attachment theories, models and consequences of attachment. Research the following and identify their key ideas:

1   Freud
2   Harlow
3   Bowlby
4   Lenneberg
5   Ainsworth
6   Rutter

Categories of attachment

There are four patterns or styles of responding to distress that have been identified in infants; one is referred to as a secure attachment, while the other three are insecure attachments (Main and Solomon, 1990). Children develop attachment security when they perceive caregivers as empathic and continuously experience caregiver responsiveness (Bretherton, 1992). This style is considered organised as the child knows what to do when distressed, and the child goes to the caregiver for comfort and security and secure attachments are considered optimal for emotional development and retain stable views of relationships and their own sense of self-worth. If an individual has an insecure or disorganised attachment, then it means that they may not feel safe within their environment and cannot trust their parents. Therefore, they are usually very independent from a young age. On the other hand, it can also lead to them being clingy and wanting constant attention from their parents, as they may feel unsafe and cannot be sure that they will return (McLeod, 2018). Both insecure and disorganised attachment can impact an individual's social development as their ability to make and maintain relationships and trust with others may be affected.

Childhood insecure attachments are categorised into three subcategories: anxious, avoidant and disorganised. Children develop attachment insecurity in the context of unresponsive, inconsistent, abusive, controlling or neglectful caregiving (Shilkret and Shilkret, 2011). Insecurely anxious individuals may perceive intimate relationships as threatening and develop maladaptive interpersonal patterns to avoid feelings of vulnerability. The child organises their behaviour in a way that displays emotional volatility and extreme neediness, such as clinginess, to get the caregiver's attention. Individuals who develop an avoidant attachment have organised their behaviours when distressed to avoid their caregivers, who tend to ignore or become annoyed by the distress of the child and withdraw. The final insecure attachment style is disorganised. These individuals have caregivers who are frightening, distressing, and/or traumatising, and the child is unsure how to respond to the caregiver or what to do when he feels distressed. Through these relationship experiences, children form the IWM, which defines their self-image and shape expectations of care and stability in future relationships.

Pause for reflection

- Why is it important to understand that there are differing categories of attachment and their importance in understanding childhood experiences?

Fonagy et al. (2002) have reinterpreted attachment as relatively secure and relatively insecure. Furthermore, they argue that attachment has been re-envisioned from an emphasis on templates of relationships, fixed in early infancy, to a model that views attachment as the context provided by evolution for the development of interpersonal understanding. Fonagy and Allison (2014) argue that the sensitivity of the carer will allow the child to experience being recognised as an 'intentional agent' as well as facilitate their building of cognitive, social-cognitive and emotion-regulating capacity. Within this conducive environment the child develops epistemic trust in the carer and as the child grows their social interactions extend beyond the carer, to epistemic trust in others which facilitates learning from the social environment.

It was suggested by Riggs and Kaminski (2010) that childhood emotional maltreatment directly predicted insecure adult attachment. The self-trauma model presented by Briere et al. (2017) showed how trauma interferes with the development of a child, particularly his/her attachment system. They found that there were significant indirect effects of Disengaged Parenting (DP) on psychological symptoms through sexual and non-sexual abuse, as well as through attachment. They suggested that although child abuse has direct and indirect impacts on psychological symptoms, exposure to DP may be especially detrimental, both by increasing the risk of child abuse and by virtue of its impacts on attachment insecurity.

Mentalizing, attachment and epistemic trust

Mentalizing is the impulse to seek to understand, to imagine other people's thoughts. The mentalizing model is concerned with the caregiver's understanding and reflection on the infant's internal world involving reflection and self-reflection. It examines the relationship between attachment processes and the growth of the child's capacity to understand interpersonal behaviour in terms of mental states (Fonagy et al., 2002). This capacity to mentalize is a key determinant of self-organisation and affect regulation, and it emerges in the context of early attachment relationships. The understanding of others depends on whether one's own mental states were adequately understood by caring, attentive, non-threatening adults. Problems in affect regulation, attentional control and self-control stemming from dysfunctional attachment relationships are mediated through a failure to develop a robust mentalizing capacity (Bateman and Fonagy, 2010).

Meins et al. (2001) have sought to link parental mentalizing with the development of affect regulation and secure attachment. They concluded that maternal mentalizing was a more powerful predictor of attachment security than, say, global sensitivity and that mind-related comments by caregivers at six months predicted attachment security at 12 months (Meins et al., 2001). Impeding or distorting open reflective communication between parent and child may disrupt mentalizing. Disturbance of attachment relationships, by inhibiting the capacity for mentalizing, may disrupt key social-cognitive capacities and create profound vulnerabilities in the context of social relationships. Missing out on early attachment experience creates a long-term vulnerability from which the child may never recover – the capacity for mentalizing is never fully established, leaving the child vulnerable to later trauma and unable to cope fully with attachment relationships (Fonagy et al., 2002).

Neuroimaging studies have confirmed the association between attachment and mentalizing: the dopaminergic reward-processing system and the oxytocinergic system have been shown to play a vital role in establishing social bonds and regulating emotional behaviour. The role of the dopaminergic reward system in attachment behaviour is considered an evolutionary mechanism to motivate reproductive mating, maternal care and offspring survival: it leads individuals to seek close relations with other humans and produces satisfaction when close relations are achieved. Oxytocin is a neuroactive hormone produced in the hypothalamus and projected to brain areas that are associated with emotions and social behaviours. It plays an important role in the activation of the dopaminergic reward system and in the deactivation of neurobehavioural systems related to social avoidance. By attenuating activity in the extended amygdala, oxytocin also acts to neutralise negative feelings towards others and enhance trust. Oxytocin can inhibit hypothalamic-pituitary-adrenal (HPA) axis activity when the attachment system is activated: secure attachment leads to 'adaptive hypoactivity' of the HPA axis, which, in turn, reduces social anxiety (Ozbay et al., 2007).

Activity

Mentalization and the theory of mind describe metacognitive processes. Mentalization mainly concerns the reflection of affective mental states. In contrast, theory of mind focuses on epistemic states such as beliefs, intentions and persuasions.

- How do these two processes operate in autism and ADHD?
- What impact might these have on social interactions?

Neuroception and attachment

Porges (2011) emphasises the significance of risk to human survival and the way in which it is assessed (which he calls neuroception). His polyvagal theory concerns the individual's neurobiological defensive response to risk (such as fight, flight or freeze). If a secure base is not communicated by the primary carer (by means of facial interaction, for example), then the infant's neuroception may be impaired and they may not develop the required sophistication to assess risk in the social environment, which may lead to a heightened sense of fear and inappropriate defensive reactions. In extreme cases this may lead to psychopathology. Children who have experienced a lack of safety and attachment may have a faulty neuroception. They may find it hard to read safety cues and to feel safe and secure with others and may struggle with relationships. Developmental trauma can cause toxic stress, a strong, frequent or prolonged activation of the body's stress management system.

Overactivation of the amygdala region in response to threat in those with experience of childhood adversity has been identified (Mothersill, Knee-Zaska and Donohoe, 2016). For these individuals, this is often subjectively experienced as feeling more easily threatened or 'triggered' in a range of situations, including 'neutral' situations not generally considered threatening by others. Dannlowski et al. (2013) found that childhood maltreatment is associated with remarkable functional and structural changes even decades later in adulthood. As well as the emotionally triggering effects of childhood trauma, many affected individuals show difference in cognitive processing even when not currently stressed or distressed and that stress exposure may increase risk for serious mental health disorders directly via a 'cognitive' pathway that is additional to the affective/threat pathway (Myin-Germeys and van Os, 2007). Early life adversity may be strongly associated with cognitive and social-cognitive difficulties including emotion recognition, theory of mind and emotional self-regulation. Rokita et al. (2020) found that accurate emotion recognition, measured in terms of facial emotion recognition, was negatively correlated with greater exposure to childhood adversity and that having one's physical needs met is likely to represent a fundamental building block on which to build a secure base from which to explore the social world.

Reactive Attachment Disorder

Reactive Attachment Disorder (RAD) (ICD-11)
Characterised by grossly abnormal attachment behaviours in early childhood, occurring in the context of a history of grossly inadequate childcare such as severe neglect, maltreatment or institutional deprivation. Even when an adequate primary caregiver is available, the child does not turn to the primary caregiver for comfort, support and nurture, rarely displays security seeking behaviours towards any adult, and does not respond when comfort is offered (WHO, 2019).

Reactive Attachment Disorder (RAD) (DSM-5)
A consistent pattern of inhibited, emotionally withdrawn behaviour toward adult caregivers.
　A persistent social or emotional disturbance. The child has experienced a pattern of extremes of insufficient care (APA, 2013).

Disinhibited Social Engagement Disorder (DSED) ICD-11
Disinhibited Social Engagement Disorder is characterised by grossly abnormal social behaviour, occurring in the context of a history of grossly inadequate childcare (e.g., severe neglect, institutional deprivation). The child approaches adults indiscriminately, lacks reticence to approach, will go away with unfamiliar adults, and exhibits overly familiar behaviour towards strangers (WHO, 2019).

Disinhibited Social Engagement Disorder (DSED) DSM-5
A pattern of behaviour in which a child actively approaches and interacts with unfamiliar adults. The behaviours are not limited to impulsivity (as in Attention Deficit Hyperactivity Disorder) but include socially disinhibited behaviour. The child has exhibited a pattern of extremes of insufficient care (APA, 2013).

Activity

DSM-5 and ICD-11 recognise both Reactive Attachment Disorder and Disinhibited Social Engagement Disorder.

- What are the main differences between them and how would they be recognised in an educational context?
- How do these attachment disorders differ from the range of attachment issues more commonly seen in an educational context?

Attention Deficit Hyperactivity Disorder (ADHD)

ADHD is a neurodevelopmental disorder present from childhood involving distractibility, impulsivity and excessive motor activity often leading to academic failure and social difficulties, in comparison with other similarly aged peers (Laver-Bradbury et al., 2010). Hughes and Cooper (2007) refer to the following characteristics:

- Inattention is the ability to sustain attention with a focus on the activity
- Impulsiveness refers to actions carried out without reference to the consequences
- Hyperactivity refers to extreme activity, being constantly on the go, talking incessantly, etc.

However, Brown (2013) considers a change that renders this old definition of ADHD as a behaviour disorder as no longer tenable. He takes the cartoon character 'Dennis the Menace' as the old paradigm of an individual with ADHD – often restless, impulsive and hyperactive, lovable but frustrating his parents and teachers. The new character is overwhelmed by a syndrome of chronic difficulties in focusing, starting a task, sustaining effort, utilising memory and regulating emotions that chronically impair their ability to manage everyday tasks of daily life. Kewley (2011) defines ADHD as a medical disorder affecting brain dysfunction that impacts individuals' educational capabilities and performance. The disorder affects 5.3 per cent of children worldwide (Polanczyk et al., 2007), with 5 per cent of children in the UK having a diagnosis. More males are diagnosed than females in the ratio of 3:1 and ADHD continues to be a commonly researched condition (O'Regan, 2014; Cortese, 2012).

Because it affects home life and school, ADHD can have a significant impact on a child's academic success and their relationships. This can mean that children with ADHD may have few friends, be socially isolated and do little in the way of constructive activities; all of which can lead to a poor quality of life. Young people who are severely affected are more likely to develop antisocial behaviour, personality dysfunction or substance misuse in later adolescence and adult life. Over time, inattentive symptoms tend to continue and hyperactive-impulsive symptoms tend to reduce (Spencer, Biederman and Mick, 2007). Diagnosis is established by exploring the extent, severity and characteristics of symptoms, how and when symptoms developed, and whether other physical, mental health and/or learning disorders are present. There are reliable (semi) structured interviews that can be used to improve the accuracy of the diagnosis.

Diagnosis

ICD-11 (WHO, 2019) refers to ADHD as a persistent pattern (at least six months) of inattention and/or hyperactivity-impulsivity, with onset during the developmental period, typically early to mid-childhood. The degree of inattention and hyperactivity-impulsivity is outside the limits of normal variation expected for age and level of intellectual functioning and significantly interferes with academic, occupational or social functioning. DSM-5 (APA, 2013), states that ADHD is a neurodevelopmental disorder, with the persistent patterns of three areas, which can then have adverse influences in academic, social and professional functioning. Hyperactivity and impulsivity: Six or more symptoms of hyperactivity-impulsivity for children up to age 16 years, or five or more for adolescents age 17 years and older and adults; symptoms of hyperactivity-impulsivity have been present for at least six months to an extent that is disruptive and inappropriate for the person's developmental level. Inattention: Six or more symptoms of inattention for children up to age 16 years, or five or more for adolescents aged 17 years and older and adults; symptoms of inattention have been present for at least six months, and they are inappropriate for developmental level.

In addition, the following conditions must be met:

Several inattentive or hyperactive-impulsive symptoms were present before age 12.

Several symptoms are present in two or more settings, (such as at home, school or work; with friends or relatives; in other activities). There is clear evidence that the symptoms interfere with, or reduce the quality of, social, school, or work functioning.

Diagnosis results in one of the following presentations:

1   Combined presentation – all three core features present
2   Predominantly inattentive presentation
3   Predominantly hyperactivity/impulsive presentation

Activity

Many people view the benefits of ADHD as 'superpowers' because they are additional skills that their neurotypical counterparts do not have. These include hyperfocus, resilience, creativity, high energy and spontaneity (Medicalnewstoday, 2021).

- What is the importance of discussing such traits?

Kazda et al. (2021) carried out a scoping review of 334 published studies and found convincing evidence that ADHD is over-diagnosed in children and adolescents. They suggest that for individuals with milder symptoms in particular, the harms associated with an ADHD diagnosis may often outweigh the benefits.

- What are the benefits and 'harms' that they refer to?
- Identify research which supports this view

Aetiology of Attention Deficit Hyperactivity Disorder (ADHD)

Heritability

ADHD is prevalent in around 5 per cent of the world population. Heritability rates range from 75 per cent to 91 per cent, which points to a strong genetic influence. Correlational studies by Kuntsi et al. (2003) identify concordance rates of 0.86 for monozygotic (MZ) twins, compared to 0.47 for dizygotic (DZ) twins, with Tripp and Wickens (2009) suggesting that multiple genes have a moderate effect on ADHD. The identification of the exact genes is still challenging but a meta-analysis of genome-wide association studies has found no genome-wide significant associations. This, of course, does not suggest that ADHD has no genetic underpinnings, rather that there are several genes which have a low but significant effect (Faraone, Biederman and Mick, 2006). Linkage and candidate gene studies have identified chromosomes 0, 5, 12, 16 and 17, chromosomal regions 5p13, 1q22e25 and 17p11 genes. Also, because the stimulants that are given to 'treat' ADHD work by raising levels of synaptic dopamine, many studies have examined the association between ADHD and several genes involved in dopamine transmission, such as the dopamine D4 receptor (DRD4) gene.

Neuroanatomy

The biomedical model views ADHD as a treatable neurodevelopmental disorder tied to lower activity in parts of the brain important for working memory (Barkley,

2014). Proponents of the biomedical model point to visible differences in brain scans for individuals with and without ADHD to characterise the disorder. Initial investigations pinpointed significant differences in the frontostriatal circuitry of children with ADHD. The first meta-analysis of MRI structural findings in children with ADHD demonstrated that the brain regions showing the largest reduction in volume in ADHD vs. controls included the posterior inferior cerebellum and the corpus callosum (Valera et al., 2007). Chandler (2010) found brain volume, along with a reduction in grey and white matter in the prefrontal cortex and hypofunctional dopamine systems. Other areas identified include the basal ganglia and the orbital prefrontal cortex responsible for controlling attention and motor planning. The cerebellum, anterior cingulate cortex and the corpus callosum are underactive and caused by neurotransmitter dysfunction or missing synapses (Shaw et al., 2007).

Attention requires that the limbic system of the brain is functioning in a coordinated way. It suppresses distractions to allow concentration and access to the executive functioning part of the cerebrum (Sousa, 2001). Barkley (2014) suggests that there are three main networks that function differently in ADHD, the connection between the frontal lobes and the striatum that processes the way someone holds information, the connection between frontal lobes and the cerebellum, which creates difficulties with time management and co-ordination connection is between the frontal lobes and limbic system. Konrad and Eickhoff (2010) suggest that neural circuits dysfunction can cause attention deficiency, along with a reduction in sustained executive control, alerting and orienting. Blood flow within the brain regions is also implicated, with Buitelaar, Kan and Asherson (2011) suggesting that for a child who has ADHD there is a lack of blood flowing towards the prefrontal regions of the brain, leading to inattentiveness and a lack of focus. Their brain has smaller and less active regions, including the orbital prefrontal cortex and cerebellum, with these functional differences persisting into adolescence and adulthood.

Neurotransmitters

Cubillo et al. (2012) identified uncharacteristic dopamine levels leading to behavioural issues such as irregular self-control and concluded that ADHD was a complex condition involving several irregular neurological pathways within the brain. This is further supported by O'Regan (2014), who suggests that there is an imbalance of dopamine, with the involvement dopaminergic and adrenergic systems. Dopamine is involved in the area of the brain responsible for executive functioning, working memory and attention (Carr-Fanning and McGuckin, 2013). An imbalance of dopamine also affects the reward pathway within the brain with the consequence that the individual will crave for the 'dopamine rush', which is further reinforced. This is supported by Sikstrom and Soderlund (2007) who in their Moderate Brain Arousal Theory suggest that a higher level of dopamine is released in response to external stimuli. This leads to hyperactivity and impulsivity and hypersensitivity with the individual seeking out stimuli which are rewarding with low levels of dopamine resulting in inattention.

Activity

Use research evidence and the lived experience of individuals to answer the following questions:

- What are the issues concerning medicating children living with ADHD made by parents, medical practitioners and teachers?
- Why do more adults seek to use medication in reducing the effects of ADHD?

Cognition and risk factors

Martinussen et al. (2005) found that individuals with ADHD had issues with working memory, resulting in language learning disorders and a lower intellectual ability. Research into the cognitive abilities in children with ADHD has found that, due to the frontal lobes being less active, deficiencies in executive functioning occur. Executive functioning is linked to many behaviours, such as decision making, response control and planning. Although some believe that the working memory model has not been widely applied to ADHD, there is evidence that the central executive has an impairment due to focused attention, divided attention and switching at the subprocesses of the central executive. Barkley (2014) proposed an integrated model of executive functioning suggesting that neurologically based problems of response inhibition lead directly to problems in four major executive functions of the brain that are essential for self-regulation, these being working memory deficits, internalised speech and weighing up the implications of behaviour, difficulties in motivational appraisal, causing decision-making difficulties in planning an issue and reconstitution, which leads to an inability to plan new behaviours. Risk factors have also been implicated in the aetiology of ADHD, these include exposure of the foetus to smoking and alcohol consumption (Han et al., 2015), exposure to environmental toxins such as nitrous oxide and other greenhouse gases, which have been found to influence dopamine receptors (Fluegge, 2016), to inconsistency in love (Lewis-Morton et al., 2014), and diet. There is no evidence to substantiate the link between sugar consumption and ADHD (Barkley, 2014).

Activity

The debate surrounding ADHD as a social construction
Saul (2014) suggests that ADHD is not an entity but a cluster of symptoms that stem from more than 20 other conditions, including depression, anxiety, bi-polar disorder, and obsessive-compulsive disorder. He criticises the

catch-all nature of an ADHD diagnosis, which he believes corrals a lot of real conditions into one and the criteria for diagnosis are arbitrary and sub-jective. Brown (2005) suggests that despite the scientific research, scepticism remains, and that ADHD is a trivial problem that is often over-diagnosed and over-treated. Some argue that ADHD is not an actual pathology and ADHD diagnosis is a socially constructed explanation to describe behaviours that simply do not meet prescribed social norms. Stolzer (2009) claimed that millions of children were diagnosed with a disease for which there was no confirmatory evidence. Timimi and Taylor (2004) go further, calling ADHD a culturally constructed diagnosis and suggests parents use ADHD labels to absolve guilt or blame for poor parenting and that ADHD mis-diagnosis is a national disaster of dangerous proportions.

Russell, Moore and Ford (2016) suggest that teachers are key in referring children who experience symptoms of hyperactivity, inattention and impulsivity, with Singh (2011) suggesting that an ADHD diagnosis represents a set of de-valued behaviours. Research has shown that the UK education system prefers learners who are compliant, obedient and can maintain attention (Swanson, 2003). Children with ADHD, or ADHD traits, are likely to struggle to behave in this manner consistently (Singh, 2008). Some of the negative connotations relating to those with ADHD are developed through societal perceptions of the condition. Hawthorne (2010) talks about institutionalised intolerance of ADHD, stating that the social perspective of those who are diagnosed with ADHD is generally negative, considering their traits as undesirable and that society relates impulsive behaviour to unpredictability and non-compliance.

You have been asked to give a presentation to a teacher and parent group at a local school on whether teachers are too quick to jump to the label of ADHD when attention, hyperactivity and impulsivity are identified in a child. Think about some of the following issues in your presentation:

- Do teachers focus too much on behaviour at the expense of focusing upon attainment?
- Are learners and parents sometimes too quick to revert to the label ADHD to justify disruptive behaviour?
- Why might the focus be on hyperactivity and impulsivity, rather than inattention?
- How might a learner who has a diagnosis of ADHD be supported?

References

Ainsworth, M. D. and Bell, S. M. (1970). Attachment, exploration, and separation: illustrated by the behavior of one-year-olds in a strange situation. *Child Development*, 41 (1), pp. 49–67.

Ainsworth, M. D. S., Blehar, M. C., Waters, E. and Wall, S. (1978). *Patterns of Attachment: A Psychological Study of the Strange Situation*. New York: Lawrence Erlbaum.

American Psychiatric Association (2013). *Diagnostic and Statistical Manual of Mental Disorders*. 5th ed. Washington, DC: American Psychiatric Publishing.

Barkley, R. A. (2014). *Attention-Deficit Hyperactivity Disorder: A Handbook for Diagnosis and Treatment*. 4th ed. New York: The Guilford Press.

Bateman, A. and Fonagy, P. (2010). Mentalization based treatment for borderline personality disorder. *World Psychiatry*, 9 (1), pp. 11–15.

Benoit D. (2004). Infant-parent attachment: definition, types, antecedents, measurement and outcome. *Paediatrics & Child Health*, 9 (8), pp. 541–545.

Berk, L. E. (2013). *Child Development*. 9th ed. Boston, MA: Pearson.

Bowlby, J. (1973). *Attachment and Loss. Vol. 2: Separation, Anxiety and Anger*. New York, NY: Basic Books.

Boullier, M. and Blair, M. (2018). Adverse childhood experiences. *Paediatrics and Child Health*, 28 (3), pp. 132–137.

Bradburn, N. (1969). *The Structure of Psychological Well-being*. Chicago: Aldine.

Bretherton, I. (1992). The origins of attachment theory: John Bowlby and Mary Ainsworth. *Developmental Psychology*, 28 (5), pp. 759–775.

Briere, J., Runtz, M., Eadie, E., Bigras, N. and Godbout, N. (2017). Disengaged parenting: structural equation modeling with child abuse, insecure attachment, and adult symptomatology. *Child Abuse & Neglect*, 67, pp. 260–270.

Brown, T. E. (2005). *Attention Deficit Disorder: The Unfocused Mind in Children and Adults*. New Haven: Yale University Press.

Brown, T. E. (2013). *A New Understanding of ADHD in Children and Adults: Executive Function Impairments*. Hove: Routledge.

Buitelaar, J., Kan, C. and Asherson, P. (2011). *ADHD in Adults*. Cambridge: Cambridge University Press.

Carr-Fanning, K. and McGuckin, C. (2013, March). *Coping with the inclusion of ADHD: the perceptions and experiences of key stakeholders*. In symposium at the Education Studies Association of Ireland (ESAI) conference, Educational Policy in Changing Times: Consultation, Implementation and Impact. The Radisson Blu Hotel and Spa Limerick: Ennis Road, Limerick, Ireland.

Cefai, C. and Camilleri, L. (2015). A healthy start: promoting mental health and well-being in the early primary school years. *Emotional & Behavioural Difficulties*, 20 (2), pp. 133–152.

Chandler, C. (2010). *The Science of ADHD: A Guide for Parents and Professionals*. Hoboken, NJ: Wiley-Blackwell.

Chess, S. and Thomas, A. (1991). Temperament and the concept of goodness of fit. In: J. Strelau and A. Angleitner (eds.), *Explorations in Temperament: International Perspectives on Theory and Measurement* (pp. 15–28). New York: Plenum Press.

Cook, A., Spinazzola, J., Ford, J., Lanktree, C., Blaustein, M., Cloitre, M., DeRosa, R., Hubbard, R., Kagan, R., Liautaud, J., Mallah, K., Olafson, E. and van der Kolk, B. (2005). Complex trauma in children and adolescents. *Psychiatric Annals*, 35 (5), pp. 390–398.

Cortese, S. (2012). The neurobiology and genetics of attention-deficit/hyperactivity disorder (ADHD): what every clinician should know. *European Journal of Paediatric Neurology*, 16, pp. 422–433.

Cubillo, A., Halari, R., Smith, A., Taylor, E. and Rubia, K. A. (2012). Review of fronto-striatal and fronto-cortical brain abnormalities in children and adults with Attention

Deficit Hyperactivity Disorder (ADHD) and new evidence for dysfunction in adults with ADHD during motivation and attention. *Cortex*, 48 (2), pp. 194–215.

Dannlowski, U., Kugel, H., Huber, F., Stuhrmann, A., Redlich, R., Grotegerd, D., Dohm, K., Sehlmeyer, C., Konrad, C., Baune, B. T., Arolt, V., Heindel, W., Zwitserlood, P. and Suslow, T. (2013). Childhood maltreatment is associated with an automatic negative emotion processing bias in the amygdala. *Human Brain Mapping*, 34 (11), pp. 2899–2909.

Department for Education and Department of Health (2015). Special Educational Needs and Disability Code of Practice: 0 to 25 years. [online] Available at: www.gov.uk/government/publications/send-code-of-practice-0-to-25 [Accessed 25. 10. 2022].

Department for Education (2022). Statistics: special educational needs (SEN). [online] Available at: www.gov.uk/government/collections/statistics-special-educational-needs-sen [Accessed 10. 12. 2022].

Dodge, R., Daly, A. P., Huyton, J. and Sanders, L. D. (2012). The challenge of defining wellbeing. *International Journal of Wellbeing*, 2 (3), pp. 222–223.

Faraone, S., Biederman, J. and Mick, E. (2006). The age dependent decline of attention deficit/hyperactivity disorder: a meta-analysis of follow-up studies. *Psychological Medicine*, 36 (2), pp. 159–165.

Fluegge, K. (2016). The possible role of air pollution in the link between ADHD and obesity. *Postgraduate Medicine*, 128, pp. 573–576.

Fonagy, P. (ed.). (2010). Attachment and personality pathology. In: J. F. Clarkin, P. Fonagy, and G. O. Gabbard (eds.), *Psychodynamic Psychotherapy for Personality Disorders: A Clinical Handbook* (pp. 37–87). American Psychiatric Publishing, Inc.

Fonagy, P., Gergely, G., Jurist, E. and Target, M. (2002). *Affect Regulation, Mentalization, and the Development of the Self.* New York, NY: Other Press.

Fonagy, P. and Allison, E. (2014). The role of mentalizing and epistemic trust in the therapeutic relationship. *Psychotherapy*, 51, pp. 372–380.

Forgeard, M. J. C., Jayawickreme, E., Kern, M. L. and Seligman, M. E. (2011). Doing the right thing: measuring wellbeing for public policy. *International Journal of Wellbeing*, 1 (1), pp. 79–106.

Fuster, J. M. (2009). Cortex and memory: emergence of a new paradigm. *Journal of Cognitive Neuroscience*, 21 (11), pp. 2047–2072.

Han, J. H., Kwon, H. J., Ha, M., Palk, K. C., Lim, M. H., Sang, G. L., Yoo, S. J. and Kim, E. J. (2015). The effects of prenatal exposure to alcohol and environmental tobacco smoke on risk for ADHD: a large population-based study. *Psychiatry Research*, 225 (1–2), pp. 164–168.

Hawthorne, S. C. C. (2010). Institutionalized Intolerance of ADHD: sources and consequences. *Hypatia*, 25 (3), pp. 504–526.

Healthwell (2023). 5 Tips for mental wellbeing. [online] Available at: https://healthwell.eani.org.uk/healthtopic/mental-health/5-steps-mental-wellbeing [Accessed 12. 01. 2023].

Hughes, L. and Cooper, P. (2007). *Understanding and Supporting Children with ADHD.* London: Paul Chapman Publishing.

Jahoda, M. (1958). *Current Concepts of Positive Mental Health.* 1st ed. New York: Basic Books.

Joseph, S. and Wood, A. (2010). Assessment of positive functioning in clinical psychology: theoretical and practical issues. *Clinical Psychology Review*, 30, pp. 830–838.

Kazda, L., Bell, K., Thomas, R., McGeechan, K., Sims, R. and Barratt, A. (2021). Overdiagnosis of attention-deficit/hyperactivity disorder in children and adolescents: a systematic scoping review. *JAMA Netw Open*, 4 (4), e215335.

Kewley, G. (2011). *Attention Deficit Hyperactivity Disorder: What Can Teachers Do?* 3rd ed. London: David Fulton Publishers.

Keyes, C. L. M. (2005). Mental illness and/or mental health? Investigating axioms of the complete state model of health. *Journal of Consulting and Clinical Psychology*, 73, pp. 539–554.

Keyes, C. L. M. (2002). The mental health continuum: from languishing to flourishing in life. *Journal of Health and Social Behavior*, 43, pp. 207–222.

Konrad, K. and Eickhoff, S.B. (2010). Is the ADHD brain wired differently? A review on structural and functional connectivity in attention deficit hyperactivity disorder. *Human Brain Mapping*, 31, pp. 904–916.

Kuntsi, J., Eley, T., Taylor, A., Hughes, C., Asherson, P., Caspi, A. and Moffitt, T. (2003). Co-occurrence of ADHD and low IQ has genetic origins. *American Journal of Medical Genetics*, 124B (1), pp. 41–47.

Laver-Bradbury, C., Thompson, M., Weeks, A., Daley, D. and Sonuga-Barke, E. J. (2010). *Step by Step Help for Children with ADHD: A Self-Help Manual for Parents.* London: Jessica Kingsley Publishers.

Lewis-Morton, R., Dallos, R., McClelland, L. and Clempson, R. (2014). There is something not quite right with Brad...: the ways in which families construct ADHD before receiving a diagnosis. *Contemporary Family Therapy: An International Journal*, 36 (2), pp. 260–280.

Liddle, I. and Carter, G. (2010). *Emotional and Psychological Wellbeing in Children: The Standardisation of the Stirling Children's Wellbeing Scale.* Stirling: Stirling Council Educational Psychology Service.

Main, M. and Solomon, J. (1986). Discovery of an insecure-disorganized/disoriented attachment pattern. In: T. B. Brazelton and M. W. Yogman (eds.), *Affective Development in Infancy* (pp. 95–124). Westport, CT: Ablex Publishing.

Mankiewicz, P. D., Gresswell, D. M. and Turner, C. (2013). Happiness in severe mental illness: exploring subjective wellbeing of individuals with psychosis and encouraging socially inclusive multidisciplinary practice. *Mental Health and Social Inclusion*, 17 (1), pp. 27–34.

Martinussen, R., Hayden, J., Hogg-Johnson, S. and Tannock, R. (2005). A meta-analysis of working memory impairments in children with attention-deficit/hyperactivity disorder. *Journal of American Academy of Child and Adolescent Psychiatry*, 44, pp. 377–384.

McLeod, S. (2018). Mary Ainsworth The Strange Situation/Attachment Styles. [online] Available at: www.simplypsychology.org/mary-ainsworth.html [Accessed 26. 01. 2023].

Medicalnewstoday (2021). 6 strengths and benefits of ADHD. [online] Available at: www.medicalnewstoday.com/articles/adhd-benefits [Accessed 12. 01. 2023].

Meins, E., Fernyhough, C., Fradley, E. and Tuckey, M. (2001). Rethinking maternal sensitivity: mothers' comments on infants' mental processes predict security of attachment at 12 months. *Journal of Child Psychology and Psychiatry, and Allied Disciplines*, 42 (5), pp. 637–648.

Mental Health First Aid (2014). Breaking down barriers with Mental Health First Aid. [online] Available at: https://mhfaengland.org/mhfa-centre/blog/breaking-down-barriers [Accessed 09. 11. 2022].

MIND (2023). Mental health facts and statistics. [online] Available at: www.mind.org.uk/information-support/types-of-mental-health-problems/statistics-and-facts-about-mental-health/how-common-are-mental-health-problems [Accessed 02. 01. 2023].

Mothersill, O., Knee-Zaska, C. and Donohoe, G. (2016). Emotion and theory of mind in schizophrenia-investigating the role of the cerebellum. *Cerebellum*, 15 (3), pp. 357–368.

Myin-Germeys, I. and van Os, J. (2007). Stress-reactivity in psychosis: evidence for an affective pathway to psychosis. *Clinical Psychology Review*, 27 (4), pp. 409–424.

National Autistic Society (2018). Autism and mental health 2018 presentations. [online] Available at: www.autism.org.uk/what-we-do/professional-development/past-confer ences/mental-health-2018-presentations [Accessed 03. 01. 2023].

NHS (2022). Five ways to well-being. [online] Available at: www.nhs.uk/mental-health/ self-help/guides-tools-and-activities/five-steps-to-mental-wellbeing [Accessed 26. 01. 2023].

O'Regan, F. (2014). *ADHD*. London: Continuum.

Ozbay, F., Johnson D. C, Dimoulas, E., Morgan, C. A., Charney, D and Southwick, S. (2007). Social support and resilience to stress: from neurobiology to clinical practice. *Psychiatry*, 4 (5), pp. 35–40.

Pilgrim, D. (2017). *Key Concepts in Mental Health*. London: SAGE.

Polanczyk, G., de Lima, M. S., Horta, B. L., Biederman, J. and Rohde, L. A. (2007). The worldwide prevalence of ADHD: a systematic review and metaregression analysis. *Am J Psychiatry*, 164 (6), pp. 942–948.

Porges, S. W. (2011). *The Polyvagal Theory: Neurophysiological Foundations of Emotions, Attachment, Communication, and Self-regulation*. New York: W.W. Norton.

Prior, V. and Glaser, D. (2006). *Understanding Attachment and Attachment Disorders: Theory, Evidence and Practice*. London: JKP.

Rayner, G., Jackson, G. and Wilson, S. (2016). Cognition-related brain networks underpin the symptoms of unipolar depression: evidence from a systematic review. *Neuroscience and Biobehavioral Reviews*, 61, pp. 53–65.

Riggs, S. A. and Kaminski, P. (2010). Childhood emotional abuse, adult attachment, and depression as predictors of relational adjustment and psychological aggression. *Journal of Aggression, Maltreatment & Trauma*, 19 (1), pp. 75–104.

Rokita, K. I., Holleran, L., Dauvermann, M. R., Mothersill, D., Holland, J., Costello, L., Kane, R., McKernan, D., Morris, D. W., Kelly, J. P., Corvin, A., Hallahan, B., McDonald, C. and Donohoe, G. (2020). Childhood trauma, brain structure and emotion recognition in patients with schizophrenia and healthy participants. *Soc Cogn Affect Neurosci*, 15 (12), pp. 1336–1350.

Ross, D., Coambs, E. and Johnson, E. (2022). Trauma of the past: the impact of adverse childhood experiences on adult attachment, money beliefs and behaviors, and financial transparency. *Journal of Financial Therapy*, 13 (1), 4.

Russell, A. E., Moore, D. A. and Ford, T. (2016). Educational practitioners' beliefs and conceptualisation about the cause of ADHD: a qualitative study. *Emotional and Behavioural Difficulties*, 21 (1), pp. 101–118.

Sadler, K., Vizard, T., Ford, T., Goodman, A., Goodman, R. and McManus, S. (2018). *Mental Health of Children and Young People in England, 2017: Trends and Characteristics*. Leeds, UK: NHS Digital.

Saul, R. (2014). *ADHD Does Not Exist: The Truth about Attention Deficit and Hyperactivity Disorder*. New York: HarperCollins.

Seligman, M. E. P. (2002). *Authentic Happiness: Using the New Positive Psychology to Realize your Potential for Lasting Fulfilment*. London: Nicholas Brealey Publishing.

Seligman, M. E. P. (2011). *Flourish: A New Understanding of Happiness and Well-being – and How to Achieve Them*. London: Nicholas Brealey Publishing.

Shaw, P., Eckstrand, K., Sharp, W., Blumenthal, J., Lerch, J. P., Greenstein, D., Clasen, L., Evans, A. J., Giedd, J. and Rapoport, J. L. (2007). Attention-deficit/hyperactivity disorder is characterized by a delay in cortical maturation. *PNAS*, 104 (49), pp. 19649–19654.

Shilkret, R. and Shilkret, C. J. (2011). Attachment theory. In: J. Berzoff, L. M. Flanagan and P. Hertz (eds.), *Inside Out and Outside In: Psychodynamic Clinical Theory and Contemporary Multicultural Contexts*. 3rd ed. (pp. 186–207). Lanham, MD: Rowman & Littlefield Publishers.

Sikstrom, S. and Soderlund, G. (2007). Stimulus-dependent dopamine release in attention deficit/hyperactivity disorder. *Psychological Review*, 114 (4), pp. 1047–1075.

Singh, I. (2008). ADHD, culture and education. *Early Child Development and Care*, 178 (4), pp. 347–361.

Singh, I. (2011). A disorder of anger and aggression: children's perspectives on attention deficit/hyperactivity disorder in the UK. *Soc Sci Med*, 73 (6), pp. 889–896.

Smith, P., Dalgleish, T. and Meiser-Stedman, R. (2019). Practitioner review: posttraumatic stress disorder and its treatment in children and adolescents. *Journal of Child Psychology and Psychiatry*, 60 (5), pp. 500–515.

Sousa, D. (2001). *How the Brain Learns*. 2nd ed. New York: Corwin Press.

Spencer, T. J., Biederman, J. and Mick, E. (2007). Attention-deficit/hyperactivity disorder: diagnosis, lifespan, comorbidities, and neurobiology. *Ambulatory Paediatrics: The Official Journal of the Ambulatory Pediatric Association*, 7 (1 Suppl), pp. 73–81.

Stolzer, J. M. (2009). Attention deficit hyperactivity disorder: valid medical condition or culturally constructed myth? *Ethical Human Psychology and Psychiatry*, 11, pp. 5–15.

Swanson, J. M. (2003). SNAP-IV Teacher and Parent Ratings Scale. In: F. Aykr (ed.), *Therapist's Guide to Learning and Attention Disorders* (pp. 487–500). New York: Academic Press.

Timimi, S. and Taylor, E. (2004). ADHD is best understood as a cultural construct. *The British Journal of Psychiatry*, 184, pp. 8–9.

Tripp, G. and Wickens, J. R. (2009). Neurobiology of ADHD. *Neuropharmacology*, 57, pp. 579–589.

Valera, E., Faraone, V., Murray, K. and Seidman, L. (2007). Meta-analysis of structural imaging findings in attention-deficit/hyperactivity disorder. *Biological Psychiatry*, 61, pp. 1361–1369.

Weinfield, N. S., Sroufe, L. A., Egeland, B. and Carlson, E. A. (1999). The nature of individual differences in infant–caregiver attachment. In: J. Cassidy & P. R. Shaver (eds.), *Handbook of Attachment: Theory, Research, and Clinical Applications* (pp. 68–88). Guilford: The Guilford Press.

Westby, C. (2018). *Adverse Childhood Experiences: What Speech-Language Pathologists Need to Know*. Word of Mouth, pp. 1–4.

World Federation for Mental Health (2011). Mental health as a priority: adopting a holistic approach to patient care. [online] Available at:www.ijpcm.org/index.php/IJPCM/article/view/26/41 [Accessed 03/12/2022].

World Health Organization (WHO) (1948). Definition of mental health. [online] Available at: www.euro.who.int/__data/assets/pdf_file/0003/152184/RD_Dastein_speech_wellbeing_07Oct.pdf [Accessed 07/11/2022].

World Health Organization (2019). *International Statistical Classification of Diseases and Related Health Problems*. 11th ed.

8 The impact of Social, Emotional and Mental Health Difficulties on individuals and families

Introduction

This chapter examines the impact that SEMH difficulties may have on an individual and their family utilising a series of case studies from a range of contexts and ages. It will examine the discourses surrounding mental health, as well as aspects relating to attachment and ADHD. It examines the importance that early experience may have on later life and the impact that this may have on education, relationships, employment and health.

Learning objectives

This chapter will:

- Introduce you how early childhood experiences impact on the lives of children, young people and adults
- Invite you examine the relationship between mental health and SEND
- Introduce you to a range of issues arising from attachment issues and trauma which may influence behaviour in adult life
- Invite you apply your understanding of issues raised in this chapter to the lived experiences of children and adults through several case studies
- Help you to understand the importance of research involving individuals and families in relation to SEMH, ADHD and attachment

Key terms

ADHD, attachment, Social, Emotional and Mental Health, education, families, adulthood, health, employment, attachment-related trauma, alexithymia, depression and anxiety, addiction, eating disorders

---

Pause for reflection

- What is the importance of the change in emphasis from Social Emotional Behavioural Difficulties (SEBD) to Social, Emotional and Mental Health (SEMH) Difficulties?

DOI: 10.4324/9781003361084-12

Mental health

The definition of positive mental health as outlined by the World Health Organization (WHO, 2014) highlights key indicators of positive states of well-being. Indicators include consideration of how individuals manage and respond to 'normal' life stressors, their abilities to fulfil their potential, make positive contributions to their own communities and abilities to work productively (WHO, 2014, p. 1). However, SEMH as a distinct category is not recognised or listed within the Diagnostic and Statistical Manual of Mental Disorders (DSM-5) (APA, 2013), but difficulties which are broadly identified as SEMH-related are recognised under the umbrella terms of trauma and stressors, anxiety and depressive disorders. Neuropsychiatric conditions are cited as the leading cause of disability experienced by children and young people (WHO, 2022). Some of the listed symptoms used to identify such conditions also include those categorised as SEMH-related, for example, ADHD, mood changes, eating disorders, depression, anxiety, and substance misuse (Shenton and Turetsky, 2010).

Attainment in school

Students who present with difficulties which impact upon their abilities to regulate their emotional and behavioural responses in social contexts have been identified as being at a higher risk of exclusion from schools (Jull, 2008) and may impact upon their level of engagement. In comparison with their peers, children and young people who have emotional difficulties are more likely to experience additional challenges and longstanding academic difficulties and are also more likely to disengage from education and schooling altogether (DfE, 2012). Such pupils are also identified as more likely to be missing or lost within the educational and welfare systems. This is particularly the case during key educational transition stages (Visser, Daniels and MacNab, 2005) and many pupils with SEMH difficulties contribute to the category of Not in Employment, Education or Training (NEET).

Resilience theory offers insights into the difference between individuals who appear to have the capacities to cope with and bounce back despite adversity, and those who manage less well under equal or similar circumstances (Rutter, 1985). Fundamental to resilience theory is the idea of the existence of protective and risk factors (Rutter, 1987) which can either help to promote resilience (protective factors) or act as risks. The experience of cumulative risks is understood as contributing significantly to the adverse psychological and social development of individuals and result in SEMH difficulties (Brown, Khan and Parsonage, 2012). There is a level of ambiguity around definitions of terms and ways of measuring risk and protective factors (Shean, 2015); some argue that school and other life transitions which require psychological and social adjustments can be experienced as traumatic events and are therefore risk factors (Jindal-Snape and Miller, 2008). Additional risk factors include familial adversity, trauma, cognitive and attention difficulties, and social disadvantage. Positive educational experiences, educational attainment and a sense of belonging to a community such as a school are regularly cited as protective factors which contribute significantly to enhancing mental health (Vaz et al., 2014).

Activity

Many children and young people experience difficult or traumatic experiences during their childhood or adolescence. These experiences can have significant effects on mental health and well-being into adulthood.

Read the document 'State of a Generation' and research the impact of the following adversities on someone's mental health:

- Children who are refugees or asylum seekers
- Children whose parents struggle with their own mental health experience
- Looked-after children
- Bullying and cyberbullying
- Exposure to acts of violence in the community (e.g. bullying, conflicts between gangs, muggings or robberies)
- Hate crime or harassment related to learning disability

The document can be accessed via the link: www.mentalhealth.org.uk/sites/default/files/2022-08/MHF-state-of-a-generation-children-young-people-report-2019.pdf

---

SEMH and young people

There is a substantial body of research evidence to suggest that young people's Social, Emotional and Mental Health (SEMH) needs have a significant impact on all aspects of their life including their learning and progress through the curriculum, behaviour in school and attendance, further training and employment and general life chances. Social media and new technology are also linked to increasing risks of poor SEMH. In 2021/22, SEMH was the second most common type of need, after Speech, Language and Communication Needs with 208,916 (20 per cent of) pupils on SEN support having this recorded as their primary type of need (DfE, 2022).

Mental health and behaviour in schools

The DfE (2018) have published a document entitled 'Mental health and behaviour in schools'. It can be accessed via the link:

https://assets.publishing.service.gov.uk/government/uploads/system/uploads/attachment_data/file/1069687/Mental_health_and_behaviour_in_schools.pdf

Chapter 3 covers aspects such as:

1   Understanding the link between mental health and behaviour
2   Mental health problems in children and young people
3   Adverse Childhood Experiences (ACEs) and other events that may have an impact on pupils
4   Mental health and special educational needs
5   You are applying for a job as a teaching assistant or teacher in a local school and have been asked to give a ten-minute presentation on mental health. From your reading of Chapters 7 and 8, along with Chapter 3 of the document above, what key points would you include?

Indicators of difficulties

Children and young people with SEMH difficulties may display passive behaviours such as anxiety, being withdrawn, unable to make choices, low self-esteem, failure to engage and being unable to make and maintain friendships. They may display active behaviours which may be challenging such as non-compliance, mood swings, physical or verbal aggression, disproportionate reactions to situations and lack of empathy. Where pupils have certain types of need, there is an increased likelihood of mental health problems. Children with autism or learning difficulties, for example, are significantly more likely to have conditions such as anxiety. Children in need, looked-after children and previously looked-after children are more likely to experience the challenge of social, emotional, and mental health issues than their peers. For example, they may struggle with forming trusting relationships, social skills, managing strong feelings and coping with transitions and change. Emerson and Hatton (2007) found that compared to a child who does not have a learning disability, a child with complex SEND is six times more likely to present with mental health problems in their lifetime and are at risk of poor psycho-social and mental health outcomes. Nearly half of the female students and one third of the male students with SEND in their study had concern for their mental ill-health.

Having SEND should be added to the risk factors of mental disorders in school-age children identified and, furthermore, female students with SEND aged 14–16 warrant a specific focus. Evidence suggests that having a disability carries a greater chance of developing a mental health difficulty. Kaptein et al. (2008) estimated that the prevalence of mental ill-health problems in children with intellectual disabilities ranged from 30 per cent to 60 per cent, in comparison to the 14 per cent prevalence of mental health difficulties in the general adolescent population (Sawyer et al., 2007). The diagnosis of mental ill-health in children with complex SEND can be extremely difficult and there is a risk of under-diagnosis. Carers may lack the skills to identify symptoms of mental ill-health and not seek the appropriate support from others. This is a phenomenon known as 'diagnostic overshadowing' whereby symptoms displayed by the individual are attributed only to their learning disability and other possibilities of the symptoms are not considered and investigated. Difficulties in communication can also pose a problem to diagnosing mental ill-health. Employing a multidisciplinary approach to diagnosis to collate comprehensive information from parents, teachers, social workers and anyone else involved with the child or young person who knows them well is crucial. The most advantageous way to manage mental ill-health in a child or young person with complex SEND is to adopt a holistic approach, where the focus not only considers the needs of the person, but also the social and environmental influences in their lives.

Activity

We often read about co-occurring conditions in relation to SEND. For example, an individual might have a primary need with respect to SEMH such as ADHD, but also be identified as autistic.

- What would the impact be on a child and an adult of being diagnosed with ADHD and autism, with respect to education, employment and social aspects of their lives?
- If you were such an individual, a parent or partner, which organisations and services could you access for information and support?

Impact of ADHD

Characterised by prolonged symptoms of hyperactivity, impulsivity and/or inattention that interfere with daily life, Attention Deficit Hyperactivity Disorder (ADHD) remains the most diagnosed mental disorder in childhood (Danielson et al., 2018). ADHD is thought to originate in childhood and is increasingly recognised as a chronic condition that can endure across the life course.

Pause for reflection

- Do you think that schools focus too much on the behavioural characteristics of ADHD, at the expense of educational attainment?

Education

ADHD is associated with poorer classroom productivity, lower grade averages, lower grades on standardised tests, and higher rates of school dropouts (Calub et al., 2019). This may be due to differences in neuroanatomy or increasing focus on behaviour rather than learning. Academic interventions result in better performance when students are actively engaged compared to passive tasks requiring attention (Raggi and Chronis, 2006). Negative assumptions suggest that lacking empathy gives greater behavioural disruptions (Singh, 2011) and that learners with ADHD thought that they were viewed as 'stupid', felt teachers ignored or had given up on them but who also exploited their ADHD as an excuse for bad behaviour. Kwon, Kim and Kwak (2018) interviewed university students and reported their findings in four themes. The first theme was lack of a daily routine. University students with ADHD symptoms did not implement their plans well because of their inattention, impulsivity, and the lack of regularity within their daily lives. The second theme was unsatisfactory academic performance and achievement. Even if the students made plans to study in advance, they failed to prioritise and complete tasks. This resulted in unsatisfactory academic performance and achievement. The third theme was unskilled interpersonal relationships. The participants reported having extreme reactions in interpersonal relationships and experienced difficulties in forming and maintaining relationships because of this impulsivity. The final theme was continuous worry. This study found that although university students with ADHD symptoms tried to overcome these tendencies, they had high levels of self-distrust because of perpetually repeating cycles involving obsessing over past events and worrying about future failures.

Liu et al. (2018) found that children with ADHD displayed significantly more problems in all aspects of school functioning and more interference with classroom learning than those without ADHD. Evidence supporting a link between ADHD and social deficits indicates that impulsivity and aggressiveness directly contribute to negative peer nominations and poor friendship stability. In a study involving three European countries, Rodriguez et al. (2007) found that there was a significant association in all cohorts between core ADHD symptoms and scholastic impairment in reading, writing, and mathematics. Particularly, inattention was related to a two to tenfold increase in scholastic impairment. Keilow, Holm and Fallesen (2018) suggest that the effect of ADHD on educational achievement is likely not only driven directly by delayed maturation of the brain, but also by secondary effects on children's life and learning circumstances, a so-called double disadvantage of biological and social consequences of ADHD.

Gray et al. (2017) carried out a review which considered academic achievement and classroom performance and showed that higher levels of inattentive behaviour as rated by teachers are associated with lower levels of both standardised test scores and classroom performance outcomes and that teacher-rated inattention is significantly predicative of poor academic achievement. Sunde et al. (2022) reported that the ADHD deficit in school performance is large, apparent in all school subjects, and not easily attributable to other factors. This strongly suggests that ADHD symptoms are an important risk factor for poor school performance independent of sex, parental education, early school performance and other psychiatric disorders. However, Carrasco, Chuang and Tripp (2022) assessed the contribution of ADHD symptom severity, IQ, semantic language, age, and memory (short-term and working memory) to variance in academic achievement in two clinically referred and two community samples of children with ADHD. After controlling for estimated IQ, semantic language skills and working memory emerged as the most consistent predictors of academic performance and severity of ADHD symptoms explained limited variance in academic test scores.

Adults

Although there is some continuity of core ADHD characteristics, the manifestation of symptoms varies in a developmental manner. For example, whereas children with ADHD may experience difficulties across all core symptom areas (inattention, hyperactivity and impulsivity), adults with ADHD are less likely to have difficulties with problems such as overt hyperactivity (Weiss et al., 1985). Approximately 10 per cent of children in the United States have been diagnosed with ADHD, more than half of which will continue to report symptoms as adults (Biederman et al., 2010). Given this propensity to persist into adulthood, multidisciplinary research increasingly considers associations between childhood ADHD and adult outcomes, finding that ADHD is linked to negative outcomes across multiple domains. For example, in adulthood, ADHD is associated with lower socio-economic achievement; more motor vehicle crashes, criminal activity and substance use; poorer physical health; an increased risk for co-morbid mental health problems and suicide attempts and less social integration (Landes and London, 2021; Roy et al., 2020). Research consistently ties childhood ADHD to more relationship uncertainty and social isolation in adulthood (Michielsen et al., 2018). This is especially the case for adult relationships linked to intimate unions such as dating and cohabiting alongside marital unions and parenthood.

Adult diagnosis

Activity

For some people, adult diagnosis of ADHD can give an understanding of past behaviour. Watch the two videoclips about two adults' experiences.

Richard Bacon can be accessed via the link: www.youtube.com/watch?v=Df3LLls6VDk

Rory Bremner can be accessed via the link: www.youtube.com/watch?v=OiKs5ADJcAg

- You have an adult friend who thinks that they may have ADHD. What messages could you take from these two videoclips when you discuss the advantages and disadvantages of seeking a diagnosis?
- Research who they would need to contact, and the procedures involved in seeking a diagnosis

---

DSM-5 (APA, 2013) provides a list of 18 symptoms that are split between two clusters, one for hyperactivity-impulsivity and another for inattention (with nine symptoms being indicative of hyperactivity-impulsivity and nine symptoms indicative of inattention). Based on the number of symptoms endorsed for each cluster, individuals can be diagnosed with ADHD that is primarily hyperactive-impulsive, primarily inattentive, or a combination of hyperactive-impulsive and inattentive. For children younger than 17, a diagnosis of ADHD requires the presence of at least six out of nine symptoms of hyperactivity-impulsivity and/or at least six out of nine symptoms of inattention. Further, the symptoms must have emerged prior to age 12, must be ongoing and cause problems on a regular basis and must interfere with daily life in more than one context (i.e., cannot only interfere with school). In addition, the symptoms should not be better explained by some other psychiatric disorder. For those aged 17 and older including adults, the diagnostic criteria are the same as for children/adolescents younger than 17, except that only five out of nine symptoms (of hyperactivity-impulsivity and/or inattention) must be present.

Ginapp et al. (2022) carried out a review of qualitative evidence on the lived experiences of adults with ADHD. They reported a range of issues including aspects relating to diagnosis such as feelings of relief, identity changes including self-acceptance and emotional turmoil, feelings of chaos as well as disorganised lives were common and difficult to manage. There were reports of struggling with interpersonal relationships and feeling different from others. Stigma surrounding legitimacy of adult ADHD was common, but ADHD was seen as promoting spontaneity, creativity, energy, and resilience. Participants were often diagnosed only after their children were diagnosed. However, after receiving a diagnosis, relief was commonly reported initially. Adults noted that receiving a diagnosis helped explain previously seemingly inexplicable symptoms and feelings of being different and allowed for participants to blame themselves less for perceived shortcomings. Toner, O'Donoghue and Houghton (2006) identified that adults with ADHD live in a state of chaos, while striving for control, and they argue that the lives of these adults are constantly cycling through chaos and control, resulting in their leading a double life.

Aoki et al. (2020) identified six themes which emerged after diagnosis: difficulties in accepting the diagnosis, interest in ADHD, feelings of relief, identity concerns, dealing with symptoms, and acceptance of ADHD. Participants felt relieved after the diagnosis, as they realised why they had experienced long-term problems and incorrect labelling, gradually beginning to accept their ADHD symptoms and deal with them better. In a qualitative study into the experiences of women who were diagnosed with ADHD after the age of 60, participants reported experiencing peer rejection, feeling different, and a tendency to become advocates for others (Henry and Jones, 2011). Although they reported difficulties in work and relationships, they also described finding creative solutions to their attention problems. Diagnosis and treatment appeared to have assisted with self-acceptance and appreciation of the strengths of having ADHD. A commonly reported late step involved acceptance, both of themselves and their diagnoses, sometimes coupled with increased interest in researching ADHD. Young et al. (2008) found that participants engage in a review of the past, the emotional impact of the diagnosis, and consideration of the future. They also regretted that they had not been diagnosed earlier, largely because of the many years they had gone without understanding their condition or receiving treatment. Hansson Halleröd et al. (2015) found that there are major positive consequences of being diagnosed with ADHD, compared to the undiagnosed situation, but that it might lead to a wish for an earlier diagnosis that could have spared suffering.

Despite the negative effects of ADHD, some people diagnosed with ADHD do not necessarily regard themselves as being impaired. Sedgwick, Merwood and Asherson (2019) argue that some aspects of ADHD can be adaptive rather than impairing and that some adults may possess certain strengths or attributes that mediate and/or compensate for their ADHD-related deficits or impairments. These include divergent thinking, hyper-focus, being nonconformist and being adventurous. Brod et al. (2005) reported that adults with ADHD consistently reported an enhanced sense of creativity and energy that, if able to be channelled, allowed them to be highly productive and focused.

However, Bjerrum, Pedersen and Larsen (2017) reviewed published and unpublished qualitative studies from 1990 to July 2015. They found that adults with ADHD had issues in relation to interacting in social relationships, academic functioning and being part of the community at the workplace and performing work tasks. They worked harder to perform tasks and strived to be accepted and to be equal members of the community.

Health

ADHD is often underdiagnosed in adults which may be due to a lack of awareness, inadequate access to ADHD care, or that DSM-5 (APA, 2013) criteria has overlapping symptomology with other co-morbid neurological conditions. Additionally, adults may mask symptoms with have learnt coping strategies. Adults with ADHD have been shown to have poorer functioning, higher rates of anxiety, depression, divorce, unemployment, and criminal convictions. Lundervold, Jensen and Haavik (2020) suggest that substance use is particularly common in adults with ADHD. They found that the severity level of alcohol consumption and number of units consumed each time of drinking were associated with severity level of ADHD symptoms. This could be due to the emotional dysregulation which can cause avoidance behaviours to be a coping strategy. Bodalski, Knouse and Kovalev (2018) found that overreliance on avoidant coping is a common issue and may be directly influenced by core symptoms of ADHD. A large proportion of children and young people diagnosed with ADHD will carry persistent symptoms into their adult life. Whilst symptoms of hyperactivity can diminish overtime, inattention and impulsivity do continue into adulthood. This can severely impact their interpersonal relationships, work performance and academic functioning and successful transition to adult mental health services. This was highlighted in a longitudinal study conducted by Singh et al. (2010), whereby most services users faced poor planning, poor execution and poor experience when transitioning from child and adolescent mental health services (CAMHS) to adult mental health services (AMHS). Hall et al. (2014) found a shortage of commissioned services for adults with ADHD, along with transitions protocols lacking definition, poor care pathways and a failure to share vital information.

NICE (2018) suggests that individuals with ADHD would benefit from improved organisation of care and better integration of child and adolescent mental health services, child health services and adult mental health services. Furthermore, multidisciplinary specialist ADHD teams and/or clinics should be formed specifically for children, adolescents, and adults. Ayyash et al. (2013), highlighted the importance of designating a care coordinator to assess the clinical and non-clinical needs of each patient and ensure proper care is carried out. Also, a person-centred approach with tracking at each stage of their patient care, appropriate training for clinical staff, early access to diagnosis and engagement with other services was needed. High co-morbidity rates, changes in presentation of symptoms and lack of recognition mean many individuals can be mis-diagnosed or in many cases remain undiagnosed. Therefore, improvements to the way information is gathered and shared within referrals and awareness on diagnostic criteria would better support adults with possible symptoms of ADHD.

Pause for reflection

- What do you think are the issues surrounding medicating children and young people in relation to ADHD?

Employment

Brod et al. (2005) suggest that being productive or effective in accomplishing tasks was a challenge for all of the participants they interviewed, regardless of whether or not they worked. Productivity in everyday life was impaired due to procrastination, poor time management, disorganisation, inability to follow through on a task, difficulty learning or remembering new material, and trouble getting to appointments on time. As a result, the participants repeatedly indicated that they were not able to accomplish as much as they wanted. Adamou et al. (2013) identified difficulties ranging from the initial job search, the interview and in employment itself. For instance, adults may be disorganised when completing their applications and have difficulties concentrating which may lead to mistakes within the forms. If they do secure an interview, adults with ADHD face the decision to disclose their ADHD status. Although much of the research regarding ADHD focuses on the negative consequences such as performance in formal education and employability issues e.g., Kuriyan et al. (2012), some prominent entrepreneurs, such as the founder of IKEA,

Ingvar Kanprad and the founder of the Virgin Group, Richard Branson, have credited their ADHD symptomology as the driving force to their decision to become self-employed. Being self-employed, Verheul et al. (2015) argue, is not merely a career choice but a manifestation of entrepreneurship which is an essential instrument in the business cycle, creating jobs as well as innovation and economic growth of societies.

Working in areas of intrinsic interest, multitasking, and self-employment were reported strategies used to achieve occupational success. Lasky et al. (2016) found that in some contexts, participants described feeling better to focus and that their symptoms such as high energy levels became strengths rather than liabilities. Jobs for which they felt best-suited often involved stress or mental challenge, novel or varied tasks, physical labour, hands-on work, and/or topics of intrinsic interest.

In contrast, Schreuer and Dorot (2017) interviewed women with ADHD who described interactions with their workplace as confusing, overwhelming, and chaotic and perceived their ADHD as a significant obstacle to success in employment that also conferred some advantages. Occupational struggles are commonly reported, with many studies detailing participant underemployment or unemployment and high job-turnover rates. Difficulties with punctuality and keeping up with tasks and deadlines were reported to generate tensions in the workplace and participants reported frequently being bored and unable to stay focused on their responsibilities, with noisy workplaces promoting distractibility.

ADHD and families

Peñuelas-Calvo et al. (2021) state that ADHD has a significant impact on the parents' quality of life (QoL), family burden, and daily functioning of the family. This impact also seems to be related to ADHD symptom severity and that inattention and combined subtypes seemed to have a greater impact on the family unit than hyperactive subtype. Poorer quality of interaction, maltreatment, divorce and single parenting, and higher child media exposure were statistically significantly associated with an increased likelihood of later ADHD symptoms and diagnosis, and thus emerged as potential risk factors. These included parenting interaction quality (sensitivity/warmth, intrusiveness/reactivity, and negativity/harsh discipline), maltreatment (general maltreatment and physical abuse), parental relationship status (divorce, single parenting), parental incarceration, and child media exposure. All factors showed a significant direct association with ADHD outcomes, except sensitivity/warmth which had an inverse association.

Activity

Family functioning
The McMaster Model of Family Functioning proposed by Epstein in 1987 assumes that the basic function of the family is to provide appropriate environmental conditions for family members to develop in physical, psychological, social, and other aspects (Epstein, Baldwin and Bishop, 1983). The six dimensions are:

1 Problem solving – the family's ability to resolve problems at a level that maintains effective family functioning
2 Communication – the ability to communicate clearly and directly with other family members
3 Family roles – how families allocate responsibilities, clarity of household tasks and provision of resources
4 Affective responsiveness – the degree of the emotional response of the family members to stimuli
5 Affective involvement – the degree of concern and attention of family members to each other's activities and interests
6 Behaviour control – the ability of family members to set and abide by rules and standards of behaviour

More negative family functioning is linked with more child ADHD symptoms and behavioural problems of children with ADHD could be less severe in families with good family functioning. Good family roles and behaviour control are associated with controlled ADHD symptoms and these two dimensions of the model provide a structured environment, including consistent house rules, expectations, and consequences clearly understood by all family members.

- How could each of the other four dimensions from the model relate to a family unit that includes a child, young person, or adult with ADHD?
- If you were a member of such a family, which dimension(s) would be your priorities and how could the family work together to address the psychological and social needs of all the group?

Breaux and Harvey (2019) found that greater maternal overreactive parenting and life stress were predictive of more child ADHD symptoms. Greater child ADHD symptoms significantly predicted greater maternal life stress and depressive symptoms and lower warmth, controlling for child oppositional defiant disorder and parent ADHD symptoms. Thirteen parents of children with ADHD participated in two focus groups. Four primary themes were identified:

- The child's behaviour feels like a 'wrecking ball'
- Coping with the 'war at home'
- A divided family: 'relationships don't survive'
- Craving support: 'it's goddamn hard work'

Parents attribute their high stress to their children's behaviour, unmet needs for support, and social stigma (Leitch et al., 2019). However, Paidipati et al. (2017) found that caregivers believed in their child's ability for future success and happiness. They did not view ADHD as a hindrance or deterrent on their child's journey towards self-actualisation or self-fulfilment, but a challenge to be overcome. Kroeger (2021) reported that with respect to family functioning, individuals with ADHD report lower relationship quality and less relationship satisfaction in intimate unions (Bruner et al., 2015). Moreover, parents diagnosed with ADHD feel less close to their children, experience less happiness in their role as parents and feel more overwhelmed as parents than their undiagnosed counterparts. Studies also note that parents with ADHD are less involved and more impatient with their children relative to parents without ADHD. Park, Hudec and Johnston (2017) reported that children of adults with ADHD also are likely to have ADHD, and there is potential for parenting to alter the developmental outcomes of these children. In relation to their parenting style, they found that greater parental ADHD symptoms were associated with less positive and more harsh and lax parenting behaviour.

Parental ADHD symptoms have been associated with more self-reported negative parenting after adjusting for child behaviour problems. Song et al. (2021) found an expected negative association between family resilience and adolescents' conduct and mental health problems. Among adolescents with ADHD, those with low family resilience scores were 1.5 to 3 times more likely to exhibit concomitant problems with conduct, depression, anxiety, and substance abuse. Additionally, they found that adolescents with ADHD who had experienced four or more Adverse Childhood Experiences (ACEs) were more than twice as likely to have anxiety and nearly three times as likely to have conduct problems and depression than their low-risk no ACEs peers. Björkenstam et al. (2018) found that all childhood adversaries (CA) increased the odds of ADHD in late adolescence and early adulthood and that familial individuals with more than four CAs had a markedly increased risk for ADHD. Craig et al. (2020) carried out a systematic review on coping strategies of parents of ADHD children and found that used more dysfunctional coping styles than other parents. The most used strategy by parents of ADHD children seemed to be avoidant-focused coping which involves cognitive and behavioural efforts oriented towards denying, minimising, or otherwise avoiding dealing directly with stressful demands, and is closely linked to distress and depression. Parental avoidant coping in ADHD children appeared to be an ineffective long-term strategy for managing parenting stress. Avoidant-type strategies may keep parents involved in a cycle of self-blame, withdrawal, and internalised frustration, rather than freeing their energies for problem solving that could lead to enhanced feelings of competence and a greater sense of control.

Activity

Read the following case studies:

Jen is a 29-year-old woman. In any stressful situation, she fidgets and has a hard time sitting still. Due to this and having a hard time with time management and personal organisation, she is on her final warning at work, and she is about to be fired from her job. She is also having a difficult time in her marriage with her husband of one year because he is ready to have children, but she fears that she is too disorganised to be a good mother. This is due to chronically misplacing everyday objects like her keys and running late to appointments. Although she wants her work to be perfect, she is prone to making careless mistakes. The struggle for perfection makes starting a new task feel very stressful, leading her to procrastinate starting in the first place. Therefore, she has recently received several warnings from her boss related to missing deadlines for assignments and errors in her work, which has led to her acute fear of being fired. As her performance at work has plummeted and she has grown increasingly anxious and doubting of herself, she has grown more pessimistic about starting a family.

Ian, 11, lives with his mum, dad and his younger brother Saul, aged seven. He gets on well with his family, he loves his little brother and really likes learning. Ian attends the local primary school and will be moving up to secondary school within the next year. At school, Ian is struggling with his schoolwork and has fallen significantly behind in some subjects. There have also been some difficulties in friendship groups, and he is often involved in arguments in the playground. Ian is often restless and finds it difficult to concentrate, even on things that he finds enjoyable; for example, it is unusual for him to be able to sit and watch a film through to its conclusion. Some teachers have described him as attention seeking and describe him as a 'butterfly' when it comes to concentrating upon the task in hand. He is very creative and can often produce novel solutions to problems set in class.

- What advice could you give to Jen and her employer with respect to them working together to support the issues raised?
- How could Ian's family and his primary school collaborate on identifying the issues that he is having at school and at home?
- What could the secondary school and his family do to support the transition from his current school?

Attachment-related traumas

Attachment-related traumas originate from events where a frightening experience is accompanied by, or results from, the appraisal of loss, rejection, or abandonment by an attachment figure. These may include both the physical or psychological loss of the caregiver or extreme forms of separations from caregivers which pose a threat to survival, since the survival of the child is closely related to the presence of, and protection provided by, the parents. Although not considered as an actual threat to survival, attachment-related traumas in adulthood are detrimental particularly since the threat to self is accompanied by the threat of loss or abandonment by an attachment figure.

Kobak, Cassidy and Zir (2004) suggest four types of attachment-related traumas. The first type of attachment-related trauma is attachment disruptions, or unanticipated and/or prolonged separations involving very little communication where there is no common plan for reunion. The second one involves the events where the child is sexually abused by the attachment figure, which is particularly detrimental due to generating a dilemma for the child who is both in need of and is afraid from the attachment figure. The third type is the loss of an attachment figure. The fourth one is attachment injuries or wounds that arise from abandonment by a present attachment figure in a situation of urgent need.

Interpersonal childhood traumas (including physical abuse, emotional abuse, sexual abuse, physical neglect, and emotional neglect) have been empirically related to various symptoms observed in adults – which have no somatic explanation – such as chronic pain, headache, and attachment problems. Styron and Janoff-Bulman (1997) found that respondents who indicated they had been abused as children reported less secure childhood and adult relationships than their non-abused counterparts, were more depressed and more likely to use destructive behaviours in conflict situations. Erozkan (2016) found that the physical, emotional, and sexual abuse, and physical and emotional neglect subdimensions of childhood trauma were positively related to fearful, preoccupied, and dismissing attachment styles. Interpersonal abuse and neglect experienced in childhood imposes a risk for individuals in terms of attachment insecurity since it significantly disturbs psychological development such as the development of positive internal working models of self and other.

Children having been exposed to interpersonal abuse and neglect grow up with more negative self-models and higher attachment anxiety and other negative models such as greater levels of avoidance from attachment (Erozkan, 2016). Interpersonal abuse experience in childhood also generates a dilemma in which children rely on an expect nurturance from people by whom they are abused (Kobak, Cassidy and Zir, 2004). Main and Morgan (1996) suggested that traumas experienced in both childhood and adolescence with associated disorganised attachment result in the vulnerability of the individual to dissociative disorders and to dissociative reactions to traumas in his/her later life. Human beings who do not experience a sufficiently secure base develop insecure patterns of attachment, including negative internal working models (IWMs) of themselves and others, along with negative expectations regarding relationships. In adults, attachment disorders can do more than disrupt relationships.

Pause for reflection

- How could we research the impact of early childhood experiences in adulthood?
- What support could be offered for adults who have experienced trauma in childhood?
- What critical life events in adulthood lead to mental health issues?

Several studies have linked attachment disorders to other physical, mental, and social problems. These include alexithymia, depression, addiction and eating disorders.

Alexithymia

This is a subclinical personality trait in which individuals lack emotional awareness and find it difficult to identify, express, or even experience emotions. They may come across as being cold and distant, which increases their difficulty forming and maintaining relationships. As a personality trait associated with deficits in the cognitive processing and regulation of affects, alexithymia has been hypothesised to correlate with insecure attachment. Troisi et al. (2001) identified that alexithymic traits were more pronounced in those participants who had patterns of insecure attachment and who reported more severe symptoms of separation anxiety during childhood, independently of the severity of their current anxiety and depressive symptoms. Schimmenti and Caretti (2018) suggest it is very likely that the genetic predisposition to alexithymic conditions may be fostered by the presence of significant stressors in an individual's life that deviate or alter the capacities for emotional understanding and processing. Zdankiewicz-Ścigała and Ścigała (2020) propose that alexithymia appears as a variable which connects non-secure attachment with trauma, dissociation, and addiction. Bekker, Bachrach and Croon (2007) found that for men, anxious attachment had a stronger direct and positive effect on antisocial behaviour than for women, and the positive effect of anxious attachment on passive-aggressive behaviour was smaller for women than for men.

Depression and anxiety

Individuals with attachment disorders tend to internalise emotions, which makes them vulnerable to developing additional psychiatric problems and unresolved attachment has been found to have a significant association with depression. Insecure and disorganised attachment representations are associated with vulnerability to psychopathology in general, including depressive symptoms. However, studies assessing the link between insecure and disorganised attachment and depressive symptoms report inconsistent results. In a meta-analysis, Dagan, Facompré and Bernard (2018) stated that attachment representations, specifically insecure-preoccupied and unresolved, are associated with depressive symptoms in adulthood. Jinyao et al. (2012) recruited university students from Hunan, China with participants completing self-report measures assessing insecure attachment (i.e., anxious and avoidant attachment), hassles, anxious symptoms, and depressive symptoms. Additionally, hassles and symptoms of anxiety and depression were assessed once a month for the subsequent six months. They found that participants with high levels of anxious, but not avoidant, attachment reported high levels of depressive symptoms when experiencing high, as opposed to low, levels of hassles. Lee and Hankin's

(2009) findings suggested that insecure attachment may in fact act as a risk factor for, and not merely as a correlate of, both depressive and anxiety symptoms.

Addiction and eating disorders

From an attachment perspective, four mental processes might be directly affected by substance abuse. For example:

1   Exploration of the environment is reduced or distorted, or risks are taken that would never have been taken in a state of sobriety
2   Mentalisation, the exploration of the inner, mental world of oneself and others is reduced
3   Age-appropriate experiences in relationships often are inhibited or even prevented. For example, Thorberg and Lyvers (2006) found that clients (who were undergoing treatment for alcoholism, heroin addiction, amphetamine/cocaine addiction or cannabis abuse) reported higher levels of insecure attachment and fear of intimacy, and lower levels of secure attachment and differentiation of self, compared to controls. Insecure attachment, high fear of intimacy and low self-differentiation appear to characterise clients enrolled in addiction treatment programmes. Such characteristics may reflect a predisposition to substance problems
4   Affect regulation and reward might be replaced by substance abuse

Schindler (2019) suggests that based on attachment theory, substance abuse can be understood as an attempt to compensate for lacking attachment strategies. Her review confirmed a link between insecure attachment and substance abuse and results of longitudinal studies show insecure attachment to be a risk factor for and that continued substance abuse impairs the ability to form close relationships. Different patterns of attachment in different groups of substance abusers have been identified, suggesting different developmental pathways. For example, fearful–avoidant attachment was frequent in heroin addicts, while alcohol abusers displayed more heterogeneous patterns.

Tasca and Balfour (2014) investigated the hypothesis that attachment insecurity may confer risk for developing an eating disorder. They found that compared to controls, those with eating disorders had higher levels of attachment insecurity and disorganised mental states. Lower reflective functioning was specifically associated with anorexia nervosa. Attachment anxiety was associated with eating disorder symptom severity, and this relationship may be mediated by perfectionism and affect regulation strategies.

Activity

Read the following case studies:

Henry is six years old. He has just joined a new primary school. He was adopted by his dads as a toddler and they seem like a happy family unit. Recently, however, Henry's behaviour has become unpredictable, and he has hurt other children on more than one occasion. Henry seems quite self-reliant and can treat other children unkindly when they are trying to make friends with him. The other children are increasingly isolating Henry and avoiding working or playing with him. He is often alone in the playground and seems unbothered by this.

Jacinda is 19 and attends university. She is predominantly happy and enjoys her course. She had a difficult childhood, as her mother left the family home at an early age and her father, unable to cope, left Jacinda with her grandparents when she was four. Jacinda's parents came in and out of her life until she was 19, at which point she made it clear to both that she felt her life was better off without them. She has a good relationship with her grandparents, although they are both quite frail now. Jacinda has a tricky time with relationships. She has had partners, but often rushes into a relationship, only to cool things after a few weeks and then end things shortly afterwards. One of her friends observed that 'She wants to be loved, but then it all becomes too much for her and she just backs away.'

The SEND Code of Practice 0–25 (DfE, DoH, 2015) promotes the use of the 'assess, plan, do, review cycle'. This graduated response cycle can be used to meet the needs of children/young people.

- Research how this could be implemented with respect to Henry; who would be involved?

Jacinda is doing well at university and is achieving good grades in her first year. However, she finds making friends difficult and her 'doomed relationships' are having an impact on her studies.

- What do you think could be the longer-term impact of this on Jacinda's progress through the course and where might she go to seek advice?

References

Adamou, M., Arif, M., Asherson, P., Aw, T. C., Bolea, B., Coghill, D., Guðjónsson, G., Halmøy, A., Hodgkins, P., Müller, U., Pitts, M., Trakoli, A., Williams, N. and Young, S. (2013). Occupational issues of adults with ADHD. *BMC Psychiatry*, 13, 59.

Aoki, Y., Tsuboi, T., Furuno, T. *et al.*, Koichiro Watanabe, K. and Kayama, M. (2020). The experiences of receiving a diagnosis of attention deficit hyperactivity disorder during adulthood in Japan: a qualitative study. *BMC Psychiatry*, 20, 373.

American Psychiatric Association (2013). *Diagnostic and Statistical Manual of Mental Disorders*. 5th ed. Washington, DC: American Psychiatric Publishing.

Ayyash, H., Sankar, S., Merriman, H., Vogt, C., Earl, T., Shah, K. and Banerjee, S. (2013). Engagement of commissioners, primary and secondary care for developing successful ADHD services. *European Child & Adolescent Psychiatry*, 22 (1), 45–46.

Bekker, M. H. J., Bachrach, N. and Croon, M. A. (2007). The relationship of antisocial behavior with attachment styles, autonomy-connectedness, and alexithymia. *Journal of Clinical Psychology*, 63 (6), pp. 507–527.

Biederman, J., Petty, C. R., Evans, M., Small, J. and Faraone, S. V. (2010). How persistent is ADHD? A controlled 10-year follow-up study of boys with ADHD. *Psychiatry Res*, 177 (3), pp. 299–304.

Bjerrum, M. B., Pedersen, P. U. and Larsen, P. (2017). Living with symptoms of attention deficit hyperactivity disorder in adulthood: a systematic review of qualitative evidence. *JBI Database of Systematic Reviews and Implementation Reports*, 15 (4), pp. 1080–1153.

Björkenstam, E., Hjern, A., Björkenstam, C. and Kosidou, K. (2018). Association of cumulative childhood adversity and adolescent violent offending with suicide in early adulthood. *JAMA Psychiatry*, 75 (2), pp. 185–193.

Bodalski, E. A., Knouse, L. E. and Kovalev, D. (2018). Adult ADHD, emotion dysregulation, and functional outcomes: examining the role of emotion regulation strategies. *Journal of Psychopathology and Behavioral Assessment*, 41, pp. 81–92.

Breaux, R. P. and Harvey, E. A. (2019). A longitudinal study of the relation between family functioning and preschool ADHD symptoms. *Journal of Clinical Child and Adolescent Psychology*, 48 (5), pp. 749–764.

Brod, M., Perwien, A., Adler, L., Spencer, T. and Johnston, J. (2005). Conceptualization and assessment of quality of life for adults with attention-deficit/hyperactivity disorder. *Primary Psychiatry*, 12, pp. 58–64.

Brod, M., Adler, L. A., Lipsius, S., Tanaka, Y., Heinloth, A. N. and Upadhyaya, H. (2015). Validation of the adult attention-deficit/hyperactivity disorder quality-of-life scale in European patients: comparison with patients from the USA. *Attention Deficit and Hyperactivity Disorders*, 7 (2), pp. 141–150.

Brown, E. R., Khan, L. and Parsonage, M. (2012). A chance to change. [online] Available at: www.researchgate.net/profile/MichaelParsonage/publication/308385529_A_cha nce_to_change_delivering_effective_parenting_programmes_to_transform_lives/links/ 57c285e808aed96fbbb26b3a/A-chance-to-change-delivering-effective-parenting-p rogrammes-to-transform-lives.pdf [Accessed 01. 02. 2023].

Bruner, M. R., Kuryluk, A. D. and Whitton, S. W. (2015). Attention-deficit/hyperactivity disorder symptom levels and romantic relationship quality in college students. *Journal of American College Health*, 63 (2), pp. 98–108.

Calub, C. A., Rapport, M. D., Friedman, L. M. and Eckridge, S. J. (2019). IQ and academic achievement in children with ADHD: the differential effects of specific cognitive functions. *J Psychopathol Behav Assess*, 41, pp. 639–651.

Carrasco, K. D., Chuang, C. C. and Tripp, G. (2022). Shared predictors of academic achievement in children with ADHD: a multi-sample study. *Journal of Attention Disorders*, 26 (4), pp. 573–586.

Craig, F., Savino, R., Fanizza, I., Lucarelli, E., Russo, L. and Trabacca, A. (2020). A systematic review of coping strategies in parents of children with attention deficit hyperactivity disorder (ADHD). *Research in Developmental Disabilities*, 98, 103571.

Dagan, O., Facompré, C. R. and Bernard, K. (2018). Adult attachment representations and depressive symptoms: a meta-analysis. *Journal of Affective Disorders*, 236, pp. 274–290.

Danielson, M. L., Bitsko, R. H., Ghandour, R. M., Holbrook, J. R., Kogan, M. D. and Blumberg, S. J. (2018). Prevalence of parent-reported ADHD diagnosis and associated treatment among U.S. children and adolescents, 2016. *Journal of Clinical Child and Adolescent Psychology*, 47 (2), pp. 199–212.

Department for Education (2012). Pupil behaviour in schools in England. [online] Available at: https://assets.publishing.service.gov.uk/government/uploads/system/uploads/attachment_data/file/184078/DFE-RR218.pdf [Accessed 01. 02. 2023].

Department for Education (2022). Special educational needs in England. [online] Available at: https://explore-education-statistics.service.gov.uk/find-statistics/special-educationa l-needs-in-england/2021-22 [Accessed 21. 12. 2022].

Department for Education and Department of Health (2015). Special educational needs and disability code of practice: 0 to 25 years. [online] Available at: www.gov.uk/gov ernment/publications/send-code-of-practice-0-to-25 [Accessed 21. 11. 2023].

Emerson, E. and Hatton, C. (2007). Mental health of children and adolescents with intellectual disabilities in Britain. *The British Journal of Psychiatry*, 191 (6), pp. 493–499.

Epstein, N. B., Baldwin, L. M. and Bishop, D. S. (1983). The McMaster Family Assessment Device. *Journal of Marital and Family Therapy*, 9 (2), pp. 171–180.

Erozkan, A. (2016). The link between types of attachment and childhood trauma. *Universal Journal of Educational Research*, 4 (5), pp. 1071–1079.

Ginapp, C. M., Macdonald-Gagnon, G., Angarita, G. A., Bold, K. W. and Potenza, M. N. (2022). The lived experiences of adults with attention-deficit/hyperactivity disorder: a rapid review of qualitative evidence. *Frontiers in Psychiatry*, 13, 949321.

Gray, S., Dueck, K., Rogers, M. and Tannock, R. (2017). Qualitative review synthesis: the relationship between inattention and academic achievement. *Educational Research*, 59, pp. 1–19.

Hall, C., Newell, K. Taylor, J., Sayal, K. and Hollis, C. (2014). Services for young people with attention deficit/hyperactivity disorder transitioning from child to adult mental health services: a national survey of mental health trusts in England. *Journal of Psychopharmacology*, 29.

Hansson Halleröd, S. L., Anckarsäter, H., Råstam, M. and Hansson Scherman, M. (2015). Experienced consequences of being diagnosed with ADHD as an adult – a qualitative study. *BMC Psychiatry*, 15, 31.

Henry, E. and Jones, S. H. (2011). Experiences of older adult women diagnosed with attention deficit hyperactivity disorder. *Journal of Women & Aging*, 23 (3), pp. 246–262.

Jinyao, Y., Xiongzhao, Z., Auerbach, R. P., Gardiner, C. K., Lin, C., Yuping, W. and Shuqiao, Y. (2012). Insecure attachment as a predictor of depressive and anxious symptomology. *Depression and Anxiety*, 29 (9), pp. 789–796.

Jindal-Snape, D. and Miller, D. J. (2008). A challenge of living? Understanding the psycho-social processes of the child during primary-secondary transition through resilience and self-esteem theories. *Educational Psychology Review*, 20 (3), pp. 217–236.

Jull, S. K. (2008). Emotional and behavioural difficulties (EBD): the special educational need justifying exclusion. *Journal of Research in Special Educational Needs*, 8 (1), pp. 13–18.

Kaptein, S., Jansen, D. E., Vogels, A. G. and Reijneveld, S. A. (2008). Mental health problems in children with intellectual disability: use of the Strengths and Difficulties Questionnaire. *Journal of Intellectual Disability Research*, 52 (2), pp. 125–131.

Keilow, M., Holm, A. and Fallesen, P. (2018). Medical treatment of Attention Deficit/Hyperactivity Disorder (ADHD) and children's academic performance. *PLoS One*, 13 (11), e0207905.

Kobak, R. R., Cassidy, J. and Zir, Y. (2004). Attachment-related trauma and posttraumatic stress disorder: implications for adult adaptation. In: W. S. Rholes and J. A. Simpson (eds.), *Adult Attachment: Theory, Research, and Clinical Implications* (pp. 388–407). New York: Guilford Press.

Kroeger, R. (2021). Childhood mental health and adult family relationships: how ADHD shapes experiences with intimate unions and parenthood. *Sociology Compass*, doi:10.1111/soc4.12865.

Kuriyan, A. B., Pelham, W. E., Molina, B. S., Waschbusch, D. A., Gnagy, E. M., Sibley, M. H., Babinski, D. E., Walther, C., Cheong, J., Yu, J. and Kent, K. M. (2013). Young adult educational and vocational outcomes of children diagnosed with ADHD. *J Abnorm Child Psychol*, 41 (1), pp. 27–41.

Kwon, S. J., Kim, Y. and Kwak, Y. (2018). Difficulties faced by university students with self-reported symptoms of attention-deficit hyperactivity disorder: a qualitative study. *Child and Adolescent Psychiatry and Mental Health*, 12, 12.

Landes, S. D. and London, A. S. (2021). Self-reported ADHD and adult health in the United States. *Journal of Attention Disorders*, 25 (1), pp. 3–13.

Lasky, A. K., Weisner, T. S., Jensen, P. S., Hinshaw, S. P., Hechtman, L., Arnold, L. E., W Murray, D. and Swanson, J. M. (2016). ADHD in context: young adults' reports of the impact of occupational environment on the manifestation of ADHD. *Social Science & Medicine*, 161, pp. 160–168.

Lee, A. and Hankin, B. L. (2009). Insecure attachment, dysfunctional attitudes, and low self-esteem predicting prospective symptoms of depression and anxiety during adolescence. *Journal of Clinical Child and Adolescent Psychology*, 38 (2), pp. 219–231.

Leitch, S., Sciberras, E., Post, B., Gerner, B., Rinehart, N., Nicholson, J. M. and Evans, S. (2019). Experience of stress in parents of children with ADHD: a qualitative study. *International Journal of Qualitative Studies on Health and Well-being*, 14 (1), 1690091.

Liu, A., Xu, Y., Yan, Q. and Tong, L. (2018). The prevalence of attention deficit/hyperactivity disorder among chinese children and adolescents. *Sci Rep*, 8, 11169.

Lundervold, A. J., Jensen, D. A. and Haavik, J. (2020). Insomnia, alcohol consumption and ADHD symptoms in adults. *Frontiers in Psychology*, 11, 1150.

Main, M. and Morgan, H. (1996). Disorganization and disorientation in infant Strange Situation behavior: phenotypic resemblance to dissociative states? In: L. Michelson and W. Ray (eds.), *Handbook of Dissociation*. New York: Plenum Press, pp. 107–137.

Michielsen, M., de Kruif, J. T. C. M., Comijs, H. C., van Mierlo, S., Semeijn, E. J., Beekman, A. T. F., Deeg, D. J. H. and Kooij, J. J. S. (2018). The burden of ADHD in older adults: a qualitative study. *Journal of Attention Disorders*, 22 (6), pp. 591–600.

National Institute for Health and Care Excellence (NICE) (2018). Attention deficit hyperactivity disorder: diagnosis and management. [online] Available at: www.nice.org.uk/guidance/ng87 [Accessed 20. 11. 2022].

Paidipati, C. P., Brawner, B., Eiraldi, R. and Deatrick, J. A. (2017). Parent and family processes related to ADHD management in ethnically diverse youth. *Journal of the American Psychiatric Nurses Association*, 23 (2), pp. 90–112.

Park, J. L., Hudec, K. L. and Johnston, C. (2017). Parental ADHD symptoms and parenting behaviors: a meta-analytic review. *Clinical Psychology Review*, 56, pp. 25–39.

Peñuelas-Calvo, I., Palomar-Ciria, N., Porras-Segovia, A., Miguélez-Fernández, C., Baltasar-Tello, I., Perez- Colmenero, S., Delgado-Gómez, D., Carballo, J. J. and Baca-García, E. (2021). Impact of ADHD symptoms on family functioning, family burden and parents' quality of life in a hospital area in Spain. *The European Journal of Psychiatry*, 35 (3), pp. 166–172.

Raggi, V. L. and Chronis, A. M. (2006). Interventions to address the academic impairment of children and adolescents with ADHD. *Clinical Child and Family Psychology Review*, 9, pp. 85–111.

Roy, A., Ferraz Dos Santos, B., Rompré, P. and Nishio, C. (2020). Dental malocclusion among children with attention deficit hyperactivity disorder. *American Journal of Orthodontics and Dentofacial Orthopaedics*, 158 (5), 694–699.

Rodriguez, A., Järvelin, M. R., Taanila, A., Miettunen, J., Moilanen, I., Henriksen, T., Pietiläinen, K., Ebeling, H., Kotimaa, A., Linnet, K. and Olsen, J. (2007). Do inattention and hyperactivity symptoms equal scholastic impairment? Evidence from three European cohorts. *BMC Public Health*, 7, 327.

Rutter, M. (1985). Resilience in the face of adversity: protective factors and resistance to psychiatric disorder. *The British Journal of Psychiatry*, 147, pp. 598–611.

Rutter, M. (1987). Psychosocial resilience and protective mechanisms. *The American Journal of Orthopsychiatry*, 57 (3), pp. 316–331.

Sawyer, S. M., Drew, S., Yeo, M. S. and Britto, M. T. (2007). Adolescents with a chronic condition: challenges living, challenges treating. *The Lancet*, 369 (9571), pp. 1481–1489.

Schimmenti, A. and Caretti, V. (2018). Attachment, trauma, and alexithymia. In: O. Luminet, R. M. Bagby and G. J. Taylor (eds.), *Alexithymia: Advances in Research, Theory, and Clinical Practice* (pp. 127–141). Cambridge: Cambridge University Press.

Schindler, A. (2019). Attachment and substance use disorders-theoretical models, empirical evidence, and implications for treatment. *Frontiers in Psychiatry*, 10, 727.

Schreuer, N. and Dorot, R. (2017). Experiences of employed women with attention deficit hyperactive disorder: a phenomenological study. *Work: Journal of Prevention, Assessment & Rehabilitation*, 56 (3), pp. 429–441.

Sedgwick, J. A., Merwood, A. and Asherson, P. (2019). The positive aspects of attention deficit hyperactivity disorder: a qualitative investigation of successful adults with ADHD . *Attention Deficit and Hyperactivity Disorders*, 11 (3), pp. 241–253.

Shean, M. (2015). Current theories relating to resilience and young people: a literature review, Victorian Health Promotion Foundation [online]. Available at: https://evi denceforlearning.org.au [Accessed 01. 02. 2023].

Shenton, M. E. and Turetsky, B. I. (eds.) (2010) Index. In: *Understanding Neuropsychiatric Disorders: Insights from Neuroimaging.* Cambridge: Cambridge University Press, pp. 559–575.

Singh, I. (2011). A disorder of anger and aggression: children's perspectives on attention deficit/hyperactivity disorder in the UK. *Soc Sci Med*, 73 (6), pp. 889–896.

Singh, S. P., Paul, M., Ford, T., Kramer, T., Weaver, T., McLaren, S., Hovish, K., Islam, Z., Belling, R. and White, S. (2010). Process, outcome and experience of transition from child to adult mental healthcare: multiperspective study. *The British Journal of Psychiatry*, 197 (4), pp. 305–312.

Song, P., Zha, M., Yang, Q., Zhang, Y., Li, X. and Rudan, I. (2021). The prevalence of adult attention-deficit hyperactivity disorder: a global systematic review and meta-analysis. *Journal of Global Health*, 11, 04009.

Styron, T. and Janoff-Bulman, R. (1997). Childhood attachment and abuse: long-term effects on adult attachment, depression, and conflict resolution. *Child Abuse & Neglect*, 21 (10), pp. 1015–1023.

Sunde, H. F., Kleppestø, T. H., Gustavson, K., Nordmo, M., Reme, B.-A. and Torvik, F. A. (2022). The ADHD deficit in school performance across sex and parental education:

a prospective sibling-comparison register study of 344,152 Norwegian adolescents. *JCPP Advances*, 2 (1), e12064.

Tasca, G. A. and Balfour, L. (2014). Eating disorders and attachment: a contemporary psychodynamic perspective. *Psychodynamic Psychiatry*, 42 (2), pp. 257–276.

Thorberg, F. A. and Lyvers, M. (2006). Attachment, fear of intimacy and differentiation of self among clients in substance disorder treatment facilities. *Addict Behav*, 31 (4), pp. 732–327.

Toner, M., O'Donoghue, T. and Houghton, S. (2006). Living in chaos and striving for control: how adults with Attention Deficit Hyperactivity Disorder deal with their disorder. *International Journal of Disability, Development and Education*, 53 (2), pp. 247–261.

Troisi, A., D'Argenio, A., Peracchio, F. and Petti, P. (2001). Insecure attachment and alexithymia in young men with mood symptoms. *The Journal of Nervous and Mental Disease*, 189, pp. 311–316.

Vaz, S., Parsons, R., Falkmer, T., Passmore, A. E. and Falkmer, M. (2014). The impact of personal background and school contextual factors on academic competence and mental health functioning across the primary-secondary school transition. *PLoS One*, 9 (3), e89874.

Verheul, I., Block, J., Burmeister-Lamp, K., Thurik, R., Tiemeier, H. and Turturea, R. (2015). ADHD-like behavior and entrepreneurial intentions. *Small Bus Econ*, 45, pp. 85–101.

Visser, J., Daniels, H. and Macnab, N. (2005). Missing. *Emotional and Behavioural Difficulties*, 10 (1), pp. 43–54.

Weiss, G., Hechtman, L., Milroy, T. and Perlman, T. (1985). Psychiatric status of hyperactives as adults: a controlled prospective 15-year follow-up of 63 hyperactive children. *Journal of the American Academy of Child Psychiatry*, 24 (2), pp. 211–220.

World Health Organization (2014). Social determinants of mental health. [online] Available at: https://apps.who.int/iris/bitstream/handle/10665/112828/9789241506809_eng.pdf [Accessed 01. 02. 2023].

World Health Organization (2019). *International Statistical Classification of Diseases and Related Health Problems*. 11th ed.

World Health Organization (2022). Mental Disorders. [online] Available at: www.who.int/news-room/fact-sheets/detail/mental-disorders [Accessed 01. 02. 2023].

Young, S., Bramham, J., Gray, K. and Rose, E. (2008). The experience of receiving a diagnosis and treatment of ADHD in adulthood: a qualitative study of clinically referred patients using interpretative phenomenological analysis. *Journal of Attention Disorders*, 11 (4), pp. 493–503.

Zdankiewicz-Ścigała, E. and Ścigała, D. K. (2020). Attachment style, early childhood trauma, alexithymia, and dissociation among persons addicted to alcohol: structural equation model of dependencies. *Frontiers in Psychology*, 10, 2957.

9 Pedagogical approaches to support these difficulties

Introduction

This chapter explores approaches to support issues associated with Social, Emotional and Mental Health (SEMH). There are several websites, organisations and textbooks which identify a range of approaches in relation to SEMH. This chapter will instead focus on the theoretical underpinning, research studies and evidence-based research and practice, for some of the main approaches used in an educational context. It will signpost you to videoclips showing how the approach is being used in practice as well as case studies and invite you to find out about past and contemporary government policies in this area. It must be remembered that although an approach is identified in a specific chapter, it can be used in other areas of need.

Learning objectives

This chapter will:

- Introduce you to a number of specific approaches which can be used to support Social, Mental and Emotional Health difficulties
- Invite you examine underpinning theory and research evidence in relation to approaches related to this area
- Invite you to research polices related to Social, Emotional and Mental Health difficulties
- Help you to understand how these approaches can support individuals in the classroom
- Invite you to review the approaches with respect to evidence-based research and practice

Key terms

Social, Mental and Emotional Health needs (SEMH), attachment, Nurture Groups, Comic Strip Conversations (CSC), Zones of Regulation, five-point scale, therapeutic, therapy, Attention Deficit Hyperactivity Disorder (ADHD), executive functioning (EF), mental health, well-being

DOI: 10.4324/9781003361084-13

Attachment issues: Nurture Groups

Nurture Groups (NG) are the best-known example of how attachment theory has been translated into an education setting. They are classes of between eight and twelve children, usually in a mainstream primary school. Nurture Groups always have two members of staff. The children spend a substantial part of each week in the group but remain part of their mainstream class, joining the other children daily for planned activities. The adults' role is to establish trust, to help children to relate to adults and to other children. Staff engage with the children at the stage they have reached, offering unconditional acceptance while teaching a balanced curriculum and better ways of coping (Bennathan and Boxall, 2000). The rationale for NGs is largely based on the principles of attachment theory (Bowlby, 1969) and the socio-cultural theory of learning. Griffiths, Stenner and Hicks (2014) argue that for children to learn successfully, they need to feel physically and emotionally secure within their environments as well as secure and connected to attuned adults that they can trust. In the absence of these conditions, children can become fearful, insecure and anxious and produce survival-related attachment behaviour which may be maladaptive in mainstream settings. A heavy emphasis in NGs is placed on structure, routine and staff responsiveness to the child's developmental stage, emotions and needs. Birch (2016) notes that an effective NG fills in attachment and developmental gaps and allows pupils to develop trusting relationships with adults, begin to self-regulate, feel secure and develop the skills and resilience they need to eventually experience mainstream learning.

The daily routine is uniform, explicit and predictable, with activities that aim to help children to develop trust, greater self-awareness, greater awareness of their own feelings and the feelings of others, communication and language skills and the growth of confidence, resilience and self-esteem. Activities include news-sharing, emotional literacy sessions, group activities, formal curriculum tasks, turn taking and the nurture breakfast (Colley, 2009). Nurture Group staff use six principles to inform their practice:

- Children's learning is understood developmentally
- The classroom offers a safe base
- Nurture is important for the development of self-esteem
- Language is understood as a vital means of communication
- All behaviour is communication
- Transitions are significant in the lives of children

Established by Marjorie Boxall, who worked as an educational psychologist in Hackney (London) in the 1960s, Nurture Groups were originally established in certain primary schools in socially deprived and poor areas in London, in response to high levels of early childhood psychosocial disorders and the attendant emotional and behavioural problems that were evident in some children on entry to primary school (Boxall, 2002). In identifying the source of these difficulties, she argued that the main parent/carer-child attachment relationship had been compromised because of the impact of challenging social circumstances in the family home; the source of which could be traced back to a range of structural factors including poverty, racism and social marginalisation. She suggested that the resulting emotional, behavioural and social difficulties experienced by children impacted on their ability to adjust to the demands of the classroom setting and to access learning opportunities. Thus the underpinning rationale is that if children's attachment relationships can be enhanced then their emotional and social well-being will improve and this, in turn, will lead to improved behaviour that will better place children to access learning opportunities with the end result that their academic scores should increase.

Nurture Groups generally take a small group of children (10–12 maximum) out of the mainstream classroom for a certain period each day and for a limited length of time over the course of one school year and, within a small group setting, model out positive attachment relationships and provide opportunities for social learning and the development of emotional literacy, whilst simultaneously enabling children to access educational learning opportunities. Underpinned by Bowlby's attachment theory, the role of the key adult in the school setting was regarded as critical in terms of establishing routines and relationships in a safe, predictable and nurturing environment. Accompanying this, the Nurture Group model placed a strong emphasis on the physical environment.

Bennathan and Boxall (2000) draw on this theory in their account of the psychological characteristics of pupils for whom NGs were initially devised. These characteristics include a range of developmentally inappropriate behaviours that correspond with Bowlby's account of attachment disorders, including severe difficulties in engaging in productive social relationships (which may manifest themselves in either withdrawn and avoidant behaviour), coercive and aggressive behaviour, or erratic and disorganised behaviour. These problems are further compounded by serious difficulties in productive engagement in solitary activities, such as individual play, which often take the form of disorganised and unproductive engagement, inability to sustain attention and difficulties in self-direction and self-regulation. Geddes (2006) has also provided an attachment theory-based analysis of learning difficulties among children with SEN and shown how many common features of learning difficulties that are often signified by the vague and stigmatising label of SEBD can be understood and remedied through an application of this perspective.

Research evidence

Cooper and Whitebread (2007) found that NGs appear to have added significantly to positive work that mainstream primary schools do with SEBD pupils. An unexpected finding was that schools with NGs appear to work more effectively with pupils who have SEBD (now SEMH) who do not attend NGs than schools where there is not an NG on site. In their systematic review of NGs, Hughes and Schlösser (2014) found that apart from the study conducted by O'Connor and Colwell (2002), most studies that examined the effectiveness of NGs did not carry out follow-up studies, making it difficult to interpret improvements in pupils as short- or long-term effects. The findings suggest that while general improvements are maintained over the long term, there is some deterioration in some areas such as showing negativism towards others, insecure sense of self and not waiting their turn. This suggests that NGs may be ineffective at promoting well-being in the long term and that for maintenance of the positive effects of the NG intervention to be optimised, pupils who had a successful experience of NGs may need top-up interventions or additional support that reflects key features of the NG set up that are not easily replicable in a mainstream classroom. However, O'Connor and Colwell (2002) were only able to carry out a follow-up on 12 of the original 68 pupils in the research, reducing the generalisability of the findings and meaning that it is difficult to conclude the overall long-term effectiveness of NG given the small sample available to the researchers in their follow-up. Nevertheless, it suggests that short-term NG for children that lack health attachment experiences at home may not be enough compensation for them in the long term if they continue to experience a less than optimal environment after leaving the NG.

Hughes and Schlösser (2014) found that all except one study in their analysis relied on teacher reports for quantitative data, arguing that using a battery of measures that consider parent/carer and child perception as well as the teacher's would triangulate the findings and create a more reliable general portrayal of the effects of NGs. Also, while many of the studies carried out on the effectiveness of NGs do not state the relationship between the researcher and the NG teachers, it is likely that studies conducted by NG teachers or researchers with a vested interest in NGs may have resulted in researcher bias. Lastly, Cunningham, Hartwell and Kreppner (2019) found that while children attending NGs used significantly more socially appropriate responses, they reported challenges engaging with peers outside of the NG, especially in the playground. This indicates that while children may learn more socially appropriate ways of interacting with their peers while in NG, pupils may need more support to help them generalise these skills beyond the context of NG.

Ofsted (2011) reported that when the Nurture Groups were working well they made a considerable difference to the behaviour and the social skills of the pupils who attended them. Through intensive, well-structured teaching and support, pupils learnt to manage their own behaviour, to build positive relationships with adults and with other pupils and to develop strategies to help them cope with their emotions. At its best, the Nurture Group was part of a genuinely 'nurturing' school, where all members were valued, but where this value was imbued with a rigorous drive for pupils to achieve their very best. The schools that were the most effective at 'nurturing' had a clearly defined, positive but firm approach to the way in which they spoke to pupils, gave them clear boundaries, praised them for their efforts and achievements, ensured that they made academic progress, and worked with their parents. They saw each pupil as an individual and planned and implemented additional support accordingly. The Nurture Groups gave parents practical support, including strategies that they could use at home with their children. Parents felt more confident about being able to help their children and they valued the Nurture Groups highly. However, ensuring that the pupils made progress in their academic learning often did not have as high a profile as the development of their social, emotional and behavioural skills. Almost all the schools saw this as part of their purpose to some extent, but its prominence varied.

Activity

Filmed over a period of one year, 'The Nurture Room' accesses three schools and follows a handful of children as they go on their journey back to full participation in the classroom via the 'nurture room'. It can be accessed via the link: https://mindreel.org.uk/video/nurture-room

- What was your overall response to the film?
- What feelings did watching the film invoke in you?
- Were you surprised by what you saw and what could be accomplished?
- What results did you note were achieved?
- How did staff achieve these results?

Social and emotional approaches

Comic Strip Conversations (CSCs) are designed for children with autism as an intervention for teaching social skills for those with limited language expression (Gray, 1994). With the use of simple figures, text and thought bubbles, a conflict situation which the child has participated can be drawn and methods of solution can be discussed (Pierson and Glaeser, 2007). Using visual aids as a support, they help turn abstract thought to concrete and allow the learner to focus, in turn reducing anxiety around the subject and they keep attention on the subject (Rao and Gagie, 2006). As CSCs were developed in the 1990s, technology has since moved on. Many professionals have deemed the creation of visual supports unproductive and time consuming and advocate the use of technology in replacing some elements of handwritten supports.

The theoretical basis for approaches such as CSCs or Social Stories is to develop 'Theory of Mind' (ToM), which is people's ability to understand thoughts and feelings to others and recognise other people's perspectives, something which those with ASD can find difficult. Bauminger, Solomon and Rogers (2010) state that due to ToM deficits children with ASD may struggle to establish friendships with peers. CSCs are designed to support ToM development by providing a framework for autistic individuals to access social information and develop social cognition to develop appropriate behaviours to follow; constructive behavioural interventions such as CSCs that address a wide range of social, communicative, and behavioural challenges associated can provide effective support (Hutchins and Prelock, 2006). They are implemented by using the following steps:

1   Sit next to the child who requires emotional support
2   Use a sheet of paper or white board
3   Work through a serious of questions such as:

- Who else was here?
- What are you doing?
- What did the other/s do?
- What did you say?
- What did the other/s say?
- What did you think when you said that?
- What did the other/s think when you said that?

4   Complete the comic strip conversation as you talk
5   Discuss what could have been meant, said, or done in that situation. Remember that autistic children have difficulties with humour, irony or implied meaning
6   Talk through what could be done next time the child is in that situation

Research evidence

Difficulty with initiating and sustaining reciprocal social interactions is one of the main symptoms of autism and social cognition is a core element of children's ability to get along with others and see the world from other perspectives. There are two important components of social cognition, the development of 'Theory of Mind' for the ability to attribute knowledge, beliefs, and desires to oneself and other, and the development of empathy. It has been argued that for autistic individuals, many of the foundation skills needed for interpersonal relationships, such as communication, understanding social cues, verbal and non-verbal gestures, and the processing of emotional signals are impaired (Pierson and Glaeser, 2007; Ahmed-Husain and Dunsmuir, 2014) and they may have difficulty in understanding humour, irony, or implied meaning as they tend to take language literally (Eckdahl, 2018). Research has shown that due to these impairments, children with ASD experience higher levels of loneliness and social dysfunction than their non-ASD peers (Pierson and Glaeser, 2007).

It is often due to games that children gain new experiences and develop social skills which affect the quality and frequency of interaction. Travis and Sigman (1998) suggest that knowledge of the specific strengths and weaknesses in social skills have can be usefully applied to interventions, such as CSCs to improve social relationships and improved communication with the peers and interactions with others. Ahmed-Husain and Dunsmuir (2014) found that the CSCs intervention is an effective and inexpensive intervention, which school staff can be trained in relatively quickly and one that can be implemented unobtrusively in mainstream secondary schools with autistic students to increase or decrease target behaviours. The successful characteristics of CSCs include the use of specific target behaviours, specific, realistic, and implementable strategies/solutions, regular reviews of the CSCs and solutions to keep the individual motivated. Pierson and Glaeser (2007) worked with one elementary special education teacher and her two paraprofessionals who used CSCs for a period of six weeks with three students who exhibited signs of loneliness. All participants became more involved socially and actively began to seek friendships. The educators working with them noted increased friendships in the classroom and on the playground as well as visible signs of social satisfaction among the participants. However, in reviewing social narratives, Leaf et al. (2020) suggest that they do not yet meet the parameters for evidence-based practice, instead proposing that research should continue to investigate and evaluate various aspects of the intervention to enable the design of a rigorous and well-defined framework from which to gain valid and repeatable findings.

Abstract

Watch the video on the theory behind and use of Comic Strip Conversations. It can be accessed via the link: www.youtube.com/watch?v=1RTVZ3kFjI0&t=270s

- What are the key reasons for the use of CSCs that the presenter suggests?
- What examples does she give?
- Identify a situation you have encountered and draw/explain how a CSC could be used

---

Activity

Zones of Regulation and the five-point scale

Watch the video 'Zones of Regulation and the 5 Point Scale'. It can be accessed via the link: www.youtube.com/watch?v=VD0o5TAc2Ts

- What do the zones represent?
- How are they portrayed?
- Give examples of how you teach the five zones and the activities you could use

Watch the video 'The Incredible Five Point Scale'. It can be accessed via the link: www.youtube.com/watch?v=Ie9xahn8pFQ&t=485s

- What is the theory behind the scale?
- How is it used?
- What are the benefits for both the learner and the teacher or support member of staff?
- Produce a five-point scale for use in your own or possible practice

Therapeutic approaches

Newmann and Wehlage (1993) defined a therapeutic approach to education that gives a level of depth and significance to the processes and products completed within the school setting. A therapeutic curriculum begins with establishing a structured environment in which a community is established amongst the child and their peers and this level of interaction and harmonious allows for the development of a creative space. The use of a therapeutic curriculum such as art allows all children regardless of disability or need to be included within the classroom. Creativity within the classroom is a prominent feature of early years teaching and is used to incorporate the curriculum in a way that is easily accessible to all, and learners may use the art tools to communicate counting or numbers, or to tell a story. Bolwerk et al. (2014) suggest that the use of art in the classroom activates several regions within the brain and that learning is best supported through a multi-modal approach in which emotional, sensory, and physical experiences can combine (Cozolino, 2013).

There is a difference between art *as* therapy, which asserts the inherent healing nature of the art-making process, versus the concept of art *in* therapy, which emphasises the importance of the psychotherapeutic relationship created between the artwork, individual, and practitioner (Edwards and Wilkins, 2014). An art-based therapeutic curriculum can be a natural fit for those on the autism spectrum as it can act as an alternative to verbal communication as well as being a pathway to establishing social skills. Within the session, children may share their artwork with teachers or peers whereas they may have felt uneasy or unable to interact before. Art-based therapy can be a form of process-based learning, and whilst the staff may prompt the learner to reach certain goals, the process is entirely student-led, and they are able to proceed at their own pace.

A drama therapy curriculum is aimed towards all individuals including those with PMLD/SLD due to the highly interactive nature and the understanding that drama therapy is not reliant on the learner's cognitive ability and verbal communications. This curriculum is a therapeutic approach and form of psychological therapy, using healing aspects of drama as part of a therapeutic process enabling the learner to engage in psychological, emotional, and social changes through physical and verbal expressions. The drama therapy curriculum includes games and improvisation, role play and enactment of stories and the expression of feelings and experiences through dramatic distance (National Institute for Health and Care Excellence, 2019). It aims to develop relationships, explore and express feelings, develop social interaction skills and improve self-image and self-confidence.

The drama therapy curriculum increases interaction skills and social participation through non-verbal communication methods to explore expression, emotions and build relationships (Scattone, Tingstrom and Wilczynski, 2006). Similarly, non-verbal communication techniques are beneficial for PMLD learners supported through research concluding that drama therapy gives PMLD learners a 'base' for learners to explore through creativity resulting in a development of relationships and expression of feelings (Ellinor, 2019). Orkibi and Feniger- Schaal (2019) carried out a systematic review the evaluate the effectiveness of the drama therapy curriculum for individuals with developmental disabilities, cognitive disabilities or both and found that it effectively enhances the learner's self-esteem and social communication, and that learners effectively express their own voice through building relationships (Geiger, Shpigelman and Feniger-Schaal, 2020). Overall, the drama therapy curriculum is viewed as an emergent discipline with an unclassified assessment methodology; however, it is evidenced that individuals with SLD/PMLD use this therapeutic framework through expression of metaphors to successful express their emotions and develop social interaction skills.

It is important to distinguish 'therapy' from 'therapeutic'. There are respectful therapeutic principles that can be used without specific training in therapy. These include:

1   Patience – change is possible, needs time
2   Trust – 'being there', reliable
3   Space – cosy contained place or freedom outside?
4   Containment – security from structure, boundaries
5   Doing and being – balance of demands and space
6   Shared language – regard through interaction
7   Timing – sensitivity over a new departure

(Chesner, 1995)

Activity

Jonah is an autistic child who has communication and sensory needs and finds it difficult to engage in sessions and is often sensory seeking throughout his time at school. He cannot appropriately engage with staff or peers and often screams as a form of communication and he also has a habit of ripping paper during lessons.

- How could an art curriculum allow him to experience a range of textures to build up his tolerance to stimuli he considers unpleasant?
- How could the act of shredding paper be incorporated into the art curriculum?

A useful document is QCA (2009), *Planning, Teaching and Assessing the Curriculum for Pupils with Learning Difficulties: Art and Design*. London: Qualification and Curriculum Authority.

- Put Jonah in a specific Key Stage and suggest how you could work with him to ensure progression by reducing direction and encouraging the formation of ideas and thought beyond the conventional, within a curriculum

Visual (art) therapy

As defined by the British Association of Art Therapists, art therapy is a form of psychotherapy that uses art media as its primary mode of communication. The main media of art therapy include painting, drawing, music, drama, dance, drama and writing and is mainly used for cancer, depression and anxiety, autism, dementia and cognitive impairment, as these patients are reluctant to express themselves in words (Deshmukh, Holmes and Cardno, 2018; Chiang et al., 2019). It plays an important role in facilitating engagement when direct verbal interaction becomes difficult, and provides a safe and indirect way to connect oneself with others (Papangelo et al., 2020). Moreover, art therapy has been gradually and successfully used for patients with mental disorders with positive outcomes, mainly reducing suffering from mental symptoms. These findings suggest that art therapy can not only be served as a useful therapeutic method to assist patients to open and share their feelings, views, and experiences, but also as an auxiliary treatment for diagnosing diseases to help medical specialists obtain complementary information different from conventional tests.

Visual (art) therapy is an established form of psychological therapy delivered by trained art therapists/art psychotherapists. It's designed to help anyone, including those whose life has been affected by adverse experiences, illness or disability, by supporting their social, emotional and mental health needs (British Association of Art Therapists, 2023). Art therapy is founded on the belief that self-expression through artistic creation has therapeutic value for those who are healing or seeking a deeper understanding of themselves and their behaviours. Art therapists are trained to understand the roles that colour, texture and various art media can play in the therapeutic process and how these tools can help reveal one's thoughts, feelings, and psychological disposition. Art therapy integrates psychotherapy and some form of visual arts as a specific, stand-alone form of therapy, but it is also used in combination with other types of therapy.

These videoclips show how a therapist uses art to support a child:
https://youtu.be/J5-_fdh7B7c https://youtu.be/SdfGbXGxxkg

It aims to allow an individual to explore self-expression creatively to either gain personal insight or to develop a coping strategy around a difficult situation., by use of techniques such as using collage, colouring, doodling and scribbling, drawing, finger painting, painting, photography, sculpting and working with clay (Kaimal, Ray and Muniz, 2016). Gussak and Rosal (2019) emphasise that this is not only relevant to children and suggest that it is beneficial for both children and adults such as those experiencing severe stress, experiencing behavioural or social problems at work, school or at home, children or adults who have experienced a traumatic event, children with learning disabilities, individuals living with a brain injury and people experiencing mental health problems (Gussak and Rosal, 2019) and in the UK, almost two-thirds of registered art therapists work with children in schools.

Research evidence

There is evidence that art therapy is effective in improving children's quality of life; anxiety; self-concept; problem-solving skills; attitudes towards school; and emotional and behavioural difficulties. Although the evidence is based on studies with high or unclear risk of bias, undertaking experimental studies in school settings is not an easy task given the lack of funding and the challenges of implementation. Visual art therapy is currently being used in the NHS for many non-psychotic mental disorders. For example, arts therapies are included in the autistic spectrum disorder (ASD) Strategic Plan for Wales as an accessible and appropriate form of psychotherapy for those with ASD. For these and other service users, it may be that art therapy is a more appropriate treatment than standard talking therapies, but the evidence base for the use and acceptability of art therapy in non-psychotic mental disorders has yet to be formally evaluated. While it is helpful for many people, the research is mixed; some studies have demonstrated its efficacy while others have found little benefit. Moula (2020) carried out a systematic review and found that visual art therapy was delivered to children with asthma, behavioural disorders, oppositional defiant disorders, separation anxiety disorders, learning disorders, and disruptive behaviours.

Haeyen et al. (2018) show that art therapy is an effective treatment for Personality Disorder (PD) patients because it not only reduces PD pathology and maladaptive modes, but it also helps patients to develop adaptive, positive modes that indicate better mental health and self-regulation. Chiang, Reid-Varley and Fan (2019) state that although literature suggests creative art therapy (CAT) to be a potentially low-risk and high benefit intervention to minimise symptoms and maximise functioning in individuals living with mental illness, the lack of methodological rigour, and inconsistency in study methods and outcome measures, have prevented the advancement of CAT for use in severe mental illness. Emery (2004) suggests that the use of non-verbal expression through the experience of making art encourages children with autism to begin to represent their experiences. Forms represent objects and the very act of drawing with intention may encourage attachment to the object. Children create art because it is rooted in the need to relate to their world.

Moghaddam et al. (2016) identified that family-based art therapy can be effective in changing stereotypical behaviours of autistic children, because these practices are so attractive, flexible and diverse. Although the signs of autism, especially stereotype behaviours, lead to limitation of their communication and interaction with others and environment, the practices like painting, melody, drawing and diversity of applying these methods help them to be flexible and more adaptive. Rather than see these three areas in isolation, an art therapist can incorporate sensory regulation using the art materials concurrent to relationship building, communication and expression (Durrani, 2019).

In a systematic review, Bernier et al. (2022) found strong evidence to support the efficacy of creative arts interventions for autistic children. Fourteen of the 15 studies used a control group for comparison. Although all creative arts interventions targeted different aspects of the child, no specific art form showed a greater effect than the others.

Schweizer, Knorth and Spreen (2014) indicate that art therapy may add to a more flexible and relaxed attitude, a better self-image, and improved communicative and learning skills in autistic children. Art therapy might be able to contribute in mitigating two main problem areas: social communicative problems, and restricted and repetitive behaviour patterns. Typical art therapeutic elements such as sensory experiences with sight and touch may improve social behaviour, flexibility and attention-abilities of autistic children.

Attention Deficit Hyperactivity Disorder

Often, approaches to support ADHD learners focus upon the behaviour which is seen in the classroom. A different approach would be to look at how you could support executive functioning. In general, learners who have executive functioning issues require structure in their daily lives, clear and simple directions on how to accomplish tasks, clear expectations, and lots of praise when they display even the smallest EF skills. Remember to create an environment that functions as a 'surrogate' frontal lobe. Examples would include graphic organisers, sticky notes, and non-verbal signals from teacher to student to help the student refocus or to inhibit behaviour. Through repetition, modelling, and engagement with the specific intervention, neural pathways develop in the student that are then used for both behavioural regulation and meta-cognitive skills.

Activity

- Read the table below which identifies some of the issues and approaches to use in relation to executive functioning and fill in the sections on working memory and monitoring

Issue	Executive function	Approach
Difficulty getting started	Initiate	Provide clear directions Break the task into small steps
Disorganised – poor time management skills Inability to plan ahead Difficulty with sequencing Misplaces books/materials Written work appears messy and lacks coherence	Organisation	External organisers Instructional chart Daily schedule, routines, rituals

---

Issue	Executive function	Approach
Distractible – poor task completion Difficulty distinguishing important information Skipping from one activity to the next	Sustained attention	Preferential seating Instruction on appropriate academic level Hands-on learning, based on interests and strength Alternating response modes Allow to work in way that suits their learning Increasing the amount of immediate feedback Using cooperative learning
Hyperactive – high level of gross-motor activity Restlessness Seeks sensory stimulation	Sustained attention	Provide acceptable opportunities for movement rather than attempting to restrict activity Provide small manipulables to channel activity from gross to fine motor Restating rules before the opportunity for rule infraction
Impulsive – shouts out answers Exhibits risk-taking behaviours Difficulty following rules Difficulty taking turns	Inhibition	Teach self-monitoring skills Teach self-regulating skills Give frequent positive feedback Teach student verbal or motor response to use while waiting
	Working memory	
	Monitoring	

Mental health and well-being

Activity

There is a range of resources to support learners with SEMH needs. An excellent website is provided by Learn Together Cambridgeshire and Peterborough, through their Ordinarily Available Provision (OAP) SEND Toolkit. The toolkit covers the four areas of need coveted in this book and hosts a vast range of resources. It can be accessed via the link: www.cambslearntogether.co.uk/cambridgeshire-send/cambridgeshire-send-oap-toolkits/send-oap-toolkit

Explore the SEMH toolkit and any other areas of need under the headings:

1   Identifying Barriers and Understanding Needs
2   Provision and Intervention
3   Strategies
4   Resources
5   Environment
6   Training
7   How To
8   Specialist Guidance
9   Curriculum

There are numerous government publications that focus on promoting and supporting mental health and well-being, including publications by DfE. In 2015, The Children and Young People's Mental Health and Wellbeing Taskforce was set up to reflect on some of the biggest challenges facing mental health provisions for children and young people and to find ways to improve eight outcomes for their mental health and well-being. Findings from the taskforce's consultation were published in their 'Future in Mind' report (2015) and highlighted the importance of recognising and promoting good mental health and well-being in all people. Furthermore, Brooks (2012) notes that interventions that take a whole school approach to well-being have a positive impact in relation to mental well-being outcomes and physical health. In 2017, the DfE and Department of Health published 'Transforming Children and Young People's Mental Health Provision: A Green Paper', outlining the government's stance in supporting the mental health of children and young people. Within the Green Paper, it was noted that schools have a key role to play in both early identification of mental health difficulties and in supporting pupils experiencing such difficulties, using early school-based interventions.

Activity

Here are more contemporary policies:

DfE (2018). Research and analysis. Mental health and wellbeing provision in schools

DfE (2021). Guidance. Promoting and supporting mental health and wellbeing in schools and colleges.

DfE (2021). Guidance Teaching about mental wellbeing.

DfE (2022). Transparency data. Transforming children and young people's mental health provision.

NICE (2022). Social and emotional wellbeing in primary and secondary education.

• Summarise the key findings or recommendations

Children and young people's mental health services (CYPMHS) is used as a term for all services that work with children and young people who have difficulties with their mental health or well-being. You may also see the term children and adolescent mental health services (CAMHS) used. This is an older term for the main specialist NHS community service within the wider CYPMHS that may be available locally.

- Find out about the role of CYPMHS nationally and your local NHS community service if available

References

Ahmed-Husain, S. and Dunsmuir, S. (2014). An evaluation of the effectiveness of Comic Strip Conversations in promoting the inclusion of young people with autism spectrum disorder in secondary schools. *International Journal of Developmental Disabilities*, 60 (2), pp. 89–108.

Bauminger, N., Solomon, M. and Rogers, S. J. (2010). Predicting friendship quality in autism spectrum disorders and typical development. *J Autism Dev Disord*, 40 (6), pp.751–761.

Bennathan, M. and Boxall, M. (2000). *Effective Intervention in Primary Schools: Nurture Groups*. London: David Fulton.

Bernier, A., Ratcliff, K., Hilton, C., Fingerhut, P. and Li, C. Y. (2022). Art interventions for children with autism spectrum disorder: a scoping review. *Am J Occup Ther*, 76 (5), 7605205030.

Birch, E. (2016). 'You do what you need for your children, don't you?': an exploration of the current range of practice and priorities of nurture groups staff in a local authority. *Educational and Child Psychology*, 33 (4), pp. 40–49.

Bock, M., Rogers, M. F. and Myles, B. S. (2001). Using Social Stories and Comic Strip Conversations to interpret social situations for an adolescent with asperger syndrome. *Intervention in School and Clinic*, 36 (5), pp. 310–313.

Bolwerk, A., Mack-Andrick, J., Lang, F. R., Dörfler, A. and Maihöfner, C. (2014). How art changes your brain: differential effects of visual art production and cognitive art evaluation on functional brain connectivity. *PLoS One*, 9 (7), e101035.

Bowlby, J. (1969). *Attachment and Loss, Vol. 1: Attachment*. New York: Basic Books.

Boxall, M. (2002). *Nurture Groups in Schools: Principles and Practice*. London: Sage Publications.

British Association of Art Therapists (BAAT) (2023). Art Therapy. [Online] Available at: https://baat.org/art-therapy (Accessed 01. 03. 2023).

Brooks, F. (2013). Chapter 7: Life Stage: School Years. In: *Chief Medical Officer's Annual Report 2012*. Department of Health.

Chesner, A. (1995). *Dramatherapy for People with Learning Disabilities: A World of Difference*. London: Jessica Kingsley Publishers.

Chiang, M., Reid-Varley, W B. and Fan, X. (2019). Creative art therapy for mental illness. *Psychiatry Res*, 275, pp. 129–136.

Colley, D. (2009). Nurture groups in secondary schools. *Emotional and Behavioural Difficulties*, 14 (4), pp. 291–300.

Cooper, P. and Whitebread, D. (2007). The effectiveness of Nurture Groups on student progress: evidence from a national research study. *Emotional & Behavioural Difficulties*, 12 (3), pp. 171–190.

Cozolino, L. (2013). *The Social Neuroscience of Education: Optimizing Attachment and Learning in the Classroom*. New York: W.W. Norton & Company, Inc.

Cunningham, L. K., Hartwell, B. and Kreppner, J. (2019). Exploring the impact of Nurture Groups on children's social skills: a mixed-methods approach. *Educational Psychology in Practice*, 35 (4), pp. 368–383.

Deshmukh, S. R., Holmes, J. and Cardno, A. (2018). Art therapy for people with dementia. *Cochrane Database of Systematic Reviews*, 9.

Durrani, H. (2019). A case for art therapy as a treatment for autism spectrum disorder. *Art Therapy*, 36, pp. 1–4.

Eckdahl, T. (2018). *Autism Spectrum Disorder: He Prefers to Play Alone*. New York: Momentum Press.

Edwards, D. and Wilkins, P. (2014). *Art Therapy*. London: SAGE.

Ellinor, J. (2019). It's the 'group' that matters: dramatherapy working with a group of parents and their children who have profound and multiple learning difficulties. *Dramatherapy*, 40 (1), pp. 5–16.

Emery, M. J. (2004). Art therapy as an intervention for autism. *Art Therapy*, 21 (3), pp. 143–147.

Geddes, H. (2006). *Attachment in the Classroom: The Links Between Children's Early Experience, Emotional Well-being and Performance in School*. London: Worth Pub.

Geiger, A., Shpigelman, C. N. and Feniger-Schaal, R. (2020). The socio-emotional world of adolescents with intellectual disability: a drama therapy-based participatory action research. *The Arts in Psychotherapy*, 70, 101679.

Gray, C. (1994). *Comic Strip Conversations: Colourful, Illustrated Interactions with Students with Autism and Related Disorders*. Jenison, Michigan: Jenison Public Schools.

Griffiths, R., Stenner, R. and Hicks, U. (2014). Hearing the unheard: children's constructions of their nurture group experiences. *Educational and Child Psychology*, 31, pp. 124–136.

Gussak, D. and Rosal, M. (2019). *The Wiley Handbook of Art Therapy*. West Sussex: John Wiley, pp. 443–450.

Haeyen, S., van Hooren, S., van der Veld, W. and Hutschemaekers, G. (2018). efficacy of art therapy in individuals with personality disorders cluster B/C: a randomized controlled trial. *J Pers Disord*, 32 (4), pp. 527–542.

Hughes, N. K. and Schlösser, A. (2014). The effectiveness of nurture groups: a systematic review. *Emotional and Behavioural Difficulties*, 19 (4), pp. 386–409.

Hutchins, T. L. and Prelock, P. A. (2006). Using social stories and comic strip conversations to promote socially valid outcomes for children with autism. *Semin Speech Lang*, 27 (1), pp. 47–59.

Kaimal, G., Ray, K. and Muniz, J. (2016). Reduction of cortisol levels and participants' responses following art making. *Art Therapy*, 33 (2), pp. 74–80.

Leaf, J. B., Cihon, J. H., Ferguson, J. L., Milne, C. M., Leaf, R. and McEachin, J. (2020). Comparing error correction to errorless learning: a randomized clinical trial. *Anal Verbal Behav*, 36 (1), pp. 1–20.

Moula, Z. (2020). A systematic review of the effectiveness of art therapy delivered in school-based settings to children aged 5–12 years, *International Journal of Art Therapy*, 25 (2), pp. 88–99.

Moghaddam, K., Zadeh Mohammadi, A., Sharifi Daramadi, P. and Afrooz, G. (2016). Effect of the family-based art therapy program on the social interactions, verbal skills and stereotypic behaviors of children with autism spectrum disorders (ASD). *Iran J Public Health*, 45 (6), pp. 830–832.

National Institute for Health and Care Excellence (NICE) (2019). Dramatherapy in early intervention in psychosis. [Online] Available at: www.nice.org.uk/sharedlearning/drama therapy-in-early-intervention-in-psychosis (Accessed 01. 03. 2023).

Newmann, F. M. and Wehlage, G. G. (1993). Five standards of authentic instruction. *Educational Leadership*, 50 (7), pp. 8–12.

O'Connor, T. and Colwell, J. (2002). The effectiveness and rationale of the 'Nurture Group' approach to helping children with emotional and behavioural difficulties remain within mainstream education. *British Journal of Special Education*, 29 (2), pp. 96–100.

Ofsted (2011). Supporting children with challenging behaviour. [online] Available at: www.gov.uk/government/publications/supporting-children-with-challenging-behaviour (Accessed 01. 02. 2023).

Orkibi, H. and Feniger-Schaal, R. (2019). Integrative systematic review of psychodrama psychotherapy research: trends and methodological implications. *PLoS One*, 14 (2), e0212575.

Papangelo, P., Pinzino, M., Pelagatti, S., Fabbri-Destro, M. and Narzisi, A. (2020). Human figure drawings in children with autism spectrum disorders: a possible window on the inner or the outer world. *Brain Sciences*, 10 (6), p. 398.

Pierson, M. R. and Glaeser, B. C. (2007). Using Comic Strip Conversations to increase social satisfaction and decrease loneliness in students with autism spectrum disorder. Special conference issue research to practice. *Education and Training in Developmental Disabilities*, 42 (4), pp. 460–466.

QCA (2009). *Planning, Teaching and Assessing the Curriculum for Pupils with Learning Difficulties: Art and Design*. London: Qualification and Curriculum Authority.

Rao, S. and Gagie, B. (2006). Learning through seeing and doing. *Teaching Exceptional Children*, 38, pp. 26–33.

Scattone, D., Tingstrom, D. H. and Wilczynski, S. M. (2006). Increasing appropriate social interactions of children with autism spectrum disorders using Social Stories^{TM}. *Focus on Autism and Other Developmental Disabilities*, 21 (4), pp. 211–222.

Schweizer, C., Knorth, E. J. and Spreen, M. (2014). Art therapy with children with autism spectrum disorders: a review of clinical case descriptions on 'what works'. *The Arts in Psychotherapy*, 41 (5), pp. 577–593.

Travis, L. L., and Sigman, M. D. (1998). Social deficits and interpersonal relationships in autism. *Mental Retardation and Developmental Disabilities Research Reviews*, 4, pp. 65–72.

Part IV

Exploring Communication and Interaction Needs

10 The underpinning theory and research evidence

Introduction

Children, young people and adults identified with Speech, Language and Communication Needs (SLCN) have difficulty in communicating with others. This may be because they have issues saying what they want to, understanding what is being said to them, or they do not understand or use social rules of communication. The profile for every individual with SLCN is different and their needs may change over time. They may have difficulty with one, some, or all of the different aspects of speech, language, or social communication at different times of their lives. Children and young people with autism spectrum disorder (ASD) are likely to have difficulties with social interaction. They may also experience difficulties with language, communication and imagination, which can impact on how they relate to others. This chapter examines theoretical perspectives, diagnosis, classification, and aetiology of a range of examples of these needs.

Learning objectives

This chapter will:

- Introduce you a range of theories relating to language acquisition
- Invite you examine underpinning theory and research evidence in relation to Communication and Interaction Needs
- Introduce you to the aetiology of language delay, language disorders and autism
- Invite you to review how Communication and Interaction Needs relate to autism spectrum disorder
- Help you to understand the importance of social interaction in communication and interaction

Key terms

Communication, interaction, Speech, Language and Communication, language acquisition, selective mutism, language delay, Developmental Language Disorder

DOI: 10.4324/9781003361084-15

(DLD), Social (Pragmatic) Communication Disorder (SCD), aphasia, Childhood-Onset Fluency Disorder (COFD) (stuttering), autism spectrum disorder

---

Pause for reflection

- What is the relationship between speech, language and communication?

Speech, Language and Communication

Speech, Language and Communication (SLC) are three terms commonly associated together, as around 50 per cent of children entering education in the UK have SLC needs (SLCN) (Gascoigne and Gross, 2017). Speech is the production of sounds used to construct sentences and words, whereas language refers to the code or understanding of the system, including the development and acquisition of complex communication systems. Communication is an umbrella term for transmission of verbal and non-verbal messages (Munodawafa, 2008). Receptive language involves receiving and decoding or interpreting language, and expressive language is the encoding or production of a message. Speech, Language and Communication (SLC) skills are crucial in the development of children and young people. According to the SEND Code of Practice (DfE, DoH 2015), children and young people with SLCN have difficulty in communicating with others. This may be because they have difficulty saying what they want to, understanding what is being said to them or they do not understand or use social rules of communication.

Theories of language acquisition

Skinner (1957) identified that language has an independent existence and is the process of a stimuli and response through positive or negative reinforcement which enables the learner's behaviour to be manipulated. Language is thus acquired through operant conditioning with reinforcement and observation and that language is a verbal behaviour in that children generalise grammatical rules based on their past experiences. It has also been proposed that there is a critical or sensitive period for language development, a period in which language is acquired, that begins after a certain maturation of the brain (Lenneberg, 1967).

In contrast, the cognitive theory of language acquisition suggests that individuals develop language alongside intellectual development. Piaget (1964) stated that the individual used their physical environment and social interactions as a basis for their understanding of language. Similarly, Bruner (1983) argued that parents provide their children with a language acquisition support system explained as a collection of strategies that facilitate the child's acquisition of language (Takaya, 2008). Vygotsky (1962) believed that cognitive processes such as those involving memory, language and thought develop through social interaction and that language was a requisite for cognitive development. The focus of language was to promote social skills and after internalisation this would lead to higher cognitive skills. Thus 'private' or internal speech eventually becomes internalised or 'inner' speech, with thought being the result of language development (Shabani, Khatib and Ebadi, 2010). It emphasises the requirement of a More Knowledgeable Other (MKO) for development, in line with his theory of the Zone of Proximal Development (ZPD). Vygotsky believed that social interaction gives way to cognitive development (Pritchard and Woollard, 2010) and it was essential for language development (van der Veer and Yasnitsky, 2016). This approach also sees the importance of the child as a social being, with the importance of skilful adults in development. Piaget's cognitive constructivist approach sees children's language developing using schemas or building blocks of the mind (Piaget, 1952), reflecting how cognition shapes language. Bruner argues that social interaction is key to stimulating language development which takes place within the Language Acquisition Socialisation System (LASS), and that parents scaffold language development (Bruner, 1983).

The modular perspective is that language development is independent of cognitive processes and therefore there must be an identifiable area of the brain associated with language acquisition (Cotterill, 2019). Previous research has highlighted that there may be areas which are designed for understanding and using language, such as the Wernicke's area (comprehension) and the Broca's area (language production). Historically Broca's area of the brain was seen to support this theory, after Broca found that patients with lesions in this area of the brain developed speech deficits (Hickok et al., 2011). However, more recently, Broca's area has been found to have two divisions, one contributing to language development and the other contributing to other cognitive processes (Fedorenko and Blank, 2020). Chomsky's (1965) view is that language is innate to humans and children are pre-programmed with the fundamental rules of grammar and language known as the Language Acquisition Device (LAD). This concept developed into his theory of Universal Grammar (UG), a concept that is triggered once a child is exposed to language which supports the identification that there are innate biological grammatical categories, such as verbs that facilitate language development in children. However, Dąbrowska (2015) argues that the empirical evidence for UG is limited, stating that studies suggest that there are differences in adults' knowledge of grammar and language and therefore individuals do not learn from the same grammatical categories.

Emergentism regards language development as a sum of smaller more simple mechanisms in the brain, interacting with the environment to produce a complex result (Khatib and Sabah, 2012), and may go some way in explaining how innate UG could be plausible. It devolves an innate knowledge of Universal Grammar to multiple less specific neurological structures which could go some way to explaining how hemispherectomy, for example, allows for language to be redeveloped (Hertz-Pannier et al., 2002) as other mechanisms in the brain learn to compensate for the missing one. Poll (2011) acknowledges the complexity of language and argues that emergentist research has identified how simple mechanisms result in complex language-learning patterns.

Pause for reflection

- Why is it important for practitioners working in the context of SEND to understand how language is acquired?

Activity

This section of the chapter has introduced you to several theories relating to language acquisition. There are others such as Usage-Based Theory, Optimality Theory and Native Language Magnet Model

- Research these newer theories and suggest how they add to our understanding of language

Genie (born 1957) is the pseudonym of an American feral child who was a victim of severe abuse, neglect and social isolation. The extent of her isolation prevented her from being exposed to any significant amount of speech, and as a result she did not acquire language during her childhood. Watch the documentary which can be accessed via: www.youtube.com/watch?v=VjZolHCrC8E

- What does this tell us about the acquisition of language?

Selective mutism

Pause for reflection

Both DSM-5 (APA, 2013) and ICD-11 (WHO, 2019) classify selective mutism as an anxiety disorder.

- Why do you think it is included in this chapter?
- What does it say about the need to consider that individuals may have issues which span more than one primary area of need?

Selective mutism (SM) is classified under anxiety disorders in DSM-5 (APA, 2013) and under anxiety or fear-related disorders in ICD-11 (WHO, 2019). SM is a rare childhood anxiety and fear-related disorder as it usually starts before the age of five; however, the problem is not normally diagnosed until the child is about six to seven years old. DSM-5 (APA, 2013) and ICD-11 (WHO, 2019) state that it is a consistent failure to communicate in social situations (however, they are able to communicate at home). This 'disturbance' occurs for at least a month, and it is not due to a lack of knowledge. It is characterised by the inability to speak in certain social situations, particularly around people and in places that the child is unfamiliar with, but the child will communicate informally and appropriately with people and places that they are familiar and feel safe with. Many children with SM do not lack linguistic knowledge or understanding and can display differing levels of speech across one setting, speaking confidently to a peer and whispering to a chosen adult but remaining silent in pressured situations (Busse and Downey, 2011). Children with SM display deficits in both receptive and expressive language, understanding of grammatical rules and visual memory, which can have an impact on academic achievement.

Aetiology of selective mutism

There is no consensus on the possible aetiology of SM (Camposano, 2011), but it is best conceptualised as the interaction of environmental and genetic factors (Cohan, Chavira and Stein, 2006). Black and Uhde (1995) proposed familial causation at a high with 70 per cent of first-degree relatives having a social phobia. Psychodynamic theory poses SM is attributed to unresolved conflict. Trauma prohibits typical emotional regulation, resulting in oral fixation as a coping mechanism for anger and anxiety (Giddan and Milling, 1999). However, Anstendig (1999) identified evidence that the sympathetic nervous system takes unconscious inhibitory control over behaviour and the ability to speak, exhibiting the interaction between anxiety and functioning responses. Other suggestions include poor family relationships, problems with sound processing, a family history of an anxiety disorder or a traumatic previous experience that causes anxiety to happen in social settings (Wong, 2010).

Nevertheless, the characteristics of SM are social anxiety which can lead to speech and language abnormalities (Vogel et al., 2019.) Milic, Carl and Rapee (2020) suggested that 20–30 per cent of children with SM have receptive or expressive language delays. Similarly, shyness and reluctance to leave parents/ carers' sides in anxiety-filled situations are signs of SM. It is important to consider that SM manifest their anxieties in different ways, resulting in some children who communicate by whispering, whereas some individuals are 'full mute'. Holka-Pokorska, Balcerzak and Jarema (2018) suggested that auditory processing deficits should be taken into consideration in the diagnosis and treatment for individuals with SM and other symptoms have been identified including clinginess to parents, challenging behaviour such as 'temper tantrums' or being isolated.

Communication and interaction difficulties

A language disorder may be diagnosed if there is consistent evidence that the individual is not following the typical pattern of development and presents significant and on-going difficulties in understanding and using the spoken language.

Activity

Children, young people and adults may have difficulty with the following:

1   Difficulties with listening, attention skills and understanding spoken language (receptive language)
2   Difficulties in conveying information in speech, sign language or gestures, or writing (expressive language)
3   Difficulty in understanding and processing language
4   Difficulty with the use of spoken language or non-verbal communication
5   Pragmatic/social communication with difficulties in the use of social language, social rules of conversation, making and maintaining friendships, understanding of others' feelings/emotions, inference, non-verbal communication such as eye contact or facial expressions
6   Speech sound difficulty
7   Difficulty with phonological skills or articulation skills

- Why is it important to focus upon non-verbal communication as well as verbal communication?
- How does the list above demonstrate the complexities of language and communication?

Language delay

Language delay may be part of overall developmental delay (in which case language is likely to move at same pace as general development). If a child has a language delay, they may not reach language milestones at the typical age. Characteristics of language delay include not babbling by the age of 15 months, not talking by the age of two years or an inability to speak in short sentences by the age of three years. Further characteristics may include failure to use gestures by 12 months of age, preference to gestures rather than vocalising after 12 months of age and difficulty imitating sounds after 18 months of age. A child with a language delay will follow the same pattern of language development as their peers. However, this would be at a slower rate and therefore not meeting the milestones for their age. Language delays are less severe than language disorders and can often be caused by issues such as hearing impairment, autism and other psychosocial issues. Additionally, language delays can have a negative impact on children, often disturbing their development socially, emotionally and academically. For example,

Schoon, Cheng and Jones (2010) found that those who had language delays in their childhood were more likely to have mental health issues in adulthood.

According to Kersner and Wright (2012), language delay concerns children who speak with fewer words by age two. Concerns grow as the child reaches age seven due to the impact this may have academically and socially. Around 10 per cent of children experience language delay. Language delay involves late talkers who catch up with or without intervention or go on to have persisting language difficulties. A language delay can be receptive, expressive or a combination of both. Wallace et al. (2015) identify a speech or language delay as being that a child has developed speech and language in the correct sequence, but at a slower rate than other children of their age, whereas a speech or language disorder means that a child's speech or language ability is significantly different from what is typical of children of their age. It may surface as a primary difficulty (where it can be accounted for by a primary condition such as autism, hearing impairment, behavioural or emotional difficulties, or neurological conditions), or as a secondary difficulty where it cannot be accounted for by any other condition.

Pause for reflection

Many children have Speech, Language and Communication Needs (SLCN), but very often they are not identified in schools. It has been estimated that 10 per cent of children have long-term SLCN. With help, many will make good progress and not have long-term difficulties.

- Why are these statistics important?
- What is the possible long-term impact of not supporting pupils with Speech, Language and Communication Needs?

Language disorders

A language delay is identified when the development of language is slow to develop, and this may be identified if the individual is not meeting the developmental milestones; for example, between six to twelve months a child should respond when individuals talk to them, and they should start using their first words. Language disorders are common in neurological practice, typically arising from focal injury to the left hemisphere and from a form of selective neuronal degeneration (O'Sullivan, Brownsett and Copland, 2019). Children with language disorders typically have no trouble hearing or pronouncing words, their challenge is mastering and applying the rules of language such as grammar. It is an impairment that makes it difficult for someone to find the correct words, form clear sentences, understand what another person says and struggle to put thoughts into words.

Developmental Language Disorder (DLD)

Developmental language disorder (DLD) occurs when a child has severe and persistent difficulties with language understanding and/or functioning that impact daily life and/or educational attainment when no other medical condition is present (i.e., hearing loss) (Lancaster and Camarata (2019). It is a heterogeneous language disorder that affects either one of, or both, expressive and receptive language (Ellis Weismer, 2013). More than 7 per cent of UK school-age children meet criteria for developmental language disorder (DLD) (Norbury et al., 2016), which is defined as language ability substantially below their peers that affects their everyday function and cannot be explained by another medical diagnosis. A variety of changes to the brain may cause a developmental language disorder (DLD) such as the processing of complex sounds that change rapidly over time (Tallal et al., 1996). The severe grammatical difficulties experienced by children with DLD suggests that the Broca's area is likely to play a role in the disorder. Deep structures in the centre of the brain known as the basal ganglia have also been implicated in DLD (Ullman et al., 2020). The basal ganglia help us to acquire the motor skills needed to perform certain tasks, such as riding a bike or typing on a computer. This type of procedural learning is also required to learn sequences of heard or spoken speech sounds. Defects in this basal ganglion system have been the basis for theories that seek to explain the cause of DLD.

Half of children with DLD have relatives with language difficulties and the concordance rate for monozygotic twins is higher than that for dizygotic twins (Bishop, North and Donlan, 1995). At least three different genetic loci (DLD1 at 16q, DLD2 at 19q, and DLD3 at 13q21) and two genes that are expressed in the brain (CMIP and ATP2C2 in chromosome 16) have been suggested to contribute to DLD. The exact role of these genes is not known but they could contribute to phonological short-term memory. There has been much research in examining the overlapping deficits and patterns of structural language components (Taylor and Whitehouse, 2016), which identify those individuals with DLD and autism as having both expressive and receptive issues. There are differences between the two, however, such as syntax deficits (Kjelgaard and Tager-Flusberg, 2001), and individuals with autism have receptive language deficits that are more severe than expressive language ones (Hulme and Snowling, 2014). However, studies have also shown there to be a varying severity in language issues specifically within the area of expressive language, but autistic individuals range from having no issues in linguistic expressive components, having a delay in expressive language, or having severe impairments (Lord and Jones, 2012). Children with DLD characteristically present with a history of delayed early communication milestones such as age of first word acquisition, production of two-word combinations and sentence generation. As these children reach primary school age, DLD manifests as low scores relative to peers, on measures of receptive and expressive language, including across vocabulary, grammar and pragmatic abilities and literacy in most instances (Conti-Ramsden, Botting and Faragher, 2001).

Social (Pragmatic) Communication Disorder (SCD)

DSM-5 (APA, 2013) introduced two diagnoses describing neurodevelopmental deficits in social communication, those being autism spectrum disorder (ASD) and Social (Pragmatic) Communication Disorder (SCD). These diagnoses are differentiated by Repetitive and Restricted Behaviours (RRB), required for an autism diagnosis, and absent in SCD (Brukner-Wertman, Laor, and Golan, 2016). According to the DSM-5 (APA, 2013), SCD can co-occur with other language and communication disorders but cannot be attributed to low abilities in vocabulary and grammar. Symptoms of SCD include problems with pragmatic skills such as topic maintenance or use of social reciprocity; social interaction skills such as code switching or adjusting speech styles are also negatively impacted, as are social cognition abilities and construction of inference (Ellis Weismer et al., 2021). A diagnosis of SCD cannot be made in combination with a diagnosis of autism, intellectual disability, or global developmental delay, or be better characterised by other mental disorders (particularly, social anxiety disorder or attention deficit hyperactivity disorder, ADHD). It is meant to capture the social elements of communication dysfunction in children who do not meet autism spectrum disorder criteria.

However, Flax et al. (2019) suggest that SCD does not capture the profiles of children who have both social communication impairment and restricted interests and repetitive behaviour. Debate exists as to whether SCD represents the condition previously identified in the literature as semantic-pragmatic deficit and subsequently as pragmatic language impairment, or whether SCD was previously identified as mild autism (Ellis Weismer, 2013) and that this condition might best be viewed in terms of the broad autism phenotype (Flax et al., 2019) and that it is not plausible yet to confirm it as a separate diagnosis (Norbury, 2014). Those who have defined it suggest that it is a lack of ability to communicate both verbally and non-verbally, particularly in social situations (Swineford et al., 2014).

It is suggested that characteristics associated with SCD are much like those presented in autism, such as lack of social communication, complication, and inability to decode and understand what is not specifically established, as well as being unable to change tone of voice and or body language to empathise with who may be speaking or listening. It is also believed that while those with SCD find it challenging to communicate socially, they do want to do so, whereas those with autism do not (Baird and Norbury, 2016). In addition, characteristics such as restricted and repetitive behaviours, those commonly found in autism are not included in the criteria for SCD (Norbury, 2014). High rates of co-morbidity between SCD and other seemingly disparate disorders (including conduct disorder, ADHD and disorders of known genetic origin) raise questions about the utility of this diagnostic category, thus SCD is probably best conceptualised as a dimensional symptom profile that may be present across a range of neurodevelopmental disorders.

Activity

Why do you think DSM-5 (APA, 2013) includes two neurodevelopmental deficits in social communication?

- What are the differences and overlapping symptoms between the two?

ICD-11 (WHO, 2019) refers to developmental language disorder with impairment of mainly pragmatic language.

- Are there any differences between the two with respect to diagnostic criteria?
- What disorders are listed in ICD-11 under the Parent 6A01.2 Developmental language disorder?

Aphasia

Language disorders can either be acquired or developed, and predominantly develop from poor language acquisition. Aphasia is an example of an acquired language disorder, which occurs due to brain injuries such as head traumas and strokes, causing dysfunctions within specific regions of the brain associated with language (Wu et al., 2020). Aphasia negatively effects communication skills, the way individuals express and understand language as well as affecting their ability to read and write; intellectual capacity, however, is not affected by this language disorder (Nicholas and Connor, 2017). However, it may negatively impair the individual within a variety of ways such as their education, social, emotional and mental health (SEMH), social skills, cognition and independence. Hoffmann and Chen (2013) identify different subtypes of aphasia, including Broca's (expressive), Wernicke's (receptive), anomic, global, and semantic aphasia. Broca's aphasia, which is in the left frontal region, which is associated with the lips and tongue, is characterised by an individual's ability to comprehend language but who struggles to articulate language effectively (Pallavi, Perumal and Krupa, 2018). Wernicke's aphasia, identified as receptive aphasia, is characterised by an individual's inability to comprehend and articulate language simultaneously, meaning the expression of language is easy; however, sentences may not make sense, as their understanding of speech is impaired. This type of aphasia has been associated with the posterior left temporal lobe, which is closely related to the area of the brain associated with auditory associations (Binder, 2015).

In DSM-5 (APA, 2013), aphasia is classed as a neurocognitive disorder, placed on a spectrum with more severe conditions, such as dementia. Godefroy et al. (2002) suggest that the fundamental determinant of aphasia is the location of lesions within the brain, and individuals with cortical lesions in the Broca's and Wernicke's areas exhibit difficulties in language function. For individuals with Broca's aphasia, fluency is poor, but comprehension is good. Additionally, speech output is reduced, short utterances are exhibited, and the use of vocabulary is limited. In comparison with Wernicke's aphasia, individuals can speak fluently, but experience poor comprehension and an unawareness of difficulties such as interpretation of numbers, pictures, and gestures.

Childhood-Onset Fluency Disorder (COFD) (stuttering)

Childhood-Onset Fluency Disorder (COFD) is a speech disorder that is characterised by frequent disruption to the normal rhythmic flow and rate of speech identified by prolongations and repetitions in sounds, words, and phrases alongside word avoidance (WHO, 2019). COFD can also be referred to as stuttering or developmental stammering. The National Health Service (NHS) (2022) further identify two types of stammering, the most common being developmental stammering that develops in early childhood alongside speech and language skills and late onset stammering that happens because of a head injury, stroke or progressive neurological condition. Frequent disruption of speech fluency and rate, leading to inappropriate speech and language skills for age (APA, 2013; WHO, 2019). It might involve sound and syllable repetition, broken words and sound pro-elongations (Coleman, 2013). Individuals with COFD may present other behaviours including nodding or eye blinking to help prevent them from stuttering. COFD can be identified through an excessive number of dysfluencies being present in their speech including part word repetitions and prolonged sounds which may be heightened by secondary emotions of shame and fear when interacting (Khan, 2015).

COFD is typically first identified during the developmental period between 18 and 24 months and the first characteristics identified include disfluency through stuttering alongside emotional and cognitive reactions to the speech difficulties (American Speech-Language-Hearing-Association (ASHA), 2023). There is no single cause for stuttering, but family history and brain differences are two possible causes that are currently being researched. It has been found that genes may play a role, but it can also be acquired through strokes, head injuries and progressive neurological conditions, although this is rare.

Pause for reflection

The Looney Tunes character Porky Pig has a stutter. Episodes show him having experienced a range of traumas and relate the impact of previous trauma to stuttering. Despite his stuttering, Porky Pig achieves success in numerous jobs including a farmer, sailor, railroad engineer, pilot, newscaster and a police officer.

- How could you use this character to support a child who stutters?

Autism spectrum disorder (ASD, autism)

Definition

Autism spectrum disorder (ASD, autism) encompasses a wide variety of symptoms, impairments, biological underpinnings, co-occurring conditions, effective interventions, supports and risks (Lord et al., 2020), and there are likely multiple categorisations within the umbrella term. With our increasing awareness of the heterogeneity in autism aetiology, neurobiology, treatment and outcomes, it seems increasingly likely that autism will at some point be divided into an array of different conditions, each with their own risk factors, pathways and treatments. It is a lifelong complex neurodevelopmental disorder, typically identified within the first three years of a child's life. It is a permanent disorder beginning in childhood affecting 1 per cent of children (Ornoy, Weinstein-Fudim and Ergaz, 2016), presenting individuals with impairments and difficulties in social, communication interactions, and repetitive behaviours and difficulties. It is widely accepted that autism lies within a complex trajectory, with its origin emerging from genetic blueprint, further determined by phenotypic variability, neuroanatomy and connectivity of the brain, manifesting in cognitive behaviours (Just et al., 2007).

Diagnosis of autism spectrum disorder

Activity

The diagnostic criteria can be accessed via the link: www.cdc.gov/ncbddd/autism/hcp-dsm.html

The ICD-11 (WHO, 2019) diagnostic requirements can be accessed via the link: https://icd.who.int/browse11/lm/en#/http%253a%252f%252fid.who.int%252ficd%252fentity%252f437815624

- Compare the diagnostic criteria for DSM-5 and ICD-11
- What is the importance of the DSM-5 severity levels?

The diagnostic criteria create the foundation for tools such as the DISCO (Diagnostic Interview for Social and Communication Disorders), the ADI-R (Autism Diagnostic Interview – Revised), the ADOS (Autism Diagnostic Observation Schedule) and 3Di (Developmental, Dimensional and Diagnostic Interview).

- How are these tools utilised in the diagnostic process?

Social interaction and communication difficulties

The 'difficulties' that autistic people experience in social communication and interaction do not arise because of their autism. Communication is a two-way process and a breakdown in communication is the result of both parties' failure to understand each other and interpret each other's intentions. The asymmetrical dynamics that exist in social relations between autistic and neurotypical people create the conditions for misunderstanding and misinterpretation. However, the assumption that autism necessarily results in 'deficits' in social interaction means that any breakdown in communication is seen as the responsibility of the autistic person. Autism has traditionally been conceptualised and defined by core deficits in social interaction and communication. A more accurate representation of autism is one of difference rather than deficit (Davis and Crompton, 2021). Sharing information with other people relies on the ability to communicate well and it may therefore be expected that autistic people find it difficult to share information with other people. Crompton et al. (2020) found that autistic people share information with other autistic people as well as non-autistic people do with other non-autistic people. These findings indicated that autistic people could experience close social bonds and empathy with other autistic people, though may experience specific difficulty interacting with non-autistic people. Morrison et al. (2020) found that social affiliation may increase for autistic adults when partnered with other autistic people, and support reframing social interaction difficulties in autism as a relational rather than an individual impairment.

This lends additional support to the Double Empathy Problem (Milton, 2012), who suggests that miscommunications between autistic people and non-autistic people result primarily from a breakdown in reciprocity and mutual understanding rather than from autism-specific deficits in social communication. It is easy to problematise the definition of autism as a 'social deficit' located within an individual's mind. Differences in neurology may well produce differences in sociality, but not a 'social deficit'. Thus, difficulties in interactions occur because of different ways of experiencing the world and processing information. For instance, autistic and non-autistic people differ in how they process sensory information, language and social cues. Social communication is a double problem experienced by both an autistic person and a non-autistic person within an interaction. Khaledi et al. (2022) suggest that autistic individuals who have communication challenges may also have trouble controlling their sensory input and have sensory processing deficits. Sensory processing difficulties in these children appear to be significantly associated with communication skills, and anxiety acts as a mediator between the two. La Valle, Chenausky and Tager-Flusberg (2021) revealed that minimally verbal autistic children and adolescents did not differ in their total number of gestures. The most frequently produced gesture across children and adolescents was a reach gesture, followed by a point gesture (deictic gesture), and then conventional gestures.

Activity

Some autistic children are delayed in their use of language, and some autistic adults don't use speech, using non-verbal communication. Using gestures may be one attempt to communicate.

- What other methods could be used?
- What is echolalia and how is it observed?

Communication may be pre-intentional or intentional.

- What is the difference between these and how are they observed?

Communication and language

Abnormal use of language (pragmatics), particularly in social communication and social interaction, is the most striking feature of autism (Belkadi, 2006), and research consistently indicates that autistic children express significant identifiable delays in language and communication development compared to other neurotypical children. Ellis Weismer, Lord and Esler (2010) found a significant difference in the profile of receptive-expressive language abilities for autistic toddlers and Bent, Barbaro and Dissanayake (2020) suggest that the recurring key markers of autism were deficits in eye contact and pointing, and from 18 months, deficits in showing became an important marker. In combination, these behaviours, along with pretend play, were found to be the best group of predictors for a diagnostic classification of autism at 24 months.

Some autistic individuals never acquire language and developmental trajectories and individual profiles are diverse with semantic difficulties the most common linguistic deficit in autistic children and adolescents (Rescorla and Safyer, 2013). By school age, an 'autism-typical' language profile emerges, with articulation and syntax least affected, and comprehension, semantics and certain facets of morphology most affected. Impaired socio-emotional-communicative relating, atypical sensory-perceptual processing, and uneven memory/learning abilities may underlie shared language anomalies across the spectrum. The speech of first-degree relatives of autistic individuals may be less grammatically and pragmatically complex than the speech of first-degree relatives of individuals with other psychiatric disorders (Landa et al., 1992). Research has shown impairment can occur in both the comprehension and production of language; however, there is greater impairment in comprehension (Hudry et al., 2010). These children have demonstrated reduced brain activation in prefrontal and temporal brain regions under scenarios that involve irony (Groen et al., 2008). They can also be impaired in their understanding of non-verbal cues from others. These non-verbal cues include discerning intentions and making rapid intuitive judgements of social context.

Pause for reflection

Research into the role of context in human information processing has revealed that contextual sensitivity is crucial in social interaction, communication, and flexibility in thoughts and behaviour. This has led to the hypothesis of context blindness as the common pathway in the cognitive deficits in autism.

- Why do you think it is useful to focus on 'context blindness' in autism, as opposed to 'mind blindness'?

The heritability of autism spectrum disorder

Studies have found that autism aggregates in families, and twin studies estimate the proportion of the phenotype variance due to genetic factors (heritability) to be about 90 per cent (Sandin et al., 2014). It is not a simple genetic transmission, however, and there may be up to 1,000 genes involved in autism and they may act in an additive way (synergistic), along with environmental risk factors to produce the final phenotype. Simplex-de novo events contribute to 52–67 per cent of cases of autism. McDonald et al. (2020) carried out a longitudinal cohort study of 445 children with multiplex (multiple individuals) and (simplex) or single-incidence family risk, finding that 68 per cent of children from multiplex families against 43 per cent of those from single-incidence families had autism or atypical development at outcome.

Hadjkacem et al. (2016) suggest that genetic factors account for only 35–40 per cent of the contributing elements to autism, whilst the remaining 60–65 per cent are likely due to other factors, including pre-natal, peri-natal and post-natal environmental factors. Environmental factors could possibly influence different stages of brain development, this includes the formation and closure of neural tube and cell differentiation as well as formation of structures such as mini-columns and myelination. Environmental factors are likely to act in concert with predisposition genes, thus altering the biochemistry of the brain. It is evident that de novo changes to DNA (alternations not hereditary from parents) linked with autism risk suggests that environmental exposure could induce damaged to the genetic code (Lyall, Schmidt and Hertz-Picciotto, 2014). Beside risk alleles there are protective alleles as well as, and Weiner et al. (2017) confirm that the genetic influences on autism are additive and suggest that they create risk through at least partially distinct aetiologic pathways.

Neurobiology

The onset of autism occurs in the early post-natal period, following a pre-symptomatic period when the defining features are not yet consolidated into the full, clinically defined syndrome that is typically observed later. Zielinski et al. (2014) found that autistic children had abnormally large head circumferences, along with increased temporal lobe grey matter, suggesting overgrowth of the brain. Cell organisation within the frontal temporal cortex is disorganised, especially within the communication area of the brain and displaced activity within the frontal cortex may lead to rigidity of thinking and obsessions. Neural pathways are affected during crucial stages of pre-natal development between the brainstem and cerebellum, resulting in deficits of intermodal attention shifting, clumsiness and imitation difficulties. The dysregulation of cell migration, synaptic pruning, insufficient apoptosis and problems with myelination are also contributing factors in the development of autism (Carper and Courchesne, 2000). It may be also due to a mutation in specific genes involved in pruning and/or a lack of socio-emotional environmental experience during a critical developmental period (Fahim et al., 2011). Overgrowth begins between 6 and 12 months of age, before the characteristics of autism fully emerge, potentially enabling the earliest identification of this condition. The defining behavioural features of autism spectrum disorder emerge over the latter part of the first and second years of life, and generally do not consolidate into the full syndrome, enabling clinical diagnosis, until 24–36 months of age (Estes et al., 2015).

Taken together, these studies illustrate a range of age-specific changes in early post-natal brain development in autism, along with dynamic changes in behaviour. This suggests that early, presymptomatic brain changes in infancy may represent a cascade of linked brain and behaviour changes that lead to the emergence of the full syndrome of autism, consolidating into a clinically diagnosable condition in the second and third years of life (Piven, Elison and Zylka, 2017). Autism characteristics change over the first two years of life, starting with a period of relatively typical brain and behaviour development at six months demonstrating relatively intact cognition and behaviour at this young age in infants who later develop autism. The increased growth rate of the amygdala between 6 and 12 months occurs prior to the emergence of the social deficits that are diagnostic for autism (Estes et al., 2015), and well before the typical age of consolidation of the symptoms of autism into a diagnosable syndrome (Ozonoff et al., 2010). This gradual onset of brain and behaviour changes suggests an age- and disorder-specific pattern of cascading brain changes leading to autism. More specifically, increased early post-natal growth rate of the amygdala, a brain structure often implicated in the social aspects of autism, occurs prior to the consolidation of the defining social deficits in autism.

Activity

There have been several areas of the brain which have been linked to autism. Use research findings to complete the table.

Area	Function	Link to autistic characteristics
Prefrontal cerebral cortex		
Hypothalamus		
Amydala		
Orbitofrontal cortex (OFC)		
Temporoparietal cortex (TPC)		
Insula		

The brain, language and autism

There are obvious differences in the brain structures between neurotypical and autistic children with respect to language. Functional imaging studies have found reduced activation in Broca's area in contrast to Wernicke's area. The reduced activation in Broca's area could indicate a deficit in integrating the meaning of words within sentences, hence, impeding comprehension. The left lateralisation, or specialisation, of language processing seen in neurotypical children can also be reversed in autistic children (Hodge et al., 2010). The two core regions of language consists of an anterior 'expressive' language region with a centre in the left pIFG, which may serve as a coordinating centre for motor planning and execution regions in the adjacent premotor and motor regions, and a posterior 'receptive' language region with a centre in the left posterior superior temporal and middle temporal gyrus, which may have different subregions that deal with auditory feedback, matching of auditory perceptions to formed templates and a lexicon. Wan and Schlaug (2010) found that increases in cortical thickness were found in the autism group in areas that are implicated in social cognition and communication, such as the inferior frontal gyrus, superior temporal sulcus, inferior parietal lobule and fusiform gyrus.

It has been proposed that the human mirror neuron system (MNS) plays an important role in the acquisition of language. The shared representations of observed and executed actions in these neurons may serve as a foundation for our capacity to understand the experiences of other people, which is crucial for effective communication and social interactions. While most autistic children exhibit impairment in social interaction or language use, nearly a quarter of them exhibit co-occurring impairments in language form and content, also referred to as language structure. Differences in language structure between autistic and neurotypical peers include shorter and simpler sentences, limited use of relative clauses and WH-questions (Durrleman and Franck, 2015). Challenges with language structure in a subgroup of autistic individuals may be associated with social communication impairments such as taking the perspective of others.

Connectivity in the brain

One frequently reported neuroanatomical feature of autism is a trajectory of generalised early brain overgrowth when aged 6–24 months. Other than increases in total brain volume, the amygdala is enlarged in young children with autism, although this enlargement is no longer present by adolescence. Early brain overgrowth tends to be reported more in boys. Many neuroscientists believe this is caused by inadequate cortical pruning of the brain during the early years of life. Some autistic children feature a significant excess in brain size and weight in the first year of life due to a high acceleration rate of brain growth observed by magnetic resonance imaging (MRI) studies. They are believed to have excess synapses and synaptic connections in the brain due to deficits in synaptic pruning during early brain development. Eltokhi et al. (2020) suggested that disturbed synaptic pruning has been linked to deficits in neuronal circuitry with behavioural impairments. The brains of autistic children have shown an increase in axons and myelination between neighbouring areas of the brain compared with more distal connections, suggesting an increase in connectivity. However, whilst social and communication skills may be compromised by unique wiring in the brain, other abilities are enhanced. Autistic people have a stellar ability to use the visual parts of the right side of the brain to compensate for problems with language processing. This may be the basis for detail-orientated processing – and may be a decided advantage!

Activity

Debate: Pathological Demand Avoidance (PDA)

Pathological Demand Avoidance (PDA), a term coined in the 1980s by Elizabeth Newson, is characterised by persistent avoidance of ordinary demands by non-autistic society, with persons frequently displaying social avoidance behaviours which can be considered manipulative or strategic. In addition to their 'pathological resistance' to the ordinary demands of everyday life and their 'socially manipulative strategies' to avoid them, children with PDA are characterised as having surface sociability but with a lack of inhibition or sense of responsibility, extreme mood swings driven by their need to be in control and obsessive behaviour usually focused on their demand avoidance (Newson, Le Maréchal and David, 2003). Newson developed a list of diagnostic criteria which included resisting and avoid ordinary demands of life, with strategies of avoidance being essentially socially manipulative, surface sociability, but apparent lack of social identity and lability of mood. The Autism Education Trust and the National Autistic Society recognise PDA as a legitimate behaviour profile on the autism spectrum and provide guidance on how best to support children.

However, PDA is increasingly, but not universally, accepted as a profile that is seen in some autistic people and the existence of PDA as a 'diagnostic term' and how it fits within the autism spectrum is widely debated. What is generally agreed upon is what is often referred to as a PDA profile. Woods (2021) argues that there is much controversy surrounding PDA, partly because there is no conclusive evidence to indicate which features comprise PDA, and how it should be conceptualised. Is it a 'rebranded autism', pathologising characteristics not assessed in an autism diagnosis, or a pseudo-syndrome resulting from the simultaneous interaction between autism and common co-occurring conditions? Wan and Schlaug (2010) state that in addition to what are defined as the core 'deficits' of autism, including assumed difficulties in social communication, difficulties in social interaction and restrictive interests, children with PDA are thought to have an extreme anxiety-driven need to control their environment and control the demands and expectations of others and can appear to have better social understanding and communication skills than some other autistic people.

Green et al. (2018) argue that the use of PDA as a diagnosis has, at times, led to altered referral practice and misunderstandings between professionals and the families of patients. The evidence does not support the validity of PDA as an independent syndrome and Woods (2022) points out that PDA is a proposed mental disorder. Despite its acceptance by some clinicians and an increasing number of 'diagnoses', PDA is not recognised in either ICD-11 (WHO, 2019) or DSM-5 (APA, 2013). As a result of its exclusion from these diagnostic manuals, PDA is best understood as a label. However, there are reports from adults that a diagnosis of PDA was both welcomed and enabled them to make more sense of their lives and from parents who have found PDA to be a reassuring diagnosis for their child.

- Should be recognised as a 'rebranded autism', or a pseudo-syndrome?
- Why do you think that several parents and schools are keen to recognise PDA?
- Does it matter if we regard PDA as a label?

References

American Speech-Language-Hearing-Association (ASHA) (2023). Stuttering. [online] Available at: www.asha.org/public/speech/disorders/stuttering [Accessed 12. 01. 2023].

Anstendig, K. D. (1999). Is selective mutism an anxiety disorder? Rethinking its DSM-IV classification. *Journal of Anxiety Disorders*, 13 (4), pp. 417–434.

Baird, G. and Norbury, C. F. (2016). Social (pragmatic) communication disorders and autism spectrum disorder. *Archives of Disease in Childhood*, 101, pp. 745–751.

Belkadi, A. (2006). Language impairments in autism: evidence against mind-blindness. *SOAS Working Papers in Linguistics*, 14, pp. 3–13.

Bent, C. A., Barbaro, J. and Dissanayake, C. (2020). Parents' experiences of the service pathway to an autism diagnosis for their child: what predicts an early diagnosis in Australia? *Research in Developmental Disabilities*, 103, 103689.

Binder, J. R. (2015). The Wernicke area: modern evidence and a reinterpretation. *Neurology*, 85 (24), pp. 2170–2175.

Bishop, D. V., North, T. and Donlan, C. (1995). Genetic basis of specific language impairment: evidence from a twin study. *Developmental Medicine and Child Neurology*, 37 (1), pp. 56–71.

Black, B. and Uhde, T. W. (1995). Psychiatric characteristics of children with selective mutism: a pilot study. *Journal of the American Academy of Child & Adolescent Psychiatry*, 34 (7), pp. 847–856.

Brukner-Wertman, Y., Laor, N. and Golan, O. (2016). Social (Pragmatic) Communication Disorder and its relation to the autism spectrum: dilemmas arising from the DSM-5 classification. *Journal of Autism and Developmental Disorders*, 46 (8), pp. 2821–2829.

Bruner, J. (1983). *Child's Talk: Learning to Use Language*. New York: Norton.

Busse, R. T. and Downey, J. (2011). Selective mutism: a three-tiered approach to prevention and intervention. *Contemporary School Psychology*, 15, pp. 53–63.

Chomsky, N. (1965). *Aspects of the Theory of Syntax*. Cambridge, MA: MIT Press.

Camposano, L. (2011). Silent suffering: children with selective mutism. *The Professional Counselor*, 1 (1), pp. 46–56.

Carper, R. A. and Courchesne, E. (2000). Inverse correlation between frontal lobe and cerebellum sizes in children with autism. *Brain: A Journal of Neurology*, 123 (4), pp. 836–844.

Cohan, S. L., Chavira, D. A. and Stein, M. B. (2006). Practitioner review: psychosocial interventions for children with selective mutism: a critical evaluation of the literature from 1990–2005. *Journal of Child Psychology and Psychiatry, and Allied Disciplines*, 47 (11), pp. 1085–1097.

Coleman, C. (2013). How can you tell if childhood stuttering is the real deal? [online] Available at: https://leader.pubs.asha.org/do/10.1044/how-can-you-tell-if-childhood-stuttering-is-the-real-deal/full [Accessed 02. 02. 2023].

Conti-Ramsden, G., Botting, N. and Faragher, B. (2001). Psycholinguistic markers for specific language impairment (SLI). *Journal of Child Psychology and Psychiatry, and Allied Disciplines*, 42 (6), pp. 741–748.

Cotterill, T. (2019). *Principles and Practices of Working with Pupils with Special Educational Needs and Disability: A Student Guide*. London: Routledge.

Crompton, C. J., Ropar, D., Evans-Williams, C. V., Flynn, E. G. and Fletcher-Watson, S. (2020). Autistic peer-to-peer information transfer is highly effective. *Autism*, 24 (7), pp. 1704–1712.

Dąbrowska, E. (2015). What exactly is Universal Grammar, and has anyone seen it? *Frontiers in Psychology*, 6, 852.

Davis, R. and Crompton, C. J. (2021). What do new findings about social interaction in autistic adults mean for neurodevelopmental research? *Perspectives on Psychological Science*, 16 (3), pp. 649–653.

Department for Education and Department of Health (2015). Special educational needs and disability code of practice: 0 to 25 years. [online] Available at: www.gov.uk/government/publications/send-code-of-practice-0-to-25 [Accessed 21. 11. 2023].

Durrleman, S. and Franck, J. (2015). Exploring links between language and cognition in autism spectrum disorders: complement sentences, false belief, and executive functioning. *Journal of Communication Disorders*, 54, pp. 15–31.

Eltokhi, A., Santuy, A., Merchan-Perez, A. and Sprengel, R. (2020). Glutamatergic dysfunction and synaptic ultrastructural alterations in schizophrenia and autism spectrum disorder: evidence from human and rodent studies. *International Journal of Molecular Sciences*, 22 (1), p. 59.

Ellis Weismer, S. (2013). Developmental language disorders: challenges and implications of cross-group comparisons. *Folia phoniatrica et logopaedica: Official Organ of the International Association of Logopedics and Phoniatrics (IALP)*, 65 (2), pp. 68–77.

Ellis Weismer, S., Lord, C. and Esler, A. (2010). Early language patterns of toddlers on the autism spectrum compared to toddlers with developmental delay. *Journal of Autism and Developmental Disorders*, 40 (10), pp. 1259–1273.

Ellis Weismer, S., Rubenstein, E., Wiggins, L. and Durkin, M. S. (2021). A preliminary epidemiologic study of Social (Pragmatic) Communication Disorder relative to Autism Spectrum Disorder and developmental disability without social communication deficits. *Journal of Autism and Developmental Disorders*, 51 (8), pp. 2686–2696.

Estes, A., Munson, J., Rogers, S. J., Greenson, J., Winter, J. and Dawson, G. (2015). Long-term outcomes of early intervention in 6-year-old children with Autism Spectrum Disorder. *Journal of the American Academy of Child and Adolescent Psychiatry*, 54 (7), pp. 580–587.

Fahim, A. T., Bowne, S. J., Sullivan, L. S., Webb, K. D., Williams, J. T, Wheaton, D. K., Birch, D. G. and Daiger, S. G. (2011). Allelic heterogeneity and genetic modifier loci contribute to clinical variation in males with x-linked retinitis pigmentosa due to RPGR mutations. *PLoS ONE*, 6 (8), e23021.

Fedorenko, E. and Blank, I. A. (2020). Broca's area is not a natural kind. *Trends in Cognitive Sciences*, 24 (4), pp. 270–284.

Flax, J., Gwin, C., Wilson, S., Fradkin, Y., Buyske, S. and Brzustowicz, L. (2019). Social (Pragmatic) Communication Disorder: another name for the Broad Autism Phenotype? *Autism: The International Journal of Research and Practice*, 23 (8), pp. 1982–1992.

Gascoigne, M., and Gross, J. (2017). Talking about a generation: current policy, evidence and practice for speech, language and communication. [online] Available at: https://speechandlanguage.org.uk/media/3215/tct_talkingaboutageneration_report_online_update.pdf [Accessed 03. 02. 2023].

Giddan, J. J. and Milling, L. (1999). Comorbidity of psychiatric and communication disorders in children. *Child Adolesc Psychiatr Clin N Am*, 8 (1), pp. 19–36.

Godefroy, O., Dubois, C., Debachy, M., Leclerc, M. and Kreisler, M. D. (2002). Vascular aphasias. Main characteristics of patients hospitalized in acute stroke units. *Stroke*, 33 pp. 702–705.

Green, J., Absoud, M., Grahame, V., Malik, O., Simonoff, E., Le Couteur, A. and Baird, G. (2018). Pathological demand avoidance: symptoms but not a syndrome. *The Lancet: Child & Adolescent Health*, 2 (6), pp. 455–464.

Groen, Y., Wijers, A. A., Mulder, L. J. M., Waggeveld, B., Minderaa, R. B. and Althaus, M. (2008). Error and feedback processing in children with ADHD and children with Autistic Spectrum Disorder: an EEG event- related potential study. *Clinical Neurophysiology*, 119 (11), pp. 2476–2493.

Hadjkacem, I., Ayadi, H., Turki, M., Yaich, S., Khemekhem, K., Walha, A., Cherif, L., Moalla, Y. and Ghribi, F. (2016). Prenatal, perinatal and postnatal factors associated with autism spectrum disorder. *Jornal de pediatria*, 92 (6), pp. 595–601.

Hertz-Pannier, L., Chiron, C., Jambaqué, I., Renaux-Kieffer, V., Van de Moortele, P. F., Delalande, O., Fohlen, M., Brunelle, F. and Le Bihan, D. (2002). Late plasticity for language in a child's non-dominant hemisphere: a pre- and post-surgery fMRI study. *Brain: A Journal of Neurology*, 125 (2), pp. 361–372.

Hickok, G., Costanzo, M., Capasso, R. and Miceli, G. (2011). The role of Broca's area in speech perception: evidence from aphasia revisited. *Brain and Language*, 119 (3), pp. 214–220.

Hodge, S. M., Makris, N., Kennedy, D. N., Caviness, V. S., Howard, J., McGrath, L., Steele, S., Frazier, J. A., Tager-Flusberg, H. and Harris, G. J. (2010). Cerebellum, language, and cognition in autism and specific language impairment. *Journal of Autism and Developmental Disorders*, 40 (3), pp. 300–316.

Hoffmann, M. and Chen, R. (2013). The spectrum of aphasia subtypes and etiology in subacute stroke. *Journal of Stroke and Cerebrovascular Diseases*, 22 (8), pp. 1385–1392.

Holka-Pokorska, J., Balcerzak, A. and Jarema, M. (2018). The controversy around the diagnosis of selective mutism: a critical analysis of three cases in the light of modern research and diagnostic criteria. *Psychiatria Polska*, 52, pp. 323–343.

Hudry, K., Leadbitter, K., Temple, K., Slonims, V., McConachie, H., Aldred, C., Howlin, P., Charman, T. and PACT Consortium (2010). Preschoolers with autism show greater impairment in receptive compared with expressive language abilities. *International Journal of Language & Communication Disorders*, 45 (6), pp. 681–690.

Hulme, C. and Snowling, M. (2014). The interface between spoken and written language: developmental disorders. *Philosophical Transactions of the Royal Society of London. Series B, Biological Sciences*, 369, 20120395.

Just, M. A., Cherkassky, V. L., Keller, T. A., Kana, R. K. and Minshew, N. J. (2007). Functional and anatomical cortical underconnectivity in autism: evidence from an FMRI study of an executive function task and corpus callosum morphometry. *Cerebral Cortex*, 17 (4), pp. 951–961.

Kersner, M. and Wright, J. (2012). *Speech and Language Therapy*. London: Routledge.

Khaledi, H., Aghaz, A., Mohammadi, A., Dadgar, H. and Meftahi, G. (2022). The relationship between communication skills, sensory difficulties, and anxiety in children with autism spectrum disorder. *Middle East Current Psychiatry*, 29 (1), 29–69.

Khan, N. (2015). The effect of stuttering on speech and learning process: a case study. *International Journal on Studies in English Language and Literature (IJSELL)*, 3 (4), pp. 89–103.

Khatib, M. and Sabah, S. (2012). On major perspectives on language acquisition: nativism, connectionism, and emergentism. *Brain: A Journal of Neurology*, 3 (4), pp. 5–12.

Kjelgaard, M. M. and Tager-Flusberg, H. (2001). An investigation of language impairment in autism: implications for genetic subgroups. *Language and Cognitive Processes*, 16 (2–3), pp. 287–308.

Lancaster, H. S. and Camarata, S. (2019). Reconceptualizing developmental language disorder as a spectrum disorder: issues and evidence. *International Journal of Language & Communication Disorders*, 54 (1), pp. 79–94.

Landa, R., Piven, J., Wzorek, M. M., Gayle, J. O., Chase, G. A. and Folstein, S. E. (1992). Social language use in parents of autistic individuals. *Psychological Medicine*, 22 (1), pp. 245–254.

La Valle, C., Chenausky, K. and Tager-Flusberg, H. (2021). How do minimally verbal children and adolescents with autism spectrum disorder use communicative gestures to complement their spoken language abilities? *Autism & Developmental Language impairments*, 6, doi:23969415211035065.

Lenneberg, E. H. (1967). *Biological Foundations of Language*. New York: Wiley.

Lord, C. and Jones, R. M. (2012). Annual research review: re-thinking the classification of autism spectrum disorders. *Journal of Child Psychology and Psychiatry, and Allied Disciplines*, 53 (5), pp. 490–509.

Lord, C., Brugha, T. S., Charman, T., Cusack, J., Dumas, G., Frazier, T., Jones, E. J. H., Jones, R. M., Pickles, A., State, M. W., Taylor, J. L. and Veenstra-VanderWeele, J. (2020). Autism spectrum disorder. *Nature Reviews: Disease Primers*, 6 (1), p. 5.

Lyall, K., Schmidt, R. J. and Hertz-Picciotto, I. (2014). Maternal lifestyle and environmental risk factors for autism spectrum disorders. *International Journal of Epidemiology*, 43 (2), pp. 443–464.

McDonald, N. M., Senturk, D., Scheffler, A., Brian, J. A., Carver, L. J., Charman, T., Chawarska, K., Curtin, S., Hertz-Picciotto, I., Jones, E. J. H., Klin, A., Landa, R., Messinger, D. S., Ozonoff, S., Stone, W. L., Tager-Flusberg, H., Webb, S. J., Young, G., Zwaigenbaum, L. and Jeste, S. S. (2020). Developmental trajectories of infants with multiplex family risk for autism: a baby siblings research consortium study. *JAMA Neurology*, 77 (1), pp. 73–81.

Milic, M. I., Carl, T. and Rapee, R. M. (2020). Similarities and differences between young children with selective mutism and social anxiety disorder. *Beh. Res. Ther*, 133, 103696.

Milton, D. (2012) On the ontological status of autism: the 'double empathy problem'. *Disability & Society*, 27 (6), pp. 883–887.

Morrison, K. E., DeBrabander, K. M., Jones, D. R., Faso, D. J., Ackerman, R. A. and Sasson, N. J. (2020). Outcomes of real-world social interaction for autistic adults paired with autistic compared to typically developing partners. *Autism*, 24 (5), pp. 1067–1080.

Munodawafa, D. (2008). Communication: concepts, practice and challenges. *Health Education Research*, 23 (3), pp. 369–370.

National Health Service (2022). Stammering. [online] Available at: www.nhs.uk/conditions/stammering [Accessed 02. 02. 2023].

Newson, E., Le Maréchal, K. and David, C. (2003). Pathological demand avoidance syndrome: a necessary distinction within the pervasive developmental disorders. *Archives of Disease in Childhood*, 88, pp. 595–600.

Nicholas, M. and Connor, L. T. (2017). People with aphasia using AAC: are executive functions important? *Aphasiology*, 31 (7), pp. 819–836.

Norbury, C. F. (2014). Practitioner review: social (pragmatic) communication disorder conceptualization, evidence and clinical implications. *J Child Psychol Psychiatry*, 55 (3), pp. 204–216.

Norbury, C. F., Gooch, D., Wray, C., Baird, G., Charman, T., Simonoff, E., Vamvakas, G. and Pickles, A. (2016). The impact of nonverbal ability on prevalence and clinical presentation of language disorder: evidence from a population study. *Journal of Child Psychology and Psychiatry, and Allied Disciplines*, 57 (11), pp. 1247–1257.

Ornoy, A., Weinstein-Fudim, L., and Ergaz, Z. (2016). Genetic syndromes, maternal diseases and antenatal factors associated with Autism Spectrum Disorders (ASD). *Frontiers in Neuroscience*, 10, p. 316.

O'Sullivan, M., Brownsett, S. and Copland, D. (2019). Language and language disorders: neuroscience to clinical practice. *Practical Neurology*, 19, pp. 380–388.

Ozonoff, S., Iosif, A. M., Baguio, F., Cook, I. C., Hill, M. M., Hutman, T., Rogers, S. J., Rozga, A., Sangha, S., Sigman, M., Steinfeld, M. B. and Young, G. S. (2010). A prospective study of the emergence of early behavioral signs of autism. *Journal of the American Academy of Child and Adolescent Psychiatry*, 49 (3), pp. 256–266.

Pallavi, J., Perumal, R. C. and Krupa, M. (2018). Quality of communication life in individuals with Broca's aphasia and normal individuals: a comparative study. *Ann Indian Acad Neurol*, 21, pp. 285–289.

Piaget, J. (1952). *The Origins of Intelligence in Children*. New York, NY: W.W. Norton & Co.

Piaget, J. (1964). Cognitive development in children: development and learning. *Journal of Research in Science Teaching*, 2, pp. 176–186.

Poll, G. H. (2011). Increasing the odds: applying emergentist theory in language intervention. *Language, Speech, and Hearing Services in Schools*, 42 (4), pp. 580–591.

Pritchard, A. and Woollard, J. (2010). *Psychology for the Classroom: Constructivism and Social Learning*. Florence, KY: Routledge.

Piven, J., Elison, J. T. and Zylka, M. J. (2017). Toward a conceptual framework for early brain and behavior development in autism. *Molecular Psychiatry*, 22 (10), pp. 1385–1394.

Rescorla, L. and Safyer, P. (2013). Lexical composition in children with autism spectrum disorder (ASD). *Journal of Child Language*, 40 (1), pp. 47–68.

Sandin, S., Lichtenstein, P., Kuja-Halkola, R., Larsson, H., Hultman, C. M. and Reichenberg, A. (2014). The familial risk of autism. *JAMA*, 311 (17), pp. 1770–1777.

Schoon, I., Cheng, H. and Jones, E. (2010). Resilience in children's development. In: K. Hansen, H. Joshi, and S. Dex (eds.), *Children of the 21st Century (Volume 2): The First Five Years* (Bristol; online edn, Policy Press Scholarship Online, 22 March 2012).

Shabani, K., Khatib, M. and Ebadi, S. (2010). Vygotsky's zone of proximal development: instructional implications and teachers' professional development. *English Language Teaching*, 3, pp. 237–248.

Skinner, B. F. (1957). *Verbal Behavior*. Acton, MA: Copley Publishing Group.

Swineford, L. B., Thurm, A., Baird, G., Wetherby, A. M. and Swedo, S. (2014). Social (pragmatic) communication disorder: a research review of this new DSM-5 diagnostic category. *Journal of Neurodevelopmental Disorders*, 6 (1), p. 41.

Takaya, K. (2008). Jerome Bruner's theory of education: from early Bruner to later Bruner. *Interchange*, 39, pp. 1–19.

Tallal, P., Miller, S. L., Bedi, G., Byma, G., Wang, X., Nagarajan, S. S., Schreiner, C., Jenkins, W. M. and Merzenich, M. M. (1996). Language comprehension in language-learning impaired children improved with acoustically modified speech. *Science*, 271 (5245), pp. 81–84.

Taylor, L. J. and Whitehouse, A. J. O. (2016). Autism Spectrum Disorder, language disorder, and Social (Pragmatic) Communication Disorder: overlaps, distinguishing features, and clinical implications. *Aust. Psychol*, 51, pp. 287–295.

Ullman, J. C., Arguello, A., Getz, J. A., Bhalla, A., Mahon, C. S., Wang, J., Giese, T., Bedard, C., Kim, D. J., Blumenfeld, J. R., Liang, N., Ravi, R., Nugent, A. A., Davis, S. S., Ha, C., Duque, J., Tran, H. L., Wells, R. C., Lianoglou, S., Daryani, V. M., … Henry, A. G. (2020). Brain delivery and activity of a lysosomal enzyme using a blood-brain barrier transport vehicle in mice. *Science Translational Medicine*, 12 (545).

Van der Veer, R., and Yasnitsky, A. (2016). Vygotsky the published: who wrote Vygotsky and what Vygotsky actually wrote. In: A. Yasnitsky and R. van der Veer (eds.), *Revisionist Revolution in Vygotsky Studies*. New York, NY: Routledge, pp. 73–93.

Vogel, F., Gensthaler, A., Stahl, J. and Schwenck, C. (2019). Fears and fear-related cognitions in children with selective mutism. *European Child & Adolescent Psychiatry*, 28 (9), pp. 1169–1181.

Vygotsky, L. S. (1962). *Thought and Language*. Cambridge, MA: MIT Press.

Wallace, I. F., Berkman, N. D., Watson, L. R., Coyne-Beasley, T., Wood, C. T., Cullen, K. and Lohr, K. N. (2015). Screening for speech and language delay in children 5 years old and younger: a systematic review. *Pediatrics*, 136 (2), e448–e462.

Wan, C. Y. and Schlaug, G. (2010). Neural pathways for language in autism: the potential for music-based treatments. *Future Neurology*, 5 (6), pp. 797–805.

Weiner, D. J., Wigdor, E. M., Ripke, S., Walters, R. K., Kosmicki, J. A., Grove, J., Samocha, K. E., Goldstein, J. I., Okbay, A., Bybjerg-Grauholm, J., Werge, T., Hougaard, D. M., Taylor, J., iPSYCH-Broad Autism Group, Psychiatric Genomics Consortium Autism Group, Skuse, D., Devlin, B., Anney, R., Sanders, S. J., Bishop, S., Mortenson, P. B., Børglum, B. A. D., Smith, G. D. and Robinson, E. B. (2017). Polygenic transmission disequilibrium confirms that common and rare variation act additively to create risk for autism spectrum disorders. *Nature Genetics*, 49 (7), pp. 978–985.

Woods, R. (2021). Pathological demand avoidance (PDA): its four schools of thought. *Developmental Psychology Forum*, 94, pp. 10–14.

Woods, R. (2022). PDA: a Preventable Delicate Activity. *The Spectrum*, 112, pp. 14–15.

Wong, P. (2010). Selective mutism: a review of etiology, comorbidities, and treatment. *Psychiatry*, 7 (3), pp. 23–31.

Wu, C., Qin, Y., Lin, Z., Yi, X., Wei, X., Ruan, Y. and He, J. (2020). Prevalence and impact of aphasia among patients admitted with acute ischemic stroke. *Journal of Stroke and Cerebrovascular Diseases*, 29 (5), 104764.

Zielinski, B. A., Prigge, M. B., Nielsen, J. A., Froehlich, A. L., Abildskov, T. J., Anderson, J. S., Fletcher, P. T., Zygmunt, K. M., Travers, B. G., Lange, N., Alexander, A. L., Bigler, E. D. and Lainhart, J. E. (2014). Longitudinal changes in cortical thickness in autism and typical development. *Brain: A Journal of Neurology*, 137 (6), pp. 1799–1812.

11 The impact of Communication and Interaction Needs on individuals and families

Introduction

This chapter examines the impact that Communication and Interaction Needs may have on an individual, their families and allies, utilising a series of case studies from a range of contexts and ages. It will take examples from areas of Speech, Language and Communication, as well as aspects relating to communication and interaction in autism, identifying the characteristics and issues raised in Chapter 10. It examines the impact that these issues may have on individuals and families, including siblings. You will be invited to examine the lived experience of individuals using case studies.

Learning objectives

This chapter will:

- Invite you to apply your understanding gained from the previous chapter to the lived experience
- Introduce you to a wide range of consequences of Communication and Interaction Needs to individuals, families and allies
- Help you to understand how these needs impact the lives of children, young people and adults
- Invite you to review research evidence which supports our understanding of the impact on the lives of individuals, families and allies
- Invite you to review how Speech, Language and Communication Needs (SLCN), expressive and receptive language, Developmental Language Disorder (DLD), aphasia, selective mutism, Child Onset Fluency Disorder (COFD) and autism spectrum disorder influence educational attainment and employment

Key terms

Impact, Speech, Language and Communication Needs (SLCN), expressive and receptive language, Developmental Language Disorder (DLD), aphasia, selective

DOI: 10.4324/9781003361084-16

mutism, Child Onset Fluency Disorder (COFD), autism spectrum disorder, gender, children, siblings, adult, families, employment

---

Pause for reflection

- What do you think are the main issues which an individual with SLCN may face in everyday life?
- Why is it important to understand the impact that interaction may have on children, young people and adults?

Speech, Language and Communication Needs

There are four aspects to Speech, Language and Communication Needs (SLCN) including speech sound production (e.g., a stammer), expressive language (the ability to express oneself through language in such a way that others are able to understand), receptive language (the ability to understand what is being said to you) and pragmatics or the social use of language (the ability to use language appropriate to a situation, e.g., talk to a teacher differently to your best friend).

Speech, Language and Communication Needs (SLCN) can affect pupils in many ways. Pupils can experience a speech sound disorder which may make their speech sound different, and, in some cases can make it so difficult to understand that it impacts on the pupil's ability to convey their message. Dysfluency or a stammer can also affect how a pupil's speech sounds. Language difficulties can take many different forms: some pupils have difficulties understanding what they've heard, while others find it hard to construct sentences or retrieve the appropriate vocabulary item. Some pupils find it hard to use their language skills to communicate with others – their grammar and vocabulary may be fine, but they struggle to interact with others. Older pupils may struggle with creative thinking skills like prediction and inference. Children with social communication needs may have difficulties taking part in a conversation, taking turns in a conversation, staying on topic, taking the listener's needs in to account, reading non-verbal cues, etc.

Expressive language difficulties may show as:

- Speech sound difficulties
- Fluency issues
- Word retrieval difficulties
- Poor vocabulary

- Immature speech may interfere with literacy development
- Selective mutism

Receptive language difficulties may show as:

- Preferring own agenda
- Attention and listening difficulties
- Unable to follow instructions
- Poor confidence and lack of self-esteem
- May need extra time to process verbal language
- May interpret language literally and may struggle to understand jokes and sarcasm

Social communication difficulties may show as:

- Mild social difficulties and conflict at unstructured times
- Frustration
- Inappropriate/immature behaviours
- Isolated or withdrawn/unhappy
- Lack of empathy/understanding feelings of others
- Impaired non-verbal communication skills such as using inappropriate body language or facial expression

Social interaction difficulties may show as:

- Lack of joint attention
- Difficulty working cooperatively in a group
- Difficulty showing awareness of others' needs
- Difficulty following group rules

Activity

Read the following case studies:

Grace is aged eight and attends a mainstream primary school. She enjoys certain lessons such as PE, using the computer and art. Her speech is clear even when she is talking to unfamiliar people. However, she finds it difficult to follow written instructions, has poor attention and listening skills and reading comprehension is weak. This impacts on her learning such that all areas of the curriculum are affected, and she does not get involved in group activities.

Kingston is aged 17 and attends his local FE college where he is studying to be a bricklayer. He can cope with the physical demands of the course and can see what his peers are doing and is able to follow visual prompts. He understands what the lecturer is saying and can decode the specific terms used in construction. However, he struggles to formulate complete oral sentences and is unable to use grammar appropriately such as verb tenses when he is assessed orally. He is reluctant to participate in class discussion and at times he lacks confidence.

- Which case study may have difficulties with expressive or receptive language?
- What impact do you think these difficulties may have on their academic and social life, including friendships?
- How could Grace and Kingston be supported at school and college?

There are four distinct and overlapping reasons for pupils to have SLCN:

1 Primary need: a persistent developmental difficulty specific to the speech and language systems associated with speech sounds, formulating sentences, understanding, social interaction or fluency
2 Secondary need: primary developmental factor related to autism, physical, hearing or cognitive impairments which affect Speech, Language and Communication
3 Reduced developmental opportunities: meaning that language is impoverished or delayed; mainly linked to social disadvantage
4 Speaking and understanding English as an additional language (EAL) does not in itself constitute a SLC difficulty

Activity

We could identify Speech, Language and Communication Needs in tiers, ranging from mild, through moderate, severe, significant to profound. Darlington Borough Council have produced such a structure and it can be found on the following website: www.darlington.gov.uk/media/7426/communication_and_interaction_-_slcn_-_final_version.pdf

- Take examples from the areas such as speech, expressive and receptive language, and social communication to identify how SLCN are identified
- Where do language and speech disorders fit in with this approach?
- What is the relationship between SLCN and autism?

Being able to understand and use language is essential for children to communicate socially and maintain friendships (Andrés-Roqueta and Katsos, 2020). This puts children with SLCN at a disadvantage where peer relationships are concerned (Craig and Evans, 1993). Findings from studies around social relationships of children with SLCN have led to conclusions that, due to differences in interacting with other children, those with SLCN are often seen as less preferred playmates than their typically developing peers (Fujiki, Brinton and Todd, 1996). Because of this, children with SLCN have been observed as having withdrawn behaviours, particularly in the classroom, as children find great importance in having and maintaining friendships. As a result of challenges both socially and academically due to SLCN, children are often faced with academic failure and social exclusion (Marton, Abramoff and Rosenzweig, 2005). All these factors can then lead to low self-esteem and a negative view towards their experiences throughout life (Jerome et al., 2002).

According to Public Health England (2020), approximately 50 per cent of children start school with a communication delay and 10 per cent have long-term Speech, Language and Communication Needs. Bishop (2017) suggests that SLCN receive less attention by researchers and professionals than other neurodevelopmental issues partly due to differing definitions and terminologies which may cause difficulties for practitioners in understanding how and when to implement appropriate interventions. Bryan et al. (2015) found that at least 60 per cent of young people in the UK who are accessing youth justice services present with Speech, Language and Communication difficulties which are largely unrecognised. The contributing reasons for this suggest that early language difficulty is a risk factor for other problems such as literacy difficulties and educational failure that may increasingly put the young person at risk of offending. Around 30 per cent of the participants presented with language difficulties, 20 per cent of the participants had a diagnosis of mental illness and 50 per cent had a history of drug abuse. Cohen, Farnia and Im-Bolter (2013) suggest that the demands on language for social and academic adjustment shift dramatically during adolescence and the ability to understand the non-literal meaning in language represented by higher order language becomes essential. In their study, clinic-referred youth scored significantly lower than comparison youth on measures of structural and higher order language, working memory, and reading. They also had lower levels of non-verbal ability and working memory as well as lower level of mothers' education, which were associated with greater risk of having higher order language impairment.

Activity

Wendy Lee, Professional Director at The Communication Trust, interviewed seven children with Speech, Language and Communication Needs about their life, their experiences at school and what it's like to have a communication difficulty. The video can be found at the following website: www.youtube.com/watch?v=Onqn_7xzp2Q

- What range of SLC needs can you identify?
- What are the implications for teaching and learning development?
- What are the implications for emotional and social development?

Developmental Language Disorder (DLD)

Developmental Language Disorder (DLD) is likely to be diagnosed when children have slow development of talking and understanding, fall behind that of other children the same age and struggle to find the right words and/or don't seem to understand other people. Indicators of DLD may include not talking as much or finding it difficult to express verbally, struggling to find words or to use varied vocabulary, not understanding or remembering what has been said, and immature language for their age. DLD could have a negative impact on friendship, self-management, assertion and cooperation. Although DLD is diagnosed most often in childhood, the associated difficulties are not restricted to this developmental period and may continue to restrict the person's social, academic, and occupational activities even beyond adolescence and into adulthood. Children with DLD are at risk for learning difficulties in school due either to the verbal load of educational instruction and tasks, or that differences associated with DLD extend beyond the verbal domain to impact other types of representations.

The findings of the few cross-sectional studies that have specifically used health-related quality of life (HRQoL) measures in children with speech and language disorders suggest that these children may have poorer HRQoL compared to typically developing peers with psychosocial domains affected more. Higher language scores were associated with better HRQoL, particularly in social and school functioning (Le et al., 2022). Eadie et al. (2018) found that children with DLD had a lower quality of life (QoL) than their typical peers at nine years and, contrary to previous studies, differences in QoL were not observed with DLD severity. Co-occurring social-emotional problems appear to play an important role in contributing to the lower QoL experienced by children with DLD. McCormack et al. (2011) found that children identified with communication impairment at age four to five years performed significantly poorer at age seven to nine years on all outcomes, parents and teachers reported slower progression in reading, writing, and overall school achievement than peers and children reported more bullying, poorer peer relationships, and less enjoyment of school than did their peers. However, children's trajectories can change over time as is clearly illustrated in a longitudinal single case study of a young boy called Cody who started out with a diagnosis of specific language impairment (now referred to as DLD) at the age of four years and ended up as an adult with significant difficulties in language, learning, social and emotional domains. At the age of 19 years, Cody compared his social skills with those of his peers and said, 'it's like they are driving sports cars and I am on a tricycle' (Brinton, Fujiki and Robinson, 2005, p. 338).

Clegg et al. (2005) identified 17 men with a severe receptive DLD in childhood, reassessed in middle childhood and early adult life, were studied again in their mid-30s with tests of intelligence (IQ), language, literacy, theory of mind and memory together with assessments of psychosocial outcome. They had normal intelligence with higher performance IQ than verbal IQ, a severe and persisting language disorder, severe literacy impairments and significant deficits in theory of mind and phonological processing. Within the DLD cohort, higher childhood intelligence and language were associated with superior cognitive and language ability at final adult outcome. In their mid-30s, the DLD cohort had significantly worse social adaptation (with prolonged unemployment and a paucity of close friendships and love relationships) compared with both their siblings and controls. Sowerbutts et al. (2021) identified that a cohort of young offenders disproportionately presented with DLD and were likely to struggle with the communication demands of the justice system. Communication barriers included exposure to unfamiliar vocabulary, repairing misunderstandings, constructing narratives and displaying the appropriate attitude. In their research with 58 juvenile offenders, Bryan, Freer and Furlong (2007) found that they had below average language skills, with the majority of these being in the poor or very poor group and had not obtained Level 1 in Literacy.

Pause for reflection

- What do you think are the short and long-term consequences of the fact that communication barriers have been identified with respect to young offenders?

Aphasia

Aphasia is defined as a language impairment which occurs because of brain injury in isolation
from other cognitive impairments (Papathanasiou, Coppens and Potagas, 2013), primarily because of stroke (Kiyani and Naz, 2018). Broca's aphasia is a form of non-fluent aphasia characterised by difficulties with speaking, writing and reading, whilst comprehension generally remains unharmed (Teng, 2017). The Broca's area is responsible for expressive language skills such as speaking and writing, thus Broca's aphasia patients may have difficulties in these areas. Research has suggested that individuals with aphasia generally have a poorer social life resulting in frustration if as they are unable to express their thoughts. Also, others may assume impaired intelligence (Cruice, Worrall and Hickson, 2006).

Within an educational context, individuals living with Wernicke's aphasia may face various struggles due to their difficulties in comprehending spoken language. Whilst Wernicke's aphasia does not affect the individual's intellectual abilities, it may affect their ability to acquire new information (Pallickal and Hema, 2020). Wernicke's aphasia could also lead to distress (Hartman et al., 2017), but despite the struggle with communication and speech these individuals can still learn effectively (Nicholas and Connor, 2016), but it may impact on social relationships and a lack of confidence in maintaining and creating friendships. Laures-Gore, Dotson and Belagaje (2020) reported socialisation as an area of difficulty for all those living with aphasia, particularly adolescents.

However, Cruice, Worrall and Hickson (2006) argue that successful social integration is equally important for older people with aphasia as it is associated with successful ageing, self-esteem, and happiness. It is apparent that, regardless of age, successful socialisation is a key aspect of living successfully with aphasia as loneliness and social isolation can lead to emotional distress and a poor QoL (Hilari et al., 2010). From this, it can be determined that depending on the individual and aphasia symptoms, independency and a higher quality of life could be quite difficult to acquire for children and young people with aphasia. Factors such as emotional distress, social isolation and depression because of loss of language can all be shown to effect independency amongst individuals (Spaccavento et al., 2014).

QoL can also be a large factor that contributes towards this. Overall, after brain damage, quality of life has been shown to worsen. This is associated with higher levels of depression, and lower levels of reacquisition in motor functions. From this, Spaccavento et al. (2014) highlight how this can affect participation within complex social activities, for example being unable to get involved within work and community interests. In addition, Lam and Wodchis (2010) found that quality of life (QoL) was rated the most negative when it came to experiencing aphasia. Bonini and Radanovic (2015) identify the interrelation between language and cognitive issues such as executive function, working memory and attention. Significant differences within cognitive profiles have been identified in relation to academic success. There is mixed evidence when it comes to academic success, but Cooper and Flowers (1987) found that children with acquired aphasia performed more poorly in academic and language tests.

A highly significant area of impact for post-stroke aphasia patients is in mental health. Baker et al. (2018) report that approximately 60 per cent of aphasic patients also develop depression. Robinson, Starkstein and Price (1988) suggested that aphasia did not cause depression, but patients with non-fluent aphasia were more likely to develop depression as both were caused by damage to similar areas of the brain. However, more recent research argues that mental difficulties in aphasic individuals are caused by emotional factors which result from the problems they encounter (Døli, Helland and Andersen Helland, 2017). Whether caused by brain damage or emotional responses, low emotional well-being is a common result of post-stroke aphasia. Developing depression can impact negatively on the rehabilitation of aphasic individuals (Robinson, Starkstein and Price, 1988). The impact of post-stroke aphasia is significant and interlinked with reports that low emotional health in post-stroke aphasia patients impacted on their relationships and that loneliness and lack of social satisfaction can lead to long-term emotional distress. Research suggests that accessing and maintaining employment after stroke is important for preserving social and personal identity (Lasker, LaPointe and Kodras, 2005); however, an average of only 28 per cent of aphasic patients successfully returned to work following their stroke and those who did return did so on significantly reduced hours and a modified workload (Graham, Pereira and Teasell, 2011).

Activity

Read the following case study:

Ayesha is a 19-year-old girl who suffered a stroke when she was 18 years old, resulting in the development of Broca's aphasia. The immediate effects of the stroke were the loss of movement in her left side, and the inability to read, write, speak or swallow. Whilst she regained movement fairly quickly, her speech did not return quickly and she sustained difficulties with expressive language. Whilst she has full comprehension and knows what she wants to say, she struggles to formulate the words. As Ayesha also has difficulties with reading and writing, she has deferred her entry to university where she was supposed to be studying Biological Sciences. Instead of attending university, she is currently focusing on intensive speech and language therapy (SLT) to aid her expressive communication. She also attends group therapy sessions with others who have faced similar experiences. Ayesha is currently single but has a close network of friends and family. She is currently looking for employment but hopes that her communication skills will improve sufficiently for her to attend university and eventually pursue a career in science despite her setback in school.

- What organisations might support Ayesha's quest for both employment and a place at university?

Lam and Wodchis (2010) suggest that aphasia has greater negative impact on a person's quality of life than cancer or Alzheimer's fisease. They studied health-related factors affecting quality of life for hospital residents in Ontario, Canada and the impact of 60 different diseases and 15 conditions in 66,193 people. The negative effects of aphasia on an individual's quality of life includes their inability to communicate with and engage their family, friends, doctors and their wider community.

- Find research evidence which may support this claim

Selective mutism

Pause for reflection

Selective mutism is a severe anxiety disorder where a person is unable to speak in certain social situations, such as with classmates at school or to relatives they do not see very often. Why do you think that this has been included in a chapter on Communication and Interaction Needs?

Selective mutism (SM) presents a significant impact on a child's social, emotional and academic function at a very critical point in their development (Bergman, 2013). As stated in DSM-5 (APA, 2013) and ICD-11 (WHO, 2019), SM is associated with severe impairment in academic functioning that will cause significant consequences on their academic achievement as it creates an inability to complete expected schoolwork. Children with SM are likely to have problems when talking to peers as they have the inability to initiate or reciprocate social interactions. Educational experience is impacted by SM, for example working memory deficits (Eysenck et al., 2007) and stress caused by reduced controlled attention resources, as they are compromised to deal with potential threat (anxiety stressor) (Klein and Boals, 2001). Cognitive function resources are allocated to 'heightened vigilance' and sensory sensitivity caused by anxious state (Eysenck et al., 2007), meaning that task performance is impaired. Moreover, individuals with SM may have inability to ask questions to gain clarification and feedback. When children get older, deficits are more evident as academic demands increase and incidental learning and collaborative conversation with peers may be impacted.

Individuals with SM often rely on friendships with peers encouraging social integration to reduce feelings of isolation and Cunningham et al. (2006) found that 32 per cent of children with SM were performing below grade level, were scored lower by teachers in terms of academic performance due to their lack of verbal communication and were often excluded from friendship groups and bullied by peers. In clinical observations, barriers to social interaction led to difficulty establishing friendships and participating in social activities (Wong, 2010). People with SM sometimes exhibit challenging behaviour and these responses may appear violent in their outbursts and this can hinder some peer relationships as there may be misinterpretation of this communication (Leo, Diliberto and Kearney, 2014). In one retrospective follow-up study, 41 children with SM were assessed on average 12 years post-referral and the majority still presented with significant fears and difficulties with communication, including fear of unknown situations, speaking with strangers, and fear of speaking on the telephone or in shops or offices. The formerly mute patients described themselves as less independent, less motivated about school achievement, less self-confident and less mature and healthy in comparison to a normal reference group (Remschmidt et al., 2001).

Activity

Read the following case study:

You are a friend to **Alex**, a 34-year-old man who, aged 20, was attacked by a dog. This was a very traumatic incident and caused him to withdraw from interacting with people at work. At work he gets anxious when colleagues give PPT presentations to the sales team in case he might be asked to present in a similar way. He physically removes himself from speaking situations, avoids eye contact, tries to hide and declines invitations to social events. When he is relaxed at home, he will talk to family and friends but will 'freeze' if someone enters the room or converses with his immediate group.

- What effect do you think that Alex's selective mutism is having on his work and social life?

You have investigated how you might help to support him, including learning non-verbal gestures and gradually exposing both Alex and you to social situations.

- Research what other strategies might help Alex in social and work situations

Childhood Onset Fluency Disorder (COFD) (stuttering)

Rice and Kroll (2006) identified that individuals with COFD perceive that their stutter has a negative impact on their employability, career advancement and job performance, being employed in a lower-status job due to their stutter and face negative attitudes from others that may impact their employment. Studies have found that job opportunities were limited for individuals with a stutter, with COFD impacting the likelihood of employment if adults are not supported effectively through relevant adaptations and training. Klein and Hood (2004) found that in their sample of 232 adults, 70 per cent of the individuals identified that the stutter reduced changes of employability and that 20 per cent had been turned down a promotion. Also, COFD can impacts the individual's social relationships and well-being, with Iverach and Rapee (2014) reporting that individuals with a stutter reported feelings of helplessness and resorted to avoidance to hide their stammer from others.

Although COFD does not directly impact an individual's cognition, it can dramatically impact their academic attainment if not supported effectively (Ribbler, 2002). Children with a stutter can have difficulty in interacting with peers and teachers and a lack of teacher knowledge and attitudes towards stuttering may be a key factor. Professional teacher-student relationships can help to support the emotional well-being of individuals, which is important for those with COFD as common emotions experienced include embarrassment, frustration and guilt, negatively impacting an individual's self-esteem and leading to avoidance within class (Khan, 2015). Therefore, without the correct support, academic achievements can be negatively impacted as individuals will not be working to their full potential, whilst increasing the chance of social isolation and poor mental health

(Samochis, Rus and Iftene, 2011). Children with COFD are commonly seen as 'slow learners' within a classroom setting, due to a lack of interaction (Ribbler, 2002).

In interview and survey studies, people who stutter report the belief that stuttering has had a negative impact on their own education and employment. McAllister, Collier and Shepstone (2012) sought objective evidence of such disadvantage for people who stutter as a group, compared with people who do not stutter. Those who stuttered at 16 were statistically more likely than those who did not stutter to be male, to have poorer cognitive test scores, and to have been bullied. For employment outcomes, the only significant association with stuttering concerned socio-economic status of occupation at 50, with those who had been reported to stutter having lower-status jobs. The higher likelihood of those who stutter working in lower-status positions may reflect their preference for avoiding occupations perceived to require good spoken communication abilities. However, Klompas and Ross (2004) indicated that most participants perceived their stuttering to have impacted on their academic performance at school, and relationships with teachers and classmates. Although their stuttering was not perceived to adversely influence their ability to establish friendships, people generally reacted negatively to their stuttering. Overall, stuttering did not appear to have influenced participants' family and marital life, but most felt that stuttering had affected their self-esteem and self-image. Silverman (2004) reports five characteristics of adults who stutter: they avoid conversation in many situations because of fear of being laughed at by others, they had an inability to express their anger, experience depression, feel guilty and they anticipate negative reaction from family members, friends and other listeners.

Autism spectrum disorder

Activity

Read the following case study:

Andrew is five years old and was a full-term baby delivered with no complications. Andrew's mother reported that as a baby and toddler, he was healthy and his motor development was within normal limits for the major milestones of sitting, standing and walking. At age three, he was described as low tone with awkward motor skills and inconsistent imitation skills. His communication development was delayed; he began using vocalisations at three months of age but had developed no words by three years. Andrew communicated through non-verbal means and used communication solely for behavioural regulation. He communicated requests primarily by reaching for the communication partner's hand and placing it on the desired object. When cued, he used an approximation of the 'more' sign when grabbing the hand along with a verbal production of /m/. He knew about ten approximate signs when asked to label, but these were not used in a communicative fashion. Protests were demonstrated most often through pushing hands. Andrew played functionally with toys when seated and used eye gaze appropriately during cause-and-effect play, but otherwise eye gaze was absent. He often appeared to be non-engaged and responded inconsistently to his name.

- What impact might these characteristics have on Andrew's communication needs?
- How could you use his understanding of signs to scaffold and develop his communication and interaction?

Impact of autism on siblings

Ward et al. (2016) found that living with an autistic sibling has an impact in both positive and negative ways. Interviewing 11 brothers and 11 sisters of autistic siblings, they recognised difficulties (decreased parental attention, extra responsibility, bothersome behaviours, communication difficulties) and positive aspects (became empathetic, loved and appreciated the child, realised the experience was life-changing) of living with an autistic young person. Similarly, Watson, Hanna and Jones (2021) found that having an autistic sibling can impact typically developing siblings' self-identity and personal development in a number of ways. Similarly, interactions with the autistic sibling and with other individuals can evoke a myriad of experiences that can both benefit and challenge typically developing siblings. Tozer and Atkin (2015) interviewed adult siblings and found that they had to fulfil other social and family obligations, alongside their 'sense of duty' to support their disabled brother or sister. Sibling experience was further mediated by negotiating their 'perceived invisibility' in social care policy and practice.

Benderix and Sivberg's (2007) interviews with siblings revealed stressful life conditions with reports of reports of precocious responsibility, feeling sorry, exposed to frightening behaviour, empathetic feelings, hoping that a group home will be a relief, physical violence made siblings feel unsafe and anxious, and relations with friends were affected negatively. Corsano et al. (2016) found that typically developing siblings expressed mixed feelings about their brother, a precocious sense of responsibility, concern about the future, friendship difficulties and troubles and the desire to talk about their experience. Most adolescents integrated their positive and negative feelings; however, three adolescents displayed rejection, denial or a sense of persecution. Gorjy, Fielding and Falkmer (2017) challenge the often widely held assumption that having a child with ASD in the family is all 'doom and gloom'. For example, they found that many typically developing (TD) siblings described the positive influence having an autistic sibling has had on their personal development, including their desire to promote the acceptance in wider society. Similarly, interactions with their autistic sibling allowed for the development of pride and appreciation of their unique personality characteristics. They reported that they had used, or wanted to use, their unique platform to raise awareness, fundraise and promote the acceptance of autism generally.

In their article 'I don't live with autism; I live with my sister', Pavlopoulou and Dimitriou (2019) found that TD siblings spoke of precocious responsibilities, including an increased amount of household chores, less access to or attention from their parents and feeling responsible for the care and protection of their sibling. They spoke about the positive impact their autistic sibling has had on their own personal attributes, such as increased empathy and understanding; developed ability to cope, compromise and feel good about helping. In contrast, many siblings spoke of responsibilities that may be above what would be expected of their developmental age and stage. For example: protecting their sibling from being bullied, hurting themselves or others, alongside an increased amount of household duties and taking responsibility for their sibling's care to allow their parents to take a break. Macedo Costa and da Silva Pereira (2019) suggest that many TD siblings are proud of their autistic sibling and appreciated how unique, smart and funny they are. TD siblings also expressed enjoyment of having someone they could play with, although difficulties with having to deal with problematic and sometimes unpredictable behaviour were often cited. For example, they reported experiencing problems with their sibling's aggression, meltdowns and social and communication difficulties. Several TD siblings express unsurprising feelings of anger, frustration, upset, hurt and embarrassment if subject to negative attitudes, or disapproving comments from others, about their sibling (Pavlopoulou and Dimitriou, 2019). Some also feel that they need to explain their sibling's behaviour (Gorjy, Fielding and Falkmer, 2017).

Impact of autism on parents

Many parents report that having an autistic child has a positive impact on their lives, for example, a new appreciation of life, relating to others, personal strength and spiritual change. Perceived social support, peer example, effective coping style and self-efficacy enhancement were facilitating factors of post-traumatic growth. Safe, Joosten and Molineux (2012) revealed that the mothers were challenged by the demands of their multiple roles while dealing with the paradox of accepting their child for who they were, and at the same time also desiring their typical growth and development. Waizbard-Bartov, Yehonatan-Schori and Golan (2019) found that parents identified empowerment, personal strength and an existential or spiritual experience. Timmons, Ekas and Johnson's (2017) research saw mothers of autistic children being divided into two groups and instructed to write letters of gratitude to either someone besides their child (general gratitude) or their child (child gratitude). Prominent themes for mothers in the general gratitude group included sources of social support, characteristics of close personal relationships, inspirational others, and other positive attributes of individuals, such as being kind-hearted. Whereas, in the child gratitude group, emergent themes were the autistic child making progress, the child's personality, inspiration, and shared experiences. Potter (2016) suggested that often fathers appreciated their children's individual qualities, valuing the strong emotional bond they had with them and their own nurturing role and associated personal development. However, other researchers had found that having an autistic child may have a negative impact on relationships.

Kuhlthau et al. (2014) describe health-related quality of life (HRQoL) of parents of autistic children who reported on their HRQoL, depression, and caregiving burden using quantitative tools. HRQoL scores were slightly worse than from those in normative populations especially related to stress and mental health. For example, parents reported average HRQoL scores which were clinically significantly lower than an average normative US population, with 40 per cent of parents reporting clinical depression symptoms. Married parents reported lower depression symptoms than parents who were not and families with three or more children with special health care needs (CSHCN) reported lower HRQoL and higher caregiving burden than families with less CSHCN. Kayfitz, Gragg and Orr (2010) suggest that mothers reported significantly more positive experiences than did fathers. Falk, Norris and Quinn (2014) found that parental mental health problems, locus of control and social support issues, perceived parent-child attachment, as well as autism symptom severity and perceived externalising behaviours in the autistic child impacted upon relationships. Schnabel et al. (2020) reported that parents of autistic children appear to experience high levels of psychological distress, such as depressive disorders, anxiety disorders and obsessive-compulsive disorder and parents of autistic children with significant autistic traits themselves described difficulties with parental mental health and navigating professional services (Marriott et al., 2022).

Gender differences in autism

The male brain is defined psychometrically as those individuals in whom systemising is significantly better than empathising, and the female brain is defined as the opposite cognitive profile. Using these definitions, autism can be considered as an extreme of the normal male profile. Baron-Cohen (2002) proposed the Extreme Male Brain Theory (EMB) to suggest that autism is more extreme manifestation of psychological due to heightened testosterone exposure in the foetus. It is suggested that this accounts for gender differences in frequency of eye contact frequency, value-laden proposition use and mediates the narrowing of interest toward systems and exerts sex-specific effects on numerical and language abilities. When attempting to account for the discrepancies in diagnosis, researchers have drawn upon two distinct ideas, which are contrasting but not mutually exclusive. One view is that there is something inherent in being female that 'protects' females from the likelihood of developing autism and that girls may require greater familial aetiologic load to manifest the phenotype. It could imply female-specific protective genetic/biological effects, such that females would have to have a greater aetiological (genetic or environmental) load than would males to reach the diagnostic threshold.

Wigdor et al. (2022) found evidence of a female protective effect from common inherited variation against autism spectrum disorder and found that mothers of autistic children carry more genetic risk than fathers, although this not mediated by a single genetic locus. Another view proposes that females may be more likely to develop autism than we currently estimate, but that diagnostic biases and variation in the ways autism is expressed mean we do not pick up autism in females to the same degree as males. In a retrospective secondary analysis of a longitudinal UK cohort study, Russell, Steer and Golding (2011) found that with the severity of autistic traits held constant, boys were more likely to receive an autism diagnosis than girls. Younger mothers and mothers of first-born children were significantly less likely to have autistic children and maternal depression before and around the time of their children's autistic difficulties was associated with a lack of diagnosis.

Difficulties with social relationships, particularly friendships, are a hallmark of autism. Some research has suggested that autistic females may have fewer social impairments than males; autistic females tend to have higher levels of social motivation (the desire and intent to form friendships with others) than males on average. Hiller, Young and Weber (2014) found that girls presented with both less and different restricted interests. However, they found that autistic females may find it harder to maintain long-term friendships or relationships than autistic males, despite having similar levels of motivation for social relationships as non-autistic females. Sedgewick, Hill and Pellicano (2019) found that in many ways, the friendships and social experiences of autistic girls are like those of neurotypical girls; however, they have significantly more social challenges.

Studies have found that autistic males' interests tend to be focused on more mechanical topics such as vehicles, computers, or physics; autistic females' interests, however, appear to focus more on topics with relational purposes, such as animals and fictional characters. McFayden et al. (2019) found that male participants reported a wider range of restricted interests, including mostly object-related interests; female participants, however, demonstrated a narrower range of topics, including mostly interests in living beings, and expressed their restricted interests in a more socially oriented manner compared to males. Autistic girls may also be more likely to model and imitate social actions around them, disguising their symptoms and resulting in missed diagnoses. Gould and Ashston-Smith (2011) found that socially immature girls tended to be 'mothered' by other girls in social play, were more worried than boys about fitting in. Many of the boys of their age and diagnoses had no friends, whereas girls tended to have one special friend, appeared shy and because they tended to be included in a group, teachers missed identifying them as loners.

Impact of autism on adults

Activity

Read the following case study:

Bobby is a 19-year-old autistic man who has recently transitioned from a post-16 special school to a work placement. It has been noted that Bobby has a very good memory, a robust sense of humour and a keen interest in movies, with an extensive collection of DVD and Blu-ray films. He has excellent computer skills and enjoys art and drawing. In line with his diagnosis, Bobby presents with difficulties in social communication skills, sensory processing, and significant challenges around flexibility and rigid thought patterns. Direct observations of Bobby, at home and in school, and from discussions with his parents, staff and Bobby himself, led to the identification of the main factors contributing to stress and anxiety. These include conversations where others have a different opinion from him on an area of focused interest, conversations with work colleagues and not joining in with their interactions, especially at break times, sensitivity to certain noises, smells, and textures and his understanding of social rules when working with colleagues.

- What information could the school provide to support Bobby in his work placement?
- Identify two of the main issues that Bobby has identified lead to stress and anxiety and identify how the placement staff could work with him to support these
- What strengths do you see in Bobby's profile and how could he use these in everyday life?

There is some evidence that the core symptoms of autism abate to some degree in adolescence and young adulthood with improvements in communication skills most common, but social impairments and repetitive behaviours tend to persist. Orsmond, Krauss and Seltzer (2004) investigated peer relationships and participation in social and recreational activities among 235 adolescents and adults with autism who live at home. The prevalence of having friendships, peer relationships, and participating in social and recreational activities were all low predictors of participation in social activities in adulthood, including greater independence in activities of daily living, better socialisation skills, and greater number of services received. In a longitudinal study, Howlin et al. (2004) found that although a minority of adults had achieved relatively high levels of independence, most remained very dependent on their families or other support services. Few lived alone, had close friends, or permanent employment. Communication generally was impaired and reading and spelling abilities were poor and stereotyped behaviours or interests frequently persisted into adulthood.

Pause for reflection

- Why do you think that it is important to listen to the voices of autistic adults?
- How would you involve them in researching the impact of autism?

Lai and Baron-Cohen (2015) refer to a lost generation of adults who were previously excluded from a diagnosis of classic autism. Making a first diagnosis of autism spectrum conditions in adults can be challenging for practical reasons (e.g., no person to provide a developmental history), developmental reasons (e.g., the acquisition of learnt or camouflaging strategies), and clinical reasons (e.g., high frequency of co-occurring disorders). In general, based on interviews or survey research, there appears to be a positive impact and relief from receiving a diagnosis of autism in adulthood. In a group of autistic adults over the age of 50, Hickey, Crabtree and Stott (2018) found that prior to diagnosis, individuals had awareness of their difficulties, attributed these to intrinsic difference and engaged in a deliberate process of reducing the visibility of this difference. Diagnosis prompted a process of life review and externalisation, whereby past negative experiences were reattributed to autism as opposed to the self. Loneliness, isolation and yearning for interpersonal connection were ubiquitous and longstanding. Tan (2018) reported that participants found explanation for their atypicality and developed a more valued self-concept. Learning of the condition did not disrupt their biography; rather, it became integral to and constitutive of it. With a new self-concept, participants re-gauged personal expectations for normalisation and accessed communities of alike others, forging relationships that affirmed identity.

Howlin et al. (2013) suggest that although severity of autism had continued to decrease during the adult period, social outcomes were poorer than in younger adulthood. In their cohort of adults first diagnosed with autism, on average, 37 years previously, social inclusion remains very limited, despite general improvements in autism symptomatology with age. Jones et al. (2014) surveyed 128 autistic adults concerning the process they went through to obtain their diagnosis and the subsequent support they received. Results suggested that routes to diagnosis were quite heterogeneous and overall levels of satisfaction with the diagnostic process were mixed with 40 per cent of respondents were 'very/quite' dissatisfied, whilst 47 per cent were 'very/quite' satisfied. The extent of delays, number of professionals seen, quality of information given at diagnosis and levels of post-diagnostic support predicted overall satisfaction with the diagnostic process. When compared with non-autistic adults, older autistic adults perform poorly on some cognitive tasks and better on other tasks, with cognitive decline occurring differently for different cognitive processes. Lever and Geurts's (2016) research involved autistic and non-autistic adults aged 50–79 years and reported more cognitive impairment in the autistic adults. However, autistic adults had higher visual memory and immediate recall than non-autistic adults.

With respect to employment, Coleman and Adams (2018) identified that the major barrier to employment was being unable to get past interviews, followed by not knowing what jobs to apply for, what they wanted to do, having difficulty keeping a job and not having proper transportation. The problem with interviews is expected to be due to the core deficits of communication and social understanding in autistic adults of knowing what jobs to apply for and what type of employment they wanted, which may be due in part to a lack of social networking, since many jobs are found through friends/colleagues, and autistic adults usually have a very limited social network. The problem with transportation is probably due to a combination of either lacking the skills to use public or personal transportation, or limited finances which require the use of public transportation which may be much slower.

Activity

Top autism tips: employment – recruitment and interviews

Watch these two videos produced by the National Autistic Society which are aimed to employers and employees. 'Employment: recruitment and interviews for employers' and 'Employment: recruitment and interviews for employees'.

They can be accessed via: www.autism.org.uk/advice-and-guidance/professional-practice/recruitment-interviews

- What key messages are contained in the videos which would support an organisation wishing to employ an autistic individual? What benefits would this person bring to an organisation?
- How would the tips support transitions into work for a potential employee?

References

American Psychiatric Association (2013). *Diagnostic and Statistical Manual of Mental Disorders*. 5th ed. Washington, DC: American Psychiatric Publishing.

Andrés-Roqueta, C. and Katsos, N. (2020). A distinction between linguistic and social pragmatics helps the precise characterization of pragmatic challenges in children with autism spectrum disorders and developmental language disorder. *Journal of Speech, Language, and Hearing Research. JSLHR*, 63 (5), pp. 1494–1508.

Baker, C., Worrall, L., Rose, M., Hudson, K., Ryan, B. and O'Byrne, L. (2018). A systematic review of rehabilitation interventions to prevent and treat depression in post-stroke aphasia. *Disability and Rehabilitation*, 40 (16), pp. 1870–1892.

Baron-Cohen, S. (2002). The extreme male brain theory of autism. *Trends in Cognitive Sciences*, 6 (6), pp. 248–254.

Benderix, Y. and Sivberg, B. (2007). Siblings' experiences of having a brother or sister with autism and mental retardation: a case study of 14 siblings from five families. *Journal of Pediatric Nursing*, 22 (5), pp. 410–418.

Bergman, R. L. (2013). *Treatment for Children with Selective Mutism: An Integrative Behavioral Approach*. Oxford: Oxford University Press.

Bishop, D. V. M. (2017). Why is it so hard to reach agreement on terminology? The case of developmental language disorder (DLD). *International Journal of Language & Communication Disorders*, 52 (6), pp. 671–680.

Bonini, M. V. and Radanovic, M. (2015). Cognitive deficits in post-stroke aphasia. *Arquivos de neuro-psiquiatria*, 73 (10), pp. 840–847.

Brinton, B., Fujiki, M. and Robinson, L. (2005). Life on a tricycle: a case study of language impairment from 4 to 19. *Topics in Language Disorders*, 25, pp. 338–352.

Bryan, K., Freer, J. and Furlong, C. (2007). Language and communication difficulties in juvenile offenders. *International Journal of Language & Communication Disorders*, 42 (5), pp. 505–520.

Bryan, K., Garvani, G., Gregory, J. and Kilner, K. (2015). Language difficulties and criminal justice: the need for earlier identification. *International Journal of Language & Communication Disorders*, 50 (6), pp. 763–775.

Clegg, J., Hollis, C., Mawhood, L. and Rutter, M. (2005). Developmental language disorders – a follow-up in later adult life. Cognitive, language and psychosocial outcomes. *Journal of Child Psychology and Psychiatry, and Allied Disciplines*, 46 (2), pp. 128–149.

Cohen, N., Farnia, F. and Im-Bolter, N. (2013). Higher order language competence and adolescent mental health. *Journal of Child Psychology and Psychiatry, and Allied Disciplines*, 54 (7), pp. 733–744.

Coleman, D. M. and Adams, J. B. (2018). Survey of vocational experiences of adults with Autism Spectrum Disorders, and recommendations on improving their employment. *Journal of Vocational Rehabilitation*, 49 (1), pp. 67–78.

Cooper, J. A. and Flowers, C. R. (1987). Children with a history of acquired aphasia: residual language and academic impairments. *The Journal of Speech and Hearing Disorders*, 52 (3), pp. 251–262.

Corsano, P., Musetti, A., and Guidotti, L. and Capelli, F. (2016). Typically developing adolescents' experience of growing up with a brother with an autism spectrum disorder. *Journal of Intellectual & Developmental Disability*, 42, pp. 151–161.

Craig, H. K. and Evans, J. L. (1993). Pragmatics and SLI: within-group variations in discourse behaviors. *Journal of Speech & Hearing Research*, 36 (4), pp. 777–789.

Cruice, M., Worrall, L. and Hickson, L. (2006). Quantifying aphasic people's social lives in the context of non-aphasic peers. *Aphasiology*, 20 (12).

Cunningham, C. E., McHolm, A. E. and Boyle, M. H. (2006). Social phobia, anxiety, oppositional behavior, social skills, and self-concept in children with specific selective mutism, generalized selective mutism, and community controls. *European Child & Adolescent Psychiatry*, 15 (5), pp. 245–255.

Døli, H., Helland, T. and Andersen Helland, W. (2017). Self-reported symptoms of anxiety and depression in chronic stroke patients with and without aphasia. *Aphasiology*, 31 (12), pp. 1392–1409.

Eadie, P., Conway, L., Hallenstein, B., Mensah, F., McKean, C. and Reilly, S. (2018). Quality of life in children with developmental language disorder. *International Journal of Language & Communication Disorders*, 53 (4), pp. 799–810.

Eysenck, M. W., Derakshan, N., Santos, R and Calvo, M. G. (2007). Anxiety and cognitive performance: attentional control theory. *Emotion*, 7 (2), pp. 336–353.

Falk, N. H., Norris, K. and Quinn, M. G. (2014). The factors predicting stress, anxiety and depression in the parents of children with autism. *Journal of Autism and Developmental Disorders*, 44 (12), pp. 3185–3203.

Fujiki, M., Brinton, B. and Todd, C. M. (1996). Social skills of children with specific language impairment. *Language, Speech, and Hearing Services in Schools*, 27 (3), pp. 195–202.

Gorjy, R., Fielding, A. and Falkmer, M. (2017). 'It's better than it used to be': perspectives of adolescent siblings of children with an autism spectrum condition. *Child and Family Social Work*, 22, pp. 1488–1496.

Gould, J. and Ashton-Smith, J. (2011). Missed diagnosis or misdiagnosis? Girls and women on the autism spectrum. *Good Autism Practice (GAP)*, 12.

Graham, J. R., Pereira, S. and Teasell, R. (2011). Aphasia and return to work in younger stroke survivors. *Aphasiology*, 25 (8), pp. 952–960.

Hartman, K., Peluzzo, A., Shadani, S., Chellquist, I., Weprin, S., Hunt, H., Smith-Benjamin, S. and Altschuler, E. L. (2017). Devising a method to study if Wernicke's aphasia patients are aware that they do not comprehend language or speak it understandably. *J Undergrad Neurosci Educ*, 16 (1), e5–e12.

Hickey, A., Crabtree, J. and Stott, J. (2018). 'Suddenly the first fifty years of my life made sense': experiences of older people with autism. *Autism: The International Journal of Research and Practice*, 22 (3), pp. 357–367.

Hilari, K., Northcott, S., Roy, P., Marshall, J., Wiggins, R. D., Chataway, J. and Ames, D. (2010). Psychological distress after stroke and aphasia: the first six months. *Clinical Rehabilitation*, 24 (2), pp. 181–190.

Hiller, R. M., Young, R. L. and Weber, N. (2014). Sex differences in autism spectrum disorder based on DSM-5 criteria: evidence from clinician and teacher reporting. *Journal of Abnormal Child Psychology*, 42 (8), pp. 1381–1393.

Howlin, P., Goode, S., Hutton, J. and Rutter, M. (2004). Adult outcome for children with autism. *Journal of Child Psychology and Psychiatry, and Allied Disciplines*, 45 (2), pp. 212–229.

Howlin, P., Moss, P., Savage, S. and Rutter, M. (2013). Social outcomes in mid- to later adulthood among individuals diagnosed with autism and average nonverbal IQ as children. *J Am Acad Child Adolesc Psychiatry*, 52 (6), pp. 572–581.

Iverach, L. and Rapee, R. M. (2014). Social anxiety disorder and stuttering: current status and future directions. *Journal of Fluency Disorders*, 40, pp. 69–82.

Jerome, A. C., Fujiki, M., Brinton, B. and James, S. L. (2002). Self-esteem in children with specific language impairment. *Journal of Speech, Language, and Hearing Research. JSLHR*, 45 (4), pp. 700–714.

Jones, L., Goddard, L., Hill, E. L., Henry, L. A. and Crane, L. (2014). Experiences of receiving a diagnosis of autism spectrum disorder: a survey of adults in the United Kingdom. *Journal of Autism and Developmental Disorders*, 44 (12), pp. 3033–3044.

Khan, M. (2015). The effect of stuttering on speech and learning process: a case study. *International Journal on Studies in English Language and Literature (IJSELL)*, 3 (4), pp. 89–103.

Kayfitz, A., & Gragg, M. and Orr, R. (2010). Positive experiences of mothers and fathers of children with autism. *Journal of Applied Research in Intellectual Disabilities*, 23, pp. 337–343.

Kiyani, H. S. and Naz, S. (2018). Development of naming, reading and imitation skills management programme for patients with Broca's aphasia. *Khyber Medical University Journal*, 10 (3), pp. 127–130.

Klein, K. and Boals, A. (2001). The relationship of life event stress and working memory capacity. *Applied Cognitive Psychology*, 15, pp. 565–579.

Klein, J. F. and Hood, S. B. (2004). The impact of stuttering on employment opportunities and job performance. *Journal of Fluency Disorders*, 29 (4), pp. 255–273.

Klompas, M. and Ross, E. (2004). Life experiences of people who stutter, and the perceived impact of stuttering on quality of life: personal accounts of South African individuals. *Journal of Fluency Disorders*, 29, pp. 275–305.

Kuhlthau, K., Payakachat, N., Delahaye, J., Hurson, J., Pyne, J., Kovacs, E. and Tilford, J. (2014). Quality of life for parents of children with autism spectrum disorders. *Research in Autism Spectrum Disorders*, 8, pp. 1339–1350.

Lai, M. C. and Baron-Cohen, S. (2015). Identifying the lost generation of adults with autism spectrum conditions. *The Lancet: Psychiatry*, 2 (11), pp. 1013–1027.

Lam, J. M., and Wodchis, W. P. (2010). The relationship of 60 disease diagnoses and 15 conditions to preference-based health-related quality of life in Ontario hospital-based long-term care residents. *Medical Care*, 48 (4), pp. 380–387.

Lasker, J., LaPointe, L. and Kodras, J. (2005). Helping a professor with aphasia resume teaching through multimodal approaches. *Aphasiology*, 19 (3–5), pp. 399–410.

Laures-Gore, J. S., Dotson, V. M. and Belagaje, S. (2020). Depression in poststroke aphasia. *American Journal of Speech-language Pathology*, 29 (4), pp. 1798–1810.

Le, H. N. D., Mensah, F., Eadie, P., Sciberras, E., Bavin, E. L., Reilly, S., Wake, M. and Gold, L. (2022). Health-related quality of life of caregivers of children with low language: results from two Australian population-based studies. *International Journal of Speech-Language Pathology*, 24 (4), pp. 352–361.

Leo, M., Diliberto, R. and Kearney, C. A. (2014). Quality of peer relationships among children with selective mutism. [online] Available at: http://digitalscholarship.unlv.edu/mcnair_posters/50 [Accessed 26. 01. 2023].

Lever, A. G. and Geurts, H. M. (2016). Psychiatric co-occurring symptoms and disorders in young, middle-aged, and older adults with autism spectrum disorder. *Journal of Autism and Developmental Disorders*, 46 (6), pp. 1916–1930.

Macedo Costa, T. and da Silva Pereira, A. P. (2019). The child with autism spectrum disorder: the perceptions of siblings. *Support for Learning*, 34 (2), pp.193–210.

Marriott, E., Stacey, J., Hewitt, O. M. and Verkuijl, N. E. (2022). Parenting an autistic child: experiences of parents with significant autistic traits. *Journal of Autism and Developmental Disorders*, 52 (7), pp. 3182–3193.

Marton, K., Abramoff, B. and Rosenzweig, S. (2005). Social cognition and language in children with specific language impairment (SLI). *Journal of Communication Disorders*, 38 (2), pp. 143–162.

McAllister, J., Collier, J., and Shepstone, L. (2012). The impact of adolescent stuttering on educational and employment outcomes: evidence from a birth cohort study. *J Fluency Disord*, 37 (2), pp. 106–121.

McCormack, J., Harrison, L. J., McLeod, S. and McAllister, L. (2011). A nationally representative study of the association between communication impairment at 4–5 years and children's life activities at 7–9 years. *Journal of Speech, Language, and Hearing Research: JSLHR*, 54 (5), pp. 1328–1348.

McFayden, T. C., Albright, J., Muskett, A. E. and Scarpa, A. (2019). Brief report: sex differences in ASD diagnosis – a brief report on restricted interests and repetitive behaviors. *Journal of Autism and Developmental Disorders*, 49 (4), pp. 1693–1699.

Nicholas, M. and Connor, L. (2016). People with aphasia using AAC: are executive functions important? *Aphasiology*, 31, pp. 1–18.

Orsmond, G. I., Krauss, M. W. and Seltzer, M. M. (2004). Peer relationships and social and recreational activities among adolescents and adults with autism. *Journal of Autism and Developmental Disorders*, 34 (3), pp. 245–256.

Pallickal, M. and Hema, N. (2020). Discourse in Wernicke's aphasia. *Aphasiology*, 34, pp. 1–2.

Papathanasiou, I., Coppens, P. and Potagas, C. (2013). *Aphasia and Related Neurogenic Communication Disorders*. Burlington, MA: Jones & Bartlett Learning.

Pavlopoulou, G. and Dimitriou, D. (2019). 'I don't live with autism; I live with my sister'. Sisters' accounts on growing up with their preverbal autistic siblings. *Research in Developmental Disabilities*, 88, pp. 1–15.

Potter, C. A. (2016). 'I accept my son for who he is – he has incredible character and personality': fathers' positive experiences of parenting children with autism. *Disability & Society*, 31 (7), pp. 948–965.

Public Health England (2020). Best start in speech, language and communication: Guidance to support local commissioners and service leads. [Online] Available at: https://assets.publishing.service.gov.uk/government/uploads/system/uploads/attachment_data/file/931310/BSSLC_Guidance.pdf [Accessed 12. 01. 2023].

Remschmidt, H., Poller, M., Herpertz-Dahlmann, B., Hennighausen, K. and Gutenbrunner, C. (2001). A follow-up study of 45 patients with elective mutism. *European Archives of Psychiatry and Clinical Neuroscience*, 251 (6), pp. 284–296.

Ribbler, N. (2002). Stuttering: its multidimensional impact on school performance. *Perspectives on School-based Issues*, 3, pp. 20–22.

Rice, M. and Kroll, R. (2006). The impact of stuttering at work: challenges and discrimination. [online] Available at: www.mnsu.edu/comdis/isad9/papers/rice9.html [Accessed 31. 01. 2023].

Robinson, R. G., Starkstein, S. E. and Price, T. R. (1988). Post-stroke depression and lesion location. *Stroke*, 19 (1), pp. 125–126.

Russell, G., Steer, C. and Golding, J. (2011). Social and demographic factors that influence the diagnosis of autistic spectrum disorders. *Social Psychiatry and Psychiatric Epidemiology*, 46 (12), pp. 1283–1293.

Safe, A., Joosten, A. and Molineux, M. (2012). The experiences of mothers of children with autism: managing multiple roles. *Journal of Intellectual & Developmental Disability*, 37 (4), pp. 294–302.

Samochis, L., Rus, L. and Iftene, F. (2011). Stuttering, a communication disorder with effects in the social life. *Medicina moderna*, XVIII, pp. 84–88.

Schnabel, A., Youssef, G. J., Hallford, D. J., Hartley, E. J., McGillivray, J. A., Stewart, M., Forbes, D. and Austin, D. W. (2020). Psychopathology in parents of children with autism spectrum disorder: a systematic review and meta-analysis of prevalence. *Autism: The International Journal of Research and Practice*, 24 (1), pp. 26–40.

Sedgewick, F., Hill, V. and Pellicano, E. (2019). 'It's different for girls': gender differences in the friendships and conflict of autistic and neurotypical adolescents. *Autism: The International Journal of Research and Practice*, 23 (5), pp. 1119–1132.

Silverman, H. (2004). *Stuttering and Other Fluency Disorders*. Long Grove, IL: Waveland Press.

Sowerbutts, A. M., Jones, D., Lal, S. and Burden, S. (2021). Quality of life in patients and in family members of those receiving home parenteral support with intestinal failure: a systematic review. *Clinical Nutrition*, 40 (5), pp. 3210–3220.

Spaccavento, S., Craca, A., Del Prete, M., Falcone, R., Colucci, A., Di Palma, A. and Loverre, A. (2014). Quality of life measurement and outcome in aphasia. *Neuropsychiatric Disease and Treatment*, 10, pp. 27–37.

Tan C. D. (2018). 'I'm a normal autistic person, not an abnormal neurotypical': autism spectrum disorder diagnosis as biographical illumination. *Social Science & Medicine*, 197, pp. 161–167.

Teng, Y. (2017). Clinical observation of scalp acupuncture plus speech rehabilitation for Broca's aphasia after cerebral stroke. *Journal of Acupuncture and Tuina Science*, 15, pp. 104–108.

Timmons, L., Ekas, N. V. and Johnson, P. R. (2017). Thankful thinking: a thematic analysis of gratitude letters by mothers of children with autism spectrum disorder. *Research in Autism Spectrum Disorders*, 34, pp. 19–27.

Tozer, R. and Atkin, K. (2015). 'Recognized, valued and supported'? The experiences of adult siblings of people with autism plus learning disability. *Journal of Applied Research in Intellectual Disabilities: JARID*, 28.

Waizbard-Bartov, E., Yehonatan-Schori, M., and Golan, O. (2019). Personal growth experiences of parents to children with autism spectrum disorder. *Journal of Autism and Developmental Disorders*, 49 (4), pp. 1330–1341.

Ward, B., Tanner, B. S., Mandleco, B., Taylor, T. and Freeborn, D. (2016). Sibling experiences: living with young persons with autism spectrum disorders. *Pediatric Nursing*, 42, pp. 69–76.

Watson, L., Hanna, P. and Jones, C. J. (2021). A systematic review of the experience of being a sibling of a child with an autism spectrum disorder. *Clinical Child Psychology and Psychiatry*, 26 (3), pp.734–749.

Wigdor, E., Weiner, D., Grove, J., Fu, J., Thompson, W., Carey, C., Baya, N., van der Merwe, C., Walters, R., Satterstrom, F., Palmer, D., Rosengren, A., Bybjerg-Grauholm, J., iPSYCH Consortium, Hougaard, D. M., Mortensen, P. B., Daly, M. J., Talkowski, M. E., Sanders, S. J., Bishop, S. L., Børglum, A. D. and Robinson, E. B. (2022). The female protective effect against autism spectrum disorder. *Cell Genom*, 2 (6), 100134.

Wong, P. (2010). Selective mutism: a review of etiology, comorbidities, and treatment. *Psychiatry*, 7 (3), pp. 23–31.

World Health Organization (2019). *International Statistical Classification of Diseases and Related Health Problems*. 11th ed.

12 Pedagogical approaches to support these needs

Introduction

This chapter explores approaches to support issues associated with Communication and Interaction Needs, including use of signs and symbols such as Makaton, communication boards, AAC and specific examples such as PECS® and Social Stories™. These are often used with autistic learners. There are several websites, organisations and textbooks which identify a range of approaches in relation to communication and interaction. This chapter will instead focus on the theoretical underpinning, research studies and evidence-based research and practice, for some of the main approaches used in an educational context. It will signpost you to videoclips showing how the approach is being used in practice. It must be remembered that although an approach is identified in a specific chapter, it can be used in other areas of need.

Learning objectives

This chapter will:

- Introduce you to a number of specific approaches which can be used to support Communication and Interaction Needs
- Invite you examine underpinning theory and research evidence in relation to approaches related to this area of need
- Introduce you to the paradigms and principles involved in communication and interaction
- Help you to understand how these approaches can support individuals in the classroom
- Invite you to review the approaches with respect to evidence-based research and practice

Key terms

Augmentative and Alternative Communication (AAC), Picture Exchange Communication System (PECS®), Makaton, Widgit™, touchscreens, Voice Output

DOI: 10.4324/9781003361084-17

Communication Aids (VOCAs), communication boards, Tacpac, Social Stories[TM], Speech and Language (S+L) Therapy (SLT), Structured Communication, expressive and receptive language, Colourful Semantics, evidence-based research

Augmentative and Alternative Communication (AAC)

AAC describes methods of communication which can be used to supplement the more usual methods of speech and writing when these are impaired. It facilitates understanding as well as expression and can be a way to help someone understand, as well as a means of expression.

Augmentative and Alternative Communication (AAC) is an intervention widely evidenced to demonstrate substantial benefits in meeting the complex communication needs of pupils with SEND (Branson and Demchak, 2009). AAC is an umbrella term that encompasses the procedures and processes used to supplement or replace speech such that an individual's communication skills, both production and comprehension, can be maximised for functional and effective communication. AAC can have a dramatic impact on an individual's life, enabling him/her to:

- Express their feelings
- Ask questions and say what they need
- Feel good about themselves
- Develop relationships with their friends and family
- Participate in school, work and play
- Be involved in decisions about their future

Individuals with PMLD and SLD can have communication impairments surrounding their speech and language. AAC can support these impairments through aided and unaided communication interventions which use of range of high to low-technology systems (Inclusive Technology, 2023). Communication interventions are used to provide support for increasing the individuals' skills and assisting individuals with PMLD and SLD with their communicational difficulties. They are commonly classified into three categories: 'no-tech' systems such as sign language systems or the use of objects; 'low-tech' systems such as printed resources of pictures and symbols in communication books; and 'high-tech' systems such as complex voice output systems based on computers and tablet devices (Trembath et al., 2014).

Low-tech approaches

Examples include:

- Makaton
- Photographs and pictures

- True Object Based Icons which can be used with individuals who have difficulty understanding two-dimensional visual symbols (i.e., photographs, line drawings). TOBIs can be any line drawing or picture that is cut out in the actual shape or outline of the object that they represent. The individual can see the symbol and the outline of the shape, which helps him/her to understand two-dimensional symbols more readily
- Widgit™ symbols which are designed to support written information and provide a way to effectively 'translate' written text into a simple and easy to understand form. They have a large vocabulary spanning standard curriculum topics, adult vocabulary and higher levels and possess a schematic structure and include grammatical markers for literacy expression. They can be accessed via the link: https://widgitonline.com/en/home
- Visual timetables
- Talking mats which are mats to which pictures or symbols are attached and re-arranged as required. They give pupils the time and the space to think about information, work out what it means and say what they feel in a visual way that can easily be recorded. Information about talking mats can be accessed via the link: www.talkingmats.com

High-tech approach: touchscreens

The use of touchscreen devices also changed how assistive technology is perceived in educational settings as digital technology has become more of a day-to-day tool than mounted into a part of the school and only accessed within the four walls of institutions (Moreno, 2020). The most useful features of tablet-assisted learning are the fun and easy to use aspects that students found to be superior to the day-to-day materials they use. However, there are also shortcomings reported around suitable mobile applications (Apps) for children with SEND. It was underlined that the software developed as a special education aid is not sufficient for the teaching of different knowledge and skill (Silman, Yaratan and Karanfiller, 2017), which means that applications were not adaptive to individual learning differences. Gasparini and Culén (2012) investigated the use of the iPad in an elementary school. The positivity and enthusiasm for using the iPad faded towards the end of the year.

Activity

Watch this journey from low-tech to high-tech for one pupil. The video can be accessed via the link: www.complexneeds.org.uk/modules/Module-3.1-Communication—augmentative-and-assistive-strategies/All/video/riv/riv2.mp4

- What were the milestones to move from one AAC technique to the next?
- How was this pupil enabled to make this journey to be able to communicate independently?

The videoclip 'Choosing the Right AAC APP' explores the range of apps to support AAC. It can be accessed via the link: www.youtube.com/watch?v=8HrkCqOw9zg

High-tech approach: Voice Output Communication Aids (VOCAs)

Voice output communication aids (VOCAs) are an AAC device that produce speech for an individual with SLCN who has limited or no verbal communication (Mueller, 2013). This device produces and stores a voice for an individual with SLCN, as it has a stored memory that allows it to be played back. Rispoli et al. (2010) explored the effectiveness of VOCAs for individuals with SLCN and suggested it increased the clarity of communication as it enabled individuals to verbally communicate and express themselves. This is supported by van der Meer and Rispoli (2010) who similarly commented on the effectiveness and suggested studies of increased verbal communication as it encouraged students to verbally communicate and repeat the words and phrases of the VOCA. This is supported by Judge and Townend (2013) who explored the benefits of verbal communication and discussed that VOCAs benefited the development of literacy in individuals with speech, language and communication needs.

However, it is important to consider Mueller (2013) who suggested the challenge it takes to teach the individual with SLCN how to effectively use the voice input machines. The study discussed the time it takes and the individual persistence and cognitive ability to understand the machine. This is because the study commented that at the start of using the machine it can take the individual a long period of time to create the sentence/phrase on the machine for a short speaking time and can dishearten the individual with SLCN. Therefore, it is important to consider that this device is meant to encourage and aid an individual's verbal communication; however, if the individual doesn't form a bond and enjoy the communication then it can result in them becoming more withdrawn and even more reluctant to use verbal communication. In addition, it is crucial to consider the impact of the cost of a VOCA, as they are personalised for an individual with SLCN, so can be costly to create an individualised voice aid. Schepis et al. (1998) explored the cost and implication of an individual's developing language and requiring an updated VOCA, highlighting the negative impact of VOCA.

Activity

These videos show how two individuals use VOCAs. They can be accessed via the link:

http://complexneeds.org.uk/modules/Module-3.1-Communication—a
ugmentative-and-assistive-strategies/All/video/bett/bett26.mp4

How do the following impact upon the use of a VOCA?

- Physical access to VOCA
- Language stored in VOCA
- The classroom environment and the activities
- Appropriate training
- Links with family and carers

High-tech approach: portable devices

An electronic tablet can offer a pupil with SLCN access to learning, information, organisational systems, communication, and emotional support. The benefits to using a touchscreen for pupils with SEND is that it enables immediate feedback from touching, shaking, rotating and other movements. Haksiz (2014) discussed the benefits of an electronic tablet and the personalisation available on a tablet and the motivation children/young people with SLCN must have in using electronic devices. Johnson (2014) explored the motivational benefits for young people with SLCN to using an electronic tablet. The study suggested that staff within a school were positive towards the use of electronic tablets as it enables communication for the non-verbal students and promoted students to think about communication and sentence structures using fun apps and activities. However, Unser (2017) discussed the challenges to consider when using electronic tablets for pupils with SLCN and highlighted that the language and speech that is used on the app might not be fully correct and the individual with SLCN may be learning it incorrectly, resulting in challenges in the future. For example, if an app used American language and phrases, this could hinder the language of the individual with SLCN as they would get corrected with the English-language translation, creating more confusing for the individual. Moreover, it is important to consider the limitations to electronic tablets regarding software, as an individual with SLCN will require specialist software to enable communication. This can be time consuming to set up and a high cost as they will require different apps and software to make the electronic tablet effective (van der Meer et al., 2012). It is important to note that even though literature suggests limitations to using electronic tablets as a form of high-technology AAC, electronic tablets present the least number of negative implications for a person with SLCN.

Communication boards

Communication boards with symbols, words or pictures to point at are effective, relatively low-technology solutions to enact, and a head pointer/eye-gaze technology to select words/pictures on a computer screen would be the high-technology version of this (Baglieri, 2017). A communication board is a visual representation of language – all organised in a very strategic way. You can use a communication board to ask question, express wants and needs, offer a choice, indicate a decision, or show a schedule. The purpose of a communication board is to help users express their wants and needs more effectively. Using illustrations, these boards can help people with limited or no language ability connect with others.

Activity

Watch the following videos on communication boards. They can be accessed via the following links: www.youtube.com/watch?v=Nib6wCDpdhM and www.youtube.com/watch?v=irH34izUmpc

- Give an example of how you could use a communication board with both an adult and a child to support communication and interaction

---

Tacpac

Tacpac is an activity that pairs music and touch to promote communication and social interaction as well as helping to heighten body awareness through proprioceptive stimulation, and being beneficial for developing anticipation, sequencing and social interaction. During these sessions, children are paired one-to-one with a familiar adult. Through linking familiar music consistently with objects, actions and people in a pattern of different activities, the partners communicate with each other. It supports those with sensory impairment, developmental delay, complex learning difficulties, tactile defensiveness, and limited or pre-verbal levels of communication (Tacpac, 2023). These two languages are highly compatible and the aim of Tacpac is to combine these to create a feeling of sensory alignment, allowing the brain to organise information to be able to communicate without interference of other stimuli. The key to aligning the senses is the integration of the touch of a textured material that corresponds with the texture (basic beat) of the music (Tacpac, 2023).

There have been few studies evaluating Tacpac's efficacy as a communication intervention. McLinden and McCall (2002) report that touch stimulates awareness, anticipation of routines, utilisation of symbols with the overall target of supporting communication. Panter (2004) describes how Tacpac was a useful resource for staff in a special school in Oxford to develop relationships between staff and children. She states that it helped staff to understand the children more, increased their awareness of each other, their likes and dislikes, and also each session was a journey of discovery.

Activity

Information can be accessed via the link: https://tacpac.co.uk/what-is-tacpac

- What are the benefits identified by the originators of Tacpac?
- Can you see any issues or difficulties in such an approach?

A Tacpac session can be accessed via the link: www.youtube.com/watch?v=6xBhMd20vyE&t=202s

---

Makaton

Makaton is a unique language programme that uses symbols, signs and speech to enable people to communicate. It supports the development of essential communication skills such as attention and listening, comprehension, memory, recall and organisation of language and expression. While Makaton is a language programme used to support those with learning and communication difficulties, British Sign Language (BSL) is a legally recognised language used by most Deaf people in the UK. The complete Makaton Language Programme comprises a Core Vocabulary of essential words or concepts presented in stages of increasing complexity, which is taught first and is the foundation of the programme. A larger, open-ended, topic-based resource vocabulary provides a bank of further signs and symbols covering broader life experiences and is used in association with the Core Vocabulary as required. It can be used in multiple settings and helps individuals communicate with peers, practitioners, and the public generally (Mistry and Barnes, 2013).

Makaton was first developed in the 1970s by Margaret Walker MBE, Kathy Johnston and Tony Cornforth, speech and language therapists. It is designed to help hearing people with learning or communication difficulties by adding hand signs and illustrated symbols on top of spoken English, to give a visual component to communication to support the development of spoken language. Makaton is flexible and can be used at any level appropriate to the individual's needs. It is an effective method of communication for anyone who has difficulties with understanding the spoken word, as it provides people with extra clues as to what is being said by using signs or gestures. Makaton can support individuals with no speech, unclear speech or those who are reluctant to communicate. Makaton is a pervasive and influential pedagogical approach for individuals with SLD which supports and facilitates language development through visual communication aids using speech, signs, and symbols based on British Sign Language (BSL) (Sheehy and Duffy, 2009). Makaton is an intervention that promotes an inclusive environment for individuals with communication needs alongside creating a positive attitude shift for individuals that communicate in alternative ways to speech (Sheehy and Duffy, 2009). Moreover, Makaton encourages social interactions and creates an accessible form of communication.

Research evidence

Makaton has been found to be effective at supporting communication across a wide range of groups including those with disabilities (Sellars, 2006), as well as Makaton peer tutoring schemes improving self-esteem, confidence and assertiveness in those with disabilities (Hooper and Walker 2002). The use of Makaton has been criticised in that its use could replace speech for children, leading to speech delay and that few people with disabilities who use Makaton progress to the level of combining signs and this limits communication (Grove and Dockrell, 2000). Hotonu, Aldous and Schafer-Dreyer (2009) argue that Makaton encourages good interaction skills such as eye contact and facial expression meaning that it encourages good communicative practice generally, rather than replacing speech. Regardless of a lack of contemporary empirical data, many people and schools around the country and world are adopting the use of Makaton and there is an attitude shift towards one of inclusion and acceptance for children who sign. Barbosa et al. (2018) suggest that Makaton is effective in facilitating flexible communication through giving individuals a voice and contributing to positive self-esteem. It is evident that even due to the limitations, the use of Makaton as an intervention for individuals with Down's syndrome is effective as it enhances communication through the simultaneous instruction of verbal speech and sign language alongside Makaton being a flexible form of communication to meet the SLCN for all individuals. Quigley and MacDonald (2022) investigated the experiences of individuals with learning difficulties who participate in Makaton choirs. Semi-structured interviews were conducted with five choir members and a leader. Participants reported increased opportunities for social connection with others, improvements in communication and social interaction. It is argued that participation in such a group may promote health and well-being by providing participants with several psychological and social benefits.

Activity

The Makaton Charity can be accessed via the link: https://makaton.org/TMC

There are several free and paid resources available, as well as information on how Makaton is used to support issues such as autism, Down's syndrome and multisensory impairment.

- Download some of the resources from the Vocabulary, Songs, Stories and Activities links and to examine the use of symbols and signs

The founder of Makaton, Margaret Walker, talks about the history of Makaton. The video can be accessed via the link: www.youtube.com/watch?v=mcGs-DlvX7k

---

Picture Exchange Communication System (PECS®)

PECS® uses visual symbols to allow a learner with little or no communication abilities to communicate with others through teaching the learner intentional and functional communication to communicate their wants and needs. The exchange of communication in PECS® involves the learner and a communication partner which in an educational setting would be a teacher or teaching assistant. The communication partner will follow phases of PECS® with the learner; when one phase is complete, the learner will move to the next, to enable more independent communication for the learner. PECS® is an alternative communication system developed by Bondy and Frost (1998) to develop communication for individuals with autism. The theoretical underpinning of PECS® is based on the principles of Applied Behaviour Analysis (ABA), and the Pyramid Approach to Education (Pyramid Educational Consultants, 2023). ABA is a therapy that defines the process of applying behavioural principles to change behaviours and simultaneously evaluate the effectiveness of interventions alongside understanding how behaviour and learning takes place. Moreover, PECS® teaches verbal causative behaviours through methodological steps using the PAE, a comprehensive model that describes elements that are required to create an effective educational environment.

It consists of pictures and symbols, often on cards or in communication books, and may be considered a low-tech AAC intervention because it requires technology to produce the images, but not to use. Through six stages, individuals are taught to present the pictures or symbols to appropriate adults to express needs or desires (Ganz and Simpson 2004; Ganz et al. 2008). Chua and Poon (2018) state that PECS® is intended for autistic individuals who have verbal communication difficulties, such as speech impairments; however, Wearmouth (2019) concludes it to be effective for individuals with various communication difficulties. A goal of PECS® is to teach functional communication, not necessarily speech, but an individual who began with PECS® could transition to a speech-generating device.

Individuals use a personalised communication book or an organised box containing all the necessary pictures to ensure they are easily and readily available for the learner in supporting the choice making for learners alongside putting vocabulary into context through using context-based communication boards enabling the learner to communicate their feelings. Often a teaching assistant will work one-to-one with an individual to implement PECS® using powerful reinforcers such as an item they resit having taken away and the teaching assistant can adapt the sentence structure through making the sentences longer and the structure of learning and go back and step if the learner makes a mistake.

Stages in PECS®

Phase One	Children will learn to exchange individual pictures for activities they wish to partake in
Phase Two	Using the above, but using the pictures in different places, showing a more persistent communication

Phase Three	A child can select two or more pictures of favourite activities and can place them in a communication book
Phase Four	Can learn to construct simple sentences on a sentence strip
Phase Five	Using the above but expanding the sentences with the use of adjectives
Phase Six	Learn to use PECS® by answering individual questions
Phase Seven	Using the above, with addition of using responses to all simple questions

(Frost and Bondy, 2002)

Research evidence

The use of PECS® with children who have little or no speech resulted in increased functional communication in a relatively short period of time (within 6 to 14 months) and sometimes, even the development of verbal ability (Magiati and Howlin, 2003; Webb, 2000). However, while it has proven highly effective in teaching children to request, other studies reported mixed results for speech outcomes (Schlosser and Wendt, 2008). Although PECS® has a positive effect towards the communication ability of autistic children, it is not yet an established evidence-based intervention for speech outcomes (Flippin, Reszka and Watson, 2010). PECS® can be interchangeable from school life to the home and lead to parents effectively communicating with their child (Tang and Winoto, 2018).

Travis and Geiger (2010) suggest that both the communicative partner and the learner benefited from PECS® being implemented as it increases the levels of intentional communication acts from individuals with autism. Similarly, Ganz et al. (2012) identified through a meta-analysis that analysed the functional communication and behavioural outcomes that it is an effective intervention to improve functional communication outcomes for all individuals; however, individuals with autism displayed the strongest outcomes. Sulzer-Azaroff et al. (2009) further suggest that PECS® is a functional intervention that provides individuals, with and without impaired speech, a functional means of communication. PECS® can be beneficially used in multiple settings including educational settings, homes and therapy settings (Collet-Klingenberg, 2008). In contrast, Flippin et al. (2010) concluded through a meta-analysis that there are concerns of generalisation in multiple settings, alongside the challenges that the individual with autism may experience in maintaining the speech and communication improvements.

Activity

Originally released in 1998, this video provides a brief overview of the potential benefits of the Picture Exchange Communication System® (PECS®) as well as the six phases of the protocol and features the developers Andy Bondy, PhD, and Lori Frost, MS, CCC-SLP. It can be accessed via the link: www.youtube.com/watch?v=rsDBJyrcyh0

Peter is aged 23 and has Fragile X syndrome resulting in limited communication abilities and reduced access to the community. He attends a local FE college where he stays for lunch. His favourite food is jacket potato and staff are keen for him to select fillings to put onto his potato.

- Using the phases of PECS®, how would you work with Peter to get to Phase Five?

Social Stories^{TM}

In the early 1990s, Carol Gray developed the concept of Social Stories^{TM}, which are highly individualised stories using visual cues and sentences, that provide social information to autistic children with autism (Gray, 1994). The primary use of a Social Story^{TM} is to describe a situation, skill or concept in the terms of social cues, perspectives and common responses (Mayton et al., 2013) and to put social situations in a 'concrete' way; this is useful for those with autism who may have a weak central coherence or struggle with appropriate social behaviours. Gray (2004) suggests that main use of Social Stories^{TM} is to describe a situation, skill or common concept in terms of relevant social cues, perspectives and common responses in a specifically defined style and format. It is a multifaceted intervention that has been an attractive tool for those who are working towards building social awareness and understanding in autistic children where a simple narrative usually paired with visual supports, assists in the identification of noticeable cues in social situations and teaches individuals how to respond appropriately (Reynhout and Carter, 2009). This intervention targets the behaviours a learner should display in a specific context and can be used by health, social and educational practitioners, and parents. Moreover, Social Stories^{TM} are normally brief and straight to the point (Reynhout and Carter, 2009). These can be individualised and be used for many things such as going out on an unfamiliar school trip or changes in routine as well as visualising expected behaviours (Sansosti, Powell-Smith and Kincaid, 2004). The objective is to ensure children know exactly how correctly respond in social situations and know exactly who, what or why is involved within the process (Ozdemir, 2008).

How to write a Social Story^{TM}

It should be written through the child's eye and the main character should somewhat represent the individual for whom the story is being created as this will allow the child to easily identify and learn ways to modify or manage their behaviours. They can include relevant and individualised photos or illustrations. Social Stories^{TM} can be conducted following Carole Gray's ten guidelines (Gray, 2015):

1 Find the Social Story^{TM} Goal: using appropriate and positive language for the learner
2 Two-Step Discovery: authors gather information about the learner
3 Three parts and a title: a Social Story has an introduction, body and conclusion
4 Format: it should be tailored to the individual's cognitive and language abilities
5 Voice and vocabulary: it can be written in first or third person and past/present and or future tense
6 Story Development: answering relevant 'wh' questions for example what, when and why
7 Sentences: the use of descriptive sentences supported by coaching sentences only
8 Formula: Social Stories^{TM} should describe more than direct the learner
9 Refine: a Social Story^{TM} is always a draft and should be reviewed against the criteria
10 10. Guide to Implementation: ensuring the goal is evident

Research evidence

Research into Social Stories^{TM} has increased over recent years and teachers and parents are looking more towards evidence-based practice when choosing relevant interventions to support autistic children. Bucholz (2012) carried out a systematic review and concluded that Social Stories^{TM} may be an effective intervention for autistic children because it allows information to be described explicitly while providing a visual representation (e.g., photographs, line drawings) of the skills being addressed in the story. They have potential to be successful interventions when practitioners consider the cognitive level, age and language ability of the student for whom the story is being written. However, Quirmbach et al. (2009) discovered through their own study of 45 autistic children aged 7–14 that only the children that were above the borderline range of the Verbal Comprehension Index were successful with Social Stories^{TM}. Crozier and Tincani (2007) highlight that it is important to keep children exposed to Social Stories^{TM} continuously for them to have the best effect. In their study, boys returned to their pre-treatment behaviours when the Social Story^{TM} approach was no longer able to be accessed.

Golzari, Hemati Alamdarloo and Moradi (2015) investigated the effects of Social Stories^{TM} on 30 autistic children, concluding that the intervention improved social skills and contributed to initiating, responding, and maintaining interactions with others. Furthermore, Qi et al. (2018) undertook a systematic review and suggested that they influence the downfall of inappropriate behaviour and promote behaviour change. In contrast, methodological flaws in the construction of Social Stories^{TM} suggest that the guidelines for implementation have been adapted without evidence-based research. Test et al. (2011) claim that although they are used by a considerable amount of special educational practitioners, the growing need for accountability of interventions could lead to a drop in usage due to the lack of obtainable favourable data. Kuoch and Mirenda (2003) explain that the main issue with the current research is that very few are looking at

Social Stories™ as a standalone intervention. Sansosti, Powell-Smith and Kincaid (2004) stipulate that the true effectiveness cannot be assessed until the additional interventions are removed. However, Bozkurt and Vuran (2014) argue that to remove the additional interventions would be detrimental as research states that the effectiveness of Social Stories™ when linked with other interventions is 65 per cent, yet this falls significantly to just 57 per cent if they are used alone. In conclusion, research suggests that the effectiveness of Social Stories™ is mixed, with Aldabas (2019) arguing that the research surrounding Social Stories™ leaves practitioners with no evidence base to support the intervention.

Activity

Social stories™ can specifically help with:

- New experiences
- Transitions
- Routines
- Expectations for behaviour
- Specific behaviour issues
- You have been tasked to write a Social Story™ for a child you are working with, to help support one of the above. Watch the following videos as a guide:

  Routines. It can be accessed via the link: www.youtube.com/watch?v=7CdjxrQSD6w
  Personal space. It can be accessed via the link: www.youtube.com/watch?v=OyDg6yK20wA
  Taking turns. It can be accessed via the link: www.youtube.com/watch?v=nvOrzh5in8o

---

Structured communication approaches

Below is a list of some of the approaches which could be used in the classroom to support communication.

Pause for reflection

- Visuals for expectation
- Visual timetables/schedules
- Task board. Break down a whole activity into manageable chunks. These can be presented in various ways: written on a whiteboard, pre-prepared and printed in advance, using Velcroed symbols or written on

Post-it notes to allow children to choose which part of the task to do first

- Help card. Sometimes when a child is stuck, they cannot work out how to ask for help, or may not even realise that this is an option. Providing a help card, which should be available on their desk, can act as a prompt that they can ask for help if they need to
- Time out card. Similarly, when a child knows that they really need to have some time out, it is likely to be at a time when they are already stressed and cannot negotiate the intricacies of asking directly
- Secret codes. As children get older, they often reject the visuals which they have used all their school lives as 'babyish' and refuse to use them. One way to get around this could be to implement a 'secret code' system
- Calming strategies. Anxiety and frustration are regular difficulties for autistic children. Teaching calming strategies to be used at these times can be a very helpful approach. You can make a visual to remind them of the strategy they have learned

Scaffolding language and modelling

Adults should be active in the role of supporting a child's learning through the practice of scaffolding. Scaffolding refers to organised interactions, between an adult and a child, that are helpful in the aim of aiding a child to reach a specific target – e.g., communication. The use of verbal scaffolding such as paraphrasing, writing prompts and effective wait times as ways of supporting language disorders, with Wasik and Jacobi-Vessels (2017) recommending scaffolding strategies such as asking questions to allow an extended response, is constructive for improving children's language development. Modelling language is also a way to increase expressive speech in autistic children. It is important to model it in a way that is straightforward for them to imitate, such that pronoun reversals do not occur because autistic children do not process prosody-related tasks well, which is crucial in social and play situations whereby modelling (e.g., turn-taking, requesting) and adult facilitation will enable a child to experience, imitate and practise these skills.

Supporting expressive language

Expressive language issues may be apparent in subjects such as literacy where a learner may struggle with their reading due to problems in syntax, word-retrieval, etc. (Hulme and Snowling, 2009). Teachers should employ high-quality, differentiated teaching strategies, and have high expectations of all students, including in group work, interactive computer sessions, or independent reading time with the teacher or teaching assistant. The child may struggle, but it is important that they are not rushed, and it also allows continuous assessment of pupils' changing abilities (McMinn, 2006). Depending on the severity, teachers could work with professionals such as the Special Educational Needs Co-ordinator (SENCo) and speech and language therapist (SLT) to provide a high level of supportive interventions (Zeng, Law and Lindsay, 2012). Comprehension difficulties may be less obvious than expressive issues, so the learner should be asked to try to explain what they have just read to ensure there are no issues in their understanding.

Supporting receptive language

Receptive language issues can affect working memory, which may be evident, for example, in maths lessons in which executive functions are required in organising, problem-solving and retaining data. Individuals with issues in this area can take longer to decode what has been said or seen – the time, efforts, and energy this takes may result in a child falling behind as the teacher may move on to another topic (Norbury, Tomblin and Bishop, 2008). Issues within auditory processing does not help in retaining information for enough time for it to be processed and for a child to understand. This is vital in school as pupils use their working memory daily. In maths lessons, teachers could use simple sentences and teach one concept at a time, while continuingly checking pupils' understanding (Hulme and Snowling, 2009). Simple strategies such as reducing distractive noises by closing the door to aid focus, using visual aids and tactile cues as a multisensory approach to giving instructions or Quality First teaching in general would support children's learning. For example, using tactile objects such as cubes instead of writing down numbers or drawing apples to represent numbers can aid in semantics (McMinn, 2006).

Colourful Semantics

Colourful Semantics is a speech and language therapy technique which uses colour-coded cards to help children to learn the important elements of a sentence, and how to join them together in the correct order. The colour-coding system is used to 'show' and teach the different elements that form a sentence, by linking the structure of a sentence (syntax) and its meaning (semantics) (Bryan, 1997). Building from simple to more complex sentences, colourful semantics can help to expand the receptive and expressive communication of children who are ready and want to go beyond requesting. It was designed to support the development of specific grammatical structures but has expanded to also support narrative and vocabulary learning (Devine, 2014). Although research shows that there is improvement in the development of expressive language (Bolderson et al., 2011), most studies were small cases studies with no control group, meaning that it cannot be certain that improvements were due to the intervention as it may be possible that it was due to the repetition of assessments or natural improvement over time (Ebbels, 2014). In addition, most research was carried out with specific language impairment rather than specifically on autistic children (Hettiarachchi, 2016).

However, findings may still be relevant as both groups of children present similar problems in developing expressive language skills, such as word order problems, lack of verb use and failure to complete sentences (Bolderson et al., 2011). Colourful semantics uses different modalities (visual and kinesthetics) to learn about the construction of sentences. This is suitable for autistic children who have high visual-perceptual skills compared to their auditory skills (Garretson, Fein and Waterhouse, 1990). In addition, it compensates for the weaker working memory and enables abstract learning by teaching fewer concrete parts of the sentence (e. g., where, what) using a visual colour-coding system. This aids receptive language and encourages children to generate responses to questions with understanding.

Activity

This video shows how teachers use colourful semantics at a speech and language school. It can be accessed via the link: www.youtube.com/watch?v=mQtmY3oqf48&t=449s

Widgit online have a similar system: Colour Coded Sentence Maker, a colour-coded symwriter environment for building sentences. It can be accessed via the link: www.widgit.com/resources/literacy-language/language-development/colour_coded_sentence_maker/index.htm

- How do the two approaches differ?

References

Aldabas, R. (2019). Effectiveness of social stories for children with autism: a comprehensive review. *Technology and Disability*, 31 (1–2), pp. 1–13.

Baglieri, S. (2017). *Disability Studies and the Inclusive Classroom. Critical Practices for Embracing Diversity in Education.* New York: Routledge.

Barbosa, R. T. A., de Oliveira, A. S. B., de LimaAntão, J. Y. F., Crocetta, T. B., Guarnieri, R., Antunes, T. P. C., Arab C, Massetti, T., Bezerra, I. M. P., de Mello Monteiro, C. B. and de Abreu, L. C. (2018). Augmentative and alternative communication in children with Down's syndrome: a systematic review. *BMC Pediatr*, 18 (1), p. 160.

Bolderson, S., Dosanjh, C., Milligan, C., Ring, T. and Chiat, S. (2011). Colourful semantics: a clinical investigation. *Child Language Teaching and Therapy*, 27 (3), pp. 344–353.

Bondy, A. S. and Frost, L. A. (1998). The picture exchange communication system. *Semin Speech Lang*, 19 (4), pp. 373–388.

Bozkurt, S. S. and Vuran, S. (2014). An analysis of the use of social stories in teaching social skills to children with autism spectrum disorders. *Kuram Ve Uygulamada Egitim Bilimleri*, 14, pp. 1875–1892.

Branson, D. and Demchak, M. (2009). The use of augmentative and alternative communication methods with infants and toddlers with disabilities: a research review. *Augment Altern Commun*, 25 (4), pp. 274–286.

Bryan, A. (1997). Colourful semantics. In: S. Chiat, J. Law and J. Marshall (eds.), *Language Disorders in Children and Adults: Psycholinguistic Approaches to Therapy*. London: Whurr, pp. 143–161.

Bucholz, J. L. (2012). Social Stories™ for children with autism: a review of the literature. *Journal of Research in Education*, 22 (2), pp. 48–73.

Chua, B. Y. E. and Poon, K. K. (2018). Studying the implementation of PECS in a naturalistic special education school setting. *Educational and Child Psychology*, 35 (Spec Iss 2), pp. 60–75.

Collet-Klingenberg, L. (2008). *Overview of Picture Exchange Communication System (PECS) for Children and Youth with Autism Spectrum Disorders*. Madison, WI: National Professional Development Institute on ASD, The Waisman Center, The University of Wisconsin.

Crozier, S. and Tincani, M. J. (2007). Effects of Social Stories on prosocial behavior of preschool children with autism spectrum disorders. *Journal of Autism and Developmental Disorders*, 37, pp. 1803–1814.

Devine, A. (2014). *Colour Coding for Learners with Autism. A Resource Book for Creating Meaning though Colour at Home and at School*. London: Jessica Kingsley Publishers.

Ebbels, S. (2014). Effectiveness of intervention for grammar in school-aged children with primary language impairments: a review of the evidence. *Child Language Teaching and Therapy*, 30 (1), pp. 7–40.

Flippin, M., Reszka, S. and Watson, L. R. (2010). Effectiveness of the Picture Exchange Communication System (PECS) on communication and speech for children with autism spectrum disorders: a meta-analysis. *Am J Speech Lang Pathol*, 19 (2), pp. 178–195.

Frost, L. A. and Bondy, A. S. (2002). *The Picture Exchange Communication System Training Manual*. 2nd ed. Newark, DE: Pyramid Educational Products.

Hettiarachchi, S. (2016). The effectiveness of Colourful Semantics on narrative skills in children with intellectual disabilities in Sri Lanka. *J Intellect Disabil*, 20 (1), pp. 18–33.

Ganz, J. B. and Simpson, R. L. (2004). Effects on communicative requesting and speech development of the Picture Exchange Communication System in children with characteristics of autism. *Journal of Autism and Developmental Disorders*, 34, 395409.

Ganz, J. B., Simpson, R. L. and Corbin-Newsome, J. (2008). The impact of the Picture Exchange Communication System on requesting and speech development in preschoolers with autism spectrum disorders and similar characteristics. *Research in Autism Spectrum Disorders*, 2, pp. 157–169.

Ganz, J. B., Earles-Vollrath, T. L., Heath, A. K., Parker, R. I., Rispoli, M. J. and Duran, J. B. (2012). A meta-analysis of single case research studies on aided augmentative and alternative communication systems with individuals with autism spectrum disorders. *Journal of Autism and Developmental Disorders*, 42 (1), pp. 60–74.

Garretson, H. B., Fein, D. and Waterhouse, L. (1990). Sustained attention in children with autism. *J Autism Dev Disord*, 20 (1), pp. 101–114.

Gasparini, A. A. and Culén, A. L. (2012). *Tablet PCs – an assistive technology for students with reading difficulties?*The Fifth International Conference on Advances in Computer-Human Interactions (ACHI 2012), Valencia.

Golzari, F., Hemati Alamdarloo, G. and Moradi, S. (2015). The effect of a Social Stories intervention on the social skills of male students with autism spectrum disorder. *SAGE Open*, 5 (4).

Gray, C. A. (1994). *The New Social Stories Book: Illustrated Edition*. Arlington: Future Horizons Inc.

Gray, C. A. (2004). Social Stories 10.0: the new defining criteria and guidelines. *Jensen Autism Journal*, 15 (4), pp. 2–21.

Gray, C. A. (2015). *The New Social Story Book. Revised*. Arlington: Future Horizons Inc.

Grove, N. and Dockrell, J. (2000). Multisign combinations by children with intellectual impairments: an analysis of language skills. *J Speech Lang Hear Res*, 43 (2), pp. 309–323.

Haksiz, M. (2014). Investigation of tablet computer use in special education teachers' courses. *Procedia-Social and Behavioral Sciences*, 141, pp. 1392–1399.

Hotonu, A., Aldous, A. and Schafer-Dreyer, R. (2009). *Including Children with Speech and Language Delay (Inclusion)*. London: Featherstone Education.

Hooper, H. and Walker, M. (2002). Makaton peer tutoring evaluation: 10 years on. *British Journal of Learning Disabilities*, 31 (1), pp. 38–42.

Hulme, C. and Snowling, M. J. (2009). *Developmental Disorders of Language Learning and Cognition*. Hoboken, New Jersey: Wiley Blackwell.

Inclusive Technology (2023). Case studies. [Online] Available at: www.inclusive.com/uk/resources/case-studies.html [Accessed 02. 03. 2023].

Johnson, D. P. (2014). *Implementing a One-to-one iPad Program in a Secondary School*. EdD Thesis. University of Nebraska at Omah.

Judge, S. and Townend, G. (2013). Perceptions of the design of voice output communication aids. *Int J Lang Commun Disord*, 48 (4), pp. 366–381.

Kuoch, H. and Mirenda, P. (2003). Social Story interventions for young children with autism spectrum disorders. *Focus on Autism and Other Developmental Disabilities*, 18 (4), pp. 219–227.

Magiati, I. and Howlin, P. (2003). A pilot evaluation study of the Picture Exchange Communication System (PECS) for children with autistic spectrum disorders. *Autism*, 20 (3), pp. 297–320.

Mayton, M. R., Menendez, A. L., Wheeler, J. J., Carter, S. L. and Chitiyo, M. (2013). An analysis of Social Stories[TM] research using an evidence-based practice model. *Journal of Research in Special Educational Needs*, 13 (3), pp. 208–217.

McLinden, M. and McCall, S. (2002). *Learning Through Touch: Supporting Children with Visual Impairment and Additional Difficulties*. London: David Fulton.

McMinn, J. (2006). *Supporting Children with Speech and Language and Associated Difficulties*. 2nd ed. London: Continuum.

Mistry, M. and Barnes, D. (2013). The use of Makaton for supporting talk, through play, for pupils who have English as an Additional Language (EAL) in the Foundation Stage. *Education 3–13*, 41 (6), pp. 603–616.

Moreno, G. (2020). Expanding definition of technology in special education: impact of training on the adoption of iPad tablets by special educators. *International Journal of Disability, Development and Education*, 69 (9), pp. 1–17.

Mueller, V.T. (2013). Voice Output Communication Aids. In: F. R. Volkmar (ed.), *Encyclopedia of Autism Spectrum Disorders*. New York: Springer.

National Health Service (NHS) (2021). Aphasia. [Online] Available at: www.nhs.uk/conditions/aphasia [Accessed 12. 01. 2023].

Norbury, C., Tomblin, J. B. and Bishop, D. V. M. (eds.) (2008). *Understanding Developmental Language Disorders: From Theory to Practice*. London: Psychology Press.

Ozdemir, S. (2008). The effectiveness of social stories on decreasing disruptive behaviors of children with autism: three case studies. *Journal of Autism and Developmental Disorders*, 38 (9), pp. 1689–1696.

Panter, A. (2004). Let the fun begin: communicating through touch the Tacpac way. *Eye Contact 39 (RNIB Journal)*, pp. 31–34.

Pyramid Educational Consultants (2023). [Online]. Available at: https://pecs-unitedkingdom.com [Accessed 02. 03. 2023].

Qi, C. H., Barton, E. E., Collier, M., Lin, Y.-L. and Montoya, C. (2018). A systematic review of effects of social stories interventions for individuals with autism spectrum disorder. *Focus on Autism and Other Developmental Disabilities*, 33 (1), pp. 25–34.

Quigley, H. and MacDonald, R. (2022). A qualitative study of an online Makaton choir for Individuals with learning difficulties. *International Journal of Community Music*, 15 (1), pp. 65–94.

Quirmbach, L. M., Lincoln, A. J., Feinberg-Gizzo, M. J., Ingersoll, B. R. and Andrews, S. M. (2009). Social stories: mechanisms of effectiveness in increasing game play skills in children diagnosed with autism spectrum disorder using a pretest posttest repeated measures randomized control group design. *J Autism Dev Disord*, 39 (2), pp. 299–321.

Reynhout, G. and Carter, M. (2009). The use of social stories by teachers and their perceived efficacy. *Research in Autism Spectrum Disorders*, 3 (1), pp. 232–251.

Rispoli, M. J., Franco, J. H., van der Meer, L., Lang, R. and Pimentel Höher Camargo, S. (2010). The use of speech generating devices in communication interventions for individuals with developmental disabilities: a review of the literature. *Developmental Neurorehabilitation*, 13 (4), pp. 276–293.

Sansosti, F. J., Powell-Smith, K. A. and Kincaid, D. (2004). A research synthesis of Social Story interventions for children with autism spectrum disorders. *Focus on Autism and Other Developmental Disabilities*, 19 (4), pp. 194–204.

Schepis, M., Reid, D., Behrmann, M. and Sutton, K. (1998). Increasing communicative interactions of young children with autism using a voice output communication aid and naturalistic teaching. *Journal of Applied Behavior Analysis*, 31, pp. 561–578.

Schlosser, R. W. and Wendt, O. (2008). Effects of augmentative and alternative communication intervention on speech production in children with autism: a systematic review. *Am J Speech Lang Pathol*, 7 (3), 212–230.

Sellars, G. (2006). Learning to communicate with children with disabilities. *Paediatr Nurs*, 18 (9), pp. 26–28.

Sheehy, K. and Duffy, H. (2009). Attitudes to Makaton in the ages on integration and inclusion. *International Journal of Special Education*, 24 (2), pp. 91–102.

Silman, F., Yaratan, H. Y. and Karanfiller, T. (2017). Use of assistive technology for teaching-learning and administrative processes for the visually impaired people. *Eurasia Journal of Mathematics, Science and Technology Education*, 13 (8), pp. 4805–4813.

Sulzer-Azaroff, B., Hoffman, A. O., Horton, C. B., Bondy, A. and Frost, L. (2009). The Picture Exchange Communication System (PECS): what do the data say? *Focus on Autism and Other Developmental Disabilities*, 24 (2), pp. 89–103.

Tacpac (2023) [Online] Available at: https://tacpac.co.uk [Accessed 03. 03. 2023].

Tang, T. Y. and Winoto, P. (2018). *An Interactive Picture Exchange Communication System (PECS) embedded with augmented aids enabled by IoT and sensing technologies for Chinese individuals with autism.* Proceedings of the 2018 ACM International Joint Conference and 2018 International Symposium on Pervasive and Ubiquitous Computing and Wearable Computers.

Test, D. W., Richter, S., Knight, V. and Spooner, F. (2011). A comprehensive review and meta-analysis of the social stories literature. *Focus on Autism and Other Developmental Disabilities*, 26 (1), pp. 49–62.

Travis, J. and Geiger, M. (2010). The effectiveness of the Picture Exchange Communication System (PECS) for children with autism spectrum disorder (ASD): a South African pilot study. *Child Language Teaching and Therapy*, 26 (1), pp. 39–59.

Trembath, D., Iacono, T., Lyon, K., West, D. and Johnson, H. (2014). Augmentative and alternative communication supports for adults with autism spectrum disorders. *Autism*, 18 (8), pp. 891–902.

Unser, C. E. (2017). *A Study on The Positives and Negatives of Using Technology in The Classroom*. Undergraduate Honors College Theses.

van der Meer, L. A. and Rispoli, M. (2010). Communication interventions involving speech-generating devices for children with autism: a review of the literature. *Dev Neurorehabil*, 13 (4), pp. 294–306.

van der Meer, L., Didden, R., Sutherland, D., O'Reilly, M. F., Lancioni, G. E. and Sigafoos, J. (2012). Comparing three augmentative and alternative communication modes for children with developmental disabilities. *Journal of Developmental and Physical Disabilities*, 24 (5), pp. 451–468.

Wasik, B. A. and Jacobi-Vessels, J. L. (2017). Word play: scaffolding language development through child-directed play. *Early Childhood Educ*, 45, pp. 769–776.

Wearmouth, J. (2019). *Special Educational Needs and Disability: The Basics*. London: Routledge.

Webb, T. (2000). Can children with autism and severe learning disabilities be taught to communicate spontaneously and effectively using the Picture Exchange Communication System? *Good Autism Practice Journal*, 1, pp. 29–41.

Zeng, B., Law, J. and Lindsay, G. (2012). Characterizing optimal intervention intensity: the relationship between dosage and effect size in interventions for children with developmental speech and language difficulties. *International Journal of Speech–Language Pathology*, 14, pp. 471–477.

Index

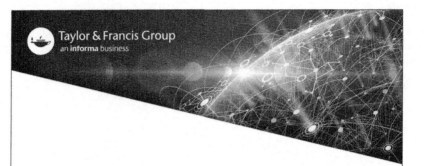

Printed in Great Britain
by Amazon

48813955R00159